Praise for Jane Mayer's

THE DARK SIDE

Winner of the J. Anthony Lukas Book Prize

"A powerful, brilliantly researched and deeply unsettling book. . . . Extraordinary and invaluable."
—*The New York Times Book Review*

"[A] very fine book. . . . To dismiss these [findings] as wild, anti-American ravings will not do. They are facts, which Mayer substantiates in persuasive detail."
—*The Washington Post Book World*

"Angry and important. . . . [*The Dark Side*] takes us, step by step through the process by which practices and methods we associate with tyrannies became official U.S. policy."   —Bloomberg

"Few tomes are as riveting or damning as Jane Mayer's *The Dark Side*. . . . It casts an unsentimental light on torture, our march to war in Iraq and the lies that continue to strangle our democracy. Essential reading."   —*Pittsburgh Post-Gazette*

"Stunning. . . . If you're a fan of *24*, you'll enjoy *The Dark Side*."
—*Slate*

"Riveting and shocking. . . . Mayer shows, not for the first time but in dismaying detail, what a catastrophic failure September 11 was on the part of the intelligence services."
—*The New York Observer*

"Mayer gives this story all the weight and sorrow it deserves. Many books get tagged with the word *essential*; hers actually is."   —*Salon*

"Reveals in greater detail the utter depravity of the Bush administration's official policy of torture."   —*The Guardian* (London)

"Some of *The Dark Side* seems right out of *The Final Days*, minus Nixon's operatic boozing and weeping. . . . Nixon parallels take us only so far, however. *The Dark Side* is scarier than *The Final Days* because these final days aren't over yet and because the stakes are much higher."   —Frank Rich, *The New York Times*

"Important. . . . Ms. Mayer, as much as anyone, is doing her part to pull back the curtain on the awful reality. *The Dark Side* is essential reading for those who think they can stand the truth."
—Bob Herbert, *The New York Times*

Jane Mayer

THE DARK SIDE

Jane Mayer is a staff writer for *The New Yorker* and the coauthor of two bestselling and critically acclaimed narrative nonfiction books, *Landslide: The Unmaking of the President, 1984–1988* and *Strange Justice: The Selling of Clarence Thomas*, the latter of which was a finalist for the National Book Award. For *The Dark Side*, Mayer was awarded a Guggenheim Fellowship, the J. Anthony Lukas Book Prize, the Goldsmith Book Prize, the Edward Weintal Prize, the Ridenhour Prize, the John Chancellor Prize, and was a finalist for the National Book Award, the National Book Critics Circle Award, and the New York Public Library's Helen Bernstein Book Award for Journalism. She lives in Chevy Chase, Maryland, with her husband, Bill, and their daughter, Kate.

ALSO BY JANE MAYER

Strange Justice: The Selling of Clarence Thomas
(with Jill Abramson)

Landslide: The Unmaking of the President, 1984–1988
(with Doyle McManus)

THE

DARK
SIDE

THE

DARK
SIDE

*The Inside Story of How the War on Terror
Turned into a War on American Ideals*

Jane Mayer

ANCHOR BOOKS
A Division of Random House, Inc.
New York

The Library of Congress has cataloged the Doubleday edition as follows:
Mayer, Jane.
Dark side: the inside story of how the war on terror turned into a war
on American ideals / Jane Mayer.
p.   cm.
1. War on Terrorism, 2001–   2. September 11 Terrorist Attacks, 2001—
Influence.   3. Military interrogation—United States.   4. War and emergency
powers—United States.   5. United States—Politics and government—2001–
6. United States—History—21st century.
HV6432.M383 2008
973.931—dc22 2008299452

Anchor ISBN: 978-0-307-45629-8

Author photograph © The New Yorker

www.anchorbooks.com

This book is for my parents, Meredith and William Mayer, and my grandparents Mary and Allan Nevins, who passed on to me a love of American history and an admiration for those who have fought to fulfill the promise of the country's ideals.

CONTENTS

1

PANIC

America should go "not abroad in search of monsters to destroy. . . . She might become the dictatress of the world: she would be no longer the ruler of her own spirit."

—John Quincy Adams, *An Address . . . Celebrating the Anniversary of Independence, at the City of Washington on the Fourth of July 1821*

If anyone in America should have been prepared to respond to the terrorist attacks of September 11, 2001, it ought to have been Vice President Dick Cheney. For decades before the planes hit the Pentagon and World Trade Center, Cheney had been secretly practicing for doomsday.

During the 1980s, while serving as a Republican congressman from Wyoming and a rising power in the conservative leadership in Congress, Cheney secretly participated in one of the most highly classified, top-secret programs of the Reagan Administration, a simulation of survival scenarios designed to ensure the smooth continuity of the U.S. government in the event of all-out nuclear war with the Soviet Union. Every year, usually during congressional recesses, Cheney would disappear in the dead of the night. He left without explanation to his wife, Lynne Vincent Cheney, who was given merely a phone number where he could be reached in the event of emergency. Along with some four or five dozen federal officials, Cheney would pretend for several weeks to be chief of staff to a designated substitute "president," bivouacked in some remote location in the United States.

As James Mann reveals in *The Vulcans,* his rich intellectual history of the neoconservative brain trust that has guided Bush foreign policy, the exercise tried to re-create some of the anticipated hardships of surviving a nuclear holocaust. Accommodations were Spartan and cuisine was barely adequate. Civilian communications systems were presumed destroyed. The challenge was to ensure civil order and control over the military in the event that the elected president and vice president, and much of the executive branch, were decimated. The Constitution, of course, spells out the line of succession. If the president and vice president are indisposed, then power passes first to the Speaker of the House, and next to the president pro tempore of the Senate. But in a secret executive order, President Reagan, who was deeply concerned about the Soviet threat, amended the process for speed and clarity. The secret order established a means of re-creating the executive branch without informing Congress that it had been sidestepped, or asking for legislation that would have made the new "continuity-of-government" plan legally legitimate. Cheney, a proponent of expansive presidential powers, was evidently unperturbed by this oversight.

Mann and others have suggested that these doomsday drills were a dress rehearsal for Cheney's calm, commanding performance on 9/11. It was not the first time he had stared into the abyss. One eyewitness, who kept a diary, said that inside the Presidential Emergency Operations Command, or PEOC, a hardened command center several hundred feet under the by-then-evacuated White House, Cheney never broke a sweat as he juggled orders to shoot down any additional incoming hijacked planes, coordinated efforts with other cabinet members, most particularly the Directors of the FBI and CIA, and resolved issues such as how to avoid charges of taking hostage two visiting foreign heads of state, from Australia and Lithuania, after all air traffic had been shut down.

Six weeks after the attacks on New York and Washington, the Bush Administration had successfully restored calm, reassured the financial markets, and rallied the sympathies and support of much of the world. But once again the White House was plunged into a state of controlled panic.

On October 17, 2001, a white powder that had been sent through the U.S. mail to Senate Majority Leader Tom Daschle's office in the Capitol was positively identified. Scientific analysis showed it to be an unusually difficult to obtain and lethally potent form of the deadly bacterial poison anthrax. This news followed less than ten days after the death in Florida of a victim in another mysterious anthrax attack. The anthrax spores in the letter to Daschle were so professionally refined, the Central Intelligence Agency believed the powder must have been sent by an experienced terrorist organization, most probably Al Qaeda, as a sequel to the group's September 11 attacks. During a meeting of the White House's National Security Council that day, Cheney, who was sitting in for the President because Bush was traveling abroad, urged everyone to keep this inflammatory speculation secret.

At the time, no one, not even America's best-informed national security leaders, really knew anything for sure about what sorts of threats loomed, or from where. The only certainty shared by virtually the entire American intelligence community in the fall of 2001 was that a second wave of even more devastating terrorist attacks on America was imminent. In preparation, the CIA had compiled a list of likely targets ranging from movie studios—whose heads were warned by the Bush Administration to take precautions—to sports arenas and corporate headquarters. Topping the list was the White House.

The next day, the worst of these fears seemed realized. On October 18, 2001, an alarm in the White House went off. Chillingly, the warning signal wasn't a simple fire alarm triggered by the detection of smoke. It was a sensitive, specialized sensor, designed to alert anyone in the vicinity that the air they were breathing had been contaminated by potentially lethal radioactive, chemical, or biological agents. Everyone who had entered the Situation Room that day was believed to have been exposed, and that included Cheney. "They thought there had been a nerve attack," a former administration official, who was sworn to secrecy about it, later confided. "It was really, really scary. They thought that Cheney was already lethally infected." Facing the possibility of his own death, the Vice President nonetheless calmly reported the emergency to the rest of the National Security Council.

Members of the National Security Council were all too well aware of the seriousness of the peril they were facing. At Cheney's urging, they had received a harrowing briefing just a few weeks earlier about the possibility of biological attack. His attention had been drawn to the subject by a war game called Dark Winter conducted in the summer before that simulated the effects of an outbreak of smallpox in America. After the September 11 attacks, Cheney's chief of staff, I. Lewis "Scooter" Libby, screened a video of the Dark Winter exercise for Cheney, showing that the United States was virtually defenseless against smallpox or any other biological attack. Cheney in particular was so stricken by the potential for attack that he insisted that the rest of the National Security Council undergo a gruesome briefing on it on September 20, 2001. When the White House sensor registered the presence of such poisons less than a month later, many, including Cheney, believed a nightmare was unfolding. "It was a really nerve-jangling time," the former official said.

In time, the Situation Room alarm turned out to be false. But on October 22, the Secret Service reported that it had found what it believed to be additional anthrax traces on an automated letter-opening device used on White House mail. By then, Cheney had convinced the President to support a $1.6 billion bioterrorism-preparedness program. Cheney argued that every citizen in the country should be vaccinated against smallpox.

During the ten days after the Vice President's scare, threats of mortal attack were nonetheless so frequent, and so terrifying, that on October 29 Cheney quietly insisted upon absenting himself from the White House to what was described as "a secure, undisclosed location"—one of several Cold War–era nuclear-hardened subterranean bunkers built during the Truman and Eisenhower Administrations, the nearest of which were located hundreds of feet below bedrock in places such as Mount Weather, in Virginia's Blue Ridge Mountains, and along the Maryland-Pennsylvania border not far from Camp David.

In a subterranean bunker crammed with communications equipment and government-issue metal desks, Cheney and other rotating cabinet members took turns occupying what was archly referred to as "The Commander in Chief's Suite."

Officials who worked in the White House and other sensitive posts with access to raw intelligence files during the fall of 2001 say it is nearly impossible to exaggerate the sense of mortal and existential danger that dominated the thinking of the upper rungs of the Bush Administration during those months.

"They thought they were going to get hit again. They convinced themselves that they were facing a ticking time bomb," recalled Roger Cressey, who then headed what was known as the Terrorist Threats Sub-Group of the National Security Council.

Counterterrorism experts knew that Al Qaeda's members had in the recent past made efforts to obtain nuclear and other horrific weapons of mass destruction in order to commit murder on an even greater scale. Unlike earlier enemies of America, they targeted innocent civilians and fought clandestinely with inhuman disregard for life. Other foes had been better organized and more powerful, but none had struck as great a blow behind the lines in America, nor spread a greater sense of vulnerability in the population. Under the circumstances, Cressey admitted, "I firmly expected to get hit again too. It seemed highly probable."

The sense of fear within the White House was understandable, but it was intensified by what was supposed to be a valuable new intelligence tool introduced after September 11, what came to be known as the "Top Secret Codeword/Threat Matrix." Having underestimated Al Qaeda before the attacks, Bush and Cheney took aggressive steps to ensure that they would never get similarly blindsided again. In the days immediately after the attacks, he and Cheney demanded to see all available raw intelligence reports concerning additional possible threats to America on a daily basis. Cheney had long been a skeptic about the CIA's skills, and was particularly insistent on reviewing the data himself. "The mistake," Cressey concluded later, "was not to have proper analysis of the intelligence before giving it to the President. There was no filter. Most of it was garbage. None of it had been corroborated or screened. But it went directly to the President and his advisers, who are not intelligence experts. That's when mistakes got made." Others who saw the same intelligence reports found the experience mind-altering. It was "like being stuck in a room listening to Led Zeppelin music," said Jim Baker, former head of the Counsel in the Department of Justice's Office of Intelligence Policy and Review. Readers suffered "sensory overload" and became "paranoid." Former Deputy Attorney General James Comey believed that the cumulative effect turned national security concerns into "an obsession."

A sense of constant danger followed Cheney everywhere. When he commuted to his White House office from the vice presidential residence, he was chauffeured in an armored motorcade that varied its route to foil possible attackers. On the backseat behind Cheney rested a duffel bag stocked with a gas mask and a biochemical surival suit. Rarely did he travel without a medical doctor in tow.

Cheney managed to make light of these macabre arrangements, joking about evading "The Jackal" by varying his routines, and teasing an old friend that, alas, he had too little survival equipment to be able to share his. Some of those around Cheney wondered if the attacks, perhaps in combination with his medical problems, had exacerbated his natural pessimism. An old family friend found him changed after September 11, "more steely, as if he was preoccupied by terrible things he couldn't talk about." Brent Scowcroft, a lifelong acquaintance, told *The New Yorker,* "I don't know him anymore." In the view of some detractors, such as Lawrence Wilkerson, the chief of staff to former Secretary of State Colin Powell, "Cheney was traumatized by 9/11. The poor guy became paranoid."

From the start of the administration, Cheney had confidently assumed the national security portfolio for a president with virtually no experience in the area. But Al Qaeda's attacks exposed a gaping shortcoming in the Vice President's thinking. The Soviet Union, whose threat had preoccupied Cheney and other doomsday planners in the 1980s, was gone. In its place another, more intangible danger had arisen. No one in the Bush Administration, including Cheney, had had the foresight or imagination to see Bin Laden's plot unfolding.

With the notable exception of Richard Clarke, the long-serving head of counterterrorism at the National Security Council, and a few counterterrorism experts at the CIA and FBI, terrorism hadn't ranked anywhere near the top of the new administration's national security concerns. Later, a number of top officials, including CIA Director George Tenet, would offer evidence that they had been keenly focused on the threat from Bin Laden before the attacks. If so, none succeeded in getting the President and Vice President's attention.

When Al Qaeda struck, Cheney and the other hardliners who had spent decades militating for a more martial and aggressive foreign policy were caught off guard. Frozen in a Cold War–era mind-set, they overlooked threats posed not by great armed nation-states, but by small, lithe rogue groups waging "asymmetric" warfare.

The Bush White House could have demanded an instant review of how they had been so badly surprised, as Franklin Delano Roosevelt did after the attack on Pearl Harbor, and the results would not have been flattering. But instead of trying to learn from what had essentially been a colossal bureaucratic failure, combined with inattention and a lack of political will at the top, the Bush White House deferred the focus elsewhere.

The lesson for Bush and Cheney was that terrorists had struck at the United States because they saw the country as soft. Bush worried that the nation was too "materialistic, hedonistic," and that Bin Laden "didn't feel threatened" by it. Confronted with a new enemy and their own intelligence failure, he and Cheney turned to some familiar conservative nostrums that had preoccupied the far right wing of the Republican Party since the Watergate era. There was too much international law, too many civil liberties, too many constraints on the President's war powers, too many rights for defendants, and too many rules against lethal covert actions. There was also too much openness and too much meddling by Congress and the press.

Cheney in particular had been chafing against the post-Watergate curbs that had been imposed on the president's powers since the mid-1970s, when he had served as Gerald Ford's chief of staff. As Vice President, Cheney had already begun to strengthen the power of the presidency by aggressively asserting executive privilege and other claims of confidentiality, most notably on his secrecy-enshrouded energy task force. He'd told Bush, who later repeated the line, that if nothing else they must leave the office stronger than they found it. Now Cheney saw the terrorist threat in such catastrophic terms that his end, saving America from possible extinction, justified virtually any means. As Wilkerson, Powell's former Chief of Staff who went on to teach National Security Affairs at George Washington University, put it, "He had a single-minded objective in black and white, that American security was paramount to everything else. He thought that perfect security was achievable. I can't fault the man for wanting to keep America safe. But he was willing to corrupt the whole country to save it."

Whether the White House fears were rational will long be debated. But it was in this feverish atmosphere that a new system of law was devised to vanquish what Bush described as a new kind of enemy in "a war unlike any other."

Beginning almost immediately after September 11, 2001, Cheney saw to it that some of the sharpest and best-trained lawyers in the country, working in secret in the White House and the United States Department of Justice, came up with legal justifications for a vast expansion of the government's power in waging war on terror.

As part of that process, for the first time in its history, the United States sanctioned government officials to physically and psychologically torment U.S.-held captives, making torture the official law of the land in all but name.

The lawyers also authorized other previously illegal practices, including the secret capture and indefinite detention of suspects without charges. Simply by designating the suspects "enemy combatants," the President could suspend the ancient writ of habeas corpus that guarantees a person the right to challenge his imprisonment in front of a fair and independent authority. Once in U.S. custody, the President's lawyers said, these suspects could be held incommunicado, hidden from their families and international monitors such as the Red Cross, and subjected to unending abuse, so long as it didn't meet the lawyers' own definition of torture. And they could be held for the duration of the war against terrorism, a struggle in which victory had never been clearly defined.

Few would argue against safeguarding the nation. But in the judgment of at least one of the country's most distinguished presidential scholars, the legal steps taken by the Bush Administration in its war against terrorism were a quantum leap beyond earlier blots on the country's history and traditions: more significant than John Adams's Alien and Sedition Acts, than Lincoln's suspension of habeas corpus during the Civil War, than the imprisonment of Americans of Japanese descent during World War II. Collectively, Arthur Schlesinger Jr. argued, the Bush Administration's extralegal counterterrorism program presented the most dramatic, sustained, and radical challenge to the rule of law in American history.

Over a lunch at a genteel Upper East Side French restaurant in Manhattan in 2006, the year before he died, Schlesinger, a liberal Democrat but also an admirer of muscular foreign policy, chose his words slowly and carefully. When asked what he thought of President Bush's policy on torture, he peered over his glasses and paused. Schlesinger's *The Imperial Presidency* had described Richard Nixon as pushing the outer limits of abuse of presidential power. Later, his book *The Cycles of American History* had placed these excesses in a continuum of pendulum swings. With his trademark bow tie askew, Schlesinger considered, and finally said, "No position taken has done more damage to the American reputation in the world—ever."

While there was nothing new about torture, its authorization by Bush Administration lawyers represented a dramatic break with the past. As early as the Revolutionary War, General George Washington vowed that, unlike the British, who tortured enemy captives, this new country in the New World would distinguish itself by its humanity. In fighting to liberate the world from Communism, Fascism, and Nazism, and working to ameliorate global ignorance and poverty, America had done more than any nation on earth to abolish torture and other violations of human rights.

Yet, almost precisely on the sixtieth anniversary of the famous war crimes tribunal's judgment in Nuremberg, which established what seemed like an immutable principle, that legalisms and technicalities could not substitute for individual moral choice and conscience, America became the first nation ever to authorize violations of the Geneva Conventions. These international treaties, many of which were hammered out by American lawyers in the wake of the harrowing Nazi atrocities of World War II, set an absolute, minimum baseline for the humane treatment of all categories of prisoners taken in almost all manner of international conflicts. Rather than lining prisoners up in front of ditches and executing them, or exterminating them in gas chambers, or subjecting them to grueling physical hardships, all enemy prisoners—even spies and saboteurs—were from then on to be accorded some basic value simply because they were human. America had long played a special role as the world's most ardent champion of these fundamental rights; it was not just a signatory but also the custodian of the Geneva Conventions, the original signed copies of which resided in a vault at the State Department.

Any fair telling of how America came to sacrifice so many cherished values in its fight against terrorism has to acknowledge that the enemy that the Bush Administration faced on September 11, and which the country faces still, is both real and terrifying. Often, those in power have felt they simply had no good choices. But this country has in the past faced other mortal enemies, equally if not more threatening, without endangering its moral authority by resorting to state-sanctioned torture. Other democratic nations, meanwhile, have grappled with similar if not greater threats from terrorism without undercutting their values and laws.

But to understand the Bush Administration's self-destructive response to September 11, one has to look particularly to Cheney, the doomsday expert and unapologetic advocate of expanding presidential power. Appearing on *Meet the Press* on the first Sunday after the attacks, Cheney gave a memorable description of how the administration viewed the continuing threat and how it planned to respond.

"We'll have to work sort of the dark side, if you will," Cheney explained in his characteristically quiet and reassuring voice. "We've got to spend time in the shadows in the intelligence world. A lot of what needs to be done here will have to be done quietly, without any discussion, using sources and methods that are available to our intelligence agencies—if we are going to be successful. That's the world these folks operate in. And, uh, so it's going to be vital for us to use any means at our disposal basically, to achieve our objectives."

Soon afterward, Cheney disappeared from public view. But his influence had already begun to shape all that followed.

2

BLAME

Safety from external danger is the most powerful director of national conduct. Even the ardent love of liberty will, after a time, give way to its dictates.

—Federalist Papers, No. 8

After the attacks of September 11, 2001, it was hard to believe that the news could get any worse for George Tenet or the CIA, the agency he had led since 1997. But when a team of analysts sorted through masses of cables and electronic communications in a conference room in the campuslike CIA headquarters in McLean, Virginia, it found some terrible news, which it soon delivered to Tenet and his chief of staff, John Moseman. Buried in the CIA's files was the trail of two of the 9/11 hijackers. The records showed that the Agency had followed the Al Qaeda suspects into the United States in 2000 and then dropped the case. For more than a year, despite the Agency's awareness that the pair was at large inside the United States, no one had alerted the FBI.

Upon hearing the news, Tenet, a warm bear of a man known for his locker-room banter and cheerleading for the CIA, reeled back in his desk chair and groaned.

"We're fucked!" is all he said.

By the night of September 11, it had already become clear that the mastermind behind the morning's four catastrophic terrorist attacks was the messianic Saudi millionaire Osama Bin Laden, the Islamic fundamentalist whom the CIA had been tracking for at least five years. Bin Laden's success at breaching American security marked perhaps the worst intelligence failure in the nation's history, rivaling the Japanese attack on Pearl Harbor in 1941. Tenet's background was in politics, as a former aide to the Senate intelligence committee, and as a close observer of earlier Washington witch hunts; he knew that recriminations over who had failed to prevent the attacks, and why, were coming—it was just a matter of time.

Later, when those investigations materialized as expected, Tenet testified that he had seen the warning signs of Al Qaeda's impending attacks, or as he put it, "the system was blinking red," and that the CIA had done all that it possibly could to get the Bush Administration's attention. But Moseman knew that the damning cable traffic would be used to tell another story—for the CIA's opponents it would be seen as "the smoking gun."

Cofer Black, the head of the CIA's terror-fighting operation, known as the Counterterrorist Center or CTC, was a lead character in the backstory. That night and for five days afterward, Black slept in his office at the CIA. He never went home. "He took it very hard—like 9/11 was a personal failure," said Tyler Drumheller, the former Chief of the CIA's Clandestine Operations in Europe, who was an old friend. To some extent, it was.

As head of the CTC, Black supervised the Bin Laden Unit. All summer he had told anyone who would listen that his gut told him, "Something terrible is going to happen! There is going to be an attack of massive proportions."

But one of the things that mystified Black's colleagues was how he could have been as alarmed as he was about Al Qaeda yet fail to piece together the many fragments of the September 11 puzzle that reached the Agency prior to the attacks.

It was a tangled story, filled with good intentions and near misses, complicated by increasingly fractious relations with the rivalrous FBI. In some ways, it began three years and one month earlier, when Al Qaeda blew up the U.S. embassy in Nairobi, Kenya, killing 247 innocent people, including 12 Americans, and injuring some 5,000 others. FBI counterterrorism agents who had been sent to the scene of the crime in Africa from the New York field office had pried loose a prized piece of intelligence that later proved key to U.S. efforts to track Al Qaeda. The agents had milked a confession out of a Saudi suspect in the bomb plot. "Without any coercion at all, other than feeding him," one of the FBI agents later said, he gave up a phone number he had called both before and after the attack. The number, 967-1-200578 in Yemen, was a rare landline belonging to a jihadi named Ahmed al-Hada.

The Saudi suspect had traded this information to the FBI in exchange for a promise not to be prosecuted in Kenya, but instead to be sent to stand trial in the United States. Despite his preference for American justice, the Saudi suspect in the bomb plot then sneeringly told the agents, "We have a plan to attack the U.S., but we're not ready yet. We need to hit you outside the country in a few places so you won't see what is going on inside. The big attack is coming. There's nothing you can do to stop it." The threat was significant, but even more so in retrospect was something the Saudi suspect didn't reveal: The phone number he had relinquished belonged to the father-in-law of one of the future 9/11 hijackers, Khalid al-Mihdhar.

Before the FBI could even finish writing up its reports on the embassy bombing case, they shared the crucial phone number with the CIA's station chief in Nairobi and the National Security Agency in Fort Meade, Maryland, which used its vast electronic eavesdropping capacity to "go up on the line." Over time, this one phone number proved an intelligence gold mine. Bin Laden and many of his lieutenants used it as a central communications hub for their planning.

While reading transcripts of NSA intercepts from this phone line approximately a year and eight months before September 11, the CIA caught word of an impending operational meeting of suspected Al Qaeda terrorists, planned for early January 2000 in Kuala Lumpur. An alert CIA desk officer immediately surmised that "something more nefarious was at foot." All the CIA had at that time were the first names of three suspects who were planning to attend the meeting. One suspect, however, was soon identified in full, as Khalid al-Mihdhar, the future hijacker, and son-in-law of the man to whom the phone was registered. Soon after, the CIA tracked his path from Yemen through Dubai to the meeting in Kuala Lumpur.

Mihdhar was a Saudi national, born in Mecca, whose fanaticism had been intensifying during years of fighting as a mujahideen in Afghanistan and Bosnia, along with his friend Nawaf al-Hazmi. The pair had applied for visas to the United States after another close friend had "martyred" himself in the 1998 suicide bombing of the U.S. embassy in Kenya. Evidently, they were bent on reviving their lost friend's cause, the infliction of maximum carnage and mayhem on America. Their aims meshed perfectly with those of Bin Laden and fellow Islamic terrorist Khalid Sheikh Mohammed, who had joined forces in Afghanistan by 1999. Bin Laden by then supported a plan proposed by Mohammed to hijack multiple airliners into symbolic American targets. With the plan, which they called "The Planes Operation," they hoped to create a demonstration of terror more spectacular than any the world had ever seen. Bin Laden selected Mihdhar and Hazmi as two of his future hijackers. Further details would be discussed among the operatives at the Kuala Lumpur meeting on January 5, 2000. On the morning of September 11, 2001, the pair would board American Airlines Flight 77 and commandeer it head-on at full speed into the Pentagon.

In Dubai, where Mihdhar changed planes on his way to the planning meeting, he was pulled aside at the request of U.S. intelligence officials. While his bags were searched, his passport was secretly photocopied. Alarmingly, it contained a valid multi-entry visa for the United States and information showing that his ultimate destination was New York. Dubai security officials sent photocopies to the CIA station in Dubai and to the Bin Laden Unit of the CIA back in Virginia.

Soon after, the CIA asked the Malaysian security service to spy on the Kuala Lumpur meeting, which took place as planned on January 5, 2000. The Malaysians' attempt to plant hidden microphones failed. But the Malaysian liaison services managed to take multiple photographs of the terrorists, all of whom were unidentified at the time except for Mihdhar. The photos were also sent to the CIA.

After the meeting, three of the suspects flew on to Bangkok, including Mihdhar and someone whose last name was known by then as Hazmi. But bafflingly, the CIA lost the future hijackers' trail at this point. According to one report, the Bin Laden Unit waited too long to get word to the CIA station in Thailand, and by the time the Bangkok agents started looking for the suspects, they had already disappeared. In March 2000, uneasy CIA officers in Malaysia prodded their counterparts in Thailand to look harder. This produced an extraordinary piece of news. One of the suspects, now fully identified as Nawaf al-Hazmi, had flown to Los Angeles six weeks earlier, on January 15, 2000. The CIA at this point found no trace of Mihdhar at all. Yet later it was discovered that he had flown to Los Angeles on the same flight.

The investigation by the independent bipartisan 9/11 Commission concluded in 2004 that although the CIA's Counterterrorist Center and its Bin Laden Unit were informed that Hazmi, a suspected Al Qaeda operative, had infiltrated the United States fully a year and a half before the attacks on New York and Washington, at this point the Agency shared this information with no one else. The CIA didn't alert the State Department's "TIPOFF" watch list to search for information of the pair's travels. Nor did the CIA share this explosive information with the FBI, which had primary domestic responsibility for protecting the United States from terrorism, and a team of agents specifically devoted to going after Al Qaeda. Instead, the Commission found "nothing more was done to track" the suspects for a year. Only then, when one of the suspects' names surfaced in the separate investigation into the 2000 *Cole* bombing, was interest reignited. The case went cold because of a bureaucratic blunder. In an oversight, Tenet later conceded, the CIA's Counterterrorist Center mislabeled the cable it got from Bangkok warning that the Al Qaeda suspect had flown to the United States. The CTC categorized it as "information"—meaning interesting, but not very—rather than "action" requiring immediate follow-up.

During this period prior to September 11, inside the CIA's Counterterrorist Center, several FBI agents were on loan from the Bureau in a deliberate effort to foster bureaucratic synergy. Given the history of animosity and rivalry between the two departments, it was jokingly referred to as "The Hostage Exchange Program." Doug Miller, one of these FBI agents on loan to the CIA, had access to what was called "bigoted"—meaning not shared—information on the CIA's Hercules computer system. There he saw the electronic communications mentioning that Hazmi had entered the United States. Twice, according to later investigations, he asked permission of his CIA supervisor to forward this disturbing information to his colleagues at the FBI. He wrote up a draft memo, to be sent to the FBI, and was ready to send it. But his boss, a CIA desk officer in the Bin Laden Unit of the Counterterrorist Center who is identified by the 9/11 Commission only as "Mike," and whose real name has never been revealed, stopped him from passing it on. After the second try, Miller dropped the matter. Oddly, three hours after "Mike" told Miller to hold off on sending the memo, formally known as a Central Intelligence Report, he nonetheless notified his bosses that the information had been shared with the FBI. The CIA assumed from then on that it had been. But it never was. The contradiction was never explained. An investigator with the 9/11 Commission who tried to sort through the details said of "Mike," "He said he couldn't remember what happened." Astonishingly, "Mike," the investigator later learned, was given a promotion by the Agency after September 11.

It was Doug Miller's unsent Central Intelligence Report informing the FBI that an Al Qaeda operative had penetrated America that Tenet and Moseman had learned about after the CIA team had reconstructed the nauseatingly damning paper trail.

In 2007, the CIA's own independent Inspector General released a report on the performance of the Agency prior to September 11 that was more damning still. It remains largely classified. But what was released was the IG's conclusion that by March 2000 fully fifty or sixty individuals within the CIA knew that two Al Qaeda suspects had come to America—but no one officially notified the FBI about this. It said the CIA had failed to inform the FBI through "prescribed channels" of Mihdhar and other terrorists' "intended or actual travel to the United States."

"The two guys' names were just sitting in someone's outbox. It just didn't get done," a former top officer in the CIA's clandestine service admitted. The Bin Laden Unit of the Counterterrorist Center, he said, "was just chaotic. There were piles and piles and PILES of un-translated intercepts." The problem, he said, was not a lack of urgency, but rather a failure of management. "When everything is a crisis, nothing is a crisis." In short, the errors were painfully mundane: misfiled paperwork, inattentive government employees, misunderstandings and miscommunications—just commonplace incompetence.

No one was more critical of the CIA's counterterrorism record than the FBI agents assigned to a New York–based squad known as "I-49." They had been tracking and arresting Middle Eastern terrorists since the mid-1990s, many of whom had been successfully convicted. Among the most articulate of these agents was a former English and Latin major named Jack Cloonan. Driving a zippy Mini Cooper, sporting an Inspector Poirot–like mustache, and telling stories with verve and humor in a thick accent redolent of his upbringing in Waltham, Massachusetts, Cloonan didn't seem the image of J. Edgar Hoover's buttoned-down FBI. In fact, Cloonan had joined the Bureau the day that Hoover died in 1972. He was one of the first FBI agents chosen to work with the CIA as part of a "fusion cell" after President Clinton signed an intelligence finding declaring war against Al Qaeda in 1996. Clinton directed the entire U.S. intelligence community, including the FBI, to work together in an effort to put together a prosecutable case against Bin Laden and his associates. Cloonan had immersed himself in the fine details of Islamic terrorism, which helped him and his colleagues recruit and debrief two major Al Qaeda informants, or as the FBI called them, "cooperating witnesses." Both informants were eventually delivered into the custody of the U.S. Department of Justice. Their statements filled hundreds of pages, teaching the American intelligence community much of what it knew about Al Qaeda.

"Clearly, something went terribly wrong," said Cloonan about September 11. "But it's never been adequately explained. Everybody talks about how the criminal process is so cumbersome and all this, but the point is, you got actionable intelligence through good old-fashioned detective spade work," he said, referring to Al Qaeda's plans for the Kuala Lumpur meeting, which were overheard on a legally tapped phone number obtained through noncoercive means by the FBI in Yemen. "The question is: What did the intelligence agency do with it? They let these people fade off the screen!"

In Cloonan's view, "What 9/11 is really all about was the lack of follow-up on these two people, Khalid al-Mihdhar and Nawaf al-Hazmi." Cloonan was realistic and self-critical enough to acknowledge that even had the FBI been informed that these two terrorists had come to America, there might still have been errors that would have prevented detection of the plot. The FBI's record, he knew better than most, left much to be desired, too. After entering America, one of the future hijackers boarded in a house with an FBI informant in California and the Bureau never learned anything about it. In addition, in August of 2001, FBI headquarters denied its Minneapolis field office permission to search the laptop computer of Zacarias Moussaoui, an Al Qaeda operative training for a second wave of attacks. An urgent memo to FBI Headquarters about potential Islamic terrorists in flight schools also went unheeded. But Cloonan ventured, "If the FBI had known sixteen months before to monitor these people, I think you can predict with a fair amount of certainty that it would have come out differently. So it wasn't some big systematic failure, it was human failure. It gets down to a couple of people not doing their jobs well. The rest is all damage control."

The near misses still haunted Cloonan years later, and undoubtedly would his whole life. "How often do you get into someone's suitcase and find multiple-entry visas? And how often do you know there's going to be an organizational meeting of Al Qaeda, anyplace in the world?" he asked. "The chances are slim to none! This is as good as it gets. It's a home run in the ninth inning of the World Series. This is the kind of case you hope your whole life for. That's why you do all this work, you have thousands of cases, you've got agents spending their lives doing all kinds of stuff, responding to every crank call that comes in, and here you are. This is what you would dream about. This is what you trained for. What you planned for, what you hope for. You want to be lucky. And that was being lucky."

Barely pausing for a breath, almost in a conversation with himself, Cloonan shook his gray head. "And then, after the group breaks up in Kuala Lumpur, and they go to Thailand, you're telling me you just lost sight of it? You just forgot to put them on the notifications list? That's as bad as it gets! You don't have to be a seasoned counterterrorism agent to know what's at stake here. It takes all of about ten seconds to sit at a keyboard and say boom, 'let's put them on the watch list.' But you say you didn't do it? You didn't think it was important? It was an oversight? Oops? It's not acceptable. And it never will be."

No one seemed to be holding the responsible individuals at the CIA and FBI accountable. Cloonan watched with a growing sense of anger and disgust, and in the days and weeks and even years after September 11, there was what he called "this big incredible mumble." Mocking the experts, he said, "It's about information sharing, and structural deficiencies, and 'the wall.' It's about the lack of preemptive philosophy, and the need to use 'enhanced interrogation methods,' and so on and so forth."

In reality, though, he insisted, "If you get into the weeds on this, you find out, you know what? It's not structural, it's not organizational—it's about human failure. It's people not doing their job. It's just that simple. And all this other stuff just obscures that fact."

The costs of this ordinary incompetence, in his view, were almost too awful for the country and the culpable individuals to face. "Was it preventable? Was 9/11 preventable?" he asked himself out loud, replaying a question that clearly ran through his head relentlessly.

"This was all preventable," he concluded. "It was all there."

Tenet certainly told the history differently. He argued strenuously in the days and years to follow that he and the Agency had done almost everything they could to warn the White House of the growing risk they saw from Al Qaeda. But the CIA's record was uneven. The

Agency had been riven by internal arguments over how aggressive it should be toward Bin Laden. The constraints had more to do with political risk and personal judgment than barriers imposed by domestic or international law.

Before leaving office, Clinton's national security adviser, Sandy Berger, had tried to emphasize in a private briefing with his successors how grave a threat Bin Laden posed. Berger was "truly obsessed with Al Qaeda," a former top Agency official who spanned both administrations said. "There was barely a day that went by that he didn't ask us for something on them. He urged the Agency to write up a plan of attack and do it as if there were no financial or other restraints—as if they had just open blue skies." At the CTC, Cofer Black responded by preparing an aggressive action plan for the incoming Bush Administration. Known as the "Blue Sky Memo," it listed a series of radical steps he believed the new administration should take against Al Qaeda. All that was missing was President Bush's authorization. Of these steps, the most crucial, he argued, was for Bush to authorize the CIA, or its partners in Afghanistan, to kill Bin Laden.

There was a long and complicated history behind the "deadly force" issue. Clinton had authorized the CIA to try to capture Bin Laden but, in accordance with an Executive Order, said the Agency could kill him only in "self-defense." At one point, Clinton reportedly authorized the Agency to allow Afghan surrogates to kill Bin Laden. But he superseded this authorization with a less aggressive one two months later.

The arguments about "kill authority" took on a surreal quality in the late 1990s, with Clinton's attorney general, Janet Reno, repeatedly questioning whether a proposed targeted killing could be classified as "self-defense." Reno was particularly sensitive to the issue. In fact, she frequently reminded the CIA that it was bound by U.S. laws like every other federal agency. The CIA had been categorically banned from carrying out assassinations in 1976 following scandalous revelations that the Agency had tried to kill Fidel Castro in the 1960s. Like police officers, however, CIA officials could kill in their own defense. Also, under rules of military engagement, some targeted killings were permissible. During the Clinton years, the line between sanctioned and illegal killing remained murky. Unless it was clarified by a new presidential finding, the CIA's lawyers were not about to let the Agency step on the wrong side of the law.

The lesson that CIA managers had learned from past scandals was to get everything in writing from the lawyers, preferably with a presidential signature at the bottom. Even those militating for more aggressive action, such as Cofer Black, were cautious about legal liability. Black was apt to cite King Henry II's famously indirect order to kill Thomas à Becket, the Archbishop of Canterbury—"Who will rid me of this meddlesome priest?"—as exactly the sort of vague presidential command to avoid. After seeing midlevel colleagues convicted for following what they thought were presidential wishes in the Iran-Contra scandal, Black warned his subordinates that the CIA was not in the "rid-me-of-this-priest business."

Some of Tenet's underlings in the Agency grew increasingly frustrated with what they regarded as an overabundance of caution at the CIA. This was particularly true of Black. But despite pressure from the counterterrorism staff, Tenet himself never advised either President Clinton or President Bush to approve the use of lethal force against Al Qaeda. To him, it seemed drastic and politically risky. Tenet acknowledged in his memoir that he had fallen short of endorsing targeted killings because he had wondered, "How would the U.S. government explain it if Arab terrorists in Afghanistan suddenly started being blown up?" Before September 11, the American public would likely have given little support for such bloody missions either. The fact that it was the Director's political judgment as much as anything else that held the CIA back was quickly forgotten after September 11.

While the CIA was locked in a tense internal stalemate about how to deal with Bin Laden, the hard-liners at the Agency found a forceful ally in Richard Clarke, the top counterterrorism official in the White House. Clarke was a secretive, acerbic workaholic who had been at the NSC since the Reagan era. He had grown increasingly alarmed about Al Qaeda by the year. In his safe was a copy of Cofer Black's Blue Sky Memo. In an effort to alert the new administration to the danger he saw, he wrote an impassioned jeremiad on January 25, 2001, essentially reprising Black's memo, titled "Strategy for Eliminating the Threat from Jihadist Networks of al Qaeda." Addressing this plea to Condoleezza Rice, Bush's new national security adviser, Clarke argued that the administration "urgently need[ed]" to "roll back" Al Qaeda. He warned that the terrorist group was not a secondary issue, as might be expected of a cult led by a medieval-seeming bearded zealot living in a mud hut half a world away, but a first-tier threat, operating in forty countries, including the United States. At the time, Clarke had no way of knowing that Mihdhar and Hazmi had already arrived in Los Angeles a few weeks earlier. But his report to Rice stated outright that Al Qaeda was known to have made inroads into America, utilizing "sleeper cells."

Clarke urged Rice to call a "Principals Meeting" of cabinet members whose portfolios dealt with national security, as soon as possible, to address Al Qaeda. He also urged the President to authorize "massive" covert military aid to the Northern Alliance in Afghanistan. It seemed the best way to take on the rival Taliban, who were Al Qaeda's protectors in the region. Inevitably, this meant secretly authorizing these surrogates to kill Bin Laden.

But Rice scheduled no cabinet meeting on Al Qaeda. Instead, not long after receiving Clarke's memo, Rice demoted him in an organizational overhaul of the NSC, stripping him of a special privilege Clinton had bestowed on Clarke, allowing him to attend cabinet-level meetings on terrorism issues. Clarke had a mixed reputation—for brilliance, but also for devious bureaucratic gamesmanship. He knew as much about Islamic terrorism as anyone in the administration, but an aide to Rice said he'd been told to keep Clarke on a tight rein, because "He had a reputation for coloring outside the lines." In the tightly managerial and narrowly political Bush White House, Clarke was regarded with suspicion. In 2003, he resigned in frustration.

As U.S. policy toward Al Qaeda chugged its way slowly through midlevels of the national security bureaucracy, Tenet claimed he kept up the pressure. In his first public congressional testimony as a member of the Bush Administration, in February 2001, Tenet later pointed out, he warned that Bin Laden and his associates posed "the most immediate and serious threat." Later, he testified before Congress again, warning that he considered a terrorist attack against the United States in the next two years "likely."

In March, Tenet's ambivalence was visible in a halfhearted effort to revive Black's aggressive Blue Sky Memo. Tenet gave a revised version of it to Rice's deputy, Stephen Hadley, again asking for broader legal latitude to kill Bin Laden. But Tenet later acknowledged that as he discussed it with Hadley, he agreed that first, before demanding this lethal authority, it made sense for the NSC to settle the administration's policy toward Al Qaeda. The NSC didn't want to take possession of the action plan at that point for political reasons—Hadley worried that along with possession would come responsibility for carrying the plan out, which the NSC didn't want. With Tenet's blessing, the Blue Sky Memo was sent back to the CIA, set aside for another day. Clarke, meanwhile, railed against the CIA's "bi-polar mood swings" and "masterful passive-aggressive behavior."

By June, with the threat of attack against U.S. interests intensifying, Tenet directed particularly imperiled U.S. embassies to close. On July 10, Tenet said he was so alarmed by the mounting clues pointing to a monstrous impending attack against U.S. interests that it "literally made my hair stand on end." For the first and only time in his seven-year career at the helm of the CIA, he picked up the secure white phone in his office, with the direct line to Condoleezza Rice, and demanded an immediate, unscheduled meeting to talk about Al Qaeda.

Tenet said that he, Black, and a CIA Bin Laden expert, identified only as "Rich," confronted Rice in her office forcefully, arguing that the government had to stop playing defense and take immediate offensive action against Al Qaeda in Afghanistan. They felt certain from warning signs they were seeing that the terrorist organization was on the verge of attack. "This country needs to go on a war footing, *NOW!*" Black boomed, according to Tenet. Black specifically said that Al Qaeda might "attack within the United States itself," according to an account of the meeting written by Bob Woodward.

Key details of the July 10 meeting have been disputed. Rice claimed she didn't recall any such urgency. Nor did she think that Tenet and his staff brought new information. She also denied anyone had told her that Bin Laden planned to attack America.

Complicating efforts to set the record straight was the fact that Tenet seemingly supplied two diametrically opposite accounts. In one account, given under oath to the 9/11 Commission prior to Tenet's departure from the Bush Administration, he praised Rice as having understood the gravity of the July 10 warning. "She got it," the notes from the 9/11 Commission quoted Tenet as saying. But after leaving the administration, Tenet appears to have given a far more critical account to Woodward. Rice is described as having given the CIA officials "the brush off." They felt "they were not getting through to her." They left feeling "frustrated."

Other top administration officials were also unmoved by the CIA's alarms in the days before 9/11. Secretary of Defense Donald Rumsfeld and his deputy for intelligence, Stephen Cambone, were skeptical of the CIA's intercepts showing a celebratory mood in the Al Qaeda training camps and excited talk of a huge event about to happen. The CIA had listened with horror as Al Qaeda members wept on tearful good-byes to one another and promised to see each other in Paradise. But Cambone and Deputy Defense Secretary Paul Wolfowitz, both of whom cast themselves as sophisticated neoconservative defense intellectuals, suggested it could just as easily be disinformation.

On August 6, the CIA's warnings indisputably reached both Rice and the President. The CIA delivered what became an infamous Presidential Daily Briefing paper, or PDB, to Bush, who was beginning a monthlong vacation at his ranch in Crawford, Texas. It was titled "Bin Laden Determined to Strike in the U.S." Tenet didn't deliver the briefing himself. He visited the ranch once that month but otherwise barely spoke with Bush during this period. Tenet admitted in his memoir that while the alarming-sounding report made clear that Bin Laden was intent on hitting America as hard as he could, "we did not have, and therefore did not convey, information about any specific ongoing plot."

Bush's reaction was reportedly dismissive. According to an account by journalist Ron Suskind in his book *The One Percent Doctrine,* after listening to the CIA's warning that day, the President responded, "All right. You've covered your ass now."

Ten days later, after a flight school in Eagan, Minnesota, alerted the FBI that a belligerent French national of Moroccan descent with thousands of dollars in cash was insisting on being taught how to steer and navigate an airliner, but wasn't interested in finding out how to take off or land, Zacarias Moussaoui was arrested. Urgent memos from the FBI's Minneapolis field office to the Bureau's headquarters suggesting Moussaoui might be part of an attack using hijacked planes were ignored, and permission to search Moussaoui's laptop computer was denied. At the time, the FBI's assistant director for counterterrorism, Dale Watson, and Thomas Pickard, the acting Director of the FBI that summer, were trying to get more funding to fight Al Qaeda. But Attorney General John Ashcroft denied their pleas. Ashcroft, a social conservative whom Bush appointed as a favor to the evangelical wing of the Republican Party, which had helped him secure the thinnest of victory margins in the 2000 election, was far more interested in obliterating gun control and executing the Oklahoma City bomber Timothy McVeigh. According to Pickard, Ashcroft assailed him that summer for talking too much about the threat from Al Qaeda, angrily remonstrating, "I don't want to hear about that anymore!"

The news of Moussaoui's arrest took days to reach the top ranks of the sclerotic FBI, but it was shared almost immediately with Tenet at the

CIA. An official with the 9/11 Commission said later that Tenet "says his hair is on fire . . . he gets information that they've captured Moussaoui in Minnesota. He actually gets that information. He gets the item in his daily briefing: a terrorist wants to learn to fly. They chuckle about it and move on. But no one is connecting these tactical fragments to the strategic warning they've all been yelling about. I mean, he'll go to a meeting that afternoon, and talk about how worried they all are."

On September 4, 2001, Clarke, who was still at the National Security Council, sent a last e-mail plea to Rice. She had finally scheduled a Principals Committee meeting that day on Al Qaeda. "Are we serious about dealing with the al Qida [*sic*] threat?" Clarke implored. "Decision makers should imagine themselves on a future day when the CSG has not succeeded in stopping al Qida attacks, and hundreds of Americans lay dead in several countries, including the U.S. What would those decision makers wish they had done earlier? That future day could happen any time."

That day, exactly one week before the terrorist attacks, the meeting of the Principals Committee of President Bush's national security advisers—a cabinet-level group that includes the Vice President, the Secretary of State, the Secretary of Defense, the Director of the CIA, the National Security Adviser, the Attorney General, and the Chairman of the Joint Chiefs of Staff—ended in a stalemate over taking more assertive action against Bin Laden. Movement was made toward arming the Northern Alliance. But no decision was made on the other issue at hand, whether to deploy a newly armed, unmanned drone aircraft, under development by the Air Force, against Bin Laden. Secret tests in the Nevada desert had succeeded in using the drone, known as the Predator, to destroy a model of Bin Laden's house. But neither the CIA nor the Air Force wanted to take the risk of using the Predator on a real mission against Bin Laden. Clarke, who attended the meeting, recalled that "Tenet said he opposed using the Predator because it wasn't the CIA's job to fly airplanes that shot missiles. And the Air Force said it wasn't their job to fly planes to collect intelligence. No one around the table seemed to have a can-do attitude. Everyone had an excuse." Roger Cressey, Clarke's deputy at the time, later admitted, "It sounds terrible, but we used to say to each other that some people didn't get it—it was going to take body bags."

Given this tragic history of missed opportunities, it is little wonder that swiftly, before anyone was in the frame of mind to call for public accountability, Tenet pinned the President down at Camp

David on the Saturday after September 11 and exacted a promise. Tenet wanted no investigations into the CIA's record on Al Qaeda. He phrased this request adeptly, telling President Bush that his people had been doing a lot of hard things, risking their lives for their country. It wasn't fair, he said, to cast them under a cloud of suspicion. As Tenet portrayed it, this wasn't about protecting himself. He just wanted to protect those beneath him. "People are working their butts off. They've saved thousands of lives," he told Bush. "The men and women who are doing the job need to know that you, Mr. President, believe in them," he said. "Let's not get into 'the failure blame game.'"

On the spot, Bush gave Tenet his word. There would be no recriminations.

Several weeks later, on September 27, Bush made good on the promise. When a Republican congressman attacked Tenet's performance, Bush rose to his rescue, saying, "We cannot be second-guessing our team, and I'm not going to. The nation's at war. We need to encourage Congress to frankly leave the man alone. Tenet's doing a good job. And if he's not, blame me, not him."

Tenet was a natural politician. He and Bush got along well. He'd been a holdover from the Clinton Administration, and at first Bush hadn't been sure about keeping him on. But Bush's father, who had been Director of the CIA himself for slightly less than a year during the Ford Administration, and David Boren, the conservative Democratic senator from Oklahoma who like the Bushes had been a member of Yale's elite secret society, Skull and Bones, and who had been a mentor and career patron for Tenet, had both urged the President to keep Tenet in place. In part, the elders thought it important to send the message that intelligence is not supposed to be political. Also, they regarded Tenet as a "straight shooter." Boren said he didn't even know what political party Tenet leaned toward. After getting what amounted to probational status, Tenet, who loved his job, worked hard at winning Bush over. Soon, Bush came to like Tenet's gregarious unpretentiousness and locker-room swagger. The son of Greek immigrant coffee-shop owners from the Queens borough of New York, Tenet was a self-made success. Also, as a career staff member, he had a gift for pleasing powerful bosses. Some at the Agency, however, scorned what they saw as his eagerness to tell the President what he wanted to hear. "He was like a puppy-dog, wagging his tail and tagging along," said one former CIA officer. "George?" said another. "His greatest wish was to hold onto his job in the Bush administration."

A foreign ambassador whose country worked closely with the Bush Administration against terrorism was astonished by what he called "a conspiracy of silence on the part of the political leaders of both parties in Washington" after September 11. "What strikes an outsider is how quiet George Bush and Bill Clinton were about each other, too." He added, "There's no need to punish people for legitimate differences of opinion about how serious the threat was from Al Qaeda before 9/11. But, you need to understand what went wrong. They didn't want to identify that. If people were grossly negligent, or intellectually lazy, or showed terrible judgment, then something should be done about it, so that there is accountability, and a learning process. It didn't happen here."

Vice President Cheney threw his considerable political clout into an effort to kill any independent, full-bore investigation, warning Democratic Senate Majority Leader Tom Daschle in 2002 that if he persisted in calling for such a probe, the White House would ensure that the Democrats were portrayed as undermining the war on terror. Given public sentiment at the time, it was a brass-knuckle threat. But Daschle persisted, strengthened immeasurably by the support of Republican senator John McCain, who, fresh from having been smeared by the Bush camp in his 2000 race for the presidency, was more than happy to expose the administration's flaws.

In Bush's decision to protect his national security team, some might see the personal loyalty for which he was known. Others might see a characteristic resistance to intellectual rigor and empirical fact-finding. Self-analysis or, as Bush derided it, being "put on the couch" was not his style. Critics, however, could suggest an ulterior motive. Like Tenet, Rice, Ashcroft, and the FBI's top officials, Bush had little to gain, and much to lose, from too close a look at his record on terrorism prior to September 11.

During the 2000 presidential campaign, Bush never publicly mentioned Bin Laden or Al Qaeda, nor had the Republican platform made fighting the terrorist organization a policy plank. Bush, whose lack of international experience was considered a political liability, stumbled on a cheap-shot question from a reporter challenging him to name Pakistan's president, General Pervez Musharraf. "The new Pakistani general, he's just been elected—not elected, this guy took over office. It appears this guy is going to bring stability to the country and I think that's good news for the subcontinent," Bush ventured when the name eluded him. Separately, when asked by a *Glamour* magazine reporter what he thought of the Taliban, Bush at first drew a blank. When the reporter offered a hint, "Because of the repression of women—in Afghanistan," Bush caught on. "Oh! I thought you said some band. The Taliban in Afghanistan. Absolutely. Repressive."

After taking office, Bush certainly was briefed by the CIA about Bin Laden prior to the session at his Texas ranch in August 2001. In fact, the 9/11 Commission revealed that he received more than forty Presidential Daily Briefings mentioning Bin Laden between January and September 10, 2001. But a witness to some of these briefings said that Bush's attention span was strikingly different from that of Cheney, who he said "would drill down" on national security information. "Cheney was the detail guy. And Cheney doesn't care how many people hate him. He's the one senior guy who had his hands on the steering wheel." In contrast, he said, "Bush was different. He had such small increments of time—they'd schedule him in five-minute increments—so he was distracted."

3

THE WARNING

The United States must not adopt the tactics of the enemy. Means are as important as ends.

—Final Report of the United States Senate Select Committee to Study Governmental Operations With Respect to Intelligence Activities, better known as The Church Committee, 1976

By the night of September 12, the sky was eerily empty over Washington. Save for low-flying military patrols, fighter jets whose radar gear could be spotted from the ground as they flew low, nonstop, nerve-racking rotations over the city, the airspace above the entire continental United States was disconcertingly deserted.

Tanks were parked in the streets downtown. The flames of the morning before had been extinguished at the Pentagon across the Potomac River in Northern Virginia. But smoke still rose from the blackened west facade of what had previously seemed an edifice as impenetrable as the Department of Defense it housed. An airliner-sized gash marked the lethal target of American Flight 77, hijacked and flown with explosive speed into the building the morning before, after Mihdhar and Hamzi had slit the throats of the pilot and crew with box cutters. Sixty-four people were killed on the plane, and 125 more at the Pentagon.

The first and only foreign flight to penetrate this unnervingly empty skyscape was a sleek private jet carrying several of America's staunchest and wisest allies, the top tier of the British intelligence services. On board were Sir Richard Dearlove, the Chief of MI6; Eliza Manninghan-Buller, the Deputy Chief of MI5; David Manning, Prime Minister Tony Blair's foreign-policy adviser; as well as a number of other covert and overt British foreign-policy experts who had more experience than they wished fighting domestic terrorism. They had come to personally deliver condolences and express solidarity in what Tenet would later describe as "an affirmation of the special relationship between our two nations and as touching an event as I experienced during my seven years as DCI."

Over a catered dinner in a private dining room at the CIA's Headquarters, the George H. W. Bush Center for Intelligence, in Langley, Virginia, and in follow-up gatherings the next few days, America's closest allies brought a more substantive and pointed message as well, which Tenet did not disclose in his memoir. As white-jacketed waiters cleared the plates, Tenet, Cofer Black, the Agency's senior counterterrorism official, and a handful of other top CIA officials listened intently as their British counterparts issued the first of several well-meant bits of advice. After an eloquent and emotional toast, and a vow to work together against this new terrorist scourge, Manning told the group, "I hope we can all agree that we should concentrate on Afghanistan, and not launch any attacks against Iraq."

The British, like the rest of the world, were waiting nervously to see how America would retaliate against Al Qaeda. They were already well aware of the preoccupation that some of Bush's foreign-policy team had with Iraq. Their message of proportionality and restraint reflected deep concern that the Bush Administration might be subject to over-reaction or, worse, the exploitation of the tragedy to advance other political agendas. Tenet gave his guests his word that action against Iraq was off the table. He said he and Secretary of State Colin Powell agreed on this. "Absolutely. Some might want to link the issues, but none of us wants to go that route." The fears of unwise retaliation, however, were not quieted that evening by the contents of a classified cable, brought in the midst of the dinner to Tenet and shared with some members of the group, according to one participant. He said it had been sent by one of Black's deputies to CIA paramilitary operatives who were already on their way to Afghanistan. It urged them to not just kill Bin Laden, but also to dismember him. Then they were directed to send a few choice body parts back to Langley.

The barbaric language was disquieting enough that the next day, in a more intimate setting, a former top British intelligence officer who had overseen the brutal British campaign to crush the IRA for ten years took the matter up over lunch at Sam and Harry's steakhouse with Tyler Drumheller, then the Chief of the CIA's Clandestine Operations in Europe. It was a coveted post, making him along with the other division chiefs one of the "barons," as they were known, of the Agency. "You need to learn from our history," the Englishman warned. He then recounted how former British Prime Minister Margaret Thatcher had become enraged and panicked following the IRA's bombing of the Conservative Party conference meeting in Brighton in 1984, in which five died and the bathroom in her own hotel room was blasted. In response, he said, "We decided to turn the terrorists' tactics back on them." He noted, "For a time, it worked. It stopped the immediate attacks. But watch out," he warned. "It's dangerous. It makes you the bad guys. And when it gets to court—and in your society, just like ours, it will—every one of these guys will get off."

Over at the White House, President Bush's reaction to the CIA's raw aggression was quite different. The same morning, September 13, the President convened his National Security Council in the Situation Room for a memorably graphic presentation from the CIA. To narrate a PowerPoint presentation, Tenet brought Cofer Black with him. In a slightly stilted accent, evidently acquired during his early years with the CIA's clandestine service in London and Africa, or perhaps during stints as a schoolboy abroad during his father's global travels as a pilot for Pan American Airways, Black finally had the opportunity to reach the audience he had been craving. Here at last was the President, whose authority he had been seeking for so long to allow his people to kill Bin Laden.

Black looked like a bull-necked tough guy, and spoke like one, too. But he had never actually been in the military other than as a volunteer in the Air Force ROTC. Nor had his CIA career placed him in combat. He had attended college in Southern California during the days of the Beach Boys; underneath the swagger, a friend said, "Cofer's just a Surfer Dude." But he had a vivid imagination and a singularly dramatic style. He dressed like the old-school spies of the Cold War days, in white button-down shirts and conservative gray suits, and wore his hair in a thinning buzz-cut. His round cheeks and babylike features, it had been observed, gave him a striking resemblance to White House political director Karl Rove. And like Rove, he had the quality most prized by presidents facing crises: boundless confidence that he knew the way forward.

First Tenet gave a summation of the CIA's proposed new action plan. Although all the talk was of the need to use new tactics against a new enemy, in truth the plan was a beefed-up version of the old Blue Sky Memo, rescued from bureaucratic limbo. To attack the Taliban, Al Qaeda's protectors in Afghanistan, the plan called for massive military assistance to their enemies, the 20,000 or so ragged troops of the Northern Alliance. Unfortunately, the Northern Alliance's charismatic leader, Ahmed Shah Massoud, had just been murdered by Al Qaeda, leaving the troops in leaderless disarray. But Tenet proposed boosting the Northern Alliance with covert on-the-ground support from CIA paramilitary teams and Special Forces teams from the U.S. military. Tenet had already warned Bush privately that the operation would be very costly. By some estimates, the CTC would run through more than $1 billion that year. Undaunted, Bush reportedly responded with a line that would later become the unofficial motto of Jack Bauer, the macho terrorist-busting hero of Fox Television's fantasy melodrama *24*. "Whatever it takes," the President replied, according to Woodward's indispensable report *Bush at War*.

After Tenet spoke, Black finally got his chance. "Mr. President, we can do this. No doubt in my mind. We do this the way we've outlined it, we'll set this thing up so it's an unfair fight for the U.S. military." But Black turned to Bush, who sat at the head of the conference table, and warned, "You've got to understand. People are going to die. And the worst part about it, Mr. President, Americans are going to die— my colleagues and my friends.

"So there should be no misunderstanding that this is going to be a bloodless activity."

Bush, who like Black was of an age to have fought in the Vietnam War but had not, responded, "That's war."

Black continued, "We've got to accept that we're going to lose people in this deal. How many, I don't know. Could be a lot." But Black promised, "You give us the mission—we can get 'em. When we're through with them, they will have flies walking across their eyeballs."

If the President and Vice President were repelled by Black's ghoulish enthusiasm, they didn't show it. Reflecting back on the moment, which surely was a rare one in the annals of White House discourse, Secretary of State Colin Powell later thought that Bush seemed eager to kill.

America's use of lethal authority was such a momentous issue, with so many moral, political, tactical, and strategic complexities, it had tied the Clinton Administration in knots for years. President Clinton had been deeply and personally involved. He knew the names of Bin Laden's top associates. Ayman al-Zawahiri, the maniacal Egyptian physician who served as Bin Laden's deputy, was framed in Clinton's mind as the evil hand behind Anwar Sadat's tragic assassination. But despite Clinton's personal investment in stopping Al Qaeda, as the record of ambivalent presidential findings and unclear legal boundaries reflected, he had been torn about what to do.

The United States had the military might to destroy Bin Laden and his followers literally at the flick of a switch. Steve Coll, in his brilliant history of the pre–September 11 U.S. involvement in Afghanistan, *Ghost Wars,* described how with the aid of the real-time video imagery transmitted by the Predator, the most powerful and technically advanced military force in the history of the world was able to stare from halfway around the globe at a tall, white-robed sheikh believed to be Bin Laden. The terrorist leader who had declared war against the United States could be watched as he walked through the primitive, undefended, mud-walled compound he and his terrorist associates and their families inhabited in the bleak, sage-brush-strewn plains outside of Kandahar, Afghanistan. The video imagery was so exquisitely detailed, U.S. officials viewing the videotapes at the CIA and White House could make out a lone child's swing hanging in the compound, known as Tarnak Farms. The robed man seemed to present an irresistible target for missile attack. But the swing haunted Clinton. It was, in a sense, the perfect symbol of the cultural, political, and strategic standoff described in Washington think tanks as "asymmetric warfare." The swing suggested innocent children lived there. The United States, for all of its military prowess, was a hamstrung Gulliver in the face of Lilliputian terrorists willing to sacrifice innocent lives in a way no civilized nation could.

Unlike Clinton, President Bush had not been exposed much to this complex policy issue. He had not attended the September 4 Principals Committee meeting on Al Qaeda. No formal debate or recommendations from it had yet reached him. There is no known indication that he was dissatisfied with this state of affairs. "I was not on point," he later admitted to Woodward with unvarnished candor.

After September 11, with the legacy of his presidency hanging in the balance, and the country—and in fact the world—waiting for his response, the contrast between Clinton's hesitancy and Bush's brashness could not have been more stark. Certainly, the heinousness of the attacks accounted for some of the contrast. But if Clinton had overthought the issue of lethal force, Bush seemed to give it virtually no thought at all. After hearing the CIA's presentation, the President asked Black simply, "How long will it take?"

To the surprise of others present at the meeting, including Tenet, Black told the President that he thought the U.S. could vanquish Al Qaeda and the Taliban in just a matter of weeks. To the dismay of Rumsfeld, the Department of Defense had no military plan for defeating Al Qaeda in Afghanistan on hand at the time, which forced the Pentagon to yield the lead role to the CIA.

As they filtered out of the White House, Tenet, according to a confidant, was a bit disconcerted. He didn't believe it was possible to deliver a decisive victory that fast. He also feared that now the CIA was "going to have to cut their heads off," a confidant said.

The radical implications of this "New Paradigm" for the rule of law in America became almost immediately clear. Shortly after September 11, Bush looked his attorney general, John Ashcroft, in the eye, according to Ashcroft's memoir, and told him icily, "Don't ever let this happen again." The command was interpreted by Ashcroft as an order to get far more aggressive, more preemptive and proactive. The President's words were few but clear: He would hold Ashcroft responsible for not thwarting the next attack. National security topped every other concern, the President implied. The top lawyer in the country was being told to do anything and everything to stop the terrorists—whatever it took.

Soon after the President's private talk with Ashcroft, Robert Mueller III, the Director of the FBI, who had assumed the post only one week before September 11, was caught off guard by this shift. Known behind his back as "Bobby Three Sticks" for the Roman numeral after his name, Mueller was an Episcopalian patrician who had prepped at St. Paul's and graduated in the Princeton class of 1966. He had also fought as a Marine in Vietnam, where he won a bronze star, before distinguishing himself as a smart and tough prosecutor in Washington, San Francisco, and New York with old-school, by-the-book values. He had run the Justice Department's criminal division, and before taking on the top FBI post, he had been the acting deputy attorney general. "Mueller has an appreciation for the Constitution and the rule of law," suggested James Baker, a career lawyer at the

Justice Department who worked closely with Mueller on complex and sensitive national security matters. Raised to be modest, Mueller was uncomfortable showboating for the press or engaging in political showmanship. But when the President called on Mueller at a national security meeting that first week, he was ready. He had just begun to launch into a progress report on the FBI's investigation of the September 11 hijackings, describing how imperative it was to follow proper police procedures and rules of evidence in order not to jeopardize the future criminal prosecution of the suspects, when Ashcroft, his boss in the Justice Department's hierarchy, abruptly cut him off.

Parroting the private talk he'd had with Bush, Ashcroft told Mueller that criminal trials were beside the point. All that mattered was stopping the next attack. Due process, it seemed, was too time-consuming.

Immediately after September 11, the Bush Administration rushed to the judgment that America's old approach to fighting terrorism, which treated it as a crime like any other, was inadequate for the post-9/11 world. Almost without discussion, it was agreed that a new kind of enemy required new kinds of tactics. As Jack Cloonan and all of the other FBI agents who had worked to convict terrorists would soon learn, their methods—which required evidence of criminality before the state could deprive a suspect of his liberty—were considered anachronistic. The mood, as Michael Rolince, head of the International Terrorism Operations Section at the FBI, put it, was "rule-of-law be damned."

The White House moved to a war footing reflexively. Remarkably little thought was given, however, to what the implications of this tectonic shift were. In reflecting back on this history later, Matthew Waxman, a young lawyer working as Rice's special assistant on the National Security Council on September 11 said, "What was incredible was how momentous a decision this is, to say we're in a state of war with Al Qaeda, because it set us on a course not only for our international response, but also in our domestic constitutional relations. You'd expect that the cabinet would have met, and that different options would have been developed, and they would have debated the pros and cons, and that allies would have been consulted. But there was little or no detailed deliberation about long-term consequences."

Before September 11, the CIA's Bin Laden Unit was a decidedly odd place. It was set up in 1996, as the Agency's only "virtual" station, in an effort to elevate the status of the unit from an ordinary task force to one that was equal in importance, at least in theory, to Paris or Rome. But unlike the foreign stations around the world, its headquarters was the fifth floor of a drab government office building in a suburban shopping mall in Tysons Corner, Virginia. "Alec Station," as it was known inside the Agency, was named after the son of its first station chief, Michael Scheuer, an analyst with a background in Europe, not Middle Eastern terrorism.

Scheuer was a noticeably rumpled-looking, middle-aged man of intense views, a style that meshed strangely with his insistence upon addressing all of the men he worked with formally as "sir." A devout Catholic, he had been trained by Jesuits and saw the terrorist threat in apocalyptic terms. He staffed Alec Station with an unusually large proportion of women, many of whom were originally Soviet analysts, who brought an intense Cold War sense of global peril to the mission. A tall, pale-skinned, spiky-haired redhead who wore bright red lipstick was particularly controversial among many of her male colleagues for her ferociousness. In a predominantly male culture where macho derring-do was cherished at least in theory, these women, some of whom called themselves "The Power Women's Club," vacationing and spending weekend social time together, were discounted by many male peers who sniped at them as man-hating fanatics. Collectively they became known around the Agency as "The Manson family."

In 1999, Scheuer was replaced after the politically smooth head of the Directorate of Operations, James Pavitt, apparently decided Scheuer was too intemperate. On the way out, Scheuer sent Pavitt a memorable parting shot. Pavitt kept Scheuer's farewell note encased in a special Lucite stand in his big seventh-floor office in Langley. "Dear Jim," it read, according to a source who examined it. Scheuer went on to accuse Pavitt, in unsparing language, of ruining his career for no reason. Pavitt explained that he liked to keep the memento because Scheuer was the only person in the Agency who had shown the balls to tell the boss the truth. The consequences of doing so, of course, were lost on no one.

The turnover in the Bin Laden Unit only went partway toward explaining the problems inside the CTC. The unit's failure to keep track of the trail of Mihdhar and Hamzi was, alas, not an isolated event. The CIA received several huge hints, for instance, that the September 11 operation's mastermind, Khalid Sheikh Mohammed, or KSM as he was later known, was plotting a terrorist attack inside the United States. One informant reported that KSM was "actively recruiting" people to travel to the United States, where colleagues were already inside the country waiting to meet them, in order to carry out terrorist-related activities. Yet almost until the end, the CTC failed to realize that KSM was associated with Al Qaeda at all. Thus, they failed to connect these clues with those they were gathering about Bin Laden.

Instead, they identified Mohammed as a freelance terrorist, putting him in a different bureaucratic box, watched not by Alec Station but instead by the smaller Extremist Branch of the CTC. At some point, his file was transferred to another unit, the Renditions Group, which organized snatch operations of wanted terrorists. But no one put the pieces together. There were numerous other similarly lost and mislaid clues.

Perfection is too much to ask of any human enterprise. But the CTC's performance was troubling, even to the CIA's loyalists. A former 9/11 investigator concluded, after sifting through all the paperwork, "that the supervisors in the CTC were not supervising." A longtime colleague described Black's CTC as "500 people running around with their hair on fire—but no system."

Nonetheless, Black was popular among the staff of the CTC because of his infectious enthusiasm. Sounding like a modern-day Teddy Roosevelt urging them to charge San Juan Hill, he would exhort his troops, "Be tough! This is no time to go 'introspective'!" Black didn't promise that the fight would be easy, but he promised it would be honorable and save thousands of American lives. "We'll just have to do the best we can. Wear seatbelts!" he would warn. "Don't drive drunk! Life is hard!" He was bombastic, of course, and colleagues discounted some of his melodramatic pronouncements, but Black was considered genuinely committed, and also unusually amiable in a bureaucracy filled with professional double-dealers. At the same time, colleagues found his record, as one put it, "a contradiction on the terrorism issue." The former CIA officer said, "They said it was our highest priority. But Cofer wasn't paying much attention."

Black had been chosen for the post partly because of a special distinction. He'd been head of the CIA station in Khartoum, Sudan, in 1994 when the terrorist known as "Carlos the Jackal" was caught. Carlos, who before Bin Laden was among the world's most infamous and wanted, secretly checked into a local hospital for surgery to fix a varicose vein in his scrotum. Black participated in Carlos's subsequent capture by the French, who wanted Carlos on murder charges. What role Black actually played was the subject of considerable backbiting inside the Agency and at the FBI. "He just happened to be there at the same time," sniped one former FBI agent. "He didn't swing through a window on a rope," a former CIA colleague agreed. But Black was sphinxlike about the details, and the legend grew. It was fed further by an apparent assassination plot on Black's life by Bin Laden and his associates, who like Carlos took shelter in the terrorist haven of Muslim radical Hasan al-Turabi's Sudan. There were reports of car chases and even shoot-outs between the guards on both sides. After this, Black took Bin Laden personally. "These people wish to kill us! I've been in situations where people wish to kill me!" he would say in his most stentorian tone.

Black's reports of life-threatening danger even ensnared the White House. He warned that a source in Khartoum had confided a sensational murder plot against Tony Lake, then Clinton's national security adviser in Washington. Lake was forced to live in a safehouse for days before the FBI was able to debunk the plot as unlikely.

Black's advancement in the CIA wasn't completely smooth. After Africa, he served as the head of the CIA's Iran Task Force. But his bellicose talk of the urgent need to go on a war footing against Iran in the late 1990s struck his superiors as over the top, a colleague recalled. Black was sidelined to Latin America, where he was made the deputy station chief, a demotion in status. His installation at the CTC revived his career.

The sad secret of the CTC, however, was that despite the fierce talk, before September 11 the CIA had no spies inside Al Qaeda or the security guard surrounding Bin Laden. They had never recruited a single agent inside his network or infiltrated any of his training camps. They had poured millions of dollars into what Richard Clarke, the counterterrorism czar at the White House, ridiculed as "rent-a-tribes"—Afghan, Uzbek, and Pakistani informants whom they relied upon to carry out a variety of ill-fated offensive actions against Bin Laden. But after four years in operation, the record of Alec Station was an embarrassment.

It was not for lack of imagination. Among other schemes, Scheuer had devised a plan to have the hired tribal leaders kidnap Bin Laden from Tarnak Farms and spirit him to a mountain cave thirty miles away. There, the Afghans were supposed to hold him for a month, until search-and-rescue teams gave up, and then turn him over to the custody of the CIA. In his mesmerizing account *The Looming Tower,* Lawrence Wright reveals that the CIA retrofitted a shipping container for the operation that could fit inside a C-130 military aircraft. Secured to its floor was a dentist's chair with specially rigged restraints. In this contraption, the CIA hoped to transport Bin Laden from the Afghan cave to Egypt, where according to Wright the CIA intended to have Bin Laden "rudely questioned." But in the days before September 11 and the "New Paradigm," the CIA's plan was angrily blocked by the FBI. John O'Neill, Chief of Counterterrorism at the FBI, convinced Clinton's attorney general, Janet Reno, that it amounted to murder. Reno approved the snatch operation only if Bin Laden was indicted first, and then he would have to be transported in his dental chair to America, not Egypt, to face criminal charges, not extermination.

It was on these sorts of legal curbs that Black blamed the CIA's failures. In truth, without better on-the-ground human intelligence, such as their own agents inside Al Qaeda, and without more efficient management and political will at the top, it's doubtful these schemes could ever have worked anyway. Clarke, an ally of Black's, later put it bluntly. "The CIA was unable to carry out the mission. The point is, they were risk-averse," he said. Tenet was "eager to kill bin Laden," he said. "He understood the threat. But the capability of the CIA's Directorate of Operations was far less than advertised. The Directorate of Operations would like people to think it's a great James Bond operation, but for years it essentially assigned officers undercover as diplomats to attend cocktail parties. They collected information. But they were not a commando unit that could go into Afghanistan and kill bin Laden."

Late in the afternoon of Sunday, September 16, Black emerged from his self-imposed exile in Langley to show the project he had been working so hard on all week to the allied British intelligence officials, who were still gathered in Washington. This time, he went to their turf, meeting at the sprawling British embassy just down Massachusetts Avenue from Cheney's official residence. Black brought a draft of a proposed new, top-secret presidential "finding" that he and the CIA lawyers had been hammering out all week. Formally called "Memoranda of Notifications" in the Bush White House, or MONs, they were legal memos detailing proposed covert actions, all of which required presidential authorization, according to laws that had been in place since the Agency's founding in 1947. Black's proposed new finding was an amalgamation of years' worth of thinking about all the powers the Agency might like to exercise in its fondest dreams. Most of the notions had been considered politically untenable before September 11.

The proposed finding included the inauguration of secret paramilitary death squads authorized to hunt and kill prime terror suspects anywhere on earth. A week earlier, these deaths would have been classified as illegal assassinations. Under the new legal analysis, such killings were sanctioned as acts of national "self-defense."

Black's proposal was nothing less than a global plan for a secret war, fought not by the military, with its well-known legal codes of conduct and a publicly accountable chain of command, but instead in the dark by faceless and nameless CIA agents following commands unknown to the American public. All new covert actions required congressional notification, but under the Bush Administration's interpretation, this would be pared down to a bare minimum of four elected representatives, none of whom were allowed to reveal publicly what they had learned. This war, as Bush later said, would be "invisible."

Black's proposal was reportedly the most aggressive, ambitious covert-action plan seen since the Cold War, maybe ever. It spanned some eighty countries in which the Agency thought terrorists or their supporters were active. To give the President deniability, and to keep him from getting his hands dirty, the finding called for the President to delegate blanket authority to Tenet to decide on a case-by-case basis whom to kill, whom to kidnap, whom to detain and interrogate, and how. After all the wrangling, the plan also called for the President to authorize the CIA to arm the Predator. It authorized the CIA's officers to break and enter into private property, and to monitor the communications and financial transactions of suspected terrorists, even inside the United States when necessary, as well.

Additionally, the CIA's lawyers floated the suggestion that the spy agency should no longer be banned from conducting espionage inside the United States. Since the Agency's inception in 1947, the curb on domestic spying had been an ironclad rule, deliberately written into the Agency's founding statute in order to ensure that America would never have a secret police service like the all-powerful and corrupt gestapos of Communist East Germany and Soviet Union. But shortly after September 11, at a meeting of general counsels to all of the various government intelligence agencies, called in the Roosevelt Room at the White House by the National Security Council's top lawyer, John Bellinger III, a CIA lawyer suggested that the curb on domestic spying be lifted. The CIA's proposal was stymied by strong resistance from the other visiting lawyers, some of whom were careerists rather than political appointees. But the proposal revealed a glimpse at the scope of the CIA's ambitions.

Virtually every other item on the CIA's wish list was approved. "Cofer Black and Dick Clarke found themselves suddenly fantastically in power," said a former administration official with inside knowledge of this period. "America was at war, but instead of the Department of Defense running it, the CIA was, so Tenet was for all intents and purposes the Secretary of Defense. Cofer was his top general, who grabbed it with both hands. They were the most powerful people in the bureaucracy."

At the time, however, the CIA had very few combat-ready paramilitary officers. The Special Activities Division, as the small paramilitary unit of the CIA was called, consisted mostly of inactive veterans of the military's Special Forces. Unlike the acrobatic Matt Damon in *The Bourne Ultimatum,* a former agent described them as "forty forty-year-olds." He added, "These were not the crack, elite squads of hunter/killers who you'd imagine being sent in to kill Bin Laden in the Hollywood version." One of the few who seemed sent by central casting, Henry "Hank" Crumpton, the young, smart, and physically buff head of operations inside the CTC, had been agitating with Black to get the unit more operational and less deskbound. The new finding gave him authority to give the CTC its own private "muscle." Under his direction, many of the best and most aggressive paramilitary officers soon joined a new secret commando team called the CTCSO, or CTC Special Operations unit. The squad ballooned to upward of a hundred gung-ho covert commandos. Tough and action-oriented, they joked among themselves, according to a former Agency colleague, that if they weren't carrying out black operations for the CIA they'd probably be robbing banks.

But as Pavitt made clear in a classified message sent out to all stations and bases around the world that week, when it came to "wreaking havoc upon and eliminating the sponsors and supporters of radical Islamic terrorism," the Agency would have to act in what he called "novel, untested ways."

The proposed presidential order described the need for "exceptional authorities to detain al Qaeda operatives worldwide." "Authorities" was an inoffensive, bureaucratic word, something from an organizational chart, not a spy novel. What it meant in practice was lost on no one familiar with the Agency's history. As John Maguire, a tough veteran of the CIA's clandestine service who welcomed the news, put it, after September 11 "Cofer and the CTC got exactly what they wanted all along, but were stopped from getting before, which was the authority and the congressional funding to do anything they wanted and needed to succeed. Before that, they had been neutered. They couldn't do anything that resulted in injury or death. But after September 11, the gloves came off."

After Black finished describing the CIA's proposed new plans to the gathered British officials, including the new capability to hunt and kill terrorists around the globe, Richard Dearlove, the coolly seasoned head of the British intelligence service, had a question. Known as one of the world's great master spies, both inscrutable and cunning, Dearlove asked Black what he planned to do "once you've hit the mercury with the hammer in Afghanistan, and the Al Qaeda cadre has spread all over the Middle East? Aren't you concerned about the potential destabilizing effect on Middle Eastern countries?"

"No," Black answered, according to Drumheller, who attended the meeting. "Our only concern is killing the terrorists."

After some three hours of conversation, Drumheller recalled, the meeting ended. On the way out, one of the British participants turned to him and said, "All rather bloodcurdling, isn't it?"

Black's comment was even more memorable. As they departed, according to Drumheller, Black turned to him and said that for the actions they were about to undertake, "We'll all probably be prosecuted." Drumheller thought that Black practically relished the possibility, casting himself as a tough but noble hero, forced to sacrifice himself for his country. "He was giving his Jack Nicholson, *A Few Good Men* speech," Drumheller concluded.

As soon as he received the paperwork, on Monday, September 17, Bush eagerly signed the new intelligence finding. He had been so enthused when he first heard about it from Tenet and Black at a cabinet meeting at Camp David that weekend, according to Bob Woodward's account *Bush at War,* the President almost shouted, "Great job!" With the stroke of the President's pen, one of the most important limitations imposed on the CIA would be erased, with only a handful of individuals' knowledge.

Gary Schroen, one of the first CIA officers to be dispatched to

Afghanistan, was among the earliest to sense the change in America's posture. Before leaving Langley, he described a memorable meeting in Black's office. "Gentlemen, I want to give you your marching orders, and I want to make them very clear," he recounted Black as saying. "I have discussed this with the President, and he is in full agreement. Your mission is to find Osama Bin Laden and his senior lieutenants, and kill them." Schroen said Black paused then to let his words sink in. "I don't want Bin Laden and his thugs captured. I want them dead. Alive and in prison here in the United States and they'll become a symbol, a rallying point for other terrorists. They have planned and carried out the murder of thousands of our citizens. They must be killed. I want to see photos of their heads on pikes. I want Bin Laden's head shipped back in a box filled with dry ice. I want to be able to show Bin Laden's head to the President. I promised him I would do that." He paused again, then asked, "Have I made myself clear?"

Schroen recounted in his memoir, *First In,* that he and his partner glanced at each other and smiled. "Perfectly clear, Cofer," they said. "I don't know where we'll find the dry ice in Afghanistan, but I think we certainly can manufacture pikes in the field."

Schroen acknowledged that it was the first time in his thirty-one-year career at the CIA that he had ever been asked to kill anyone.

Not long after, the Russians warned Black in a secret meeting that Afghanistan was the geopolitical equivalent of quicksand. Black scoffed at their pessimism. "We're going to kill them," Black retorted. "We're going to put their heads on sticks. We're going to rock their world."

Black savored the anticipated details of Bin Laden's death in an interview with *The New Yorker* magazine, as well. "You'd need some DNA," he said, to prove to the world Bin Laden was slain. "There's a good way to do it. Take a machete, and whack off his head, and you'll get a bucketful of DNA, so you can see it and test it. It beats lugging the whole body back!"

Inside the Agency, Drumheller and a few others were worried. The September 17 Memorandum of Notification had moved much faster than usual. Generally, after the Agency's lawyers drafted a proposed covert-action finding, it was reviewed by "The Lawyers' Group," which was chaired by the NSC's legal counsel and included lawyers from the State Department, Defense Department, Justice Department, and CIA. After the lawyers flyspecked it, the proposed finding was reviewed further by the cabinet-level national security policy makers, where among others the Vice President weighed in. Only then did it move to the President's desk. But in this critical instance, the CIA would be gaining fearsome new powers with very little debate—none of it public. The Agency was taking on new responsibilities in areas where it had no expertise, such as interrogation and detention. Within the Agency, there was a fair amount of underground dissent, particularly among the older veterans who remembered the CIA scandals of the past. "A number of people said, 'Be very careful. What are we talking about here?" Drumheller recalled.

Drumheller himself worried that despite years of caution regarding the CIA's legal limits, "We were basically telling ourselves it's okay to do this."

"But the proponents," he recalled, "said, 'It's not so bad, it's not so much.' The truth," he said, "is that the President wanted it. So everyone else wanted to be the most aggressive. A lot of ambitious people played on Cheney and the President's fascination with this. The President *loved* it."

The redefinition of America's standards for the treatment of its enemies took place almost entirely out of public view. But Cofer Black offered one public hint. On September 26, 2002, a year into what came to be known as the CIA's "program," he addressed the House and Senate Intelligence Committees. The arrest and detention of terrorists, he said, was "a very highly classified area." But he added, "All you need to know is that there was a 'before 9/11' and there was an 'after 9/11.' After 9/11, the gloves come off."

4

MEN OF ZEAL

The greatest dangers to liberty lurk in insidious encroachment by men of zeal, well-meaning but without understanding.

—Justice Louis Brandeis,
Olmstead v. United States (1928)

Tom Daschle, the Democratic Senate Majority Leader, was anxious in the days immediately after the September 11 attacks to do almost anything that the President asked. But he drew the line on September 14, 2001, when his Republican counterpart, Senate Minority Leader Trent Lott, delivered a special request from Alberto Gonzales, the White House Counsel.

Congress was on the verge of authorizing Bush to go to war against the perpetrators of the attacks. The language had already been written and the vote was pending. But at the last moment, the White House presented an urgent new proposal, "a draft that gave the White House virtually unchecked authority and the ability to do virtually anything," Daschle recalled.

Specifically, Gonzales demanded that Congress expand the President's war authority even further than had already been agreed upon. President Bush wanted authorization to wage war against suspected terrorists not just abroad but also inside the United States.

"We were just dumbfounded," Daschle said.

As Daschle knew, Congress had already turned back an earlier effort by the White House to expand the definition of the enemy. The White House wanted to target not just those terrorists who could be linked to the September 11 attacks, but anyone whom the President deemed a terrorist. After considerable haggling, the White House had appeared to accept compromise language. It was not quite as broad as the White House wanted, but it nonetheless gave the President the authority to treat the war on terror as an armed conflict with very few boundaries. He could use "all necessary and appropriate force" to wage war against any "nations, organizations, or persons" he determined had "planned, authorized, committed, or aided the terrorist attacks that occurred on Sept. 11, 2001." He was also free to target any who had "harbored such organizations or persons," in order to prevent future acts of terrorism.

Now, minutes before Daschle was about to submit the approved language to Congress for a vote, the White House was back again with a new gambit. Lott appeared on Gonzales's behalf, insisting that the words "in the United States" needed to be added to the scope of the President's proposed battle zone. It seemed to Daschle a bizarre request. The wording would have given President Bush the authority to round up American citizens as enemy combatants, potentially stripping them of their civil liberties.

Daschle refused to give the President what he regarded as a blank check. Instead, that day the Senate voted unanimously, and the House voted 420–1, to authorize the more limited war powers. But if Daschle assumed that this was the end of the matter, he was mistaken.

That afternoon, President Bush delivered a somber address from the main pulpit of the National Cathedral. The sanctuary, a soaring replica of Europe's high Gothic style, had often served in times of crisis as a hallowed meeting place in Washington. Addressing an audience of dignitaries that included most of the members of Congress as well as former presidents Clinton, Bush, Carter, and Ford, the President spoke eloquently of his new resolve to "rid the world of evil." For a moment the capital seemed unified, transcending the clash of partisan politics that had threatened to ensnare Bush's presidency only days before.

As Bush called for a new spirit of common purpose, however, his legal team, which was ideologically extreme and intensely partisan, was busy across town composing secret legal memos that would grant the President all the powers, and more, that Congress had just denied his administration.

Without informing either Congress or the public, which would not learn of these extraordinary memos for at least three more years, the

President's lawyers dismissed the notion that Congress could limit the President's conduct of warfare at all. The new legal interpretation wiped out years of checks and balances, eviscerating among other laws the post-Vietnam War Powers Resolution prohibiting the president from engaging in military hostilities for more than ninety days without congressional authorization.

Daschle may have been left with the impression that he had fended President Bush off from using his augmented war powers as commander in chief inside America. But the same day, the President's lawyers sought alternative advice from the Justice Department on just this issue. They wanted to know about "the legality of the use of military force to prevent or deter terrorist activity inside the United States," according to a confidential Justice Department memorandum.

Within a week, the Justice Department delivered a secret answer that would shock Daschle when he found out about it. The memo argued that in times of national emergency, which had been declared since September 11, "If the president decided the threat justified deploying the military inside the country," the federal government could legally "raid or attack dwellings where terrorists were thought to be, despite risks that third parties could be killed or injured by exchanges of fire." The government could also shoot down civilian airliners hijacked by terrorists and set up military checkpoints inside American cities. In this and related memos, the Justice Department said that the executive branch could ignore both Fourth Amendment protections against illegitimate searches and, without court warrants, specific laws passed by Congress prohibiting wiretaps and other surreptitious surveillance of Americans' communications. Such warrantless eavesdropping had been illegal since 1978.

"The government may be justified in taking measures which in less troubled conditions could be seen as infringements of individual liberties," the Office of Legal Counsel lawyers told the White House. In fact, the lawyers advised, "We think that the Fourth Amendment should be no more relevant than it would be in cases of invasion or insurrection." When this position became public in 2008, Bush's third attorney general, Michael Mukasey, repudiated the argument that no law could regulate military searches within the United States, assuring outraged senators in a public hearing that "the Fourth Amendment applies across the board, regardless of whether we're in wartime or peacetime."

Bush's legal team was arguing that the President not only had power to defend the nation as he saw fit in ways that were not limited by any laws, he also had the power to override existing laws that Congress had specifically designed to curb him. The opinion trampled this distinction between unrestricted presidential power and regulated presidential power, where Congress had purposefully imposed limits. In doing so, the Justice Department turned the most famous Supreme Court ruling on this subject on its head. During the Truman Administration, the eminent Justice Robert Jackson had set the precedent balancing the competing claims of the President and Congress during wartime. In 1952, a labor dispute had threatened to cut off steel supplies needed to wage the Korean War. Truman, citing his presidential powers as commander in chief, had authorized the government to seize the steel mills to keep the production lines moving. But Congress had previously passed laws defining how strikes could be settled, barring such interference. Jackson ruled that since Congress had already legislated in this area, even the commander in chief had no authority to disobey the law. "No penance would ever expiate the sin against free government of holding that a President can escape control of executive powers by law through assuming a military role," Jackson ruled.

In contrast, in the view of Bush's lawyers, all such statutes, including those prohibiting torture, secret detention, and warrantless surveillance, could now be set aside.

Wars have always aggrandized presidential power in America's history. Some of the country's greatest presidents, including Abraham Lincoln and Franklin Roosevelt, trampled civil liberties in the name of safeguarding national security. Lincoln infamously suspended habeas corpus during the Civil War. Roosevelt interned 120,000 Japanese-American citizens. By comparison, President Bush's infringements of Americans' civil liberties during the war on terror have been modest. But the constitutional arguments made by Bush Administration lawyers in justifying its policies have been of a whole new order. While earlier presidents arguably overstepped boundaries in times of emergency, neither Lincoln nor Roosevelt claimed the routine presidential right to do so. Nixon set the closest precedent. He argued that he had the inherent right as President to exercise such power, or as he infamously put it, "When the President does it, that means that it is not illegal." But he was forced to resign in disgrace. The Bush White House, in contrast, seized on historical aberrations, such as the darkest moments of Lincoln and Roosevelt, and turned them into a doctrine of presidential prerogative.

The Justice Department's legal advice on these sensitive matters was kept secret, but hints of Bush's sense that he was entitled to disregard Congress began to be sprinkled into his public pronouncements. Less than a week after Daschle turned the White House's request down, for instance, President Bush gave an address that reportedly reached 80 million Americans. The wording was telling. Bush promised, "Whether we bring our enemies to justice, or bring justice to our enemies, justice will be done." Then, despite the few limitations set by Congress, the President added, "Our war on terror begins with Al Qaeda, but it does not end there." He said America's target was not just Bin Laden and those responsible for the September 11 attacks but, more broadly, "the global terror network." Americans, Bush warned, "should not expect one battle, but a lengthy campaign, unlike any other we have ever seen."

After the speech, Bush called his gifted speechwriter, Michael Gerson, and told him that he had "never felt more comfortable in my life."

One reason President Bush may have been at peace with this new role as crisis manager is that he had previously contemplated the unparalleled opportunity that wars hand to presidents. He had learned by watching his father. According to a family biographer, who interviewed Bush in 1999 when he was still governor of Texas, Bush felt that his father had squandered this opportunity presented by the success of the first Gulf War, and he was determined that if ever he had the chance, he would do better. "One of the keys to being seen as a great leader is to be seen as a commander in chief," Bush told biographer and *Houston Chronicle* journalist Mickey Herskowitz. "My father had all this political capital built up when he drove the Iraqis out of Kuwait and he wasted it . . . If I had that much capital, I'm not going to waste it. I'm going to get everything passed that I want to get passed, and I'm going to have a successful presidency."

The war on terror certainly was not the battle that Bush had contemplated. But amid the awful strain and loss after September 11, the President confided to associates that it had given him new purpose. As he had anticipated, it also gave him greater stature. In the privacy of the White House, some noticed, Bush had begun to refer to himself in the third person, as "the Commander in Chief."

The lead architect of the Bush Administration's idiosyncratic interpretation of American law was a tall and bespectacled government lawyer who had the look of an irascible sea captain. It was said that from the moment David Addington walked into a room, his presence was palpable, in part because of the power of his unwavering conservative convictions. "No one stood to his right," as one colleague put it. And no one was better positioned to translate the President's impulse to get tough into the Bush Administration's controversial legal strategy for the war on terror than Addington, who was then Vice President Cheney's legal counsel.

Within minutes of the September 11 terrorist attacks, Addington began to assert himself as the war on terror's indispensable man. For years, Addington had carried a dog-eared copy of the U.S. Constitution in his pocket; taped onto the back were photocopies of extra statutes that detailed the legal procedures for presidential succession. Like his patron, Cheney, Addington was a regular participant in "continuity-of-government" exercises. As such, he was steeped in the fine points of how to prevail in a state of national emergency. On September 11, no lawyer in the White House was more ready.

The day of the attacks, Addington was evacuated with most of the rest of the White House staff and had begun to walk toward the Memorial Bridge, on his way home to the Virginia suburbs. But he was soon summoned by phone to join Cheney in the Presidential Emergency Operations Center beneath the West Wing. Down in the subterranean bunker, there were waiters serving sandwiches and cookies, and photographers immortalizing the moment for history. "The amenities were really surprisingly nice," an eyewitness recalled. But, he said, there were no law books. Addington's worn, pocket-sized copy of the U.S. Constitution served as the only legal text on hand during the crisis.

Before long, others noticed that Addington and Cheney were deeply engrossed in an intense legal discussion. The burning question of the moment, which would develop into the signature issue of the coming Bush years, was how far the President's powers could be extended in order to fight this new foe. The pressures felt by the White House lawyers to push the limits were extraordinary.

"Feelings were very raw," Bradford Berenson, a deputy in the Bush White House Counsel's Office, later recalled. "There were thousands of bereaved American families. Everyone was expecting additional attacks. The only planes in the air were military. At a moment like that, there's an intense focus of responsibility and accountability on the person of the President. It's a responsibility to protect the nation. It's visceral. You feel the President owes all of his power to preventing another attack." He said the lawyers knew that they had to guide the

President's response "always within the law." But, he noted, they felt that "if you have to err on the side of being too aggressive, or not aggressive enough, you'd err on being too aggressive."

By the end of the day on September 11, Addington had joined forces in this legal discussion with two other lawyers who shared many of his rigidly conservative views. Timothy Flanigan, who was a lawyer in the White House Counsel's Office, and John Yoo, who was a deputy chief in the Justice Department's Office of Legal Counsel, were both patched in by remote video from their respective secure perches in the White House Situation Room and the Justice Department's fourth-floor Command Center.

Flanigan was a hard-fighting veteran of many of Washington's bitterest partisan political wars. Like many of the top Bush Administration lawyers, he had proven his loyalty by volunteering in *Bush v. Gore,* the scorched-earth legal brawl settling the tainted 2000 presidential election. He'd also been involved in the politically divisive legal investigation of Bill Clinton's sex life, defending former independent counsel Kenneth Starr, whom Clinton sympathizers regarded as a political zealot, as having conducted his investigation "in a moderate and appropriate fashion." A Mormon and anti-abortion activist, Flanigan was the father of fourteen children, some of whom were homeschooled. A friend said he drove the family in his own school bus.

Both Flanigan and Yoo were active in the Federalist Society, a group of conservative lawyers devoted to reestablishing the "original" interpretation of the Constitution. Both had clerked for conservative Supreme Court justices, Flanigan for former Chief Justice Warren Burger (he had reportedly been paid $700,000 by the Federalist Society to write a biography about him), and Yoo for Clarence Thomas. Yoo, too, had passed the partisan litmus test by working for the Republican side in *Bush v. Gore.* He was only thirty-four in 2001. But at Berkeley, where he had been a law professor prior to joining the Bush Administration, Yoo had won a national reputation for holding cleverly provocative views. Like many conservatives whose suspicion of international rights stretched back over the decades to Wilson's League of Nations and Roosevelt's United Nations, Yoo was dismissive of the claims of international law and institutions, instead championing the need for America to assert its supremacy without apology or hindrance in the world.

Yoo's specialty was the area of presidential power during war. Unlike most mainstream academics, he likened the president's powers to that of British kings, arguing that America's founders had meant for presidents to be able to wage war almost as unilaterally. Yoo's views were not widely accepted. Critics accused him of "fictionalizing the founding" history of the country. The Constitution divides the war powers between the president, who is assigned the role of "Commander in Chief of the Army and Navy," and Congress, which is given the power to declare war, raise and govern the Army and Navy, and regulate the taking of prisoners. Most mainstream historians interpret the extensive record laid out in the *Federalist Papers* as proof that the framers deliberately split these responsibilities specifically to avoid monarchical concentrations of power, which they feared could lead too easily to unnecessary and damaging wars. As Bruce Fein, a Republican legal activist who voted for Bush in both presidential elections and who served as associate deputy attorney general in the Reagan Justice Department, pointed out, "If you read the *Federalist Papers,* you can see how rich in history they are. The founders really understood the history of what people did with power, going back to Greek and Roman and biblical times. Our political heritage is to be skeptical of executive power, because, in particular, there was skepticism of King George III." Fein believed that the founders "would have been shocked" by the Bush White House.

Yoo was nonetheless a facile and polished advocate, with sterling Ivy League credentials. In the weeks before the terrorist attacks, Yoo had been bored at the Justice Department and talked with friends about leaving. But the tragedy of September 11 presented an extraordinary opportunity to all three lawyers for putting their extreme principles into practice.

The legal doctrine that Addington espoused—that the president, as commander in chief, had the authority to disregard virtually all previously known legal boundaries if national security demanded it—rested on a reading of the Constitution that few legal scholars shared.

Liberal historians like Schlesinger were not the only experts who questioned what came to be known as "The New Paradigm." High-ranking and very conservative administration lawyers who worked closely with Addington found themselves astonished by his radical absolutism. One later recalled sitting in meetings with Addington wondering, "How did this lunatic end up running the country?"

The New Paradigm began with a sensible-sounding rationale. As John Yoo, who had a soft, singsong voice and eminently reasonable manner, explained it, "When a foreign entity for political purposes can kill 3,000 Americans and cause billions of dollars' worth of damage and try to eliminate the leaders of the American government, that sounds like war to most people, not a crime," explained Yoo. Thus, the overarching intent of the legal strategy was to transform the fight against terrorism from a criminal justice matter to a full-fledged military war, thereby allowing the CIA and Pentagon to kill or capture and question terrorist suspects as swiftly as possible, with as much latitude as possible. The assumption on all sides was that getting accurate, fast, "actionable" information would be the key to defeating the terrorists. By emphasizing interrogation over due process, the government intended to preempt future attacks before they materialized. Although there was no serious effort to examine whether this political preconception was accurate, the administration proclaimed that criminal and military courts, with their exacting standards of evidence and their emphasis on protecting defendants' rights, including the right to remain silent, were too cumbersome. Rather than seeing the American legal system as the country's greatest strength, it was instantly regarded as a burden.

Cheney, the patron of this harsh new legal regime, said, "We think it guarantees that we'll have the kind of treatment of these individuals that we believe they deserve." But under this New Paradigm, the President gave terror suspects neither the rights of criminal defendants nor the rights of prisoners of war. Instead, he authorized a new, ad hoc system of detention and interrogation that operated outside any previously known coherent body of law. The administration designated terrorists as "illegal enemy combatants" whose treatment would ultimately be decided by the President. As Eric Lewis, an expert in international law who represented several detainees, later put it, "The administration's lawyers created a third category and cast them outside the law."

That the Vice President's lawyer, who had no line authority on national security matters, no staff—not even an assistant—and only secondary bureaucratic rank, would end up shaping much of the administration's legal strategy on terrorism was one of the oddities of the nation's plunge into the dark side. Addington's path to power defied nearly all of Washington's conventions. He didn't serve the President directly, and although he had been a government lawyer for most of his career, he had never worked in the Justice Department. He kept the door to his office locked at all times, and never spoke to the press or posed for photographs for news stories. (He and Cheney declined repeated requests to be interviewed for this book.) In a city where social networks translated into power, Addington was a loner, commuting to work every day on the subway from a modest suburban house in Alexandria, Virginia. He seemed to revel in being anonymous and abstemious, refusing the lavish invitations that accompany top White House jobs in favor of a simple bowl of gazpacho eaten most days for lunch. "He didn't care about advancement in the Washington world," a colleague noted. "He was interested in certain outcomes."

Colleagues speculated endlessly about how Addington attained such power. Certainly, his intellect was strong and his personality was forceful. He worked tirelessly long days and nights, and he had a prodigious memory for the minutiae of federal legal statutes. More important, undoubtedly, was his closeness to Cheney, whose political views he clearly shared and was assumed to be representing. When a White House colleague in conflict with Addington challenged officials at the Office of Management and Budget, asking why they allowed Addington to single-handedly rewrite their budget proposals before they were passed on to the President for his signature, they responded, "We have to! It's what the Vice President wants!" As Cheney grew into the most influential vice president in American history, Addington, as his surrogate, became one of the most powerful unelected officials in the government—"Cheney's Cheney."

Addington's talent for bureaucratic infighting was such that even his admirers tended to invoke metaphors involving knives. Juleanna Glover, Cheney's former press secretary, called Addington "efficient, discreet, loyal, sublimely brilliant," but also noted that "as anyone who worked with him knew, he was someone who, in a knife fight, you wanted covering your back." Bradford Berenson, the former White House lawyer, said, "He was powerful because people knew he spoke for the Vice President, and because he was an extremely smart, creative, and aggressive public official. Some engage in bureaucratic infighting using slaps. Some use knives. David fell into the latter category. You could make the argument that there are some costs. It introduced a little fear into the policy-making process. Views might be more candidly expressed without that fear. But David was like the Marines. No better friend—no worse enemy."

People who sparred with Addington agreed. Colonel Lawrence Wilkerson, Secretary of State Powell's former chief of staff, described Addington as "utterly ruthless." A former top national-security lawyer said, "He took a political litmus test of everyone. If you were not sufficiently ideological, he would cut the ground out from under you."

Addington's singular influence, though, in the days and weeks immediately after September 11 could also be traced to a curious vacuum. In a war that would rely as much on exploiting legal loopholes as it did on bullets and bombs, there were few law degrees among the top officials. Neither the President, the Vice President, the Secretary of Defense, the Secretary of State, nor the National Security Adviser was a lawyer. In contrast, during the Clinton Administration, all of these posts were held by lawyers, with the exception of the Vice President, and even he had attended law school briefly. Bill Clinton liked to remind other lawyers in his administration that he had taught constitutional law.

There were, of course, other lawyers in the Bush Administration whose power on paper exceeded that of Addington. But none, including Attorney General Ashcroft and the White House Counsel, Alberto Gonzales, had anything like Addington's familiarity with national security law. Ashcroft's relations with the White House grew increasingly strained, leaving him out of the inner circle that decided the most important legal strategies in the war on terror. Gonzales, whom the President nicknamed "Fredo" and referred to as *"mi amigo"* or *"mi abogado"* ("my lawyer" in Spanish), in reference to Gonzales's humble Mexican origins and decade of personal legal service to him in Texas, had more influence because of his longtime ties to the President. But as an administration lawyer put it, "He was an empty suit. He was weak. And he doesn't know shit about the Geneva Conventions."

As a result, it was Addington who offered legal certitude at a moment of paramount political and legal confusion. "He was supremely confident," another Bush Administration lawyer recalled. Participants in meetings in the White House Counsel's office in the days immediately after September 11 described Gonzales sitting in a wingback chair, asking questions, while Addington sat directly across from him, holding forth. "Gonzales would call the meetings," the former high-ranking lawyer recalled. "But Addington was always the force in the room." In Bruce Fein's estimation, the Bush legal team was strikingly unsophisticated. "There is no one of legal stature, certainly no one like Bork, or Scalia, or Elliot Richardson, or Archibald Cox," he said. "No one knew the Constitution—certainly not Cheney."

Addington's admirers saw him as he saw himself, as a selfless patriot, a believer in hard power who was not afraid to make unpopular choices—altogether the necessary answer to threatening times. One such admirer was Steve Berry, a Republican lawyer and Washington lobbyist who hired Addington to work with him as the legislative counsel to the House Intelligence Committee in 1983. Berry had been a career patron and close friend ever since. He said, "I know him well, and I know that if there's a threat he will do everything in his power, within the law, to protect the United States." Berry added that Addington was acutely aware of the legal tensions between liberty and security. "We fought ourselves every day about it," he recalled. But, he said, they concluded that a "strong national security and defense" was the first priority, and that "without a strong defense, there's not much expectation or hope of having other freedoms."

The impact of reading the Matrix Threat Reports daily weighed heavily on Addington, Berry said, as it did on others in the White House. "I've talked to David about this a little. Psychologically, it's really taxing to read every day not about one or two but about a dozen, or two dozen, legitimate reports about efforts to take out U.S. citizens. . . . There's a little bit of a bunker mentality that set in among some of the national-security-policy officials after 9/11," he said. "For Dave, protecting America isn't just a virtue. It's a personal mission. I feel safer just knowing he's where he is."

Addington had a dazzling ability to recall decades' worth of intelligence and national security legislation. Though few people doubted Addington's knowledge of national security law, even his admirers questioned his political instincts. "The only time I've seen him wrong is on his political judgment," a former colleague said. "He has a tin ear for political issues. Sometimes the law says one thing but you have to at least listen to the other side. He will cite case history, case after case. David doesn't see why you have to compromise."

This might not have mattered had the White House looked elsewhere for policy recommendations. But, almost by default, starting right after September 11, the lawyers filled much of this void. Both Bush and Cheney made clear they wanted to be as aggressive as the law would allow. But it was left to their deputies, the lawyers, to fill in the details. What was missing was a discussion of policy—not just what was legal, but what was moral, ethical, right, and smart to do. This discussion rarely if ever happened.

Conventional wisdom held that September 11 changed everything, including the thinking of Cheney and Addington. But a close look at the twenty-year collaboration between the two men suggests that they had long imagined many aspects of the program they put in place after the terrorist attacks. Cheney's writings and speeches suggest he had been laying the political groundwork for years. "This preceded 9/11," said Fein, who has known both men professionally for decades. "I'm not saying that warrantless surveillance did. But the idea of reducing Congress to a cipher was already in play. It was Cheney and Addington's political agenda."

The Addingtons were a military family. They moved frequently; David's father, Jerry, an electrical engineer in the Army, was assigned to a variety of posts, including Saudi Arabia and Washington, D.C., where he worked with the Joint Chiefs of Staff. As a teenager, Addington told a friend that he hoped to live in Washington himself when he grew up. Jerry Addington, a 1940 graduate of West Point who won a Bronze Star during the Second World War, also served in Korea and at the North American Air Defense Command in Colorado; he reached the rank of brigadier general before he retired in 1970, when David was thirteen. David attended public high school in Albuquerque, New Mexico, and his father began a second career teaching middle-school math. His mother, Eleanore, was a housewife; the family lived in a ranch house in a middle-class subdivision and regularly attended Catholic church. His mother continued to live there after his father died in 1994. "We are an extremely close family," one of Addington's three older sisters, Linda, recalled. "Discipline was very important for us, and faith was very important. It was about being ethical—the right thing to do whether anyone else does it or not. I see that in Dave." She was reluctant to say more. "Dave is most deliberate about his privacy," she added.

Addington had been a hawk on national defense since he was a teenager. Leonard Napolitano, an engineer who was one of Addington's close childhood friends, and whose political leanings were more like those of his sister, Janet Napolitano, the Democratic governor of Arizona, joked, "I don't think that in high school David was a believer in the divine right of kings." But, he said, Addington was "always conservative."

Socially, Napolitano recalled, he and Addington were "the brains, or nerds." Addington stood out for wearing black socks with shorts. He and his friends were not particularly athletic, and they liked to play poker all night on weekends, stopping early in the morning for breakfast. Their circle included some girls, until the boys found them "too distracting to our interest in cards," Napolitano recalled.

When he and Addington were in high school, Napolitano said, the

Vietnam War was in its final stages and "there was a certain amount of 'challenge authority' and alcohol and drugs, but they weren't issues in our group." Addington's high-school history teacher, Irwin Hoffman, whom Napolitano recalled as wonderful, exacting, and "a flaming liberal," said that Addington felt strongly that America "should have stayed and won the Vietnam War, despite the fact that we were losing." Hoffman, who is retired, added, "The boy seemed terribly, terribly bright. He wrote well, and he was very verbal, not at all reluctant to express his opinions. He was pleasant and quite handsome." But even in high school, his teacher noticed a characteristic that would cause some colleagues in the White House to regard him as a bully. "He also had a very strong sarcastic streak," Hoffman said. "He was scornful of anyone who said anything that was naive or less than bright. His sneers were almost palpable."

Addington graduated in 1974, a particularly tumultuous period for conservatives. In the aftermath of Watergate's lawlessness, reformers in Congress imposed tighter restraints on future presidents and reined in the FBI and CIA. Nixon had argued that he had "inherent authority" to spy on American citizens whom he deemed enemies. The FBI eavesdropped on Martin Luther King Jr.'s private life, using tapes of his intimate behavior in an unsuccessful effort to blackmail him into committing suicide. Nixon's henchmen broke into the private office of the psychiatrist to anti–Vietnam War activist Daniel Ellsberg, in hopes of finding material with which they could discredit him. Congressional hearings led by Senator Frank Church and Representative Otis Pike, meanwhile, exposed scandalous abuses of power, revealing details of CIA assassination plots, coup attempts, mind-control experiments, and domestic spying. Congress passed a series of measures aimed at reinvigorating the system of checks and balances, including an expanded Freedom of Information Act and the Foreign Intelligence Surveillance Act, the law requiring judicial review before foreign security suspects inside the country could be wiretapped. It also created the House and Senate Intelligence Committees to oversee all covert CIA activities. And it passed the War Powers Resolution, limiting the president's ability to commit troops to war without congressional authorization.

After high school, Addington pursued an ambition that he had had for years: to join the military. Rather than attending West Point, as his father had, he enrolled in the U.S. Naval Academy in Annapolis.

But he dropped out before the end of his freshman year. He went home and, according to Napolitano, worked in a Long John Silver's restaurant.

Addington then went to Georgetown University, graduating summa cum laude in 1978 from the School of Foreign Service; he went on to earn honors at Duke Law School. After graduating in 1981, he married Linda Werling, a graduate student in pharmacology. The marriage ended in divorce. His second wife, Cynthia, did not work outside of the home, caring for the couple's three girls full-time.

Soon after leaving Duke, Addington started his first job and made his first steps toward becoming an expert in national security law. Under William Casey's directorship, Addington joined the general counsel's office at the CIA. There, he was described as loving the "go-go guys," with their hunting licenses to conduct covert operations around the globe. A former top Agency lawyer who later worked with Addington said that Addington strongly opposed the reform movements that followed Vietnam and Watergate. "Addington was too young to be fully affected by the Vietnam War," the lawyer said. "He was shaped by the postwar, post-Watergate years instead. He thought the presidency was too weakened. He's a believer that in foreign policy the executive is meant to be quite powerful."

These views were shared by Cheney, who followed his friend and mentor, Donald Rumsfeld, as White House Chief of Staff in the Ford Administration. "On a range of executive-power issues, Cheney thought that presidents from Nixon onward yielded too quickly," said Michael J. Malbin, a political scientist who has advised Cheney on the issue of executive power. Kenneth Adelman, who was a high-ranking Pentagon official under Ford, said that the fall of Saigon in 1975 was "very painful for Dick. He believed that Vietnam could have been saved—maybe—if Congress hadn't cut off funding. He was against that kind of interference."

Cheney described those post-Watergate years as "the nadir of the modern presidency in terms of authority and legitimacy." He told *U.S. News & World Report* that the need for a strong president "has been a continuing theme, if you will, in terms of my career."

Jane Harman, the ranking Democrat on the House Intelligence Committee, who spent considerable time working with Cheney and Addington during the Bush years, came to believe that they were stuck in a time warp, still fighting Watergate. "They were focused on

restoring the Nixon presidency," she said. "They persuaded themselves that, following Nixon, things went all wrong." She said that in
meetings Addington was always courtly and pleasant. But when it
came to accommodating Congress, "his answer is always no."

In a revealing interview that Cheney gave in December 2005 to reporters traveling with him to Oman, he explained, "I do have the
view that over the years there had been an erosion of presidential
power and authority. . . . A lot of the things around Watergate and
Vietnam both, in the seventies, served to erode the authority I think
the president needs." Further, Cheney explained, it was his express
aim to restore the balance of power. The president needed to be able
to act as Alexander Hamilton had described it in the *Federalist Papers,*
with "secrecy" and "dispatch"—especially, Cheney said, "in the day
and age we live in . . . with the threats we face." He added, "I believe
in a strong, robust executive authority, and I think the world we live
in demands it."

At the CIA, where Addington spent two years, he focused on fights
aimed at limiting Congress's interference in intelligence gathering.
Addington viewed the public airings of the CIA's covert activities as
"an absolute disaster," Berry recalled. He found a political hero in the
CIA's director, Casey, who also regarded congressional constraints on
the Agency as little more than impediments to be circumvented.

Using their constitutional authority over appropriations, the Democrats in Congress forbade the CIA to spend federal funds to support the Contras, a rightist rebel group in Nicaragua. But Casey's
attitude, as Berry recalled it, was "We're gonna fund these freedom
fighters whether Congress wants us to or not." Berry, then the staff director for the Republicans on the House Intelligence Committee,
asked Casey for help in fighting the Democrats. Soon afterward, the
Agency sent Addington to join Berry on Capitol Hill.

When the Iran-Contra scandal broke in 1986, it exposed White
House arms deals and foreign fund-raising designed to help the anti-
Sandinista forces in Nicaragua, in contravention of the will of Con-
gress. Members of Congress were furious. Summoned to Capitol Hill,
Casey lied outright, denying that funds for the Contras had been so-
licited from any foreign governments, although he knew that the
Saudis, among others, had agreed to give millions of dollars to the
Contras at the request of the White House. Even within the Reagan
Administration, the foreign funding of these U.S. covert operations

was controversial. Secretary of State George Shultz had warned Reagan that he might be committing an impeachable offense. But, under Casey's guidance, the White House went ahead with the plan anyway.

As a demonstration of presidential power, the Iran-Contra scandal was a spectacular failure. It substantially weakened Reagan's popularity, and eventually seven people were convicted of seventeen felonies. Cheney, who was then a Republican congressman from Wyoming, worried that the scandal would further undercut presidential authority. In late 1986, he became the ranking Republican on a House select committee that was investigating the scandal, and he commissioned a report on Reagan's support of the Contras. Addington, who had become an expert in intelligence law, contributed legal research. The scholarly sounding but politically outlandish Minority Report, released in 1987, argued that Congress—not the President—had overstepped its authority by encroaching on the President's foreign-policy powers. The President, the report said, had been driven by "a legitimate frustration with abuses of power and irresolution by the legislative branch." The Minority Report sanctioned the President's actions to a surprising degree, considering the number of criminal charges that resulted from the scandal. The report also defended the legality of ignoring congressional intelligence oversight, arguing that "the President has the Constitutional and statutory authority to withhold notifying Congress of covert actions under rare conditions." And it condemned "legislative hostage taking," noting that "Congress must realize . . . that the power of the purse does not make it supreme" in matters of war. The president, the report noted, "will on occasion feel duty bound to assert monarchical notions of prerogative that will permit him to exceed the laws." While the report did not condone turning the presidency into a monarchy, its lessons were still very much on Cheney's mind fifteen years later.

In his December 2005 interview with reporters, Cheney proudly cited this document. "If you want reference to an obscure text, go look at the minority views that were filed in the Iran-Contra committee, the Iran-Contra report, in about 1987," he said. "Part of the argument was whether the President had the authority to do what was done in the Reagan years."

For Addington and Cheney, therefore, executive power was personal. Both had experienced the loss of power firsthand in the post-Watergate period, and they were still chafing over the constraints they were forced to accept by self-styled Democratic reformers. Unable to win the political fight in the court of public opinion, conservatives cast it instead as a matter of legal principle. As Justice Oliver Wendell Holmes Jr. wrote dryly, "If you have no doubt of your premises or power, and want a certain result with all your heart, you naturally express your wishes in law, and sweep away all your opposition."

Conservative legal scholars such as Samuel Alito and Steven Calabresi, one of the founders of the Federalist Society, elevated the issue to an academic-sounding doctrine called the theory of the "unitary executive." In November 2000, for instance, well before the terrorist attacks, while most of the country was transfixed by the competing claims of victory in the presidential election between Bush and Gore, Judge Alito championed the theory at a meeting of the Federalist Society in Washington. Alito, whom Bush would later appoint to the Supreme Court, proclaimed that the president should not just exercise "some executive powers—but *the* executive power—the whole thing." Even Calabresi later admitted, however, that the Bush Administration had "pushed the envelope" on this theory so far, "If I were a judge, I am not at all sure that I would uphold everything they have done."

Fundamentally, the drive for expanded presidential authority was about power. Cheney and Addington "viewed power as the absence of restraint, which is why they didn't go to Congress," Jack Goldsmith, a conservative legal scholar and former Justice official, explained. In the days after 9/11, they spoke often of wanting "maximum flexibility." What was lost in this view, however, was any appreciation for the legitimacy in a democracy that stems from winning consensus, including the consent of the governed. Also overlooked was the original reason for checks and balances; they were designed to offset human fallibility.

In 1989, President George H. W. Bush appointed Cheney Secretary of Defense. Cheney hired Addington first as his special assistant and, later, as the Pentagon's general counsel. At the Pentagon, Addington became widely known as Cheney's gatekeeper—a stickler for process who controlled the flow of documents to his boss. Using a red felt-tipped pen, he covered his colleagues' memos with comments before returning them for rewrites. His editing invariably made arguments sharper, smarter, and firmer in their defense of Cheney's executive powers.

Addington and Cheney became a formidable team, but it was soon clear that Addington would not match Cheney as a politician. Adelman recalled Addington's personality as "dour," adding, "Unlike with Dick, I never saw much of a sense of humor. Cheney can be witty and funny. David is sober. I didn't see him at social events much." But, he added, "Dick wasn't looking for friends at work. He was looking for performance. And David delivers. He's efficient and dedicated. He's a doer." He went on, "Cheney's not a lawyer, so he would defer to David on the law."

At the Pentagon, Addington took a particular interest in the covert actions of the Special Forces. A former colleague recalled that after attending a demonstration by Special Forces officers, Addington mocked the CIA, which was constrained by oversight laws. "This is how real covert operations are done," he said.

Cheney, throughout his tenure as Defense Secretary, shared with Addington a pessimistic view of the Soviet Union and other threats. Both remained skeptical of Gorbachev long after the State Department, the National Security Adviser, and the CIA had concluded that he was a reformer. "They were always, like, 'Whoa—beware the Bear!'" Wilkerson recalled.

During the Clinton presidency, both Addington and Cheney worked in the private sector, and in 1994, Addington led an exploratory presidential campaign for Cheney.

Cheney went on to become the chief executive at Halliburton, the huge Texas-based oil services company, where he became wealthy and enjoyed the clear lines of authority in the private sector. He earned $4.4 million during his last year at Halliburton, 1999, and left with stock options and retirement benefits worth a reported $20 million. But evidently, he missed Washington.

After pivoting from Bush's adviser on vice presidential selection to Bush's pick as running mate, a process that Cheney's old friend Stu Spencer joked about as "the most Machiavellian fucking thing I've ever seen," Cheney asked Addington to help oversee the new administration's transition. Together they set up the most powerful vice presidency in American history.

By then, both men had far more experience and savvy about how to work the levers of power in Washington than the incoming Texans. In his stint as Chief of Staff to Ford, Cheney had witnessed the marginalization of Vice President Nelson Rockefeller. Friends said Cheney had studied the vice presidency closely, deciding that the best route to power was to control the process shaping the decisions before they reached the president.

Famously, Bush would describe himself as "The Decider." But Cheney had a more sophisticated understanding of how Washington works. Without drawing attention to himself, he often drastically narrowed Bush's choices. In the White House, there are two spigots controlling the president's choices. One is the paper flow—determining what the president gets to read. The other is access—determining whom he sees and talks with. Cheney almost invariably had the final word with the President. But Addington frequently had the final say about the paperwork that reached him. As Berenson put it, Addington "would dive into a 200-page bill like it was a four-course meal."

Addington's would be the last box before paperwork reached the President. According to another lawyer on the White House staff, he would "review every proposed executive order before it reached the President for his signature. Frequently he would single-handedly rewrite the entire thing, even though it had already been vetted by the interagency process. He'd slash a red line straight through it and start over from scratch, making it read the way he wanted. Only then would he send it on to the President."

When this lawyer complained, Addington told him that he was free to put in his own drafts if he wanted. But Addington noted that if anyone got in his way, the Vice President would likely take it up with the President, in private, later.

From the start, Bush delegated much of the national security portfolio to Cheney, handing the Vice President an unusually important responsibility. The Vice President's office thus saw virtually every important document relating to national security. Addington regularly attended White House legal meetings with the CIA and the National Security Agency. He received copies of all National Security Council documents, including internal memos from the staff. And, as a former top official in the Defense Department, he exerted influence over the legal office at the Pentagon, helping his protégé William J. Haynes III, more commonly referred to as Jim Haynes, secure the position of general counsel. A former national security lawyer, speaking of the Pentagon's legal office, said, "It's obvious that Addington ran the whole operation."

Almost immediately after the terrorist attacks, other administration lawyers noticed that Addington dominated the internal debates. His assumption, shared by other hard-line lawyers in the White

House Counsel's Office and in the Justice Department's Office of Legal Counsel, was that the criminal justice system was insufficient to handle the threat from terrorism. The matter was settled without debate, Berenson recalled: "There was a consensus that we had to move from retribution and punishment to preemption and prevention. Only a warfare model allows that approach."

Richard Shiffrin, who was the Pentagon's deputy general counsel for intelligence, said that during a tense White House meeting held in the Situation Room after September 11, Addington was strikingly strident. "He'd sit, listen, and then say, 'No, that's not right.' He was particularly doctrinaire and ideological. He didn't recognize the wisdom of the other lawyers. He was always right. He didn't listen. He knew the answers." The details of the discussion are classified, Shiffrin said, but he left with the impression that Addington "doesn't believe there should be coequal branches." Another participant recalled, "If you favored international law, you were in danger of being called 'soft on terrorism' by Addington." He added that Addington's manner in meetings was "very insistent and very loud." Yet another participant said that whenever he cautioned against executive-branch overreaching, Addington would respond brusquely, "There you go again, giving away the President's power."

On September 25, 2001, the Office of Legal Counsel issued another in a series of secret legal memos. It declared that it was the President's prerogative to take whatever military action he deemed necessary, including preemptive action, not just in response to the September 11 attacks but also in prevention of any future attacks from terrorist groups, whether they were linked to Al Qaeda or not. The memo, like Bush's address of a few days earlier, unapologetically crossed the line that Congress had drawn. The twenty-page memo, titled "The President's Constitutional Authority to Conduct Military Operations Against Terrorists and Nations Supporting Them," was written by John Yoo in close consultation with Addington. In a rather solipsistic bit of scholarship, among the many authorities it cited in its footnotes in support of its arguments was Yoo himself.

Some of the arguments that Yoo made were legal boilerplate. But others were astounding. He concluded, for instance, that Congress had no right at all to interfere with the President's response to terrorist threats. Without citing any authority for this view, Yoo simply asserted that no one could limit "the method, timing, or place" of the

President's war on terror. He wrote, "These decisions, under our Constitution, are for the President alone to make."

Bursting with creative though idiosyncratic interpretation, and written impressively fast, the memo was vintage John Yoo. His passion for these issues, like that of Addington, was partly personal. Born in South Korea in 1967, Yoo had been brought to America as an infant by his immigrant parents, both of whom were psychiatrists who had survived the Korean War and become staunch anti-Communists. Quite directly, Yoo's family owed its freedom and prosperity to Harry Truman's controversial decision to wage the Korean War without obtaining congressional authorization. Had Truman not used military force, without Congress's permission, Yoo reflected on occasion, he would not have attended Harvard College and Yale Law School, nor, like so many other immigrants to America, had the fortune to have escaped Communism. Yoo left early mentors feeling deceived about the depth and extremism of his views—he had learned apparently to mask them behind moderate-sounding language—but in time it became clear that he acted less as a lawyer judiciously guiding the government than as a single-minded advocate for a cause.

Yoo's contentious opinion might have been dismissed as the interesting work of an academic provocateur, except for the imprimatur at the top of the page. Printed neatly above the margin were the words "The Office of the Legal Counsel, U.S. Department of Justice." The OLC plays a unique role in the federal government. Sometimes referred to as the Attorney General's law firm, its small but often brilliant staff of lawyers, many of whom are political appointees, issue opinions that are legally binding on the rest of the executive branch. If the OLC interprets the law in a certain way, unless the attorney general overrules it, the government must too. If the OLC says a previously outlawed practice, such as waterboarding, is legal, it is nearly impossible to prosecute U.S. officials who followed that advice on good faith. As Jack Goldsmith, who headed the OLC in 2003, put it, OLC memos were virtual "golden shields." The office wields "one of the most momentous, and dangerous powers in the government: the power to dispense get-out-of-jail-free cards." At the same time, OLC decisions also stripped dissenters of the ability to make opposing legal arguments, as doubters in the State Department, Defense Department, and the CIA would find.

For Yoo's allies in the White House, his position at OLC was a political bonanza. It was like having a personal friend who could write medical prescriptions. With Yoo's authority to issue official opinions, their views could be transformed into the law of the land. Flanigan, who had headed OLC during the first Bush Administration, clearly understood this as well as anyone. Before long, Yoo was a charter member of a self-selected, secretive, five-man club that called itself "The War Council." In addition to Yoo, its members were Addington, Flanigan, Gonzales, and Jim Haynes, the general counsel to the Pentagon who owed his job to Addington. Like a high-school clique, some of the members played squash and racquetball together and took secret trips together, while mocking those they excluded as "soft" and "leakers" to the press.

None of this would have been of more than passing interest except that this insular, unelected, self-reinforcing group, with virtually no experience in law enforcement, military service, counterterrorism, or the Muslim world, was in position to make many of the most fateful legal decisions in the post-9/11 era. In some instances, the group gave itself oral legal advice without so much as writing it down. "It's incredible," a colleague later said, "but John Yoo and David Addington were running the war on terror almost on their own." They had help from Haynes, whom they could always count on at the Department of Defense. Flanigan, too, was more important than most people realized, because he had inside knowledge of the OLC, having run it, and he used that. "The bottom line is that when you have the Department of Justice—in particular OLC—you don't really need anything else. They understood this," noted Goldsmith.

As interesting as who was in this club was who was left out.

An early glimpse was visible on October 25, 2001. That day, the top four congressional experts on intelligence matters—the chairmen and ranking minority members of the Senate and House Intelligence Oversight Committees—were ushered into the White House for a top-secret briefing. The purpose was to learn one of the President's most closely guarded secrets—but, oddly, not from the President. When they arrived at the White House for the briefing, they had expected to meet in the Oval Office, as they always had for such grave moments in earlier administrations. But instead, after arriving in the West Wing's VIP lobby, a chandeliered holding room filled with oversized historic oil paintings and Chippendale-style antique couches often filled with anxious-looking, well-dressed supplicants, they were led instead to the Vice President's office.

Once seated, Cheney, with Addington at his side, outlined the basic elements of a brand-new and powerfully intrusive eavesdropping program, allowing for the NSA to intercept phone calls and other communications—including private e-mails—to and from the United States without first getting a warrant. The specifications of this program, known as the Terrorist Surveillance Program, or TSP, remain classified. But the original focus of these intercepts was reportedly communications between the United States and Afghanistan, where the Taliban and Al Qaeda were based. However, there were no geographic barriers placed on the program. Nor were there the usual requirements for finding probable cause of wrongdoing, as required by the Constitution. "They wanted to go on fishing expeditions," said a former federal prosecutor who later learned the details of the program. "It was incredibly sneaky; they argued that 9/11 proved they needed this, when there was no evidence that it had."

Prior to the 1978 Foreign Intelligence Surveillance Act, the CIA had authorized its own wiretaps. But after the abuses revealed during the Church Committee hearings, Congress decided to set up a special, secret court composed of non–intelligence officials, appointed by the Chief Justice of the Supreme Court, to review the Agency's surveillance requests. "It was a curb on abuse," said a career Justice Department official with firsthand knowledge of the TSP, who asked to remain anonymous because of the classified nature of the program. "There was no evidence that the process didn't work in wartime. It did. In my experience, it never hurt our ability to get the bad guys."

John Yoo's specific legal analysis authorizing the NSA program has never been released to Congress or the public. But evidently it argued that the President's authority to conduct warrantless surveillance inside America was a presidential prerogative, and also that it was "incidental" to Congress's vote authorizing the use of military force. In other words, while not a single member of Congress realized it, and in fact some, like Senator Tom Daschle, had explicitly resisted it, Yoo argued that Congress had implicitly allowed the President to ignore the Foreign Intelligence Surveillance Act.

Walter Dellinger, the Solicitor General in the Clinton Administration and a professor of constitutional law at Duke University, described the Bush Administration's theories as "insane." "I don't think anyone has ever taken the theory of presidential power and distorted it this way," he said. "Is it conservative? It's a particular brand of conservatism. It has nothing to do with respect for tradition. In it is the embodiment of power for the executive, it's like Mussolini in 1930."

During their White House briefing on October 25, the four intelligence committee members were not shown Yoo's legal reasoning. Nor did they get to see it at any time after. Neither did many other experts inside the government who would likely have found fault with it, including the top lawyer for Condoleezza Rice's National Security Council, John Bellinger III. In fact, Bellinger was not told about the Terrorist Surveillance Program at all. This was strange, because unlike Addington, who had no line authority over national security matters, Bellinger was the ranking lawyer in the White House on intelligence affairs, with statutory purview over the subject.

Bellinger and his aides had heard through friends that something was going on from which he was being deliberately cut out. "Don't tell John" was the whisper from the War Council. Bellinger, a Princeton graduate, had a reputation as a moderate Republican. He had close ties to such Washington establishment figures as William Webster, the former Director of both the FBI and CIA, and unforgivably from the standpoint of the War Council, he was rumored to have occasional lunches with liberal Democratic legal icon Lloyd Cutler, at whose law firm Bellinger had worked. As it became clear that the Office of the Vice President was in charge of a critically important program involving national security, which it was not sharing with Bellinger, he asked to be included. It was a demeaning position to be put in. He was supposed to be in charge of this area. According to a well-informed source, after Bellinger asked to be "read in," Cheney personally screened Bellinger's record for political loyalty, reviewing his past legal work. Evidently, Cheney found him insufficiently reliable. The top NSC lawyer was kept in the dark about the secret program.

Bellinger declined to comment about the NSA program, but friends said he was relegated to complaining bitterly to White House Counsel Alberto Gonzales about this and a series of other secret activities of the War Council. He told a colleague that sometimes he would discover them making critical decisions on issues he was hard at work on. Gonzales, who was never particularly communicative, would just nod. "Judge," Bellinger would implore, "you always say there's one team. So is there one team? Or two?"

If he answered at all, Gonzales would reply, "Well, John, we have one team, but there are certain matters where it's important to have smaller meetings."

Addington, whom a well-informed source called "the father of the eavesdropping program," refused to show the OLC legal memos to the NSA, as well, even though the program was to be run by the agency, putting its personnel at legal risk. "It's contrary to everything OLC is about—you're supposed to show the client the opinion," said a well-informed source. "No one at the NSA period had access to the legal opinions in support of the program, in contravention of the whole culture of the NSA," he said. Later, when the Inspector General of the NSA, who was conducting an audit, asked to see the legal work on which the program rested, Addington declared, "The President decides who sees what." The message, said the witness, "was none of your fucking business. Butt out!" After that, evidently, the NSA did.

General Michael Hayden, the NSA's director, whom Bush appointed head of the CIA in 2006, assured critics that his lawyers didn't need to see John Yoo's reasoning because they had done their own analysis of the program and found it legal. But a knowledgeable source said that without being able to read the OLC legal work, it was questionable how they could have reached any sound conclusions. Moreover, their independence was somewhat suspect given that the program had originated with Hayden. The NSA had wanted to extend its surveillance powers as soon as Bush had taken office, proposing in a transition report to the incoming administration that its reach should include a "powerful, permanent presence" on the commercial communications networks. "After 9/11 the White House asked Hayden what he wanted, and he said this. They said, 'Presto—you got it,'" recounted the source. Hayden believed, as he put it, that the government needed to "live on the edge." He liked to say, "My spikes will have chalk on them. . . . As a professional, I'm troubled if I'm not using the full authority allowed by law."

Richard Shiffrin was also not informed about the domestic spying program, which was remarkable, because Shiffrin was the Pentagon lawyer in charge of supervising the legality of the NSA's programs. As such, any legal question involving the NSA should have been checked with him. "It was exceptional that I didn't know about it—extraordinary," Shiffrin later said. "In the prior administration, on anything involving NSA legal issues I'd have been made aware. And I should have been in this one."

A reason he was cut out of the loop may have been that Shiffrin was a career lawyer, not a political appointee. As such, his expertise in the law would likely have led him to find the Terrorist Surveillance Program illegal. He had had earlier run-ins with the Bush political appointees on other surveillance issues. He had tried to be polite, but he had been shocked by what he regarded as the amateurism of John Yoo's legal work. "A high school student could have done better," he later said.

Ashcroft's deputy attorney general, Larry Thompson, the second-ranking lawyer in the Department of Justice, was excluded from the list of those "read in" to the eavesdropping program, too. He reportedly refused to sign the wiretap permission forms brought to him not long after September 11 because he didn't know what lay behind them. This was phenomenal, given that he was John Yoo's boss.

"It was unfathomable," said Jack Goldsmith, who became the head of the Office of Legal Counsel in late 2003. He finally became one of the very few people in the country with access to Yoo's secret legal work on the surveillance program when he took over. After reading it for himself, Goldsmith was shocked. In his book *The Terror Presidency,* Goldsmith wrote that the top Bush Administration officials had dealt with FISA "the way they dealt with other laws they didn't like: they blew through them in secret based on flimsy legal opinions that they guarded closely so no one could question the legal basis for the operations."

Quite simply, he later said, "It was the biggest legal mess I had ever seen in my life."

Goldsmith believed that Addington influenced the administration's legal positions "to a remarkable degree." Shiffrin said that after September 11, Addington simply became "an unopposable force."

Some Bush Administration lawyers came to believe the President and Vice President were deeply ill-served by Addington. "He was more like Cheney's agent than like a lawyer. A lawyer sometimes says no," one lamented. "Addington never said, 'There is a line you can't cross.'" As a result, he concluded later, the Bush Administration was led astray. "George W. Bush was damaged by incredibly bad legal advice," he argued.

In time, Addington and his cohorts' legal excesses succeeded in uniting liberal champions of civil liberties and conservative critics of statism in opposition. Scott Horton, a professor at Columbia Law School and the head of the New York Bar Association's International Law committee, accused them of attempting to "overturn two centuries of jurisprudence defining the limits of the executive branch. They've made war a matter of dictatorial power." Bruce Fein, the Republican legal activist, said that Addington and other presidential legal advisers had "staked out powers that are a universe beyond any other administration." Bush, he said, had "made claims that are really quite alarming. He's said that there are no restraints on his ability, as he sees it, to collect intelligence, to open mail, to commit torture, and to use electronic surveillance. If you used the President's reasoning, you could shut down Congress for leaking too much. His war powers allow him to declare anyone an illegal combatant. All the world's a battlefield—according to this view, he could kill someone in Lafayette Park if he wants! It's got the sense of Louis XIV: 'I am the State.'"

5

DETAINEE 001

The Constitution has never greatly bothered any wartime president.

—President Franklin Roosevelt's Attorney General
Francis Biddle, writing in 1962

Oblivious to the legal machinations in Washington, a gaunt twenty-year-old from Marin County, California, carrying a Koran in a cloth sack, squatted in a foxhole in Afghanistan, sipping tea. John Walker Lindh, or "The American Taliban," as he became known, had traveled halfway around the world, and to another universe culturally and politically, to take up sentry duty on the Taliban's front line in the Northeast Takhar Province on September 6, 2001. His guard post was atop a 2,000-foot-tall hill not far from the Tajikistan border. To the left was the Oxus River, which Alexander the Great had crossed; to the right were the snowcapped peaks of the Hindu Kush. In the distance lurked the remnants of the Northern Alliance, which before the CIA's cash infusion reached it was close to losing Afghanistan's civil war. What was left of the Northern Alliance's defensive line was a battery of hulking Soviet tanks, mementos of the force's former sponsor during the years of Soviet occupation.

The territory was so desolate, a private investigator from San Francisco who later traced Lindh's footsteps said, "If there had been a sign saying, 'World Ends Here,' I would not have been surprised." One could walk for days, in all directions, and see no lights, no cars, and no phones. "It felt to be about 500 B.C.," said the detective, David Fechheimer, who was hired by Lindh's legal defense team.

Lindh hoisted a rifle and carried two grenades, which he had been taught how to use that summer in an Afghan training camp called Al Farooq, a camp that was funded by Osama Bin Laden. A Muslim convert who had come to the region to study Arabic, Lindh had become convinced that a proper Muslim needed to do more than read and pray. "I believed it was the part of every good Muslim to train" for military jihad, he later said. His intention was to help the Taliban defeat the Northern Alliance, then create a "pure" Muslim state.

At the camp, Lindh had been taught how to shoot rocket-propelled grenades and guns. He had also personally met Bin Laden. The Saudi terrorist was a legend in the region, but Lindh said he'd only been vaguely aware of his reputation. He claimed that he had never heard of Al Qaeda, which terrorism experts found plausible. "There were two kinds of training at Al Farooq—Al Qaeda training, to fight civilians, and military training, to fight the Northern Alliance," explained Bruce Hoffman, a terrorism expert at the Rand Corporation in Washington. "Lindh took only the military training. Seventy thousand people were trained in general warfare at these camps, but perhaps only a tenth received advanced terrorist training."

Lindh met Bin Laden, but it proved something of a letdown. Bin Laden gave an evening lecture at the camp. Arriving in a swirling, dusty motorcade of Land Rovers, he had been treated like a rock star. But Lindh had been less than enraptured. Asked what Bin Laden had been like, Lindh later told his defense team, "To tell you the truth, he was really boring. I was so tired. The training was really grueling. I thought he seemed sick. Most of the speakers stood up when they spoke, but he sat down, and talked in a really soft voice about the history of Afghanistan, and how everyone had invaded it starting with the Greeks. I listened to the beginning, but it wasn't very interesting. So I fell asleep."

Lindh professed to be oblivious to the terror plotting around him. But he admitted that he had been taken aside toward the end of his training by an Egyptian official at the camp named Abu Mohammed al-Masri, who was later identified as a confirmed member of Al Qaeda, for a private talk. "He asked me whether I'd like to do a martyrdom operation" in the United States or Israel, Lindh later admitted. "I said no, I'm not interested in that. I came to fight the Northern Alliance, not other countries." The Egyptian accepted Lindh's demurral but warned him that, whatever else he did, he was not to mention their conversation to anyone.

At his sentry post, Lindh had never had the occasion to use his weapons. But he had won something of a reputation among his fellow soldiers for another skill. He had a knack for cooking macaroni. A shipment of the dried pasta had arrived, but few of the other Taliban had known what to do with it.

News of the September 11 attacks took a while to reach Lindh. Details were sketchy. It wasn't clear who had perpetrated the violence. Lindh did notice, however, that just around September 11, a handful of the better-connected Arab fighters in his unit seemed to vanish from the front, as if perhaps they knew something.

Exactly what Lindh knew about Bin Laden and his attack plans, and how far the United States could go in trying to wring this and other precious intelligence out of him, were at the heart of a roiling debate back in Washington that had only just reached the Bush White House. The misfit son of a liberal upper-middle-class family, from a part of Northern California better known for hot tubs than mosques, would become the first experiment in detainee treatment in the war on terror, literally prisoner number "001."

As a test, Lindh's case was both unique, because of his American citizenship, and typical in the sense that the way that he was stripped, humiliated, and deliberately exposed to cold and hunger and other mistreatment would in time become quite familiar to the world after the photos of Abu Ghraib emerged. But in the furor immediately after 9/11, questions about his rough handling were seldom asked. At the time, photos that appeared of him naked, bound in duct tape to a stretcher, with a homemade sign reading "Shit Head" affixed to his blindfold, seemed funny to most Americans in a fittingly sadistic way.

Before the details of his case were known, even moderate Democrats such as Hillary Clinton denounced him as a "traitor" in an interview on *Meet the Press,* a crime meriting the death penalty. Lindh's parents, who had supported the Clinton presidency, frantically tried to reach Senator Clinton without success, instead leaving a message with an aide asking her to withhold judgment. Interestingly, among the few sympathetic words for him, after he was first captured, were those from President Bush. "I don't know what we're going to do with the poor fellow," the President said in an interview with Barbara Walters. His father, George Herbert Walker Bush, was less understanding, perhaps reflecting the difference between their roles in the family as patriarchal paragon and wayward son. "He's just despicable," said the elder President Bush on *Good Morning America*. "I thought of a unique penalty: Make him leave his hair the way it is and his face as dirty as it is, and let him go wandering around this country and see what kind of sympathy he would get."

"It was a bipartisan campaign without the facts," complained Frank Lindh, John's father, a former Justice Department lawyer who had gone into private legal practice in San Francisco. "This was a time to show that they were über-patriots, and if it took John to do that, they were willing."

Lindh had no way of knowing it, but in the midst of his strange journey the rules in Washington were changing in a way that would drastically affect his life. When Lindh arrived in Afghanistan in the summer of 2001, crossing the Khyber Pass from Pakistan, where he had been studying Arabic and the Koran, the United States was engaged in an informal diplomatic rapprochement with the Taliban. This warming of relations took place despite the sect's repellent human rights record and protection of Bin Laden, who was well known to be living in the Taliban's midst. In the spring of 2001, Secretary of State Colin Powell personally announced a grant of $43 million to the Taliban government for opium eradication, which the *New York Times* referred to as "a first cautious step toward reducing the isolation of the Taliban by the incoming Bush Administration." The State Department issued a press release at the time in which Powell said, "We will continue to look for ways to provide more assistance to the Afghans." Scott Carrier, a freelance radio journalist for public radio among other outlets, who was based at the time in Afghanistan, said, "When Lindh went there, we were buddies with the Taliban. We were giving them money to not grow opium, and letting them grow it anyway. We wanted them to stabilize their position. But then the world changed."

The American bombing campaign against Afghan targets began in October, after the Taliban refused to turn over Bin Laden. By then, as Cofer Black had promised the President, stealth teams of CIA officers and military Special Forces soldiers had landed in Afghanistan, where they had linked up with Northern Alliance units. The lead CIA advance officer, Gary Schroen, had flown in with three cardboard boxes weighing about forty-five pounds between his legs, containing $3 million in hundred-dollar bills—all used, and in nonsequential order—to buy tribal support. After landing and setting up a secure communications line, Schroen's unit, known by the code name "Jawbreaker," had sent a cable back to Langley jocularly following up on Black's demand for Bin Laden's head. It requested the necessary cardboard container and dry ice. If available, "pikes" were requested as well.

Bombs started falling on Lindh's outpost on November 5. By November 10, the Taliban's front line had broken and Lindh's unit was in retreat. Lindh said later that the political situation was unclear to him from the ground. "He just didn't have a clue," said Tamara Sonn, an expert on Islam who teaches at the College of William and Mary in Virginia, and who examined Lindh for his defense team. "He said he saw American planes overhead. I asked, 'Didn't you know you were at war with America?' He said, 'No. I couldn't figure out why the Americans were helping the Northern Alliance against the Taliban.'" Lindh told Sonn that, at the time, he saw no connection between Afghanistan's civil war and terrorism. Caught up in his religious cause against the Northern Alliance, he claimed, he was blind to the broader truth. In its court filings, the government described Lindh's claim of ignorance as "simply not credible."

Terrified of being captured by the Northern Alliance, Lindh's unit fled fifty miles on foot over two days. They lacked food and water. A third of his comrades died on the way. Most of the Afghan Taliban soldiers deserted, after which they were welcomed as brothers by their compatriots on the other side. Members of the Taliban, meanwhile, were rescued in droves by Pakistan's intelligence service, which had spent years aiding the Taliban for strategic reasons. Left behind were the foreign fighters, like Lindh. He said he was unable to walk without assistance by the time he reached the town of Kunduz, where he learned that a surrender had been negotiated for his unit.

The deal had been struck with an infamous Afghan warlord, Rashid Dostum. Cofer Black had described Dostum to the President in his earliest briefings on the war plan as a wily rogue who at one time or another had been on virtually everyone's payroll, including the Iranians' and the Russians'. Now the blue-turbaned tyrant with the bushy jet-black mustache and eyebrows was getting fistfuls of cash from the United States. By mid-October a CIA team had given him what they described as "a big chunk of money." American Special Forces soldiers were staying in the incongruous luxury of his guesthouse, next to a palace decorated with a fountain in the shape of a poppy flower bud. Dostum's brutality was infamous, even in Afghanistan. Rumors circulated that he mashed opponents in the treads of his tanks for display. But virtuous allies were hard to find in the chronically corrupt and war-torn country of Afghanistan, and for the moment Dostum was the CIA's man.

Lindh's Taliban commander, Mullah Faisal, agreed to pay Dostum around $500,000 in exchange for his unit's safe passage across Dostum's territory to the Taliban-controlled town of Herat. (Classified government cables confirmed this cash transaction.) From there, Lindh said, he planned to escape to Pakistan and return to America.

But Mullah Faisal, it turned out, was double-crossed. General Dostum collected the cash, but his men detained the prisoners, who had been disarmed, in a cavernous, nineteenth-century fortress that he commanded, called Qala-i-Jangi, near the town of Mazar-i-Sharif. Its walls were sixty feet high and many yards thick. It held a garrison stocked with weapons. Given Dostum's reputation for savaging his enemies, the prisoners panicked. An Uzbek Taliban soldier exploded a hidden grenade.

In retaliation, Northern Alliance guards herded Lindh's unit into the basement of the fortress, which the Soviets had turned into a bomb shelter. They then rolled a grenade down an airshaft, the first round of what would turn out to be one of the most hard-fought battles of the entire Afghan campaign. "The whole thing was a huge fuckup," said Carrier, who was there at the time. The next morning, the surviving Taliban soldiers, including Lindh, were marched out and interrogated in the fort's courtyard by Dostum's men and two Americans—later identified as Johnny "Mike" Spann and a second CIA officer, Dave Tyson, sometimes referred to as "Dawson."

Videotape shot that day, November 25, showed Lindh on his knees, with matted hair covering his face and his arms bound behind his back. He was kicked in the head by Dostum's troops as the two Americans moved among them.

"I didn't know who the American guys were," Lindh told Fechheimer, the private investigator. Neither Spann nor Tyson identified himself. Lindh thought they were mercenaries working with Dostum. Spann wore blue jeans and a black sweatshirt. Tyson wore a *shalwar kameez*. Both carried Russian-made automatic rifles.

Lindh remained mute as the two American officers, cognizant of his Western appearance and trying to identify fleeing Al Qaeda members, tried to interrogate him. The videotape captured the CIA officers warning Lindh that he might die if he didn't talk. Death threats and mock executions are considered war crimes under the Geneva Conventions, and felony offenses under U.S. anti-torture laws. But in an amateurish good-cop/bad-cop routine, Spann asked Lindh, "You believe in what you're doing here that much, you're willing to be killed here?"

Tyson told Spann within Lindh's earshot that "he's got to decide if he wants to live or die, and die here. We're just going to leave him, and he's going to fucking sit in prison the rest of his fucking short life. It's his decision. We can only help the guys who want to talk to us."

Soon afterward, in a spontaneous uprising, several hundred Taliban prisoners overpowered Dostum's guards. In the melee they killed Spann, making him the first U.S. casualty of the war on terror. Cofer Black was tragically right in warning the President that Americans, including his own dear colleagues, were going to die.

Spann's father said later that he learned that his son "fired his AK-47 until its ammo ran out, then fired his Glock pistol until its ammo ran out, and then continued to fight them hand-to-hand until they overtook him." He said, "We could never prove that John Walker Lindh touched Mike or pulled the trigger." But he added, "As far as I'm concerned, everyone who was part of Al Qaeda is guilty."

In the mayhem, Tyson managed to escape. An eyewitness said he borrowed a German journalist's satellite phone to call for military help. But in the chaos, some of the American bombs went astray and destroyed a combined U.S.-Uzbek-British command post. The errant missile flipped an Uzbek tank, killing its crew, which had been allied with the United States, and sending streams of British and U.S. Special Forces soldiers out of the post spitting blood and dust. In just the first day of the battle, some 230 people were killed, including thirty Afghan and Uzbek allies of the United States. Mangled along with them were the bodies of dozens of Dostum's horses, which had been stabled in the fortress. The carnage, eyewitnesses said, was unforgettable.

Lindh, who was bound and unarmed when the melee broke out, was shot in the leg. Terrified, he played dead for twelve hours in the yard before crawling at night into the fortress's basement. He and 300 other Taliban remained there for the next week as Northern Alliance soldiers tried to expel them with gunfire, grenades, bombs, diesel fuel—which they ignited—and then freezing water, which flooded the basement by several feet. Anyone who couldn't stand drowned. Lindh leaned on a stick to stay upright, but slipped on a body at one point, falling and swallowing some water, which was contaminated with blood, human remains, and waste.

On December 1, Lindh and eighty-five other survivors crawled out to surrender. This time, when Lindh saw American journalists and Red Cross workers, he identified himself as a fellow American citizen and in stilted, Arabic-accented English, he begged for their help.

Mercy for terror suspects was not high on the list of Cheney's priorities at that point. Two weeks before Lindh's surrender, well before the President had determined what legal approach his administration would take, Cheney delivered a hard-edged speech at the U.S. Chamber of Commerce in Washington declaring that terrorists do not "deserve to be treated as prisoners of war." Cheney evidently staked out this position on his own. It would be ten more weeks before President Bush formalized this policy with his signature on an order declaring that America would deny Al Qaeda, the Taliban, and other prisoners in the war on terror the protections outlined under the international standards established by the 1949 Geneva Conventions. One hundred and ninety-nine countries, including the U.S. and Afghanistan, had ratified the Conventions, pledging to abide by universally acceptable rules for armed conflict. But the Vice President seems to have felt no compunction about publicly announcing his view that this pledge didn't cover prisoners in the war on terror, whether it had been approved by the President or not. Of all the complicated legal arguments made by the Bush Administration in the first months after September 11, none more directly cleared the way for torture than this.

The bloody battle surrounding Lindh's capture added urgency to the debate in Washington about what to do with the new enemy prisoners. "Get them out of there!" General Tommy Franks, head of the U.S. Central Command overseeing the Afghan theater, beseeched top Pentagon officials after seeing the fanaticism of the Islamic fighters captured along with Lindh. Spann's death made clear that adequate security couldn't be maintained in makeshift battlefield prisons filled with terrorists who would rather die than be taken alive.

While the problem was clear, answers were less so. "The following conundrum occurred to all of us," Bradford Berenson, the Associate White House Counsel, explained later. "When you capture a suspected Al Qaeda terrorist, what do you do with him? You can't kill him once you have him in custody and he's been captured. That would be a violation of international law. You can't let him go, because he's far too dangerous and potentially far too valuable as a source of intelligence. And," the Bush White House believed, "you can't, in many cases, try him in the ordinary civilian court system."

The Bush Administration's solution to this complex "conundrum" was forged in a highly unusual process. It was cloaked in secrecy and it excluded much of the government, including almost all of the administration's most experienced experts in military and international law. Cheney, Addington, and the handful of other like-minded conservative members of the self-appointed War Council, none of whom were military veterans let alone experts in military law, stealthily usurped the decision making. Their solution—the imposition of an alternative legal system following rules of the executive branch's own devising—has proven the origin of almost all of the Bush Administration's most vexing legal problems in the war on terror.

Almost from the start, these key policies were forged in an abnormal way. For fifty years, since the end of World War II, in both Democratic and Republican administrations, most major national security initiatives had been debated collectively in an "interagency" process involving experts from all affected departments. Typically, experienced officials from the Departments of Defense, Intelligence, State, Justice, and the National Security Council all weighed in on major policy issues. Initially, White House Counsel Alberto Gonzales assigned the question of how to treat prisoners in the war on terror to exactly this sort of inclusive group. The designated leader was Pierre-Richard Prosper, Ambassador-at-Large for War Crimes issues at the State Department.

But Cheney's staff and the other members of the War Council largely abstained from participation in this consultative group process. They disdained Prosper as soft, slow, and unduly mindful of international law. Prosper had won the first genocide conviction before the International Criminal Tribunal for Rwanda. It was a dubious distinction in the eyes of the unilateralists who distrusted what they regarded as the anti-American interference of human rights organizations and international institutions like the International Criminal Court. Addington, in particular, mocked Prosper and other State Department officials as "pin-striped" squishes. A White House colleague recalled him saying, "Fuck the interagency process."

Nonetheless, in the weeks immediately after September 11, Gonzales asked the interagency group to come up with multiple options for how America should bring terror suspects to justice. One idea that particularly intrigued Cheney and Addington was the notion of using military commissions to try suspects. They felt that putting the Pentagon in charge sent the correct message, that the fight against terrorism was not a law-enforcement matter but a war. They also liked the tremendous latitude that such commissions could give the President to hold, interrogate, and prosecute the suspects in any way he saw fit. Unlike the U.S. courts, military commissions concentrated all power in the hands of the executive branch. There were a few problems with the approach, however. Military commissions hadn't been used in the United States since World War II, for the simple reason that in 1951, the Uniform Code of Military Justice had been instituted, modernizing and rationalizing military law and rendering military commissions a crude relic of the past. Another downside was the likelihood that the White House would need to get Congress to authorize the system if it was going to withstand legal challenges.

Timothy Flanigan, the Deputy White House Counsel, told the *New York Times* that the inspiration came from William P. Barr, the former attorney general under whom Flanigan had served during the first Bush Administration. Barr had considered using military commissions then as a possible way to try suspects in the bombing of Pan Am Flight 103 over Lockerbie, Scotland. When he suggested it shortly after September 11, Flanigan said he immediately "thought it was a great idea."

Prosper's interagency group was not so quickly convinced. Hard at work in a windowless conference room on the seventh floor of the State Department, the group wanted to explore all of the other options, too. Some members of the group argued that terror suspects could still be tried in the regular criminal courts. Justice Department representatives argued that they had a strong track record on getting criminal convictions in domestic terrorism cases; all over Europe, this criminal approach was used. The uniformed military lawyers in the group proposed military courts-martial, as prescribed under the Uniform Code of Military Justice. A third option weighed by Prosper's group was a tribunal composed of both civilian and military experts, like those used for Nazi war criminals in Nuremberg. The arguments went round and round.

Meanwhile, at a time of pressing fear, when, as Berenson put it, "the watch word was forward-leaning," the War Council had no patience for such dithering. It was an article of faith in the hard-line group that the criminal courts were not up to the challenge of handling terrorism. Evidence against the terror suspects might be too slight, or it might need to be kept classified, which could prove too challenging in an open court. More important, Cheney and the War Council believed it was an urgent matter of life and death to not just solve crimes but instead to preempt them before they were committed. They had no time to establish guilt beyond a reasonable doubt. They also had no use for laws that stretched back to the founding of the country protecting defendants from being coerced into self-incrimination. As Flanigan put the choice to the *Times*: "Are we going to go with a system that is really guaranteed to prevent us from getting information in every case—or are we going to go another route?"

On November 13, 2001, the administration's radical answer became clear.

"What the hell just happened?" demanded Powell, who learned of the decision from a news report on CNN that night. He, like National Security Adviser Rice, was stunned and incensed. So was the highest-ranking lawyer at the CIA, as well as many judge advocate generals, or JAGs, the top uniformed—as opposed to civilian—lawyers in the military services. Virtually none of them had seen the order before it was a fait accompli. Michael Chertoff, the head of the Justice Department's Criminal Division, who had argued for trying terror suspects in the U.S. courts, was also bypassed. So was John Bellinger III, the National Security Council legal adviser and Deputy White House Counsel, who was still actively involved in what he thought was the ongoing interagency process at the time.

Attorney General Ashcroft had only learned of the military commission plan two days earlier, when he discovered to his outrage that John Yoo, his subordinate, had vouched for a confidential legal memorandum cutting the Justice Department and U.S. Courts out of the picture. Yoo had sanctioned White House plans to give the Defense Department—not the Justice Department—sole authority to decide which terrorists would be tried in military commissions. Furious, Ashcroft demanded a confrontation with the top decision makers at the White House. But, according to the *Washington Post,* when he arrived in the Roosevelt Room on Saturday, November 11, in the midst of the Veterans Day weekend, the President was not present. Instead, Cheney was presiding. Cheney had neglected to invite either Rice or Powell, evidently preferring to tell them about the military commissions only after President Bush had signed the order into law.

The meeting became so heated that Ashcroft, who was known for a prickly temper, was reduced to shouting that he was the President's top law-enforcement officer and as such he should play a part in the prosecution of terrorists, both within the United States and in the military tribunals. One of Cheney's allies at the meeting was scandalized that Ashcroft had been "rude" to the Vice President.

Afterward, Addington rewrote the draft of the executive order slightly to give the White House, not the Defense Department, authority to pick which terrorists were tried and how. Despite Ashcroft's outburst, however, the Justice Department remained sidelined.

It was becoming clear that behind the scenes Cheney and the War Council had short-circuited Prosper's interagency group by secretly composing both the draft of the executive order and a thirty-five-page OLC memo, dated November 6, declaring that the President had "inherent authority" as commander in chief to establish military commissions.

Preempting what would become one of the fiercest debates dividing the administration during the rest of Bush's presidency, the memo nonchalantly dismissed international law, suggesting that the President could abide by it or not, selectively. In a preview of Cheney's speech two days later, the memo also stated that terror suspects were not automatically entitled to "receive the protections of the Geneva Conventions or the rights that laws of war accord to lawful combatants."

In saying so, the memo signaled a fundamental and egregious misunderstanding of the Geneva Conventions. These laws of war, dating back centuries but codified first in 1864 and updated most recently in 1949, laid out civilized rules of treatment for all categories of people caught in international armed conflicts, not just regular soldiers—or, as they were called, "lawful combatants." There were rules for the treatment of citizens and other rules for the treatment of spies and saboteurs—or "unlawful" combatants. Drafted after World War II with the French Resistance in mind, these nonuniformed, "unlawful" combatants could be interrogated. If found guilty in brief hearings, they could be executed. But they still could not be subjected to "cruel treatment." Nor could they be tortured either physically or psychologically.

The distinction—between killing an enemy as the result of a legitimate legal process (including warfare) and torturing a defenseless enemy captive—was woven deeply into the fabric of America's military history and sense of honor.

In the Revolutionary War, George Washington and the Continental Army were regarded by the British as treasonous, "illegal combatants" undeserving of the protections of legitimate soldiers, the same category into which the Bush Administration was casting terror suspects. As a result, the British freely brutalized and killed American prisoners of war, in conditions considered scandalous even in that day. In contrast, Washington ordered American troops to take a higher road, in keeping with the ideals of the new republic. He insisted that enemy captives must be given food and medical attention and be housed in conditions that were no worse than those of the American soldiers. In directives still eloquent today, he ordered his troops to treat British war prisoners "with humanity, and let them have no reason to complain of us copying the brutal manner of the British Army . . . While we are contending for our own liberty we should be very cautious of violating the rights of conscience in others, ever considering that God alone is the judge of the hearts of men, and to Him only in this case, are they answerable."

Washington's orders, which became the backbone of American military doctrine until 2001, were not simply gestures of kindness or even morality. They sprang also from a shrewd calculation that brutality undermines military discipline and strengthens the enemy's resolve, while displays of humanity could be used to tactical advantage. As David Hackett Fischer wrote in *Washington's Crossing,* his Pulitzer Prize–winning history, the superior treatment of enemy captives by American soldiers bolstered their morale and fomented desertion among the British and Hessian soldiers. In so doing, he wrote, "They reversed the momentum of the war. They improvised a new way of war that grew into an American tradition. They chose a policy of humanity that aligned the conduct of the war with the values of the Revolution."

America continued to blaze the high road during the Civil War, when Francis Lieber, a Columbia University professor, drafted the first comprehensive legal code for modern warfare, including strict rules calling for the humane treatment of military prisoners. The "Lieber Code," which remained in force well into the twentieth century, established the principle that soldiers are not the same as criminals, so must not be detained in punishing conditions. Soldiers could be held for the duration of hostilities and interrogated. But intentional suffering and indignity, as well as starvation, mutilation, torture, and "other barbarity," were all prohibited. As he famously wrote, "Military necessity does not permit of cruelty . . . nor of torture to extort confessions."

Lieber's code was adopted by two seminal international diplomatic conferences in The Hague in 1899 and 1907, putting American ideals at the core of future international humanitarian law.

After World War I, America actively participated in the 1929 conference that produced the first Geneva Convention governing the humane treatment of prisoners. Under huge duress, the United States complied with these laws of war in World War II. Historian Niall Ferguson has written that "it is not too much to say that it saved the lives of millions." By his estimation, a third of the 96 million people who served in the armed forces of the belligerent states were held captive at some point, during which their treatment was safeguarded by the Allied powers. The record of the Axis powers was far less noble. Japan systematically violated these laws, finding loopholes and exceptions whenever useful. But Germany, according to Ferguson, largely observed these protocols when it came to the treatment of prisoners of war. Winston Churchill championed the Geneva Conventions, and denounced torture, in part because of this reciprocity factor. Some 90,000 American soldiers became prisoners of the Third Reich, making the argument for enlightened self-interest painfully clear.

"History," Ferguson wrote, "provides a powerful counter argument" to those who think that the laws of war coddle the enemy at the expense of domestic security. "Any dilution of the Geneva Convention," he warned the Bush Administration, "could end up having the very reverse effect of what the administration intends. Far from protecting Americans from terror, it could end up exposing them to it."

In 1949 at an international gathering in Geneva, humanitarian law was rewritten by several nations, including the United States. These new "Geneva Conventions" strove to close any loopholes, ensuring that all categories of people caught in international armed conflicts were protected from the shockingly inhumane abuse of captives practiced by the Nazis and the Japanese. America was at the forefront of this effort. U.S. negotiators advocated that the rules be absolutely clear, even specifying food rations, barracks conditions, and athletic requirements—provisions later mocked by the Bush legal team. Having lived so recently through the horrors of war, the U.S. Senate eagerly ratified the new conventions, making them binding U.S. law.

But none of this rich history, which had so infused America's military ethos, was reflected in the legal memos advising the President to abandon the Geneva Conventions.

Technically, the November 6 memo supporting military commissions was authored by Patrick Philbin, a friend and colleague of John

Yoo's in the Office of Legal Counsel. Philbin and Yoo had attended Harvard College and Yale Law School at roughly the same time. They both had followed the same conservative expressway to the top rungs of legal power in Washington by clerking for Supreme Court Justice Clarence Thomas and an even better-connected hard-line insider, U.S. Appeals Court judge Laurence Silberman, who served as a godfather to the right-wing legal movement in the capital. Silberman, like his friend Cheney, had been a partisan political warrior as far back as the Nixon Administration, in whose Justice Department he served during the Watergate scandal. His protégé, Philbin, was young, eager, and bright. However, he had no experience in military or national security law. So Yoo, Addington, and Flanigan had helpfully bolstered his effort.

On the Tuesday after Ashcroft's angry Veterans Day showdown, Cheney presented the draft of the military commission order, which had been secretly written by his legal allies, to President Bush during their weekly private White House lunch. It was apparently the first time that Bush had seen it. The draft ran some four pages. The language was arcane and the subject matter more so. But after the lunch, Cheney advised Addington and the other lawyers that the President was on board. An hour or so later, with no further vetting or debate, and without circulating the draft to any of President Bush's other top advisers on national security matters, the finished document was presented back to the President, this time for his final signature. Deputy White House Staff Director Stuart Bowen told the *Washington Post* that he had bypassed all of his usual procedures, which called for more review, because of intense pressure to get it signed quickly from the lawyers who had secretly written the order. As a result, in the span of little more than a luncheon, Addington's text became U.S. law.

As this remarkable end run around White House protocol was under way, Cheney evidently stepped back and let others seem to be taking the lead. As former Bush speechwriter David Frum observed about Cheney's power, in a profile written by Barton Gellman and Jo Becker in the *Washington Post,* "A lot of it was a black box, and I think designedly so. It was like—you know the experiment where you pass a magnet under the table and you see the iron filings on the top of the table move? You know there's a magnet there because of what you see happening. But you never see the magnet."

The November 13 order proclaimed a state of "extraordinary emergency." It allowed the military to detain and try any foreigner whom the President or his representatives deemed to have "engaged in" or "abetted" or "conspired to commit" terrorism. If convicted, defendants could be sentenced to death. They would have no avenue of appeal except to the President or the Secretary of Defense, who would simultaneously serve as the prosecuting authorities. The accused would have no access to review by the federal courts or any other independent body. Detainees would be treated "humanely" and would be given "full and fair trials," the order said. They would be given "adequate food, drinking water, shelter, clothing, and medical treatment," and "allowed the free exercise of religion." Yet the order noted that "it is not practicable" to apply "the principles of law and the rules of evidence generally recognized in the trial of criminal cases in the United States district courts." The death penalty, for example, could be imposed even if there was a split verdict.

In December 2001, the Department of Defense circulated internal memos suggesting that, in the commission system, defendants would have only limited rights to confront their accusers, see all the evidence against them, or be present during their trials. There would be no right to remain silent and hearsay evidence would be admissible, as would evidence obtained through physical coercion. Guilt did not need to be proved beyond a reasonable doubt. The order firmly established that terrorism would henceforth be approached on a war footing, endowing the President with enhanced powers.

These rules for the military commissions would be dictated on an ad hoc basis by the Secretary of Defense, the order said. Despite warnings from the Prosper group that Congress might need to authorize the process if it was to withstand court challenge, the order said the commander in chief could assert his prerogative to establish the military commission process without review by Congress or the courts. To the War Council, the claims of Congress and the courts in wartime were comparatively negligible. As Colin Powell would later say caustically of Addington, "He doesn't believe in the Constitution."

The precedent for the order was an obscure 1942 case, *Ex parte Quirin,* in which Franklin Roosevelt created a military commission to try eight Nazi saboteurs who had infiltrated the United States via submarines. The Supreme Court upheld their convictions, 8–0, but even the conservative Justice Antonin Scalia has called it "not this Court's finest hour." Roosevelt was later criticized for creating a sham process.

Moreover, while he used military commissions to try a handful of suspects who had already admitted their guilt, the Bush White House was proposing expanding the process to cover a large, unknown universe of "enemy combatants." It was also ignoring the Uniform Code of Military Justice and developments in international law that had rendered *Quirin* out of date.

Berenson explained that he and the other White House lawyers believed that "The legal foundation was very strong. F.D.R.'s order establishing military commissions had been upheld by the Supreme Court. This was almost identical. What we underestimated," he later acknowledged, "was the extent to which the culture had shifted beneath us since World War Two." Concerns about civil liberties and human rights, and anger over Vietnam and Watergate, he said, had turned public opinion against a strong executive branch. "But," he said, "Addington thought military commissions had to be a tool at the President's disposal."

It was not just civil libertarians who were alarmed. Uniformed military lawyers were galvanized by the order into taking the first steps in what would become a remarkable role as defenders of America's honor and its rule of law against what they saw as illegitimate and ruinous incursions by the Bush Administration's political appointees. Rear Admiral Donald Guter, who was the Navy's Judge Advocate General, its chief lawyer, until June 2002, said that he and the other members of the Judge Advocate General's Corps, who were experts in the laws of war, tried unsuccessfully to amend parts of the military-commission plan when they first learned of it, days before the order was formally signed by the President.

Major General Thomas Romig, the Judge Advocate General for the U.S. Army, was astonished when William Haynes, the civilian General Counsel at the Pentagon, gave him a sneak preview of the executive order the weekend before Bush signed it. Romig predicted accurately that the United States was "going to be perceived as unfair, because it was unnecessarily archaic." He and several other top military lawyers threw themselves into an effort to fix and avert what they saw as a looming disaster. But the opinions of the military lawyers clearly were not valued. Addington, according to Romig, was overheard to have said, "Don't bring the TJAGs into the process. They aren't reliable."

"We were marginalized," Guter said. "We were warning them that we had this long tradition of military justice, and we didn't want to tarnish it. The treatment of detainees was a huge issue. They didn't want to hear it." Guter said that when he and the other JAGs told Haynes they needed more information, Haynes replied, "No, you don't."

Some of the civilian lawyers at the Defense Department were equally nonplussed. Shiffrin, the Deputy General Counsel for Intelligence, who had been shut out of the domestic spying initiative, was taken aback when Haynes showed him the order. Earlier in Shiffrin's career, at the Justice Department, his office had been in the same room where the Nazi defendants were tried and he had become interested in the case, which he said he regarded as "one of the worst Supreme Court cases ever." He informed Haynes that he was skeptical of the administration's invocation of *Quirin*. "Gee, this is problematic," Shiffrin told him. But by the time Haynes showed him the order, any doubts were moot; the President had already signed it.

Marine Major Dan Mori, the uniformed lawyer later assigned to defend one of the first Guantánamo detainees, an Australian kangarooskinner and adventurer named David Hicks, said of the commissions, "It was a political stunt. The administration clearly didn't know anything about military law or the laws of war. I think they were clueless that there even was a UCMJ and a Manual for Courts-Martial! The fundamental problem is that the rules were constructed by people with a vested interest in conviction."

Mori said that the designers of the military commissions evinced a profound legal confusion. "A military commission can try only violations of the laws of war," he said. "But the administration's lawyers didn't understand this." Under federal criminal statutes, for example, conspiring to commit terrorist acts is a crime. But, as the Nuremberg trials established, under the laws of war it is not, since all soldiers could be charged with conspiring to fight for their side. Yet, Mori said, a charge of conspiracy "is the only thing there is in many cases at Guantánamo—guilt by association. So you've got this big problem." He added, "I hope that nobody confuses military justice with these 'military commissions.' This is a political process, set up by the civilian leadership. It's inept, incompetent, and improper."

In a bohemian brownstone in the heart of New York's Greenwich Village, Michael Ratner, a graying pillar of America's left-wing legal bar, who was in some ways the ideological equal and opposite of David Addington, read the military commission order on November 14, the morning after it was issued. He said he immediately realized that the war on terror had expanded from a response to September 11 into a political battle at home, one that would define the heart and soul of America. "I woke up November 14 and saw that the President on his own could detain anyone he alleged to be an international terrorist and try them in military tribunals," he recalled, "and I was really shocked." Ratner thought the executive order was so much broader than Congress's September 14 Authorization to Use Military Force that in his opinion "it was illegal."

Since the Vietnam War years, Ratner had been a leader of the legal brigade of the progressive movement, defending civil liberties by challenging what he and his organization, the Center for Constitutional Rights, saw as violations of all manner of legal rights. He had taught at Columbia and Yale Law Schools and gotten under the skin of foreign dictators and multinational corporations by suing them for human rights violations in the U.S. courts. Few were as familiar with the legal arguments propounded by John Yoo and David Addington as Ratner was.

Later that day, in his office at the Center for Constitutional Rights, Ratner recalled, "All of us were sitting around saying, 'What is going on here?'" On a hunch that the new legal rules emanating from the Bush White House were actually retreads of old political ideas, Ratner went to the remote reaches of his bookshelves. He pulled out a copy of a fat, self-published compendium called *Mandate for Change.* It was a musty relic of the Reagan era. Published by the right-wing Heritage Foundation, it was a wish list of everything the newly empowered conservative movement had wanted in the 1980s, when Ronald Reagan was in the White House. Many of the ideas were too radical and outlandish to have survived political debate. As he flipped through the pages, Ratner came across many of the expanded military, intelligence, and executive powers that the Bush Administration was now proposing. To Ratner it was clear that the war on terror was a political battle cloaked in legal strategy, an ideological trench war that would have to be fought by lawyers like himself.

In Minneapolis, Joe Margulies, another tall lawyer with thinning hair, prominent ears, and a weakness for lost causes, was equally stricken. Margulies, a fair-minded, independent thinker, had warned against overreaction toward the Bush Administration in a panel discussion, arguing that the Patriot Act was nowhere near as repressive as past wartime measures such as the Alien and Sedition Acts. But on November 14, after reading about the new executive order, he changed his mind. "I got the sense that America had lost its moral bearings," he said. The military tribunals "bore no resemblance to what you or I would call a trial. There was no jury, no presumption of innocence, and no right to counsel." The atmosphere was crackling with emotion, and there was open discussion among not just extremists but respected mainstream commentators, such as *Newsweek* columnist Jonathan Alter and Harvard Law School professor Alan Dershowitz, about the merits of torture. "Everybody understood the phenomenon of executive overreaching during times of perceived crisis," he said. All the elements were gathering, he worried, for "a gross abuse of power."

Margulies was in private practice at the time, doing a combination of civil rights work and death-penalty cases. In nearly two decades of defense work, he'd come to regard the rule of law as "a great accomplishment, but a fragile one." He had argued capital cases in Texas, while Bush was governor, so as he put it, "I'd gone face-to-face with Bush justice before." Years of death-penalty cases had taught Margulies that there was no question that the government had the power and often the right to take away individuals' liberty. What mattered most to him, and the country, he believed, was that this great and terrible power was exercised lawfully. Experience had honed what he called his "really refined sense of outrage at what I call official misconduct, or abuse of the process."

Margulies believed that the Bush Administration's legal strategies—with their emphasis on preventing crimes that had yet to be committed and holding prisoners without evidence that could hold up in an open court—called out for a serious challenge. But he could see it would be too much for one lawyer to take on. It would require a group with a variety of areas of expertise.

Within forty-eight hours, Margulies had reached Ratner, whom he knew only by reputation, by phone. In the weeks to come, their group would expand ever so slightly to include, among others, a free-spirited British death-penalty lawyer named Clive Stafford Smith, whom Margulies described admiringly as "a freak of nature." Trained at Columbia Law School, Smith lived in New Orleans with his family. He had represented more than 300 capital defendants at the trial stage in hard-core death-penalty states like Louisiana and Mississippi, and he had never had a client executed. Margulies came to regard him as "one of the most talented capital defense lawyers the country has ever seen." Also in the group would be a loquacious, maverick white-collar criminal lawyer, who had overlapped with Bush at Yale and was now a partner at Shearman & Sterling, one of Washington's most prestigious firms, named Tom Wilner. Many other brilliant and patriotic lawyers who regarded the American Constitution as the country's greatest strength would in time volunteer their time as well. But at the moment their outrage was just hot air, because they realized they were missing the most essential ingredient in any case: clients.

It was against the backdrop of these momentous legal changes that John Walker Lindh was taken into U.S. custody on December 1, 2001. Frank Lindh later said he couldn't figure out exactly what was happening behind the closed office doors in Washington, but he sensed that "there was a decision-making process going on about how to treat him. Ultimately, it must have been the President's decision to go with the hard-line approach," he concluded.

As soon as Lindh's parents heard media reports about their son's capture, they hired James Brosnahan, a prominent San Francisco trial lawyer, to represent him. On December 3, two days after Lindh was taken into custody, Brosnahan sent letters to Ashcroft, Rumsfeld, Tenet, and Powell informing them that he represented Lindh and wanted to meet with him. But for fifty-four days, during which Lindh asked repeatedly to speak to a lawyer, he was denied counsel.

Meanwhile, Lindh had given a series of interviews to reporters and government interrogators in the first several days after his capture that supplied virtually all of the incriminating evidence against him. Lindh evidently didn't comprehend the legal peril he was in—or, if he did, he felt coerced into talking. CNN was the first television news organization to interview him.

Robert Pelton, a freelance contributor to CNN, interviewed Lindh at a hospital to which he'd been taken after surrendering. Lindh still had a bullet in his thigh (U.S. officials left it in for weeks, claiming that they needed to preserve the chain of custody of the evidence against him). He also had shrapnel wounds, and intestinal problems from the contaminated water he had swallowed. An American Special Forces officer at the hospital later described Lindh, who was lying on the floor to recover from his wounds, as "delirious." Another American officer jokingly offered to shoot Lindh on the spot. But transcripts obtained by Lindh's lawyers show that Pelton told them not to kill Lindh "yet." He wanted to interview him first.

Lindh asked Pelton not to film or interview him, but the transcript shows that Pelton did anyway, even after Lindh had been given morphine, which Pelton told Lindh was "happy juice."

By the time Pelton left, he had a tape of Lindh saying that his "heart became attached" to the Taliban and that "the goal of every Muslim" was to be a *shahid,* or martyr. At the time, so soon after September 11, most people understood Muslim martyrdom to mean suicide terrorism—not dying in battle against the Northern Alliance. Lindh also said that he disapproved of the uprising that had led to Spann's death, because it was un-Islamic to break an agreement to surrender. That part wasn't news, however.

Pelton's interview, which portrayed Lindh as a committed traitor, was televised around the world. Within days, Rumsfeld declared that Lindh "was fighting on the Al Qaeda side."

For the next eight weeks, Lindh was held incommunicado and interrogated by the United States government. After being detained for two weeks in Afghanistan, Lindh was confined aboard an amphibious assault ship in the northern Arabian sea, the USS *Peleliu.* By the end of December, he was joined there by seven others. Some 3,000 other U.S. prisoners by then were in Afghan jails, many having been rounded up for cash bounties by warlords like Dostum.

The Justice Department, in particular, promoted a view of Lindh as a hardened terrorist who had embraced anti-American beliefs, taken up arms with people who hated his own country, and contributed to the death of Mike Spann, the young CIA officer from Georgia. Perhaps anxious to prove his relevance in the unfolding drama, on February 5 Attorney General Ashcroft personally announced plans to charge Lindh with "conspiracy to kill nationals of the United States" and nine other terrorism-related counts, carrying the possibility of three life sentences plus an additional ninety years in prison. Ashcroft noted that Lindh's rights had been "scrupulously honored." Lindh had been read the Miranda warning, Ashcroft noted, and had waived his right to a lawyer before being interviewed by the FBI. Ashcroft proclaimed that Lindh had no attorney at the time, so the statements he gave interrogators should be admissible.

But government documents suggested a different story. In Afghanistan, Lindh asked for counsel almost immediately. According to declassified government documents, a Navy medic who was present when Lindh arrived at the hospital on December 1 sent a cable to the United States saying that Lindh had asked, "When will I be able to speak to a lawyer?" Yet Lindh wasn't told that his parents had hired a lawyer for him until January. Frank Lindh tried to send word about Brosnahan to his son in a letter he entrusted to the Red Cross, whose mandate is to communicate with soldiers across battle lines. But American officials blocked the delivery of the letter. His parents also tried to get word to him through the State Department, the Defense Department, and their representatives in Congress. "He was behind a wall of silence," Lindh's father said.

During this time, Lindh was often kept blindfolded, naked, and bound to a stretcher with duct tape, according to a declassified account from a Navy physician. One document quotes the physician saying that the lead military interrogator believed that "sleep deprivation, cold, and hunger" could be applied to make Lindh talk. For days, Lindh was fed only a thousand calories a day and was left cold and sleep-deprived in a pitch-dark steel shipping container. The physician described Lindh as "disoriented" and "suffering lack of nourishment," adding that "suicide is a concern."

Nonetheless, Lindh was interrogated repeatedly. Early on, an unidentified Army interrogator had qualms and evidently asked through his superiors in the chain of command what the rules were regarding extracting a confession from Lindh. His understanding was that he could not collect incriminating information from Lindh that could be used against him in a criminal trial unless Lindh had a lawyer or had waived his rights. But after checking with the admiral in charge, he was told otherwise. The order came straight from the top of the Pentagon. A government document obtained by Lindh's lawyers shows clearly that the admiral told the interrogator that William Haynes, the General Counsel to the Secretary of Defense, had authorized him to "take the gloves off" and ask anything he wanted.

On December 9, an FBI agent assigned to Pakistan, Christopher Reimann, began extracting the confession from Lindh that became the basis for the criminal case. The encounter took place at Camp Rhino, a Marine base near Kandahar. Lindh, still blindfolded and handcuffed, was taken from his steel container to a nearby tent. Lindh's blindfold was removed. Reimann flashed his FBI badge and began to question Lindh. At this point, more than a week after his capture and repeated interrogation, Reimann read Lindh the Miranda warning. But, when noting the right to counsel, the agent acknowledged, he ad-libbed, "Of course, there are no lawyers here."

At no point did Reimann mention that Lindh's family had hired counsel for him. Under these circumstances, Lindh, still in handcuffs, signed a waiver of his right to counsel. "He thought it was the only way he was ever going to get out of that metal box," said George Harris, one of his defense lawyers.

But back in Washington, as Ashcroft surely knew, two days before Reimann began the interrogation, the Justice Department was notified by the FBI that an agent planned to question Lindh without the presence of counsel. It set off a legal skirmish. John De Pue, a trial attorney in the Terrorism and Violent Crime Section of the Justice Department, was not sure if this was proper and consulted with the Professional Responsibility Advisory Office, an internal-ethics unit. The legal adviser on duty that Friday who handled such questions was Jesselyn Radack. A thirty-year-old graduate of Brown University and Yale Law School, Radack had recently joined the internal-ethics unit after being selected for the Attorney General's prestigious Honors Program. Ambitious, idealistic, and proud to have graduated from Brown with honors in three majors, she had dreamed about this sort of high-profile case. After researching the matter and discussing it with a superior, she sent an e-mail to De Pue offering advice. "I consulted with a Senior Legal Advisor here," she wrote, "and we don't think you can have the FBI agent question Walker. It would be a pre-indictment, custodial overt interview, which is not authorized by law." Radack pointed out that Lindh's father had already retained a lawyer for him, which made it improper to approach Lindh without approaching his counsel, too.

"Thanks much," De Pue wrote back. "I have passed you [sic] assessment along and will keep you posted."

On December 10, Radack was surprised to learn that Reimann had questioned Lindh anyway. Alarmed, she advised De Pue that Lindh's confession might "have to be sealed" and "only used for national security purposes," not in a criminal case against him. She pressed for more information.

"Ugh," De Pue e-mailed back. "We are trying to figure out what actually transpired and what, if anything, Walker said."

Ten days later, Radack learned that the prosecution was ignoring her unit's advice and intended to use Lindh's confession. It argued that, because Lindh had been read his Miranda rights, the confession had been properly obtained. Radack was still troubled. "It was like ethics were out the window," she said. "After 9/11, it was, like, 'anything goes' in the name of terrorism. It felt like they'd made up their minds to get him, regardless of the process." Radack believed that the role of the ethics office was to "rein in the cowboys" whose zeal to stop criminals sometimes led them to overstep legal boundaries. "But after 9/11 we were bending ethics to fit our needs," she said. "Something wrong was going on. It wasn't just fishy—it stank."

Radack recalled that at her office "I was getting the vibes: Don't take this further. Drop it."

On January 15, when Ashcroft announced the government's complaint against Lindh, it became clear why. Ashcroft stated that the Justice Department had concluded that the FBI's interrogation of Lindh was legal because "the subject here is entitled to choose his own lawyer, and to our knowledge, has not chosen a lawyer at this time." The lawyer whom Lindh's father had hired to represent him, Ashcroft reasoned, wasn't legitimate because Lindh hadn't personally retained him. Ashcroft did not mention that Brosnahan's efforts to communicate with Lindh had been blocked.

Ashcroft's statement was an unequivocal contradiction of the Professional Responsibility Advisory Office's advice. Radack, who was appalled by Ashcroft's statement, said that she soon learned how costly it was to buck "the party line." Two weeks after the government's complaint was filed, she received a "blistering" performance review. It never mentioned her advice in the Lindh matter, but it severely questioned her legal judgment. She was advised to get a new job; otherwise, the performance review would be placed in her permanent file. Radack, who had received a merit bonus the year before, quickly found a job with a private law firm.

Just before she left the Justice Department, though, Radack learned that the presiding judge in the Lindh case had asked to see all Justice Department documents pertaining to the case, including internal e-mails. But she discovered, to her surprise, that the crucial e-mails she had written advising that Lindh's statement couldn't be used against him had not been given to the judge. More alarming, when she tried to check the paper file she had compiled in the case, which had included printouts of these e-mails, they were missing. "I felt instantly sick," she said. "The e-mails were definitely relevant." In her view, "Someone deliberately purged them from the file. In violation of the rules of federal procedure, they were going to withhold these documents from the court."

The situation dissolved into a flurry of mutual recriminations. When leaked copies of her internal e-mails later turned up in *Newsweek,* Radack's life became unbearable.

The Justice Department contacted her new employers and warned the firm that she was the target of a criminal leak investigation, even though the e-mails were not classified. Eventually, the firm rescinded its job offer. The Bush Administration then opened a yearlong criminal investigation of her and also referred her for disciplinary action in the states where she was licensed to practice law. Radack believed her name was also added to the "no-fly" list of possible terror suspects, resulting in full body searches every time she tried to travel by air. As such, she was one of the first of many loyal officials inside the administration whose consciences and senses of legal fair play landed them stunned and cast out, powerless to moderate the White House's self-destructive course.

What Radack didn't know was that Gonzales, at the White House, had decided that the administration didn't need to comply with the defense lawyers' discovery requests. The White House evidently feared details of Lindh's treatment would prove embarrassing. Radack was caught in the crosshairs of this fight.

In July 2002, a year and a half after the indictment and two days before Lindh's lawyers planned to challenge the legitimacy of his FBI confession in court, claiming that it had been coerced under shocking conditions, the prosecutors offered them a surprise deal. The case was hastily settled in a weekend-long flurry of negotiations that ended at 2 A.M. on the day that key evidence against Lindh was to be challenged in open court. By the time it was over, the Justice Department had dropped nine out of the ten counts against Lindh. As part of a plea agreement, Lindh accepted guilt on only two charges, and they were not directly related to terrorism: violation of a statute forbidding American citizens from contributing "services" to the Taliban. Ashcroft continued to cite Lindh's conviction as a major success, but there was no doubt that the first high-profile prosecution effort had mysteriously imploded.

"The Defense Department was really worried about the claims of mistreatment," said George Harris. "They said the deal had to be struck before the suppression hearing so the details wouldn't get out. They really wanted us to agree to drop any claims of intentional mistreatment. That was key to Rumsfeld." The surfacing of the directive from his general counsel, Haynes, encouraging interrogators to "take the gloves off" was not ideal publicity, even before the photographs of Abu Ghraib surfaced.

Paul McNulty, the U.S. Attorney in the Eastern District of Virginia, who had brought the case against Lindh, acknowledged that "there were risks to going forward" to trial. Yet, even though his office dropped nine of the ten original charges, McNulty said he was "satisfied with the outcome."

In retrospect, the reasons for the collapse of the overblown terror charges against Lindh are obvious. The military's mistreatment of him proved a huge liability to prosecutors once he finally faced trial. The Justice Department's denial of his basic rights also damaged the case. The lack of evidence to support the gravity of the charges against him exposed shameless political grandstanding by the Department of Justice. In fact, the case provided a first glimpse into high-level intrigue by Bush political appointees in the Department of the sort that would eventually claim the job of Attorney General Alberto Gonzales. But these lessons went largely unheeded. Instead, what John Walker Lindh taught the Bush Administration was that open criminal trials under the strict rules of the American legal system were not worth the risk. In the future, enemy prisoners would have to be held safely outside the reach of U.S. law, where they could be questioned without legal interference and tried under rules more favorable to the prosecution—if they were tried at all. In looking back, Harris said that "their experience with our case likely led to the idea that there should be an 'Unlawful Enemy Combatant Doctrine'—so there wouldn't be any more challenges like ours."

Clearly, Lindh's attorneys also thought there were risks, since they accepted a guilty plea and a twenty-year sentence. One major factor was that, after the indictment, prosecutors added a subsequent count, charging Lindh with committing a felony while carrying grenades. This charge alone carried a thirty-year minimum sentence. His lawyers thought the twenty-year plea was the best they could do. But one of Lindh's attorneys, Tony West, later criticized the deal as unjust. "It's part of the change in approach to law in this country, to prevention," he said. "You can detain people without evidence, make allegations, then develop the evidence later. If you have no evidence, you drop the charges. The only problem is, you've destroyed someone's life in the process."

Rohan Gunaratna, a prominent Sri Lankan terrorism expert who advised Lindh's lawyers and became genuinely convinced that Lindh was not a terrorist, saw the case as a cautionary tale. Lindh's prosecution was warped, he said, by American officials' poor understanding of the difference between fervent Muslims and Al Qaeda terrorists. He found the U.S. government worrisomely unsophisticated about Islam. During the early period after September 11 when Lindh was captured, he said, "They were like babies. They didn't know enough about Islam or Afghanistan. It was totally alien to them." Instead of punishing converts like Lindh, from whom they could learn, Gunaratna believed U.S. officials should have first used him as a resource. Perhaps they could have explored how he managed to effortlessly penetrate Al Qaeda's training camps when the CIA never got remotely close. If handled right, he argued, Lindh and other detainees could "provide enormous insight into how young Muslim converts get sucked in."

It was not just Lindh's defense team that considered the Bush Administration's first major prosecution in the war on terror to be deeply flawed. The weakness of the case was also signaled by U.S. District Court Judge T. S. Ellis III, who was presiding over it. In a sentencing hearing after the settlement, Ellis noted that the case linking Lindh to Al Qaeda "was not strong" and that there was "no evidence" tying him to Spann's death. When Spann's heartbroken father objected to this statement, Judge Ellis responded gently. "He clearly is a hero," he said, speaking of Spann. But he added pointedly, "Of all the things he fought for, one of them is that we don't convict people in the absence of proof beyond a reasonable doubt."

For years after Lindh's guilty plea, his lawyers tried to get his sentence commuted. They argued that another terror suspect seized at the same time as he, in the same circumstances, had been treated far more leniently. Yaser Hamdi, who had dual U.S. and Saudi citizenship, surrendered along with Lindh in Afghanistan, where he too had been a Taliban foot soldier. Unlike Lindh, however, after Hamdi was held in solitary confinement for two years without charges, he was stripped of his U.S. citizenship and turned over to the Saudi government, which in turn reportedly set him free.

The contrast rankled Lindh's family, underscoring the irrationality and unfairness of the Bush Administration's arbitrary legal process. In all likelihood, Hamdi was freed because without a confession of the type Lindh gave, there wasn't enough evidence to convict him. Unfortunate though Lindh was, comparatively speaking, he was lucky. He was well represented by some of the best lawyers in America and charged in a recognized criminal justice system. The exercise of those most elementary rights was a privilege that few of the terror suspects whose cases followed his could claim.

For the Bush Administration, Lindh's case was a learning experience. Evidently, the lesson learned was that trials of terror suspects in regularly constituted courts of law were too big a risk. But it's worth asking: risk to whom? As the full story of the case shows, putting Lindh on trial posed less of a threat to national security than it did to the government's reputation for justice. A trial would have exposed exaggerated charges, political posturing, willful mistreatment directed from the Pentagon's top lawyer, and, if Gunaratna was correct, an amateurish understanding of Al Qaeda.

In fact, while the White House was focusing on Lindh, the United States finally deployed the armed Predator to help destroy a high-level Al Qaeda meeting outside Kabul. In many respects, the trial run was a brilliant success. The strike killed Al Qaeda's military chief, Mohammad Atef, who left behind valuable documents. But evidently, Bin Laden was spared. A few weeks later, his voice was reportedly detected by agents on a satellite telephone near the Tora Bora cave complex. American B-52 bombers pounded the area. Afterward, Secretary of State Colin Powell declared, "We've destroyed Al Qaeda in Afghanistan." But the verdict was premature. Bin Laden escaped. The best estimates were that he either walked, rode a donkey, or took a bus across the border into Pakistan sometime in the third week of December 2001.

In Adelaide, Australia, meanwhile, a clever criminal defense lawyer named Stephen Kenny had been retained by the family of David Hicks, the onetime kangaroo skinner and militant Muslim convert captured in Afghanistan around the same time as Lindh. Hicks, who would be designated detainee 002, was believed to be in U.S. custody, but the government refused to acknowledge it was holding him. For help, Kenny got in touch with Ratner at the Center for Constitutional Rights. The Americans were waiting for individual suspects to be charged so that, in the usual manner, they could represent them. But in a conversation with his American counterparts, the Australian lawyer had what Margulies later called "a lightning strike" insight. Kenny wondered out loud if in fact the U.S.-held detainees would ever actually face military commissions or any other form of trial. "They'll never charge anyone," Kenny predicted. "There's no incentive to. The way they've set things up, they can hold and interrogate them forever."

6

OUTSOURCING TORTURE

One by one, the terrorists are learning the meaning of American justice.

—President George W. Bush, January 28, 2003,
State of the Union Address

We don't kick the {expletive} out of them. We send them to other countries so they can kick the {expletive} out of them.

—a U.S. official quoted in the *Washington Post,*
December 26, 2002

It began almost like a hallucination. At one in the morning in mid-October, six weeks after Vice President Cheney proclaimed that winning the war on terror meant "We've got to spend time in the shadows," a sleek, white private Gulfstream V jet landed amid the cracked and dusty runways of the international airport in Karachi, Pakistan, and taxied into a remote spot in the dark shadow of the old terminal. The plane was a vision of incongruous luxury—forty feet long with room for a dozen passengers. Its plush leather seats were the color of champagne, the beverage ordinarily expected on board. But instead of corporate jet-setters, a mysterious team of muscular male figures, dressed head to toe in black and wearing black masks, disembarked. One of the men carried a video camera and filmed the entire operation.

An hour and forty minutes later, as overnight desk clerks stared past the empty baggage carousels, the masked men in black returned to the jet, this time with their cargo. Dragging between them was an unidentified extra figure. His slumping head was hooded, and his feet and hands were shackled. He sagged like deadweight. None of the airport authorities seemed to know much about it, except that he was said to be a foreign deportee. Curiously, the jet was serviced by its own private ground crew, working for a company with an unfamiliar corporate name. As stealthily as it had come, the executive jet was gone almost without a trace. Except for one detail. An alert observer at the airport jotted down the internationally required registration number on the jet's tail, N-379 P, and passed it on to a local news reporter.

Soon after, on October 26, 2001, Masood Anwar, a reporter for the *News International* in Pakistan, publicized the first small piece of what would in time become a global jigsaw puzzle, revealing a secret program that has been a source of pride inside the Bush Administration and a growing international scandal in the eyes of many others. The Pakistani paper described the airport incident under the headline "Mystery Man Handed Over to US Troops in Karachi." Neither the team nor its extra passenger was identified. But the story noted that the plane was registered to the United States. It had flown from and returned to Amman, Jordan. Rumor had it that the men in black were U.S. officials and their quarry was a Yemeni microbiology student suspected of links to the *Cole* bombing.

After reading the bizarre airport story in Pakistan, Rajiv Chandrasekaran, a young and enterprising foreign correspondent for the *Washington Post,* was intrigued enough to run the plane's tail number through an FAA database. "I tried finding the number for the company listed, and couldn't get anything," Chandrasekaran later said. Almost immediately, he suspected that the company was a front, suggesting that the CIA was involved. "I thought, 'Why the hell would they fly in the middle of the night?'" But with the world on edge as it braced for America's response to the attacks of September 11, he was overloaded with other assignments. "That was it," he recalled of the first odd report. "It was all I had time to do back then."

It took almost a half a year before Chandrasekaran and another colleague at the *Washington Post,* Peter Finn, were able to piece the puzzle together further, bringing into focus the dim outlines of one of the most controversial clandestine programs run by the CIA's Counterterrorist Center, known as "extraordinary rendition." Devised as a means of extraditing criminal suspects from one foreign country to another outside of the recognized legal process, it would be cited by President Bush and George Tenet as among the most valuable weapons in the war on terror. Renditions, Tenet testified in Congress, "shattered terrorist cells and networks, thwarted terrorist plans, and in some cases even prevented attacks from occurring." But critics contended that the intelligence was purchased at an unconscionable cost. The true unstated purpose of the abductions, they said, was to subject the suspects to aggressive methods of persuasion that were illegal in America—including torture. Over time, the extraordinary-rendition program produced a file of confessions forced out of prisoners claiming to have suffered unimaginable torment. Much of this intelligence, however, proved demonstrably false, leading the United States tragically astray. But in the first months after the terrorist attacks on New York and Washington, all that was visible was a series of inexplicable human snatches, scattered around the globe.

A glimpse surfaced in Sweden, for instance, at 9 o'clock on the moonless evening of December 18, 2001. With little warning, a half-dozen masked men in black whisked two Egyptian asylum seekers, Muhammad Zery and Ahmed Agiza, into an empty office at Stockholm's Bromma Airport. Working in swift, synchronized lockstep, the masked men cut off the Egyptians' clothes with scissors and placed the shreds in bags. They forcibly administered sedatives by anal suppository, swaddled the prisoners in diapers, and dressed them in orange jumpsuits and hoods, with no cutouts for their eyes. As was reported by *Kalla Fakta,* a Swedish television news program, the suspects were placed in handcuffs and leg irons and photographed. Then, according to a declassified Swedish government report, the men were flown to Cairo on a U.S.-registered Gulfstream V jet, again with the tail number N-379 P.

A border police officer working the late shift at the airport found the whole episode "a little extraordinary," as he later put it. All non-European aircraft were supposed to contact the police before landing. Somehow, this American jet had evaded all of the usual red tape. He thought it odd, too, that on the jet, along with the masked men, had been a handful of U.S. and Egyptian officials and a doctor, all of whom seemed to be carrying out some sort of forcible secret operation on Swedish territory without obeying Swedish laws.

The next day, in Pakistan, an additional piece of the story began to unfold that in time would reveal the true destination and fateful consequences of these and other mysterious disappearances. On that day, December 19, 2001, Pakistani security forces, blocking the chaotic escape of those fleeing Afghanistan over what were called "rat trails" through the mountains, captured what was considered the first big prize in the war on terror. He was an alleged Al Qaeda commander by the name of Ali Abdul Aziz al-Fakhiri, better known by his *nom de guerre,* Ibn al-Shaykh al-Libi. The Pakistanis quickly turned al-Libi over to the Americans. "The Pakistanis were great. They gave us everything," a former CIA officer in Afghanistan said. "Mind you, it took balefuls of cash. Cash by the barrel for the head of a big fish." Once al-Libi was transported to the central interrogation center at Bagram Air Base in Afghanistan, U.S. authorities ran his name through the FBI's computer system in New York. Information came pouring out.

Al-Libi had tried to play dumb, but the records showed that he had been the chief of Bin Laden's Khalden training camp. He had trained hundreds, possibly thousands, of jihadis in terrorist tactics. He knew Bin Laden personally and likely had inside knowledge of his operations. At the FBI's field office in New York, Jack Cloonan thought they had a possible gold mine. He knew that Zacarias Moussaoui and Richard Reid, the so called "Shoe Bomber," who attempted to detonate plastic explosives while in-flight on American Airlines Flight 63 from Paris to Miami on December 20, 2001, both of whom were in U.S. custody, had spent time at the Khalden camp. Cloonan worried that "neither the Moussaoui case nor the Reid case was a slam dunk." But if they could turn al-Libi into a state's witness, he thought, it could make all the difference. Cloonan became intent on securing al-Libi's testimony as a future witness. With the criminal justice model in mind, he advised his FBI colleagues in Afghanistan to question al-Libi respectfully "and handle this like it was being done right here, in my office in New York." He recalled, "I remember talking on a secure line to them. I told them, 'Do yourself a favor, read the guy his rights. It may be old-fashioned, but this will come out if we don't. It may take ten years, but it will hurt you, and the Bureau's reputation, if you don't. Have it stand as a shining example of what we feel is right.'"

Soon after, in a freezing-cold office at the Bagram Air Base, heated only by a small coal brazier that they constantly had to stoke, Russell Fincher, an FBI terrorism agent from New York, and Marty Mahon, a New York City detective who had been working terrorism cases with the joint terrorism task force since the *Cole* bombing, found themselves talking with al-Libi. The tough native New Yorkers almost liked him. They had to keep reminding themselves that he would just as soon stick a pencil through their eye and kill them (which another

U.S.-held Al Qaeda suspect had tried to do) as talk to them. Al-Libi was a small man who liked to smile a lot, in a way that seemed genuinely friendly, not malicious. He spoke a bit of English, so they called in translators only when they were really stuck. Once he got started, he just talked and talked. In fact, he talked so much that they had to keep pocketfuls of pens warmed by their body heat, because in the frosty Spartan cell they were using as an office, the ink kept freezing before he was done. They could barely keep up.

It was Fincher who forged the first personal connection. A devout Christian, he'd asked al-Libi if he prayed. "Of course!" the terrorist had replied. What followed were joint prayer sessions and rambling discussions about Mohammed, Jesus, and God. As the captors drank hot coffee with their prisoner, they delicately flattered and cajoled him. The approach seemed to be succeeding. "He was expecting us to pull out his fingernails or something," a source familiar with the interrogation, who was not authorized to describe it on the record, recalled. "But when he found out that we were really there to listen, and that he was stuck, with no way out, he just opened up."

What he had to say, as far as they were concerned, was invaluable. Al-Libi told the FBI duo enough about Reid to convince them that he'd make a devastating witness in any future trial against him. He also gave them many new details about how the training camps were run and how the Arabs had dominated. He was himself from Libya, and it emerged that he hadn't actually liked Bin Laden, who had tried to force him to train only Al Qaeda fighters, not all Muslims, which was his preference. Most important, they claimed, al-Libi gave the agents specific, actionable intelligence—information that could save American lives. Defenders of coercion in the Bush Administration would go on to argue that the extreme urgency of getting such operational information justified their aggressive approach. But without coercion, al-Libi told the FBI team of an approved plot by Al Qaeda that was in the final stage before execution, to blow up the U.S. embassy in Aden, Yemen. A source close to the interrogation maintained that this was corroborated, averting what would likely have been a deadly attack.

Almost as important as what al-Libi said was what he didn't say. Although Fincher reportedly pressed al-Libi hard on any ties between Al Qaeda and Saddam Hussein's regime in Iraq, the Al Qaeda commander told the investigators he knew of none.

In exchange for his cooperation, there was something al-Libi wanted. Word had reached him, even as far away as the caves of Afghanistan, that the United States had offered emigration help to some Al Qaeda informers and their families. He had a Syrian wife. He wanted for her, and her family, to be able to come to the United States. He was willing to be prosecuted himself if a deal could be struck. The agents made no promises, but they confirmed how well the witness-relocation effort was going with others. As one inside source put it, "The carrot was dangled."

"It was going well," said Cloonan. Maybe, he later thought, too well. Al-Libi's statements were being transcribed and shared almost instantaneously with other agencies, including the CIA. "Remember," he said, "at that time, court rooms were the enemy. They didn't want him walled off, and put into the criminal system." Another law-enforcement officer close to the case claims the CIA "was jealous" of the mother lode of information that the FBI succeeded in seducing out of al-Libi. CIA sources have suggested that, to the contrary, they suspected al-Libi was holding back too much. Whatever the motive, several days into what the FBI regarded as winning al-Libi's trust, a young Arabic-speaking CIA officer named "Albert," who had previously worked for Cloonan at the FBI as a junior language specialist, burst into the cell where Fincher was questioning al-Libi and started shouting at the prisoner. "You're going to Egypt!" he yelled. "And while you're there, I'm going to find your mother, and fuck her!"

Soon after, he and other CIA officers returned, accompanied by military personnel, and grabbed al-Libi. "They literally came into the room, strapped him to a stretcher, wrapped his feet, his hands, and his mouth in duct tape," and took him away, a senior FBI official said. Al-Libi was hooded and loaded into a waiting pickup truck, which drove directly into the hold of a waiting plane. "He was transferred," an eyewitness deadpanned with a smirk. As a former CIA officer in Afghanistan at the time put it, "The FBI tells us not to set foot in the U.S., but outside, it's our rules."

Cloonan retired from the FBI soon after in disgust. Before walking away from a twenty-seven-year career, he confronted Mueller in a huge staff meeting in New York about the Bureau's response to illegal interrogation techniques being used on U.S.-held captives abroad. According to Cloonan, the FBI's top man replied, "I'm not concerned about due process abroad." Cloonan said, "I knew then it was a new day, and time for me to leave." In looking back at the al-Libi fight, he added, "At least we got information in ways that wouldn't shock the conscience of the court. And no one will have to seek revenge for what I did."

In Washington, Cloonan discovered, the FBI had lost another round on the bureaucratic front of the war on terror. The jurisdictional fight over which agency would get custody of al-Libi, he later heard, reached the Oval Office, where the President sided with Tenet. Unlike Mueller, Tenet had a seat at the cabinet table. And, clearly, Bush preferred the CIA's tough-guy approach. When Tenet had first described the burgeoning rendition program back at the end of September, Bush was so excited he'd wanted to know, "At what point are we going to feel comfortable talking about these things?" He was hoping to go public, as the terror suspects were snatched one by one around the world, so that Americans could keep score, like a sporting event. Tenet explained disappointingly that many of the countries secretly aiding the United States in these operations lived in fear that their populations would find out. Evidently, the controversial nature of the program had not occurred to the President. Tenet consoled Bush with the possibility that in the future, when perhaps hundreds of suspects had been "rendered," they could at least release the aggregate numbers. Bush was pleased.

With the President's encouragement, in the months after the September 11 attacks the rendition program boomed. The Counterterrorist Center, which ran the program, was seen as the hot place to be inside the CIA. There were so many volunteers, they had to be turned away. "All the others at CTC were second-class citizens," one former officer recalled. The staff at the CTC, meanwhile, mushroomed from 300 to 1,200 in a matter of weeks. The budget seemed limitless. At one point, an officer from another part of the Agency questioned Cofer Black about how fast he seemed to be burning through the millions of dollars of new congressional appropriations he had been allocated. Black, he recalled, told him a little defensively, "George [Tenet] told me to spend as much as we needed."

"But were you supposed to spend the whole budget all at once?" the officer said he retorted. Caution was part of the discredited past.

As a former counterterrorism officer told the *Washington Post,* "It was the Camelot of counterterrorism. We didn't have to mess with others—and it was fun."

After the CIA took custody of al-Libi, the FBI lost track of him. There were rumors that he was rendered to Egypt, where he was being tortured. One memorable but unconfirmed detail that made the rounds was that he had been buried alive in the desert, with sand up to his neck. He was said to have lost his mind. But both he and his influence on America were far from finished.

On January 27, 2005, President Bush, in an interview with the New York Times, assured the world that "torture is never acceptable, nor do we hand over people to countries that do torture." This assurance would have surprised al-Libi and hundreds of other U.S.-held captives who suddenly found themselves imprisoned after the attacks of September 11 in ghastly foreign dungeons, seemingly with no way out. For many, the program itself was a form of torture.

Renditions were not invented for the war on terror. The U.S. government had carried out renditions at least since the Reagan era. But they were originally used on an extremely limited basis and for a different purpose. After September 11, the program expanded beyond recognition, becoming what John Radsan, a lawyer in the CIA's Office of General Counsel during the first years of the Bush Administration, later admitted to be "a nightmare."

What began as a program aimed at a small, discrete set of suspects—people against whom there were outstanding foreign arrest warrants—came to include the wide and ill-defined population that the administration termed "illegal enemy combatants." Many of them had never been publicly charged with any crime. Before September 11, the program was aimed at rendering criminal suspects to justice, but afterward it was used to render suspects outside the reach of the law. Instead of holding suspects accountable for previously committed crimes, it was used to gather evidence of future crimes not yet committed—for which there was not sufficient evidence to prove guilt under the ordinary rule of law, which all over the civilized world requires transparency, fairness, and independent review. Rendition thus became an enforcement mechanism for the Bush Administration's preemptive criminal model, disrupting and punishing suspects before they were provably guilty.

Because of the classified nature of the program, no accurate statistics have ever been made available about its size. Before September 11, Tenet testified that the CIA had carried out some seventy renditions, about two dozen of which had involved bringing suspects to the United States to face charges. Afterward, though, the estimates ranged from upward of one hundred to possibly in the low thousands. Peter Bergen and Katherine Tiedemann of the New America Foundation documented 117 rendition cases after September 11, piecing together research from such organizations as Human Rights Watch, Amnesty International, the American Civil Liberties Union, and the Center for Human Rights and Global Justice at NYU Law School.

Scott Horton, an expert on international law who helped prepare a report on renditions issued by NYU Law School and the New York City Bar Association, estimated that at least 150 people were renditioned between 2001 and 2005. Representative Ed Markey, a Democrat from Massachusetts and a member of the Select Committee on Homeland Security, said that a more precise number was impossible to obtain. "I've asked people at the CIA for numbers," he said. "They refuse to answer. All they will say is that they're in compliance with the law."

The program's legality, however, rested on a rather contorted reading of the law, one that seemed to violate its spirit and possibly its letter, too. In 1990, the Senate ratified the Convention Against Torture, which declares that it is the policy of the United States "not to expel, extradite, or otherwise effect the involuntary removal of any person to a country where there are substantial grounds for believing the person would be in danger of being subjected to torture." The law explicitly prohibited the United States from transferring prisoners to other countries without first reviewing "all relevant considerations, including . . . a consistent pattern of gross, flagrant or mass violations of human rights." It applied to people in U.S. custody anywhere in the world, not just within the borders of America.

Yet the extraordinary-rendition program operated in obvious disregard of these legal barriers. Terrorism suspects all over Europe, Africa, Asia, and the Middle East were abducted by unidentified, and thus unaccountable, hooded or masked American agents and forced onto planes like the one first described in Karachi. The aircraft, which were flown by pilots with false identities and registered to a series of dummy American corporations, had clearance to land at U.S. and allied bases in places as far-flung as Greenland and Diego Garcia. Upon arriving in foreign countries, rendered suspects simply vanished. Detainees were not provided with lawyers, were rarely charged with crimes, and were not given any means of informing their families or anyone else of their whereabouts. Only a fraction of these cases have fully surfaced, but judging from those, it is clear that torture was omnipresent. A former CIA agent in the Middle East who was involved in a number of the post–September 11 cases maintained that torture was not the purpose of these transfers. "We had no place to hold all of these people," he said. Also, the CIA lacked the language skills and detailed knowledge of indigenous terror organizations that foreign intelligence agencies could bring to bear. Getting information was the CIA's goal; the means, he suggested, were incidental.

The most common destinations for rendered suspects were Egypt, Morocco, Syria, Jordan, Uzbekistan, and Afghanistan, all of which have long been cited for human rights violations by the State Department and are known to torture suspects. To justify sending detainees to these countries, the administration appeared to be relying on a very fine reading of the law requiring "substantial grounds for believing" that a detainee will be tortured abroad. Martin Lederman, a lawyer who left the Justice Department's Office of Legal Counsel in 2002 after eight years, and who became an expert in these issues while teaching law at Georgetown University, explained the loophole he believed the Bush Administration had exploited. "The Convention only applies when you know a suspect is more likely than not to be tortured," he said. "But what if you kind of know? That's not enough. So there are ways to get around it." This wiggle room seems to have been what Alberto Gonzales was alluding to during his January 2005 confirmation hearings to become Attorney General. Asked about rumors of torture in the rendition program, Gonzales, then the top lawyer in the White House, chuckled and noted that the administration "can't fully control" what other nations do.

Almost from the start, the Bush Administration's aggressive use of "extraordinary renditions" stirred fierce internal resistance, much of it coming from surprising quarters—not just human rights activists but rather hard-line law-and-order stalwarts in the criminal justice system with years of experience fighting terrorism. Their concerns were as much practical as ideological. Firsthand experience in interrogation led most to doubt the effectiveness of physical coercion as a means of extracting reliable information. They also warned the Bush Administration that once it took prisoners outside the realm of the law, it would have trouble bringing them back in. By holding detainees indefinitely, without counsel, without charges of wrongdoing, and under circumstances that could, in legal parlance, "shock the conscience" of a court, the administration, they warned, would jeopardize its chances of convicting hundreds of suspected terrorists, or even of using them as witnesses in almost any court in the world.

"It's a big problem," said Jamie Gorelick, a former deputy attorney general and a member of the 9/11 Commission. "In criminal justice, you either prosecute the suspects or let them go. But if you've treated them in ways that won't allow you to prosecute them you're in this no-man's-land. What do you do with these people?"

The criminal prosecution of terrorist suspects, of course, was not a priority for the Bush Administration in the immediate aftermath of September 11. But even some who had led the fight against Al Qaeda in the administration worried about the unintended consequences of the White House's radical legal measures. Surprisingly, among these critics was Michael Scheuer, the Jeremiah-like former head of the Bin Laden Unit at the CIA who helped establish the practice of rendition in the first place.

"It was begun in desperation," he later explained. During the 1990s, under the Clinton Administration, the stated mission of his job had been to "detect, disrupt, and dismantle" terrorist operations. His unit spent much of 1996 studying how Al Qaeda operated; by the next year, Scheuer said, they had determined the need to try to capture Bin Laden and his associates. The problem, in his view, was that Clinton's reluctance to authorize lethal operations against Bin Laden put the CIA in a bind. He recalled, "We went to the White House and they said, 'Do it.'" He added that Richard Clarke, who was in charge of counterterrorism for the National Security Council at the time, offered no advice. "He told me, 'Figure it out by yourselves,'" Scheuer said. (Clarke did not respond to a request for comment about Scheuer.)

Scheuer sought the counsel of Mary Jo White, then the U.S. Attorney for the Southern District of New York, who, along with a small group of FBI agents in New York, was pursuing the 1993 World Trade Center bombing case. In 1998, White's team obtained an indictment against Bin Laden authorizing U.S. agents to bring him and his associates to the United States to stand trial. This formally established that Bin Laden was a wanted fugitive who could be legally rendered to stand trial in the United States. From the start, though, the CIA was wary of granting terrorism suspects the due process afforded by American law. The agency did not want to divulge secrets about its intelligence sources and methods, and American courts demanded transparency. Even establishing the chain of custody of key evidence—such as a laptop computer—could easily pose a significant problem: foreign governments, fearing retaliation from their Muslim populations, might refuse to testify in U.S. courts about how they had obtained the evidence, for fear of having their secret cooperation exposed. The provenance of a laptop computer had in fact been the center of an extraordinarily bitter tussle between the CIA and the FBI. Filled with details of Al Qaeda's structure, it was considered the Rosetta Stone of counterterrorism in the pre-9/11 period. But the CIA had refused to share it with the FBI for months, because of the Agency's fears that the computer's foreign sourcing would leak out.

The CIA also felt that other agencies sometimes stood in its way. In 1996, for example, the State Department stymied a joint effort by the CIA and the FBI to question one of Bin Laden's cousins in America because he had a diplomatic passport, which protects the holder from U.S. law enforcement. An FBI agent arrived in the Falls Church, Virginia, office of the cousin, Abdullah Mohammed Bin Laden, demanding to question him. But he suavely said that he would be "more than happy" to talk, except for this: he produced a diplomatic passport. He was not a diplomat, he was working for a suspicious nongovernmental organization. But the Saudi government had accredited him to the embassy as an "attaché." Describing the CIA's frustration, Scheuer said, "We were turning into voyeurs. We knew where these people were, but we couldn't capture them." And even if they could, he noted, "we had nowhere to take them." The Agency realized that "we had to come up with a third party."

The obvious choice, Scheuer said, was Egypt. The largest recipient of U.S. foreign aid after Israel, Egypt was a key strategic ally, and its secret police force, the Mukhabarat, had a reputation for brutality. Egypt had been frequently cited by the State Department for torture of prisoners. According to a 2002 report, detainees were "stripped and blindfolded; suspended from a ceiling or doorframe with feet just touching the floor; beaten with fists, whips, metal rods, or other objects; subjected to electrical shocks; and doused with cold water [and] sexually assaulted." Hosni Mubarak, Egypt's leader, who came to office in 1981 after President Anwar Sadat was assassinated by Islamist extremists, was determined to crack down on terrorism. His prime political enemies were radical Islamists, hundreds of whom had fled the country and joined Al Qaeda. Among this radical Islamic diaspora was Ayman al-Zawahiri, the Cairo physician who after having been brutally tortured in Egyptian prisons went on to Afghanistan, where he eventually became Bin Laden's top deputy.

In 1995, Scheuer said, America proposed the rendition program to

Egypt. In Cairo that summer, Edward S. Walker Jr., the U.S. Ambassador to Egypt, learned about the plan from the CIA's Cairo station chief. It was considered so secret, the two met in a special secure area of the fortresslike embassy, a room encased by electronically impenetrable walls and regularly swept for eavesdropping equipment. Given Egypt's difficulties halting terrorism on its own, using more conventional police methods, Walker endorsed the plan.

Soon after, the United States offered Egypt its rich resources to track, capture, and transport terrorist suspects globally—including access to a small fleet of aircraft. Egypt embraced the idea immediately. "What was clever was that some of the senior people in Al Qaeda were Egyptian," Scheuer said. "It served American purposes to get these people arrested, and Egyptian purposes to get these people back, where they could be interrogated." Technically, U.S. law required the CIA to seek "assurances" from Egypt that rendered suspects wouldn't be tortured. But even during the Clinton Administration, this obligation appears to have been little more than a sham. Scheuer insisted that the assurances were obtained, but he acknowledged that he was "not sure" if any documents confirming the arrangement were signed. In a congressional hearing, he acknowledged candidly that even if the assurances not to torture were written in indelible ink, coming from Arab police states, "they weren't worth a bucket of warm spit."

Each rendition was authorized at the very top levels of both governments. Tenet or the head of the CTC was required to sign off on each case. The National Security Adviser, too, was apprised of many of the renditions. The long-serving chief of the Egyptian central intelligence agency, Omar Suleiman, negotiated directly with top Agency officials. Walker described the Egyptian counterpart, Suleiman, as "very bright, very realistic," adding that he was cognizant that there was a downside to "some of the negative things that the Egyptians engaged in, of torture and so on. But he was not squeamish, by the way."

A series of spectacular operations followed almost immediately from this secret pact. On September 13, 1995, U.S. agents helped kidnap Talaat Fouad Qassem, one of Egypt's most wanted terrorists, in Croatia. Qassem had fled to Europe after being linked by Egypt to the assassination of Sadat; he had been sentenced to death in absentia. Croatian police seized Qassem in Zagreb and handed him over to U.S. agents, who interrogated him aboard a ship cruising the Adriatic Sea and then took him back to Egypt. Once there, Qassem disappeared.

There is no record that he was put on trial. Hossam el-Hamalawy, an Egyptian journalist covering human rights issues, said, "We believe he was executed." He was far from the only rendered suspect presumed dead.

A more elaborate operation was staged in Tirana, Albania, in the summer of 1998. According to the *Wall Street Journal,* the CIA provided the Albanian intelligence service with equipment to wiretap the phones of a suspected cell of Muslim militants led by Ayman al-Zawahiri's brother, Mohammed. Tapes of the conversations were translated into English, revealing lengthy discussions between the Zawahiri brothers. There were no outstanding indictments in the case, so the United States pressured Egypt for assistance; in June, Egypt issued an arrest warrant for Shawki Salama Attiya, one of the militants. Over the next few months, Albanian security forces, working with U.S. agents, killed one suspect and captured Attiya and four others. These men were bound, blindfolded, and taken to an abandoned air base, then flown by jet to Cairo for interrogation. Attiya later alleged that he suffered electrical shocks to his genitals, was hung from his limbs, and was kept in a cell in filthy water up to his knees. Two other suspects, who had been sentenced to death in absentia, were hanged. Egypt also sentenced both of the Zawahiri brothers to death in absentia. Meanwhile, however, the brutalization of what were referred to as the "Albanian returnees" became a rallying cry for Islamic militants in Egypt—radicalizing sentiment against America.

On August 5, 1998, a month after the Albanian rendition, in what was beginning to take on the aura of a very personal vendetta, an Arab-language newspaper in London published a letter from Zawahiri threatening retaliation against the United States—in a "language they will understand." He warned that America's "message has been received and that the response, which we hope they will read carefully, is being prepared." Two days later, the U.S. embassies in Kenya and Tanzania were blown up, killing 224 people.

Meanwhile, the rendition program was becoming bureaucratized in Washington, like any other government function. In 1997, a "Rendition Branch" was formally added to the CIA's Counterterrorist Center. In 1998, President Clinton signed a still-classified directive giving Clarke, the national coordinator for counterterrorism, detailed guidelines for "Apprehension, Extradition, Rendition and Prosecution" of wanted fugitives, including Bin Laden. Renditions became almost routine. While waiting for one such abduction to take place on the other side of the globe, Clinton's National Security Council staff whiled away the late-night hours watching movies, including, memorably, *The Mouse That Roared.*

The United States began rendering terror suspects to other countries, too, but the most common destination remained Egypt. The partnership between the American and the Egyptian intelligence services was extraordinarily close: The Americans could give the Egyptian interrogators questions they wanted put to the detainees in the morning, Scheuer said, and get answers by the evening. The Americans asked to question suspects directly themselves, but, Scheuer said, the Egyptians refused. "We were never in the same room at the same time."

Scheuer claimed that "there was a legal process" undergirding these early renditions. Every suspect who was apprehended, he said, had been convicted in absentia. Before a suspect was captured, a dossier was prepared containing the equivalent of a rap sheet. The CIA's legal counsel signed off on every proposed operation. Scheuer said that this system prevented innocent people from being subjected to rendition. "Langley would never let us proceed unless there was substance," he said. Moreover, Scheuer emphasized, renditions were pursued out of expedience—"not out of thinking it was the best policy."

Since September 11, as the number of renditions grew and hundreds of suspected terrorists were deposited indefinitely not just in foreign prisons but also in U.S.-run facilities in Afghanistan, Cuba, and the CIA's top-secret "black site" prisons, the shortcomings of this approach became manifest. "Are we going to hold these people forever?" Scheuer asked. "The policy makers hadn't thought what to do with them, and what would happen when it was found out that we were turning them over to governments that the human-rights world reviled." Once a detainee's rights had been violated, he said, "you absolutely can't" reinstate him into the court system. "You can't kill him, either," he added. "All we've done is create a nightmare."

On a bleak winter day in Trenton, New Jersey, Daniel Coleman, an ex–FBI agent, scoffed at the idea that Scheuer was now having compunctions about renditions. The CIA, Coleman said, liked rendition from the start. "They loved that these guys would just disappear off the books and never be heard of again," he said. "They were proud of it."

Few could speak with more authority on the subject. For ten years, Coleman worked closely with the CIA on counterterrorism cases, including the embassy attacks in Kenya and Tanzania. He had been the earliest of the agents from the FBI's New York field office to be assigned to the "fusion cell" at Langley. Coleman's gruff manner and middle-aged midriff had won him the nickname "Grumpy Santa" among his colleagues, but they knew that underneath he was the most decent and dedicated of agents. He became the FBI's first case agent assigned to Bin Laden in the mid-1990s. He'd been instrumental in starting the FBI's Bin Laden Unit. He'd spent years in solitary study of Islamic radicalism, mastering the names of hundreds of suspects and absorbing their profiles and culture. He retired in July 2004 partly because the dust from the collapsed World Trade Center towers, where he had sped to help out on September 11, had exacerbated his asthma. He breathed heavily and walked slowly, but he was quick to grasp the big picture, which was that after September 11, his methodical style of detective work, in which interrogations were aimed at forging relationships with detainees, was unfashionable. Like his friend and colleague Jack Cloonan, he saw that overnight the rules of the game had changed.

Yet the more patient approach used by Coleman and other agents had yielded major successes. In the embassy bombings case, they helped convict four Al Qaeda operatives on 302 criminal counts; all four men pleaded guilty to serious terrorism charges and were sentenced to life in prison. The confessions the FBI agents elicited, and the trial itself, which ended in May 2001, created an invaluable public record about Al Qaeda, including details about its funding mechanisms, its internal structure, and its intention to obtain weapons of mass destruction. They felt they had done their job—and that it was the political leadership in Washington that had failed by not paying sufficient attention.

The key to solving the embassy bombings case had nothing to do with torture. The secret was getting inside cooperation from an informer named Jamal Ahmed al-Fadl, better known among the counterterrorism experts at the FBI's New York field office as "Junior." For nearly a decade, Junior had been living in the United States' Witness Protection Program under an assumed identity. A Sudanese citizen and onetime confidant of Bin Laden's, he had served as the FBI's chief witness in the embassy bombings case and had cooperated as much as he could on every Al Qaeda case since. A dark-skinned man with close-cropped hair and a mischievous smile, al-Fadl entered government custody in 1996 after walking into the U.S. embassy in Eritrea and confessing to membership in Al Qaeda. Coleman had succeeded in getting him to confess that he had become disaffected from the terrorist organization, which he said discriminated against non-Arabs like himself, after he had stolen money from it. Since then, in a plea agreement for a still-to-be-determined sentence, he had lived under false identities in at least a half dozen American towns, including spending his first eighteen months in the country in a Residence Inn in New Jersey, where he was guarded by several long-suffering FBI agents who lived with him around the clock. They were armed, but it took more than firepower to protect them from unpredictable antics. Subsequently, his wife and children joined him in America, moving with him to a series of undisclosed locations.

Al-Fadl, who was arguably America's most valuable informant on Al Qaeda, was a living example of both the pros and cons of the old paradigm. He provided crucial information about the terrorist organization's operations and made numerous positive identifications of suspected members before and after the attacks of September 11. He served also as a textbook on Al Qaeda's inner workings. At the same time, al-Fadl's upkeep had been expensive, and he was an incessant troublemaker, "a lovable rogue," in Coleman's words. His incessant womanizing, financial scheming, and emotional ups and downs had become almost a full-time job for his chief handlers at the FBI.

Coleman had learned from it that "people don't do anything unless they're rewarded." He said that if the FBI had beaten a confession out of al-Fadl with what he called "all that alpha-male shit," it would never be able to talk to him again and again. Brutality may yield a timely scrap of information, he conceded. But in the longer fight against terrorism, such an approach is "completely insufficient," he said. "You need to talk to people for weeks. Years."

Coleman was a political nonpartisan with a law-and-order mentality. His eldest son was a former Army Ranger who served in Afghanistan. Yet Coleman was troubled by the Bush Administration's New Paradigm. Torture, he said, "has become bureaucratized." Bad as the policy of rendition was before September 11, Coleman said, "afterward, it really went out of control." He explained, "Now, instead of just sending people to third countries, we're holding them ourselves. We're taking people, and keeping them in our own custody in third countries. That's an enormous problem." Egypt, he pointed out, at least had an established legal system, however harsh. "There was a process there," Coleman said. "But what's our process? We have no method over there other than our laws—and we've decided to ignore them. What are we now, the Huns? If you don't talk to us, we'll kill you?"

From the beginning of the rendition program, Coleman said, there was no doubt that Egypt engaged in torture. He recalled the case of a suspect in the first World Trade Center bombing who fled to Egypt. The United States requested his return and the Egyptians handed him over—wrapped head to toe in duct tape, like a mummy. In another incident, an Egyptian pilot who had worked for Bin Laden but later cooperated with the U.S. government in a terrorism trial, needed to be rescued by U.S. diplomats after he returned from a brief visit to Cairo. The FBI learned that Egyptian authorities had imprisoned him. For days, he had been chained to a toilet, where, according to Cloonan, his guards had urinated on him.

Under such circumstances, it might seem difficult for the U.S. government to legally justify dispatching suspects to Egypt. But Coleman said that since September 11 the CIA "has seemed to think it's operating under different rules, that it has extralegal abilities outside the U.S." Agents, he said, "told me that they have their own enormous office of general counsel that rarely tells them no. Whatever they do is all right. It all takes place overseas."

Coleman was angry that lawyers in Washington were redefining the parameters of counterterrorism interrogations. "Have any of these guys ever tried to talk to someone who's been deprived of his clothes?" he asked. "He's going to be ashamed, and humiliated, and cold. He'll tell you anything you want to hear to get his clothes back. There's no value in it."

The FBI had an embarrassing firsthand reminder of why such tactics are illegal when, immediately after September 11, they coerced an Egyptian national who had been staying at a hotel near the World Trade Center into falsely confessing to a role in the attacks. Abdallah Higazy, like the other hotel guests, fled when the hijacked planes smashed into the towers. Soon after, the hotel told the FBI it had found in his closet a radio communication system for air pilots. The FBI took Higazy into custody. According to Higazy, an FBI agent told him that if he didn't confess that the equipment was his, and that it connected him to the Al Qaeda attacks, his family in Egypt would be tortured. After first denying the charges, Higazy confessed under the pressure. Luckily for him, an airline pilot who had also been a guest at the same hotel soon returned to ask for his radio back. The charges were dropped, and Higazy sued the hotel and the FBI in a case in which the government argued that the damning details had to be sealed to protect national security.

Years of experience had taught Coleman to treat even the most despicable suspects as if there were "a personal relationship, even if you can't stand them." He said that many of the suspects he had interrogated expected to be tortured and were stunned to learn that they had rights under the American system. Due process made detainees more compliant, not less, Coleman argued. He had also found that a defendant's right to legal counsel was beneficial not only to suspects but also to law-enforcement officers. Defense lawyers frequently persuaded detainees to cooperate with prosecutors in exchange for plea agreements. "The lawyers show these guys there's a way out," Coleman said. "It's human nature. People don't cooperate with you unless they have some reason to." He added, "Brutalization doesn't work. We know that. Besides, you lose your soul."

As 2002 began, al-Libi and the two Egyptian nationals whom the Rendition Unit had abducted from the airport in Sweden took up residence in what was known infamously as the Scorpion maximum-security prison in Cairo. Swedish officials have maintained that they received assurances from the Egyptian government that the two prisoners they helped rendition, Zery and Agiza, would be treated humanely. But both suspects have said, through lawyers and family members, that almost immediately upon disembarking from the U.S. jet, they were tortured with excruciatingly painful jolts of electrical charges to their genitals, under the watchful supervision of a medical doctor. Zery, who was released two years later without charges on the condition that he not discuss his mistreatment, said that he was also forced to lie on an electrified bed frame. Agiza, a physician, accused of having been allied with Zawahiri, was convicted on terrorism charges by Egypt's Supreme Military Court and sentenced to fifteen years in prison.

For the time being, al-Libi's fate remained largely unknown outside of the CIA. In his memoir, Tenet wrote blandly: "We believed that al-Libi was withholding critical threat information at the time so we transferred him to a third country for further debriefing."

Meanwhile, the redefinition of legal standards for the treatment of captives cleared another hurdle in the Bush White House. In early January 2002, soon after the CIA took custody of al-Libi, a handful of

CIA officers at a high-level legal meeting in the Situation Room voiced a problem they were facing. "The CIA guys said, 'We're going to have some real difficulties getting actionable intelligence from detainees' if the Agency's interrogators were required to respect the limits for treatment demanded by the Geneva Conventions," John Yoo told the *Washington Post.* In Yoo's version of events, the impetus to break out of Geneva's strictures thus came from the CIA. Many at the Agency, however, saw this differently, suggesting it was Cheney and his lawyer, Addington, who pushed the Agency to take the path toward torture.

In the Situation Room meeting, the CIA reportedly asked White House Counsel Alberto Gonzales for authorization to get tougher than the law allowed. But Gonzales had little experience in the complicated area of the laws of war. Addington, however, who sat at his side, actually knew more about the topic than many realized. He had had a little-known brush with interrogation abuse before. In 1992, when he was General Counsel to the Department of Defense under Cheney, an investigation found that U.S. military training manuals used in Latin America were promoting prohibited techniques for questioning captives, including executions, beatings, false imprisonment, and other abuses. When the manuals surfaced, an outcry ensued. In response, Cheney promised to destroy the offending manuals. Only seven copies were kept—all of which were given to Addington, who locked them in his safe.

When the legal discussion turned to the Geneva Conventions, Addington, a colleague said, "was probably the only person in the White House who really knew the rules."

If so, he would have understood immediately that renditions were a potential problem. Under Geneva's rules, prisoners could be held indefinitely until the end of armed conflict. But they had to be treated humanely. They couldn't be punished for refusing to cooperate with interrogators and they had to be given access to the Red Cross. "No physical or mental torture nor any other form of coercion may be inflicted on prisoners of war to secure from them information of any kind whatever," the treaties stated.

In addition, every captive was entitled to a hearing before a competent tribunal in order to determine his status. There were many categories of captives in armed conflicts, ranging from innocent refugees to war criminals. But under the Geneva Conventions, all were guaranteed some basic human rights. In keeping with American values and traditions, these rules had been respected scrupulously by both Republican and Democratic administrations since 1949, even during the most trying times. Undoubtedly, there had been individual lapses in every conflict, but the unwavering policy—and usually the practice—of the United States had been to comply with these laws of war.

During the Vietnam War, this commitment was sorely tested. The North Vietnamese refused to respect U.S. pilots as legitimately covered by the Geneva Conventions, calling them "pirates" in an illegal war. Hundreds of downed American flyers, including John McCain, were tortured; many died. The Viet Cong, meanwhile, defied conventional rules of warfare, often fighting without uniforms, disguised as civilians. The United States nonetheless gave the Viet Cong the protection of the Third Geneva Convention. Rather than dismissing them as illegal enemy combatants who were not entitled to the protections of the laws of war, as President Bush did with terror suspects after September 11, the United States devised a formal system of status hearings to separate the real civilians from the combatants. Known as Article 5 tribunals, they guaranteed prisoners the fundamental right to be individually charged and to confront the evidence in a fair process. By 2001, such hearings were more than custom; they had become binding U.S. military law. Article 5 hearings were held with great success in U.S. conflicts ranging from Panama to Grenada. In the Gulf War, the United States conducted almost 1,200 such hearings, finding 310 detainees were POWs and the rest refugees. These hearings were not simply a display of kindness—they were the best-known method to avoid mistakenly imprisoning innocent bystanders.

Ironically after September 11, Addington advised the President to scrap these rules; in doing so, the former Vietnam War hawk was reprising arguments that had been used against America by the Viet Cong. Laying the foundation for this shift was a famous set of internal legal memos by Yoo, Addington, and other members of the War Council, many of which were later leaked to the public. Taken together, the memos enshrined the political position already expressed by Cheney, advising the President that he did not have to comply with the Geneva Conventions or other customary international laws in handling detainees in the war on terror. These memos denied legal protections not just to Al Qaeda, but to the entire Taliban. All were described as "illegal enemy combatants." Afghanistan, like the United

States, had signed the Geneva Conventions, but the President's lawyers argued that this was of no concern because the country was now a "failed state."

One of the earliest and most ardent proponents of this unusual legal interpretation was Douglas Feith, the third-ranking civilian official in the Department of Defense, with the title Under Secretary for Policy, whom Rumsfeld had referred to as "an intellectual engine." A neoconservative, Feith prided himself on being "unfashionable," by which he evidently meant breaking with the more centrist foreign-policy establishment. As far back as the 1980s, when he had been a midlevel Reagan Administration official, Feith had argued that terrorists did not deserve to be protected by the Geneva Conventions. The issue had first arisen in regard to the Palestinian Liberation Organization. Feith, a passionate Zionist, had helped to convince the Reagan Administration to oppose international efforts to protect anti-Israeli terrorists as soldiers. John Yoo and other Bush Administration lawyers seized on this position as a precedent. It seemed sensible—after all, terrorists were not conventional soldiers. But it failed to take into account several other factors, including the Bush Administration's determination to deny terror suspects the protection of the criminal legal system as well. In the Reagan era, terrorists were either dealt with as criminals or were covered by Geneva's lowest standard, known as Common Article Three. But in the absence of both legal systems, Feith's argument left captives in the war on terror in legal limbo. Feith nonetheless packaged his argument with Orwellian cleverness as a defense of the Geneva Conventions, arguing in a memo, which Rumsfeld shared with President Bush, that it would defile the Geneva Conventions to extend their rights to such disreputable warriors.

At the State Department, Powell and his legal adviser, William Howard Taft IV, fought a rear-guard action against Bush's lawyers and lost. This fierce fight took place almost entirely outside the public's view. In a confidential forty-page memo to John Yoo dated January 11, 2002, Taft argued that Yoo's analysis was "seriously flawed." Taft told Yoo that his contention that the President could disregard the Geneva Conventions was "untenable," "incorrect," and "confused." Taft disputed Yoo's argument that Afghanistan, as a "failed state," was not covered by the Conventions. "The official United States position before, during, and after the emergence of the Taliban was that Afghanistan constituted a state," he wrote. Taft also warned Yoo that if the United States took the war on terror outside the Geneva Conventions, not only could U.S. soldiers be denied the protections of the Conventions—and therefore be prosecuted for crimes, including murder—but President Bush could be accused of a "grave breach" by other countries, which would mean he could be prosecuted for war crimes. Taft wrote, "In previous conflicts, the United States has dealt with tens of thousands of detainees without repudiating its obligations under the Conventions. I have no doubt we can do so here, where only a relative handful of persons is involved."

Taft sent a copy of his memo to Gonzales, hoping that his dissent would reach the President. Within days, Yoo sent Taft a lengthy rebuttal.

Others in the administration worried that the President's lawyers were shirking their obligations to uphold the laws. "Lawyers have to be the voice of reason and sometimes have to put the brakes on, no matter how much the client wants to hear something else," David Bowker, a former top State Department lawyer said. "Our job is to keep the train on the tracks. It's not to tell the President, 'Here are the ways to avoid the law.'" He went on, "There is no such thing as a non-covered person under the Geneva Conventions. It's nonsense. The protocols cover fighters in everything from world wars to local rebellions."

But Taft's access to the President was no match for that of Cheney, who, as an administration source put it, "always got both the first and last bite of the apple." It remains unclear, in fact, whether anyone ever fully explained the countervailing arguments to President Bush before he signed off on the plan. According to top State Department officials, Bush decided to nullify the Geneva Conventions on January 8, 2002. This was three days before Taft sent his memo to Yoo. Evidently, the State Department was too far out of the loop to catch up.

On January 18, Rumsfeld sent an order to the Joint Chiefs of Staff declaring that the military no longer needed to follow Geneva's rules in their handling of Al Qaeda and Taliban prisoners. For half a century, soldiers had been trained in the rules. Now they would be left to their own devices. The next day, Rumsfeld rescinded an earlier order by General Tommy Franks, commander of the Coalition Forces in Afghanistan, which had set up Article 5 hearings to screen captives individually. Now that America was no longer following the Geneva Conventions, there would be no more need for Article 5 hearings. The President had determined unilaterally that all prisoners captured in the war on terror were unlawful combatants.

Powell made a last-ditch effort, calling Rice on January 25, 2002, and insisting that they couldn't do this, that he had to see the President in person about it. His office was already inundated with cables from allied countries in shock that America would ignore its treaty obligations. Many warned that this would inhibit their ability to fully cooperate with the United States in the war on terror. But unknown to Powell, the same day that he demanded to see the President, the Vice President's office ginned up a remarkable preemptive memo anticipating and rebutting all of the arguments Powell was sure to make.

The infamous January 25 memo appeared to have been authored by Bush's old friend, White House Counsel Alberto Gonzales, over whose signature it appeared. It cleverly used Bush's own words to convince the President. "As you have said, the war against terrorism is a new kind of war. . . . In my judgment, this new paradigm renders obsolete Geneva's strict limitations on questioning of enemy prisoners," the author wrote. He dismissed amenities that he claimed Geneva demanded for captured enemies, such as "athletic uniforms and scientific instruments," as "quaint." The tone of the memo was caustic, not unlike its true author, who was later revealed to be Addington.

Addington's critique of the State Department position was either ignorant or intellectually dishonest. It omitted any mention of handling terror suspects in the war on terror as spies and saboteurs. Under Geneva's rules, such unlawful combatants could be given battlefield trials and executed on the spot if found guilty. No "athletic equipment" or "scientific instruments" were required. The State Department was only arguing for status hearings to ensure that the United States was holding the right people before depriving them of their liberty.

The following day, Washington's conservative newspaper, the *Washington Times,* a favorite outlet for the White House, ran a curious front-page news story lampooning Powell's position as pro-terrorist—"bowing to pressure from the Left." It seemed to most astute readers an obvious leak from the Addington camp. Yet Addington made a great show inside the White House of claiming that the State Department itself had leaked the story, an accusation he used to further marginalize Powell and Taft, who he argued could not be trusted to keep national security secrets from the press.

On February 7, President Bush struck what was described as a compromise. America would abandon its commitment to abide by the Geneva Conventions in the war on terror. But Bush promised that "as a matter of policy"—not law—"the United States Armed Forces shall continue to treat detainees humanely" . . . so long as it was consistent with "military necessity."

It didn't take long for critics, including many of the military's own uniformed lawyers, to realize that this last phrase was a caveat flexible enough to sanction almost anything. What battlefield decisions couldn't be described as "military necessity"? It was, in fact, the same legalistic language used by the Japanese in World War II to justify the Bataan Death March.

After losing the battle to uphold the Geneva Conventions, Powell concluded that Bush was not stupid but was easily manipulated. A confidant said that Powell thought it was easy to play on Bush's wish to be seen as doing the tough thing and making the "hard" choice. "He has these cowboy characteristics, and when you know where to rub him, you can really get him to do some dumb things. You have to play on those swaggering bits of his self-image. Cheney knew exactly how to push all his buttons," Powell confided to a friend.

Colonel Wilkerson, Powell's chief of staff, was more scathing. "You can slip a lot of crap over on someone who doesn't read a lot or pay attention to the details if you have no scruples," he said. "And David Addington doesn't."

There was another curious loophole in the President's February 7 order, one that took longer for the outside world to spot. A close reading of the directive to treat detainees "humanely" revealed that it referred only to military interrogators—not to CIA officials. This exemption allowed the CIA to argue that it had the full legal authority of the U.S. government to treat prisoners in cruel, inhumane, and degrading ways—just as long as the torment stopped short of torture.

As the Bush Administration swept away the old rules, becoming unfettered and unchecked, it began to authorize the rendition of suspects for whom it had little or no solid evidence of guilt. One early example was Mamdouh Habib, an Egyptian-born citizen of Australia who ran a small coffee shop in Sydney and who was apprehended in Pakistan in October 2001. According to his wife, Habib, a radical Muslim with four children, had left Australia that summer for Pakistan in search of a job and religious schools for their children, who he felt were growing up in too secular an environment. Habib had expressed support for Islamist causes. But a spokesman at the Pentagon claimed that Habib was a terrorist who had spent most of his trip in Afghanistan "either supporting hostile forces, or on the battlefield fighting illegally against the U.S."

In 2005, however, after a three-year ordeal, Habib was released without charges. A top Australian intelligence official who was intimately involved in the case admitted, on background, that "Habib was of no intelligence value. He knew nothing about terrorism."

Habib, it turned out, had been leaving Pakistan aboard a bus after September 11 when Pakistani security forces spotted him and took him into custody for questioning as a suspicious foreigner. According to unsealed legal documents, Habib was interrogated in Pakistan for three weeks, in part at a facility in Islamabad. There, he said, he was hung from the ceiling by his arms as he stood on a cylindrical drum that was attached to an electrical charge. When his interrogators didn't like his answers, they could flip a switch, shocking his feet to make him "dance," which would cause him to slip so that his full weight would pull on his arms. He recounted that this routine became so painful, he fainted.

Some of his interrogators, he claimed, spoke English with American accents. (Having lived in Australia for years, Habib was comfortable in English.) After a week in Islamabad, he said, he was handcuffed, blindfolded, and turned over to the custody of unidentified American authorities. In a scuffle, his blindfold slipped, allowing him to see muscular men wearing black short-sleeved shirts, several of whom had distinctive tattoos: One depicted an American flag attached to a flagpole shaped like a middle finger, the other a large cross. Then, he said, the Americans took him to an airfield, cut his clothes off with scissors, dressed him in a jumpsuit, covered his eyes with opaque goggles, and placed him aboard a private plane. He was flown to Egypt. The Pakistani Interior Minister, Makhdoom Hayat, later confirmed that Habib was sent to Egypt, disclosing that the United States, not Pakistan, had initiated the rendition. They "wanted him for their own investigations," he said.

Habib was held and interrogated in Egypt for six months, during which time he claimed to have been subjected to horrific conditions. He said that he was beaten frequently with blunt instruments, including an object that he likened to an electric "cattle prod." He said he was told that if he didn't confess to belonging to Al Qaeda he would be anally raped by specially trained dogs. (Human rights activist Hossam el-Hamalawy and other experts have said that Egyptian security forces train German shepherds for police work, and that other prisoners have also claimed to have been threatened with rape by trained dogs, although there are no known recorded cases of assault in this way.) Habib said that he was shackled and forced to stand in three torture chambers: One room was filled with water up to his chin, requiring him to stand on tiptoe for hours; another chamber, filled with water up to his knees, had a ceiling so low that he was forced into a prolonged, painful stoop; in the third, he stood in water up to his ankles and within sight of an electric switch and a generator, which his jailers said would be used to electrocute him if he didn't confess. He was also kicked and beaten with a stick repeatedly. Frequently, he said, he lapsed into unconsciousness. (Egyptian authorities have described such allegations of torture as "mythology.")

Then, without explanation, he said, he was suddenly treated better. He was fed meat and allowed to sleep. He was even given candy and cigarettes. In just enough time for his scars to heal over, he was told he was going home. Instead, however, he was transported first to Bagram Air Base in Afghanistan, and then to Guantánamo Bay, where he was detained until 2005.

While he was being tormented in Egypt, Habib submitted to his interrogators' demands and made multiple confessions. These "confessions" formed virtually all of the U.S. case against Habib in Guantánamo. Evidently, U.S. officials believed that the facts were not reliable enough to withstand scrutiny, however. The day before the United States planned to bring charges against Habib, Joe Margulies, who by this time had won the right to represent him, called Dana Priest at the *Washington Post* and told her the story of Habib's rendition and torture. On January 11, immediately after the *Washington Post* published a shocking front-page article on Habib's case, the Pentagon, offering virtually no explanation, agreed to release him into the custody of the Australian government. Margulies learned that after seeing the news story, the CIA feared legal exposure if Habib's case was ever heard in an open court. "Habib was released because he was hopelessly embarrassing," Eric Freedman, a professor at Hofstra Law School who organized legal representation for the Guantánamo detainees, said. In 2005, he called the case "a large crack in the wall in a house of cards that is midway through tumbling down."

A Pentagon spokesman, Lieutenant Commander Flex Plexico, said there was "no evidence" that Habib "was tortured or abused" while he was in U.S. custody. He also said that Habib had received "Al Qaeda training," which included instruction in making false abuse allegations. Habib's claims, he suggested, "fit the standard operating procedure."

The U.S. government never responded directly to Habib's charge that he was rendered to Egypt. However, several other men who were released from Guantánamo were able to confirm aspects of Habib's tale and noted that Habib told them about it at the time. Jamal al-Harith, a British detainee who was sent home to Manchester, England, in March 2004, said that at one point he had been placed in a cage across from Habib. "He said that he had been in Egypt for about six months, and they had injected him with drugs, and hung him from the ceiling, and beaten him very, very badly," Harith recalled. "He seemed to be in pain. He was haggard-looking. I never saw him walk. He always had to be held up." Another former inmate in Guantánamo, Shafiq Rasul, later reported that Habib "used to bleed from his nose, mouth and ears when he was asleep."

There was also evidence supporting Habib's story. A set of flight logs documenting the travels of the white Gulfstream V jet with the tail number N-379 P, showed that on April 9, 2002, the jet left Dulles Airport outside of Washington and landed in Cairo. This was the same period when Habib said he had been released by the Egyptians in Cairo and flown to Bagram Air Base. The flight logs, which were obtained by Stephen Grey, the British journalist, were incomplete. But they chronicled some 700 flights over four years by the fourteen-seat jet, whose tail number was later changed to N8068V. All the flights appeared to have originated from Dulles Airport.

In actuality, the rendition flights originated a bit farther south. At first glimpse, the paperwork suggested the planes were registered to a company called Premier Executive Transport Services of Dedham, Massachusetts. But in fact, further investigation by journalists revealed that the company was just a CIA-fabricated front for the real base, a company called Aero Contractors Ltd., which was owned and operated by the CIA. Aero's headquarters was based at the tiny Johnston County Airport, a patch of runways surrounded by pine trees and tobacco fields in the otherwise unremarkable town of Smithfield, North Carolina. Reporters' phone calls to Aero went unreturned. Pleasant, southern-accented desk clerks apologized that they would not be able to comment, or pass on messages to anyone who could. Smithfield seemed to be an odd place to center a high-stakes, covert global abduction operation, but in fact it had two geographic advantages. It was near Fort Bragg, home to the Special Forces who assisted many of the CIA's covert counterterrorism missions after September 11. And the little airport was just a half hour, as the jet flew, from

Langley, where the black-masked men of the CIA's Special Activities Division could hop on board.

While Aero operated the CIA's fleet of planes, a little-known subsidiary of the huge blue-chip aerospace company Boeing, called Jeppesen International Trip Planning, secretly handled the computerized flight plans for many of the rendition trips. According to Sean Belcher, a former employee of the company in San Jose, California, while the Bush Administration was insisting that it did not render suspects to be tortured, executives at Jeppesen had no such illusions. He described a meeting in which one of his bosses, Bob Overby, the managing director of Jeppesen International Trip Planning, said, "We do all of the extraordinary-rendition flights—you know, the torture flights. Let's face it, some of these flights end up that way." Overby and other Jeppesen executives declined to comment. Boeing officials also declined to comment on the company's role as the CIA's travel agent. But the company evidently felt that it accrued enough benefits from the business to offset the distasteful aspects. Belcher, the former Jeppesen employee, recalled his boss, Overby, saying of rendition, "It certainly pays well. They"—the CIA—"spare no expense. They have absolutely no worry about costs. What they have to get done, they get done."

Maher Arar, a Canadian telecommunications engineer, had occasion to experience the CIA's largesse firsthand. On September 26, 2002, American officials, suspecting Arar of being a terrorist, apprehended him on his return to Canada from a family vacation in Tunisia during a layover at John F. Kennedy Airport in New York. By happenstance, it was the same day that Cofer Black stood in front of Congress testifying that when it came to renditions, "there was a before September 11 and an after September 11, and after September 11, the gloves came off."

Arar, who at the time was a thirty-four-year-old graduate of McGill University whose family had emigrated to Canada when he was a teenager, was detained because his name had been placed on the terrorist watch list. He was held for the next thirteen days, as American officials questioned him about possible links to two other suspected terrorists. Arar said that he barely knew them, although he had worked with the brother of one suspect. Arar did not know it at the time, but he had been falsely implicated when these suspects were tortured in Syria.

Evidently, on the basis of these forced confessions alone, Arar was shackled and chained at three in the morning and driven in what he recalled as "a very impressive motorcade" to a small airport full of private planes in New Jersey. Without affording Arar a chance to confront any charge or evidence, J. Scott Blackman, Director of the Eastern Region of the Immigration and Naturalization Service, had determined that Arar was an Al Qaeda member who must be forcibly deported. The deportation order was signed by Deputy Attorney General Larry Thompson.

Soon, Arar found himself on a luxurious private executive jet. There were about a dozen leather seats. During the flight, Arar said, he heard the pilots and crew identify themselves in radio communications as members of "the Special Removal Unit." They were dressed like civilians, so he couldn't figure out what part of the government they worked for. Nor was he sure where he was being taken. But with growing horror he watched a small screen with a real-time map showing the plane's progress from New Jersey to Washington, D.C., then to Bangor, Maine, and on to Rome, Italy, and finally on toward the Middle East.

"All the time," he said, "I was thinking I was being sent to get tortured. My God, I thought, how am I going to avoid it?" The Americans, he learned, planned to take him to Syria. Having been told by his parents about the barbaric practices of the Syrian police, Arar begged the crew not to send him there, arguing that he would surely be tortured. His captors did not respond to his request; instead, they invited him to join them in watching what he recalled as "a CIA-type Hollywood spy thriller" that was aired on board. He watched, but he admitted, "I had trouble paying attention." He also had trouble swallowing what he described as "a very nice dinner of shish kebab."

The crew exhibited a strange mixture of concern and indifference. Realizing that Arar's luggage had been left behind, one of the American crew gave him a pair of jeans and the sweater off his back. Yet the man insisted on accompanying him inside the tiny bathroom on board, despite the indignity. "Sorry, those are the rules," the crew member said.

As Arar begged the head of the crew not to take him to Syria, telling him again and again that he would surely be tortured, he recalled, "I could see sympathy in his eyes." But it made no difference. As they approached the Middle East, Arar could hear that there was a problem: Syria had refused to accept him directly. Despite the legal fiction that rendition suspects were "wanted" by foreign legal authorities, Arar had to be forced on Syria. Rather than getting there directly, he was required to be dropped first in Amman, Jordan. But ten hours after landing in Jordan, Arar said, he was driven to Syria, where interrogators, after a day of threats, "just began beating on me." They whipped his hands repeatedly with two-inch-thick electrical cables and kept him in a body-sized slot of a windowless underground cell—his was cell no. 2—which he likened to being buried alive in a casket. "Not even animals could withstand it," he said. Although he initially tried to assert his innocence, he eventually confessed to anything his tormentors wanted him to say. "You just give up," he said. "You become like an animal."

In Syria, Arar was incarcerated in one of the most notorious prisons on earth, known as Far-Filastin, Arabic for "The Palestinian Branch," or as it was more colloquially known in its home city of Damascus, "The Grave." Sometimes likened to an iceberg, its most fearsome feature, a catacomblike web of airless, lightless cells no wider than the length of a human arm, was hidden from above ground. This was the heart of the Syrian intelligence service's dungeonlike interrogation center. Later, an official investigation by the Canadian government found Arar and other prisoners' descriptions credible—of cats urinating on the prisoners through grates in the ceiling, and of rats and cockroaches infesting the cells, which were so cold and damp in the winter that the prisoners resorted to wrapping their underwear around their ears for warmth.

The State Department's human rights report in 2003 deplored the Syrians' use of torture—"administering electrical shocks, pulling out fingernails, forcing objects into the rectum . . . and hyper-extending the spine" to the point of "fracture." Four months before the United States transported Arar to Damascus, the State Department had added Syria to the list of outlaw states that President Bush described as "The Axis of Evil."

But when it came to fighting the war on terror, the State Department's decorousness was considered old-think. Cheney himself signaled the new realpolitik, to the surprise of some White House colleagues shortly after the September 11 attacks, when he embraced a proposed alliance with Uzbekistan without hesitation. Cheney was known as the coldest of Cold Warriors, distrustful of the "Evil Empire" to the bitter end. But despite warnings from Rice and Powell about President Islam Karimov's brutal repression of opponents, Cheney felt they had to put national security first. The Pentagon and CIA needed Uzbekistan as a forward base. If that meant joining forces with a torture regime, known on occasion to literally boil political prisoners alive, he was ready. "We need to get Al Qaeda before they get us," Cheney explained. Craig Murray, the former British Ambassador to Uzbekistan, complained that he tried to warn the CIA station chief in Tashkent that much of the intelligence out of Uzbekistan was derived from torture, most of which he said was "rubbish." In at least three instances he said he knew of, U.S.-rendered suspects were "almost certainly" tortured. But he said that while the station chief did not dispute that intelligence was being obtained under torture, the CIA did not consider this a problem. "There was no reason to think they were perturbed," Murray said.

The new way of thinking was reflected by Tenet at a closed-door meeting of top intelligence officials of the English-speaking world, gathered on March 10, 2002, in Queenstown, New Zealand. "Gentlemen," Tenet had reportedly said with a dramatic pause, "we are at war." What this meant, he had gone on to explain, was "As for the CIA, I can tell you this. There's nothing we won't do, nothing we won't try, and no country we won't deal with to achieve our goals— to stop the enemy. The shackles, my friends, have to be taken off." He added, "We're going to have to work with others in a way we haven't before . . . Egypt, Syria, Russia—very much Russia . . . China, Pakistan, India, and Saudi Arabia." He noted, "Risks are going to have to be taken. These countries are our partners now, like it or not. We're going to have to shed old habits."

Other top American officials in attendance included Lieutenant General Michael Hayden, then head of the NSA; Mueller, the Director of the FBI; and the CIA's head of covert operations, James Pavitt. Pavitt evidently amplified the tough talk, noting, "We're going to be working with intelligence agencies that are utterly unhesitant in what they will do to get people to talk."

From his cell, Arar could hear others screaming, among them Ahmed El Maati, the acquaintance from Ottawa whose previous confession under torture appears to have falsely implicated Arar. (El Maati told interrogators, among other falsehoods, that he had met Arar in Afghanistan. In truth, Arar had never been to the country.) The most upsetting screams, he told the Canadian investigators later, were from women, evidently locked up and being beaten while their infants wailed. As the months went on, the treatment of Arar grew less severe, particularly after he had several visits, at his wife's insistence, from the Canadian consul. But psychologically, the torment only grew. After a while, he found himself screaming as well, completely without control. He banged his head against the wall, becoming dizzy, and felt his heart racing. His mind, he said, was "bombarded by memories." The treatment was so unbearable, Arar later invoked an Arabic expression to describe it. "You forget the milk that you have been fed from the breast of your mother," he said. "That's exactly how I felt. It was just so painful."

More than a year later, in October 2003, Arar was released without charges, after his wife forced the Canadian government to take up his cause. Once he was released, Imad Moustapha, the Syrian Ambassador in Washington, announced that his country had found no links between Arar and terrorism. No evidence was found against him other than the confessions of the other two Syrian prisoners, both of whom were also eventually released without charges. After Arar's release, a man convicted of immigration fraud in the United States, Mohamed Kamal Elzahabi, made accusations against Arar to the FBI.

A thorough official investigation by the Canadian government cleared Arar of any links to terrorism and concluded that he had, as he claimed, been egregiously tortured. As a result, the Canadian government awarded him $10.5 million in compensatory damages. The Canadian government also sternly disciplined the responsible public officials.

In contrast, the United States government refused to clear Arar's name from its terrorist watch list but would not explain why. The Justice Department also argued successfully that Arar's attempt to sue for gross violations of his civil rights posed too much of a threat to national security to be heard in court. U.S. District Judge David Trager, a Clinton appointee, dismissed Arar's lawsuit in February 2006 on what the press described as "state secret privilege" grounds, but which was actually an even more repressive argument. As legal expert David Luban wrote, "Judge Trager . . . argues, amazingly, that even invoking the state secret doctrine might prove embarrassing to the government," because "it could be construed as the equivalent of a public admission that the alleged conduct had occurred in the manner claimed. Therefore, the lawsuit must be tossed out without forcing the government to use the nuclear option."

"They are outsourcing torture because they know it is illegal," Arar charged. "Why, if they have suspicions, don't they question people within the boundary of the law?" The U.S. government provided no answers.

Arar, who remained psychologically shattered, bedeviled by night-mares, afraid to fly, and seized by the fear that random strangers were the men who had tortured him, had no avenue of redress and no means of holding any Americans accountable.

Despite his innocence, Arar had signed numerous false confessions by the time he was released. He had admitted, among other crimes, to having trained with Al Qaeda in Afghanistan, confirming El Maati's lie, although he'd never been to the country. Torture thus pro-duced not only falsehoods but false corroboration. "I was ready to do anything to get out of that place, at any cost," he later admitted. Arar's provably false confessions underscore what virtually every ex-pert in and outside the government agrees upon, which is that torture and lesser forms of physical coercion will make people confess some-thing. "But the truth is another matter," as Tom Parker, a former MI5 security officer and war crimes investigator, put it. The problem, he said, is distinguishing true confessions from lies. In his view, "The marginal amount of intelligence gained is outweighed by the damage done. The U.S.," he warned, "is doing what Great Britain did in the 1970s. They violated people's civil liberties, and it did nothing but radicalize the entire population."

Scientific research on the efficacy of torture is extremely limited be-cause of the moral and legal impediments to experimentation. Before endorsing physical and psychological abuse, the Bush Administration did no empirical study. The policy seems to have been based on some combination of political preference and intuitive belief about human nature. Yet from the start, top White House officials were utterly con-vinced that coercion was foolproof. John Yoo, in an informal aside at a book signing in Washington, said unabashedly, "It works—we know it does. The CIA says it does and the Vice President says it does." Pressed further about the widespread doubts many professionals in the military and law-enforcement communities had about the relia-bility of forced confessions, he argued, "There are other ways to cor-roborate the details."

Al-Libi's case, however, illustrates that false confessions had huge consequences for the Bush Administration's war on terror. Many of the details of al-Libi's story, including his final destination, remain uncertain. Unconfirmed reports suggest that he was eventually trans-ferred to Libya, where he was stricken with tuberculosis. No official U.S. account exists and there has never been a public investigation of his case. But on September 8, 2006, the Senate Select Committee on

Intelligence released an astonishing report documenting that top Bush Administration intelligence officials had known for years that in his case rendition, torture, and bad intelligence were inextricably entwined. The bipartisan report disclosed that after the CIA "rendered" al-Libi to a foreign intelligence service—which Tenet in his memoir disclosed to be Egypt—he was physically and psychologically brutalized into fabricating what he thought his captors wanted to hear. The report concluded that as far back as early 2002, al-Libi "lied . . . to avoid torture."

In 2004, after al-Libi was returned to the custody of the United States, he told the CIA that Egyptian security officials had threatened him with "a long list of methods that could be used against him which were extreme." He said the Egyptians pressed him in particular to admit to knowing about ties between Al Qaeda and Saddam Hussein in Iraq. This pressure occurred in the crucial months prior to the U.S. invasion of Iraq, when the Bush Administration was trying to substantiate the case for war. Al-Libi told the CIA that he "knew nothing" about the subject so he "had difficulty even coming up with a story." Dissatisfied with his nonresponsiveness, he said, the Egyptians locked him in a tiny cage for more than eighty hours. Al-Libi still didn't know what to say when they let him out. At this point, al-Libi said, the Egyptians knocked him over and punched him for fifteen minutes. Then, when again they asked him about links between Saddam Hussein and Al Qaeda, according to the report, he admitted to the CIA that he had made a story up. He accused three Al Qaeda figures he knew—using their real names—of going to Iraq to learn about nuclear weapons.

The Egyptian interrogators wanted more, though. Al-Libi told the CIA that the Egyptians pressed him about Saddam Hussein supplying Al Qaeda with anthrax and other biological weapons. According to the Senate report, al-Libi said he "knew nothing about the subject and didn't understand the term biological," so he couldn't even invent a confession. "He could not come up with a story." Again he was beaten, this time, he said, "in a way that left no marks." He subsequently fabricated additional details, which were piped into the Vice President's office, among other places, and used by the Bush Administration to buttress its allegations that Iraq was on the verge of supplying Al Qaeda with potentially terrifying weapons of mass destruction. President Bush fanned these fears on October 7, 2002, in a speech in Cincinnati, Ohio, announcing, "We've learned that Iraq has trained Al Qaeda members in bomb-making and poisons and deadly gasses."

"Of all of the pieces of intelligence assembled in the lead-up to the war, this was the most chilling," Rand Beers, former counterterrorism adviser to the National Security Council during the Clinton and Bush Administrations, later wrote.

One of the most startling revelations in the report is that almost from the start of al-Libi's rendition, there were high-level suspicions in some United States intelligence circles that he was a fabricator. On February 22, 2002, the report said, an unnamed official at the Defense Intelligence Agency who had access to al-Libi's confessions in Egypt issued an analysis warning that al-Libi's confession lacked specificity and that he "might be intentionally misleading his debriefers." The warning pointed out that al-Libi had given no specific names of Iraqis that Al Qaeda had worked with and no specific kinds of chemical or biological weapons they had ostensibly used. He also had failed to detail where Iraqi training for Al Qaeda had taken place. "It is possible that he doesn't know any further details; it is more likely that this individual . . . may be describing scenarios to debriefers that he knew will retain their interest."

The DIA issued a second such warning in July 2002. The report documented that these concerns were shared with, among others, Douglas Feith, the top intelligence official at the Pentagon and an avid proponent of going to war against Iraq. There is no indication that Feith passed the DIA's doubts about al-Libi's confession on this subject any further.

None of these doubts were shared with Secretary of State Powell in the fall of 2002 as America weighed whether to go to war. As a result, the former Al Qaeda commander played an improbably crucial role in Powell's momentous February 2003 address to the United Nations Security Council arguing the case for a preemptive war against Iraq. In his speech, Powell did not refer to al-Libi by name, but he announced to the world that "a senior terrorist operative" who "was responsible for one of Al Qaeda's training camps in Afghanistan" had told U.S. authorities that Saddam Hussein had offered to train two Al Qaeda operatives in the use of "chemical or biological weapons." Powell assured the audience that "every statement" he made was "based on solid intelligence . . . from human sources."

In truth, Powell had been highly skeptical about much of the intelligence underlying the case for war. His chief of staff, Wilkerson, recalled the Secretary of State remonstrating against earlier drafts of the speech, some of which were supplied by the Vice President's office, as too flimsily sourced. The intelligence was so tenuous that Powell had protested, "This is like Genesis—it's Mohammed met Ahab who met Ahmed who met Abu—everything is twenty-six years ago!" It was a very weak chain of information on which to base a war.

Powell ordered Wilkerson to cut everything that was not substantiated out of the speech's terrorism section. They got it down to eight pages, Wilkerson recalled, but Powell "was still frustrated. He was about to throw the whole thing out," Wilkerson said, "when Tenet dropped the bombshell. He said they had a high-level Al Qaeda figure who had just told them that Al Qaeda and Saddam Hussein's secret police trained together in Baghdad—and chemical and biological weapons were involved."

"How high-level?" asked Powell. "Bin Laden? Zawahiri?"

"No," Tenet told him. "But high-level."

"It was a very dramatic moment," Wilkerson later revealed. "It changed Powell's mind."

With Tenet's personal assurance that the informant was reliable, Powell went forward and put his name and reputation behind the most fateful speech of his life.

But when Tenet vouched for al-Libi to Powell, he made no mention of the DIA's doubts. A well-informed Republican source familiar with the details said top CIA officials had to have known about the warnings. "The entire intelligence community would have had access to the DIA analysis. If you were on Intel-Link"—the classified government computer system—"anyone reading about that case would see it," he said.

Wilkerson said later that when challenged about this omission, CIA officials told Powell that there had been a "computer glitch" that prevented them from seeing the damning DIA report at the time they were assembling the speech.

Others, too, had doubts, including some of the experts inside the CIA. Paul Pillar, the senior national intelligence officer in charge of the Near East at the Agency from 2000 until 2005, spent the better part of a Saturday after Powell's speech reading the debriefing reports on al-Libi's interrogations. "Setting aside the issue of whether he was a fabricator," Pillar said, "it just wasn't there." Pillar said that al-Libi's account "was just so confusing, it was James Joycean. It required a leap to get to the conclusions his reporting was used for. You could read and reread his reports and not reach the same conclusion. It was confused, and unclear."

Almost a year to the day after Powell's speech, al-Libi recanted. At that point, al-Libi was back in the CIA's custody in Afghanistan. On February 4 and February 5, 2004, CIA officers in Afghanistan sent cables back to Langley acknowledging that his story of links between Al Qaeda and Iraq was no longer reliable. There is no evidence that the CIA shared this news with top policy makers, even though it clearly contradicted the Agency's repeated assurances to the White House and Congress that coercion worked. A former congressional intelligence expert said, "Those cables sat around an awful long time before anyone looked at them." In any case, by then the first anniversary of the U.S. invasion of Iraq had passed and the 9/11 Commission had declared that there was no known "collaborative relationship" between Saddam Hussein and Al Qaeda.

Daniel Coleman was disgusted when he heard about al-Libi's false confession. "It was ridiculous for interrogators to think Libi would have known anything about Iraq," he said. "I could have told them that. He ran a training camp. He wouldn't have had anything to do with Iraq. Administration officials were always pushing us to come up with links, but there weren't any. The reason they got bad information," he said, "is that they beat it out of him. You never get good information from someone that way."

According to two FBI officials, al-Libi later explained his subsequent lies matter-of-factly. "They were killing me," he said. "I had to tell them something."

7

INSIDE THE BLACK SITES

More than 3,000 suspected terrorists have been arrested in many countries. Many others have met a different fate. Let's put it this way: They are no longer a problem to the United States and our friends and allies.

—President George W. Bush,
State of the Union Address, January 28, 2003

John Kiriakou, a boyish-looking CIA officer, had eagerly volunteered to help fight Al Qaeda after September 11, but he had never imagined that he would see so much blood. "There was blood everywhere. It was all over him. It was all over the bed. It pooled underneath the bed. It was all over us, every time we had to move him. It was just an incredible amount of blood that he lost."

The "he" in question was the purported Al Qaeda logistics chief, Abu Zubayda, and the time and place were March 28, 2002, at a hospital bedside in the overcrowded and unlovely city of Faisalabad, Pakistan. Kiriakou, a George Washington University graduate who had been recruited into the CIA by a professor a decade earlier, was fluent in Greek and nearly fluent in Arabic. At that moment, he was poised to be the first American to talk with Zubayda, who was slipping in and out of consciousness. The accident of these circumstances placed Kiriakou precisely in the center of what another counterterrorism expert describes as one of the most critical choices facing the United States government in the war on terror. "It was right there that there was a fork in the road—they could go left or right—and it set the course."

Zubayda was America's first "high-value detainee," the crucial test case for all that followed. His treatment would set the precedent for the abuse of U.S.-held prisoners, transforming U.S. practices starting with the CIA, but eventually spreading through the U.S. military, too. For over six months, the Agency had been stalking the footsteps of major Al Qaeda suspects, and with Zubayda's capture they believed they finally had one in custody. Lesser suspects, such as al-Libi, could be "rendered" elsewhere, but the Agency wanted to interrogate the most important ones itself.

Zubayda, whose real name was Zayn al-Abidin Muhammed Hussein, had left fingerprints all over Al Qaeda operations for years. Born in Saudi Arabia, Zubayda had migrated to the West Bank as a teenager, where he became militantly involved in the Palestinian uprising against Israel. Later, he had joined the anti-Soviet jihad in Afghanistan, where he was known to have grown personally close to Bin Laden. The Agency believed he might well know where Bin Laden and Zawahiri were hiding. By the spring of 2002, their elusiveness was rankling the White House as reports began to appear in print that Bin Laden had escaped from Tora Bora several months before. The Agency also believed he would certainly know the inside details of many Al Qaeda operations. For all of these reasons, teams of Agency and Special Forces officers had been hunting for him since September 11. "We thought if we could capture him it would deal a significant blow to the Al Qaeda leadership," Kiriakou later told ABC News.

Several weeks earlier, the Agency had gotten a lucky break in the case. On the outskirts of Pakistan's militant tribal area, along the mountainous border with Afghanistan, Pakistani intelligence officers had noticed a caravan carrying several exceptionally tall burka-clad women who turned out to be male Islamic extremists in disguise. They were bound for Faisalabad. For a bribe, their driver gave away their destination. This enabled the U.S. government to mount a major surveillance operation on their neighborhood. In the NSA's headquarters in Fort Meade, Maryland, translators and analysts among the agency's 38,000 employees pored over every fragment of electronic information vacuumed by enormously powerful eavesdropping equipment trained on the spot, until they could pinpoint what they believed was a nest of top Al Qaeda suspects.

In the predawn hours of March 28, dozens of armed CIA, FBI, and Pakistani law-enforcement and intelligence officers raided a shambling compound on the suburban outskirts of Faisalabad, taking Zubayda by surprise along with some twenty-five other suspected Al Qaeda followers, including one with a valid Arizona driver's license. In an attempt to escape, Zubayda leapt from the roof to that of a neighboring house, where a gun battle ensued before he dropped twenty-five feet to the ground. By the time it was over, Zubayda had been shot in the thigh, stomach, and groin. A Pakistani doctor told Kiriakou that he'd never seen anyone with such egregious injuries survive. In truth, Zubayda had nearly slipped into sepsis in the back of a pickup truck where, unrecognized, he had been piled with several other wounded suspects after the gunfight. An agent with a flashlight identified him just in time to rush him to the hospital for resuscitation.

The raid was a triumph due in part to what law-enforcement agents call "pocket litter," the incriminating detritus scattered around a criminal scene. Zubayda left behind computers, cell phones, computer disks, phone books, and two Western-style bank cards for accounts in Kuwait and Saudi Arabia. He also left behind a voluminous personal diary—in all, there were nearly 10,000 pages of potentially invaluable intelligence. Adding urgency, according to Kiriakou, were the remnants of a bomb that he and two other men had been building on a table, along with plans for what appeared to be an attack on a British school in Lahore. The soldering iron, Kiriakou said, "was still hot."

This scene of bomb builders disrupted mid-soldering is as close to the Hollywood-style "ticking time bomb" scenario as any that U.S. authorities have described in the war on terror. In the Agency's view, Zubayda possessed lifesaving, actionable intelligence. Cases like his were the justification for the new "robust" powers enumerated by Cofer Black in the first sleepless week after September 11 and authorized by President Bush's classified Memorandum of Understanding.

Yet, on closer examination, Zubayda's capture provides a strong argument in favor of softer methods. What put Zubayda in CIA custody was not toughness, it was money. The Pakistani intelligence service bought the original tip leading to his whereabouts with a small bribe to the taxi driver. Afterward, the CIA bought Pakistan's help for a much larger sum. A CIA source involved at the time disclosed, "We paid $10 million for Abu Zubayda." He said the money went to the ISI, Pakistan's intelligence service. "They built a new headquarters on thirty-five acres they bought outside of Islamabad, and they got themselves a helicopter. We funded the whole thing." The first big break in the war on terror confirmed what the Israeli security service had also concluded by 2001, which is that the best way to make reluctant informants talk was to give them what the Israelis referred to in Hebrew as the "three Ks": *kesef*, or money; *kavod*, respect; and *kussit*, a crude sexual term for a woman.

In the hospital, where Kiriakou was the first to speak with Zubayda, other approaches were in store. "We knew he was the biggest fish we had caught," said Kiriakou, "and he was full of information. Frankly, there were lives at stake. He had information, and we wanted to get it." The immediate questions following his capture were where to take such a high-value detainee and how much force they could use on him afterward. A special CIA interrogation squad had been training in "enhanced" techniques for a moment such as this. Kiriakou himself had been tapped to join it. But a senior figure at the Agency who had acted as his mentor, gave him pause. "Do you really want to take the risk?" he asked. He warned Kiriakou, "It's a slippery slope." He predicted that "someone's going to go too far, and then someone's going to get killed. And when that happens, there are going to be congressional investigations, and eventually people are going to go to jail. So it may not be the best career path." Kiriakou turned down the offer to become an interrogator, eventually leaving the counterterrorism unit and, finally, the Agency itself. But at the time, he supported the harshest of treatment for Zubayda. "I was so angry," he said, acknowledging an emotional current underlying the rush toward torture that is rarely admitted.

Physical and ethical complications arose immediately because of the seriousness of Zubayda's injuries. In his military hearing in Guantánamo Bay in 2007, Zubayda said he had lost a testicle and had ongoing medical complications from bullet wounds to his head and thigh. He complained that one foot was perpetually cold, requiring him to wrap it in his skullcap during the hearing and to beg for socks. He also suffered from seizures and speech problems. In his memoir, Tenet described flying a top trauma surgeon in from Johns Hopkins in Baltimore to save Zubayda's life. It was from any standpoint an extraordinary feat of medicine. But what Tenet did not describe was a discovery that the CIA made at the same time. "The mere fact that Zubayda was weakened from being in critical condition, they learned from that," said a retired senior Agency official who was involved at the time. "It broke his resistance." The CIA has adamantly denied reports that it refused medical care for Zubayda in violation of international law and medical ethics. But Zubayda's near-death nonetheless taught the CIA an important lesson: Pain could be manipulated to their advantage.

Zubayda's extremis also taught the Agency about President Bush's mind-set. According to *New York Times* reporter James Risen, Tenet explained to Bush not long after Zubayda's capture that intelligence gathering was going poorly because Zubayda had been sedated with painkillers. Bush retorted, "Who authorized putting him on pain medication?"

Risen writes that there is some dispute about the anecdote. But while the exact details of Bush's private conversation remain shrouded in secrecy, Bush's gusto for playing rough was evident in remarks he made to Republican supporters in Greenwich, Connecticut, on April 9, 2002. "The other day," he said, "we hauled in a guy named Abu Zubayda. He's one of the top operatives plotting and planning death and destruction on the United States. He's not plotting and planning anymore. He's where he belongs," the President said.

Bush also knew about, and approved of, White House meetings in which his top cabinet members were briefed by the CIA on its plans to use specific "enhanced" interrogation techniques on various high-value detainees. The meetings were chaired by Rice, who was then the National Security Adviser, in the Situation Room. The participants were the members of the Principals Committee, the five Bush cabinet members who handled national security matters: Vice President Cheney, Secretary of State Powell, Secretary of Defense Rumsfeld, CIA Director Tenet, and Attorney General Ashcroft. Knowing how the Agency had been blamed for ostensible "rogue" actions in the past, Tenet was eager to spread the political risk of undertaking "enhanced interrogations." However, some members of the group became irritated with Tenet's insistence upon airing the grim details. "The CIA already had legal clearance to do these things," a knowledgeable source said, "and so it was pointless for them to keep sharing the details. No one was going to question their decisions—they were the CIA—they knew more than anyone else about each case. It's not as if any of the principals were debating the policy—that was already set. They wanted to go to the limit that the law required. But Tenet would say, 'We're going to do this, this, and this.'" Ashcroft in particular took offense at discussing such distasteful matters inside the White House. "History will not judge us kindly," he reportedly warned. There is no indication, however, that any Bush cabinet members objected to the policy. Cheney was described as "totally pushing it," and Rice, during the early period when Zubayda was captured, was described by a knowledgeable source as "a total hard-ass." The source suggested, "She was probably reflecting what the President wanted."

Behind the tough talk, however, was a bureaucracy in disarray. Despite the CIA's sweeping new authority to create paramilitary teams to hunt, capture, or kill suspected terrorists almost anywhere in the world, at the time the CIA had virtually no trained interrogators. It had been years since the Agency had questioned hostile witnesses. The CIA had numerous polygraphers and psychological profilers, as well as agents skilled in debriefing defectors. But "after Vietnam," says an outside adviser to the CIA, "they had very little experience with interrogation. When 9/11 hit, it was fifty-two-card pick-up."

A former CIA operative involved at the time said that at first the Agency was crippled by its dearth of expertise. "It began right away, in Afghanistan, on the fly," he recalled. "They invented the program of interrogation with people who had no understanding of Al Qaeda or the Arab world. You hear all this hubbub about hanging people upside down," he said. "But the key to interrogation is knowledge, not techniques. We didn't know anything. And if you don't know anything, you can't get anything."

At the same time, the operative said, the pressure from the White House, and in particular from Vice President Cheney, was intense. Cheney and his chief of staff, I. Lewis "Scooter" Libby, were over at the CIA so often, a special reading room was set aside for them. "They were pushing us: Get information! Do NOT let us get hit again!" In Cheney's single-minded focus, he searched the CIA's archives to see what worked in the past. He was particularly impressed with the Vietnam War–era Phoenix Program. Critics, including military historians, have described it as a program of state-sanctioned torture and murder. A Pentagon-contract study later found that 97 percent of the Viet Cong it targeted were of negligible importance. But after September 11, inside the CIA the Phoenix Program served as a model. "It was completely unconventional, it was very effective, and it stayed below the radar a really long time," the former CIA operative explained admiringly.

A. B. "Buzzy" Krongard, who was Executive Director of the CIA from 2001 to 2004, said the Agency turned to "everyone we could, including our friends in Arab cultures. We reached back to the whole alumni association." Specifically, the CIA asked Arab allies about which techniques for handling terror suspects worked best in Arab cultures. The Agency's belief was that interrogation was a cultural matter, much dependent on indigenous mores. "We talked to police and to other governments—Jordan, the Saudis, the Egyptians," Krongard said. The State Department regularly criticized all of these countries for chronic human rights abuses, but this was not a deterrent. Another former CIA official active at the time said the Agency also consulted closely with Israel. The Israeli Supreme Court prohibited torture and other forms of coercive interrogations in 1999 after more-permissive rules resulted in abuse. But a former CIA officer said the lesson derived from Israeli sources was less enlightened: "The Israelis taught us that you can put a towel around a guy's neck and use it like a collar, to propel him headfirst into a wall." It was a technique that the CIA would try out on Zubayda as soon as he recovered enough from his wounds to be hurt again.

The CIA knew even less about running prisons than it did about hostile interrogations, but it had to hold its prisoners somewhere beyond the reach of the American legal system, and that was the impetus for its "black site" program. Tyler Drumheller, the former Chief of European Operations at the CIA, said, "The Agency had no experience in detention. Never. But they insisted on arresting and detaining people in this program. It was a mistake, in my opinion. You can't mix intelligence and police work. But the White House was really pushing. They wanted someone to do it. The military didn't want to. So the CIA said, 'We'll try.'"

Drumheller regarded Tenet as a friend, but he also knew him well enough to see how the Director's weaknesses set the Agency on what he considered a ruinous course after September 11. "George Tenet," he said, "came out of politics, not intelligence. His whole modus operandi was to please the Principal. We got stuck with all sorts of things. This is really the legacy of a Director who never said no to anybody." Another former Agency operative who was involved in the Afghan campaign concurred. "It was a terrible mistake for George Tenet to have taken this mission on. I always objected to the CIA being a jailer," he said. "Why did this task fall to the Agency? Partly because we can work with the foreign services to set up the prisons. But really, the whole thing should have fallen to the DOD. Rumsfeld and [Stephen] Cambone fought like hell to stay out of it. They didn't want any part of it. I like George, but he's just not a strong leader. He's a politician. He should have said, 'Find someone else. I don't want to besmirch the Agency's reputation.'"

Many inside the CIA had misgivings. "A lot of us knew this would be a can of worms," said another former operative who was involved at the time. "It was going to get a lot uglier. We warned them, it's going to become an atrocious mess." The problem from the start, he said, was that no one thought through what he called "The Disposal Plan." "What are you going to do with these people? The utility of someone [like Zubayda] is at most six months to a year. You exhaust them. Then what?" He said, "It would have been better if we had executed them."

The audacious notion of the Central Intelligence Agency secretly holding terror suspects itself outside the reach of any law was a new one, forged in the frantic weeks immediately after September 11. The expectation of a second wave of attacks was almost universal. Many, including Cofer Black, were all but certain that nuclear weapons in the hands of terrorists were a genuine threat. He told colleagues at one point that in the NSA intercepts "pearls" stood for nuclear weapons and "weddings" stood for attacks. Both were seen as so imminent, he warned a colleague not to travel to New York for the weekend. By late winter, the Agency was feverishly trying to prevent what it had convinced itself was a threat of unimaginable proportions. Under the circumstances, they felt that anything they could do to keep the terrorists out of action was fair game.

The CTC already had a list of its most wanted suspects, and as the Taliban fell and the fleeing Al Qaeda sympathizers were caught and questioned, many new names were added. Prisoners were flooding into U.S. hands in Afghanistan. There alone, the United States processed an estimated 6,000 captives. Pakistan has said it handed 500 more to the United States. Iran claims to have sent an additional 1,000 over the border to Afghanistan. With no Afghan tradition of taking prisoners alive, the prison facilities were primitive and inadequate. Scores of those captured by the Northern Alliance along with Lindh, for instance, simply suffocated to death in airless shipping containers, a horror show that shocked human rights groups.

Some inside the Agency argued that the CIA would be better off killing Al Qaeda members. The operations chief at the CTC wanted to send teams of assassination squads around the globe to hunt and kill top terror suspects, one by one. The plan got as far as training a covert paramilitary assassin team under the code name "Operation Box Top." But the concept of a global hit squad was reportedly abandoned as too challenging logistically, ethically, and legally. For tactical reasons, too, many in the Agency preferred to keep valuable Al Qaeda suspects alive for questioning.

The issue of where to put CIA prisoners was vexing from the start. "Originally," a former top Agency official disclosed, "they had plans to put the detainees on a ship" sailing in international waters. "That way they'd never have to put them on trial. They could manipulate the legal process. It was going to be like the Flying Dutchman— they'd just sail forever." He disclosed that the CIA covertly used merchant marine vessels for such secret missions.

The idea of perpetually circumnavigating the globe, however, proved impractical. Other options considered by the Agency included an attempt to convince an unspecified African country, believed to be Zambia, to take the prisoners. At first the country agreed, a CIA source said. But evidently, when it figured out what sorts of prisoners were in question, the country backed out. "Finally," he recalled, "someone at the White House said, 'What about Guantánamo?'"

By January 2002, the U.S. military had established a prison camp at the U.S. base in Guantánamo Bay, Cuba, for the "illegal enemy combatants" it was capturing in Afghanistan and elsewhere. The White House lawyers had picked the location because of its unique legal status. Leased in perpetuity to the United States by the pre-Castro Cuban government in 1903, it was arguably under U.S. control but not under U.S. law. This rare set of circumstances allowed the executive branch to hold and interrogate foreign prisoners there in any manner it deemed necessary, beyond meddling from Congress and courts. Or so the White House hoped.

Early on, the CIA sent scouts to check out Guantánamo as a location for its high-value detainees, but the Agency reportedly turned against it as too visible. The site was aswarm with U.S. military and law-enforcement personnel. Visiting CIA officers reported back that Camp X-Ray, as the prison was called, was "a goat fuck." (Later, the CIA set up its own private prison on the island, separate from the main military encampment, but it was hastily closed when the Supreme Court ruled that the prisoners there were in fact covered by U.S. law.)

What the Agency was seeking for its most valuable prisoners was total isolation, total secrecy, and total control. An Agency source close to Tenet recalled the quest as a puzzle. "Where else in the world could we put them, outside of Guantánamo?" A CIA task force was launched to scour the globe. The mission was an international exercise, as another Agency source put it, in researching "how to make people disappear."

One obvious choice was Afghanistan. For the same reason that the White House could argue that Afghanistan was "a failed state," unbound by international law, it was also an ideal spot for secret CIA prisons. Several other allied countries, including a number of former Soviet satellite states who were hoping to win U.S. favor for their ambitions to join NATO, also agreed to host ghost prisons. Although their leaders have denied it, multiple credible reports have identified Poland and Romania in particular as host countries. The irony of the United States rewarding striving democracies, with histories as police states, for their help in secretly interrogating prisoners outside the protection of the law evidently was not dwelled upon. "We told them we'd help them join NATO if they helped us torture people," a cynical former CIA officer said.

The precise locations of these clandestine prisons, which are referred to in classified documents as "black sites," remain among the government's most tightly held secrets. But at least eight countries have participated, according to Dana Priest's 2005 Pulitzer Prize–winning investigative report in the *Washington Post.* For the host countries, there were both political and legal liabilities. State-enforced disappearances are not only illegal in the United States, but such practices also violate laws in almost all of the allied countries whose cooperation the United States sought.

There were financial rewards for the host countries, however. One year of the Afghan prison operation alone cost an estimated $100 million, which Congress hid in a classified annex of the first supplemental Afghan appropriations bill in 2002. Among the services that U.S. taxpayers unwittingly paid for were medieval-like dungeons, including a reviled former brick factory outside of Kabul known as "The Salt Pit." In 2004, a still-unidentified prisoner froze to death there after a young CIA supervisor ordered guards to strip him naked and chain him overnight to the concrete floor. The CIA has never accounted for the death, nor publicly reprimanded the supervisor. Instead, the Agency reportedly promoted him.

Within three days of his capture, Zubayda was stabilized enough for the Renditions Team to remove him from Pakistan. A CIA officer on the ground said he had no idea where his colleagues were taking the suspect. His destination was available only on a "need-to-know" basis. The CIA's "high-value detainee" program was extraordinarily compartmentalized in order to maximize secrecy, even to a degree unusual for the spy agency. Internal communications dealing with the program were segregated into a separate cable channel with its own encryption codes. Typical of this high level of secrecy, the Agency went to extraordinary lengths to cover its tracks in the transport of Zubayda. Rather than flying him directly from Pakistan to the intended "black site," a well-informed source said the Agency flew him around the world for three days. The CIA rotated the pilots so that none would know the whole itinerary. Before the final destination was reached, landings were made on several continents, including Latin America. Finally, after this dizzying trek, the CIA installed Zubayda in a new facility in Thailand. The Thai government's only stipulation was that there must be absolutely no publicity about its cooperation. If the operation could be kept completely covered up, however, the CIA could have the run of the Thai facility. It boasted, among other features, subterranean cells.

Before Zubayda left Pakistan, Kiriakou managed to draw him out in English. Zubayda refused to speak Arabic under the circumstances, because it would defile what he called "God's language." To his surprise, Kiriakou found the terrorist to be "a friendly guy" who was "willing to talk. It's funny to say," he noted, "but we never exchanged a harsh word." He said Zubayda openly admitted his role in the September 11 attacks and claimed to regret having killed so many Americans. Zubayda expressed an all-consuming hatred for Israel, however, which he claimed justified the mass murders. If released, Zubayda admitted, he would commit more of them, killing every American and Jew that he could, adding sheepishly, "It's nothing personal. You're a nice guy. It's just who I am." Such sentiments convinced Kiriakou that terrorists such as Zubayda were unlike enemies of the past and so needed to be treated differently. "They hate us more than they love life," he said. Kiriakou also believed that while he was willing to be chatty, Zubayda was "unwilling to give us actionable intelligence." It would take the special CIA interrogation team, Kiriakou believed, "to get him to open up."

First, however, another matter had to be dealt with. "What can we do with him?" the Agency needed to know. "They had to figure out if he had any due-process rights," said John Radsan, the law professor who worked in the CIA General Counsel's Office at the time but who was not directly involved. In his memoir, Tenet notes, "Despite what Hollywood might have you believe, in situations like this you don't call in the tough guys; you call in the lawyers."

Shortly after Zubayda's capture, John Yoo was summoned to the White House again. Gathered in Gonzales's second-floor corner office in the West Wing along with the White House Counsel were the familiar members of the War Council—Addington, Flanigan, and Haynes. They tossed around ideas about exactly what sorts of pain could be inflicted on Zubayda. The CIA had sent a wish list of "stress techniques" it wanted to use. They, too, saw themselves as justified in pushing the edges of the law to save the country from mortal enemies. As usual, Gonzales barely spoke. But Flanigan said later, "Everyone was focused on trying to avoid torture, staying within the line, while doing everything possible to save American lives."

From most points of view, torture would never have been an option. Torture and degrading treatment were clearly prohibited by two bodies of international law, and by domestic law as well. In addition to the Geneva Conventions, the United States took the lead in drafting and ratifying the 1984 Convention Against Torture and Other Cruel, Inhuman or Degrading Treatment or Punishment, which provided international law's first explicit definition of torture. "The CAT" is about as categorical a piece of legislation as is possible to write. It bans torture absolutely. It stresses that there are "no circumstances whatsoever, whether a state of war or a threat of war, internal political instability or any other public emergency," that could be "invoked as a justification of torture" or "other acts of cruel, inhumane or degrading treatment" used to get prisoners to divulge information. The language in the Convention Against Torture is plain and clear. It defines torture as "severe pain or suffering, whether physical or mental."

The treaty had been a logical cause for America to lead. It reflected ideals of the European Enlightenment that had coursed through America's history since its founding. John Adams, Benjamin Franklin, and Thomas Jefferson, among other founders of the country, greatly admired the eighteenth-century Italian philosopher Cesare Beccaria's work *On Crime and Punishments,* weaving his notions of justice into the Bill of Rights. These were the origins of the Fifth and Eighth Amendment prohibitions against compelling criminal suspects to testify against themselves, or subjecting them to "cruel and unusual punishments."

To blur this bright legal line, the White House lawyers turned not to law but to language. The soft spot in the CAT, as they saw it, was the definition of torture. It might be banned, but what if the Bush Administration described the psychic stress and physical duress they hoped to exert on captives as something else? Among the euphemisms that the President would employ in the years to follow were "enhanced" interrogations, "robust" interrogations, and "special" interrogations. The redefinition of commonly understood crimes enabled Cheney to describe "waterboarding," a process of partial drowning and asphyxiation that had been classified as a criminal form of torture in the United States at least since 1901, as "a no-brainer for me," while at the same time insisting, "We don't torture." As William Safire, the conservative language columnist at the *New York Times,* wrote, "Some locutions begin as bland bureaucratic euphemisms to conceal great crimes. As their meanings become clear, these collocations gain an aura of horror. In the past century, the *final solution* and *ethnic cleansing* were phrases that sent a chill through our lexicon. In this young century, the word in the news . . . is *waterboarding.* If the word *torture,* rooted in the Latin for 'twist,' means anything (and it means the deliberate infliction of excruciating physical or mental pain to punish or coerce), then *waterboarding* is a means of torture."

The Bush Administration's corruption of language had a curiously corrupting impact on the public debate, as well. It was all but impossible to have a national conversation about torture if top administration officials denied they were engaged in it. Without access to the details of the CIA's secret program, neither Congress nor the public had the means to argue otherwise. The Bush Administration could have openly asked Congress for greater authority, or engaged the public in a discussion of the morality and efficacy of "enhanced" interrogations, but instead it chose a path of tricky legalisms adopted in classified memos.

On August 1, 2002, in an infamous memo written largely by Yoo but signed by Assistant Attorney General Jay S. Bybee, the OLC redefined the crime of torture to make it all but impossible to commit. They argued that torture required the intent to inflict suffering "equivalent in intensity to the pain accompanying serious physical injury, such as organ failure, impairment of bodily function, or even death." Mental suffering, they wrote, had to "result in significant psychological harm" and "be of significant duration, e.g., lasting for months or years." This last bit, about the amount of time that the suffering had to span, stretched a reservation to the CAT that the Senate added in 1990 at the urging of the first President Bush, requiring the mental pain to be "prolonged" to qualify as torture.

The Bush legal team provided seven examples of prohibited abuse, such as "electric shocks to genitalia, or threats to do so." But what of electric shocks to less-sensitive parts of the body? This was not addressed. The authors wrote, "There is [a] significant range of acts that though they might constitute cruel, inhuman, or degrading treatment or punishment fail to rise to the level of torture."

The memo was studded with additional loopholes. To qualify as torture, the infliction of pain had to be the "precise objective" of the abuse, rather than a by-product. An interrogator could know that his actions would cause pain, but "if causing such harm is not the objective, he lacks the requisite specific intent" to be found guilty of torture.

Most strikingly, perhaps, the memo then argued that even where officials *did* commit torture, they could be protected from criminal prosecution by invoking the defenses of "necessity" and self-defense. According to Martin Lederman, the Georgetown professor and former OLC lawyer, the notion that the statute recognizes such defenses was patently implausible. The OLC failed to cite major legal impediments including a recent Supreme Court case indicating that Congress must clearly specify it before a necessity defense can be invoked. It also ignored the official U.S. position established three years earlier that the torture prohibition is absolute: "No exceptional circumstances may be invoked as a justification of torture," the United States had represented to the United Nations. "U.S. law contains no provision permitting otherwise prohibited acts of torture . . . to be employed on grounds of exigent circumstances (for example, during a 'state of public emergency'). . . ."

If all else failed, Yoo and Bybee advised, the President could argue that torture was legal because he authorized it. The commander in chief, according to the OLC, had inherent powers to order any interrogation technique he chose. Under this interpretation, U.S. laws and treaties banning torture—despite having been signed into law by earlier presidents—were deemed unconstitutional and therefore null. By this logic, the President was literally above the law. It made the President so omnipotent, as former Supreme Court Justice Robert Jackson wrote in striking down similar claims to inherent power asserted by Harry Truman, the president's "power either has no beginning or it has no end."

The memo was accompanied by a still-secret classified list, specifying permitted CIA interrogation techniques, including waterboarding.

When the torture memo leaked into the public domain in 2004, it was widely and vehemently condemned. Harold Koh, the dean of Yale Law School, described it as "perhaps the most clearly erroneous legal opinion I have ever read." Even Ruth Wedgwood, a conservative supporter of the Bush Administration's tough anti-terror program, called it a relic of the Dark Ages, like "the 14th century, when an outlaw was treated like a beast."

Yoo, however, was undeterred by his critics. In a soft, eminently reasonable voice he argued that terror suspects deserved no legal protection. "Why is it so hard for people to understand that there is a category of behavior not covered by the legal system?" he asked. "What were pirates? What were slave traders? They weren't fighting on behalf of any nation. Historically, there were people so bad that they were not given protection of the laws. There were no specific provisions for their trial or imprisonment. If you were an illegal combatant, you didn't deserve the protection of the laws of war." Yoo, who often bolstered seemingly unprecedented positions by citing dubious historic precedents, argued that "the Lincoln assassins were treated this way, too." He said, "They were tried in a military court, and executed."

Yoo also argued that the Constitution granted the president plenary powers to override laws banning torture when he was acting in the nation's defense. As Yoo explained it, Congress doesn't have the power to "tie the president's hands in regard to torture as an interrogation technique." He continued, "It's the core of the commander in chief function. They can't prevent the president from ordering torture."

Yoo expanded on this theory when questioned about it by the director of Notre Dame's Center for Civil and Human Rights, law school professor Doug Cassel. If the president's right to torture was so absolute, Cassel asked, could no law stop him from "crushing the testicles of the person's child"? Yoo responded, "No treaty." Pressed on whether a law, rather than a treaty, could prohibit the President from doing so, Yoo wouldn't rule out the possibility that no law could restrain the President from barbarism. "I think it depends on why the president thinks he needs to do that," he said.

The only way to block a president from torturing, Yoo argued, was to impeach him. He went on to suggest that President Bush's victory in the 2004 election, along with the relatively mild challenge from Democrats to Gonzales's nomination as Attorney General, was "proof that the debate is over." He said, "The issue is dying out. The public has had its referendum."

His declaration of victory may have been premature. In 2008, the *New York Times* ran a front-page story revealing that the Justice

Department's Office of Professional Responsibility was investigating the Bush Administration's secret embrace of waterboarding and other interrogation methods widely denounced as torture. The office was trying to determine if Yoo's torture memos fell below the professional standards required of the Justice Department's Office of Legal Counsel, an office renowned for its probity and political independence.

Yoo has been singled out for his lead role in justifying torture. Former Attorney General John Ashcroft derided him, for instance, as "Dr. Yes." But many other Bush Administration officials were involved as well. Michael Chertoff, who was the head of the Justice Department's Criminal Division when Zubayda was caught, downplayed his role during his 2005 confirmation hearings to become Secretary of Homeland Security, claiming that his only part had been to warn the CIA that it "better be very careful" because "you are dealing in the area where there is potential criminality." But according to a top CIA official directly involved at the time, as well as a former top Justice Department official involved in a secondhand way, Chertoff was consulted extensively about detainees' treatment. The former senior Agency official said with disgust, "Chertoff, and Gonzales, and all these other guys act like they know nothing about this now, but they were all in the room. They're moonwalking backwards so fast, Michael Jackson would be proud of them." The source alleged that "Chertoff was on the phone" with the CIA's general counsel, Scott Muller, "almost every day. Sometimes several times a day. He had to advise them at every turn about what was criminal."

The former Justice Department lawyer who was involved on these issues with the Bush White House said that Chertoff spoke frequently with William Haynes, the Pentagon's General Counsel, about where to draw the line on military interrogations as well. In his confirmation hearings, however, Chertoff said he had played a very limited role, and he criticized the torture memo, saying, "I do not believe that definition is a sufficiently comprehensive definition of torture."

The Bush legal team, as former *New York Times* columnist Anthony Lewis observed, spent an extraordinary amount of effort figuring out how to steer top administration officials around criminal conduct. Their "memos," Lewis wrote, "read like the advice of a mob lawyer to a Mafia don on how to skirt the law and stay out of prison. Avoiding prosecution is literally a theme of the memoranda." Behind these contortions was the reality that the White House lawyers, like criminal litigators, were using their skills to provide rationales for a path their clients had already taken. The secrecy surrounding Zubayda's handling makes it difficult to know for certain, but it appears that in May, June, and July—in other words, months before the infamous torture memo provided legal cover—the CIA had already begun to treat him in ways that were deeply troubling.

In September 2006, President Bush admitted for the first time in public that the CIA had run a secret global detention and interrogation operation along rules of its own making. At the time, Bush specifically defended the harsh treatment of Zubayda in particular. ". . . We knew that Zubayda had more information that could save innocent lives, but he stopped talking," Bush said. ". . . And so the CIA used an alternative set of procedures. . . . The Department of Justice reviewed the authorized methods extensively and determined them to be lawful."

FBI agents, who were the first to question Zubayda at the black site, before the CIA interrogation team arrived, saw it rather differently. They thought that what they glimpsed of the CIA's treatment of him was disgraceful, disastrously counterproductive, and criminal.

Two of the FBI agents questioning Zubayda had extensive knowledge of Islamic terrorism. One was Ali Soufan, a passionate young émigré to America who, having been born in Lebanon, was a native Arabic speaker and also a Muslim. The other agent was Steve Gaudin, who had worked on terrorism cases all over the world. Neither would comment. But colleagues said that both had been tracking Al Qaeda doggedly and at times brilliantly before September 11. Both were brimming with anger at the intelligence failure that the attacks represented, blaming their FBI bosses, the CIA, the politicians in Washington, the laws and red tape, and really, when they were honest, also themselves.

Both believed it was making progress using the traditional FBI "rapport-building" techniques of questioning. They sent back early cables describing Zubayda as revealing inside details of the attacks on New York and Washington, including the nickname of its central planner, "Mukhtar," who was identified as Khalid Sheikh Mohammed. This tidbit, later trumpeted by the Bush Administration as a significant breakthrough, actually only confirmed information previously received but inadequately processed by the CIA in the months before the attacks. The 9/11 Commission report documents this.

During this early period, Zubayda also described an Al Qaeda associate whose physical description matched that of Jose Padilla. The information led to the arrest of the slow-witted American gang member in May 2002, at O'Hare International Airport in Chicago, on charges that he planned to detonate a radiological "dirty bomb." Abu Zubayda disclosed Padilla's role accidentally, apparently. While making small talk, he described an Al Qaeda associate he said had just visited the U.S. embassy in Pakistan. That scrap was enough for authorities to find and arrest Padilla.

These early revelations were greeted with excitement by Tenet, until he was told they were extracted not by his officers but by the rival team at the FBI. Tenet, according to an account given by Ron Suskind, was under extraordinary pressure from Bush to produce breakthrough intelligence from Zubayda, whose capture the President had sold to the country as a major coup.

"AZ," an informed source said of Zubayda, "was talking a lot." The FBI agents believed they were getting "phenomenal" information. In a matter of days, a CIA team arrived and took over, freezing out the FBI. The apparent leader of the CIA team was a former military psychologist named James Mitchell, whom the intelligence agency had hired on a contract. Oddly, given the Agency's own dearth of experience in the area of interrogating Islamic extremists, he had no background in the Middle East or in Islamic terrorism. He spoke no Arabic and he knew next to nothing about the Muslim religion. He was himself a devout Mormon. But others present said he seemed to think he had all the answers about how to deal with Zubayda. Mitchell announced that the suspect had to be treated "like a dog in a cage," informed sources said. "He said it was like an experiment, when you apply electric shocks to a caged dog, after a while, he's so diminished, he can't resist."

The FBI agents, with their traditions of working within the U.S. criminal legal framework, were appalled. They argued that Zubayda was not a dog, he was a human being.

Mitchell, according to the informed sources, retorted, "Science is science."

Horrified, the agents demanded to know if he had ever read anything about the Middle East. Had he ever worked with Islamic extremists? They reported back to their bosses at the FBI that the psychologist had admitted he hadn't but had argued that it made no difference.

According to the version of events that circulated through the FBI, what happened next was that Zubayda completely shut down. After ten to fifteen days, the FBI agents had to be brought back in, at which point he began talking again. But, FBI sources claimed, they were once again expelled on orders from Washington, because President Bush had chosen the CIA as the lead agency. Mitchell then reappeared.

By then, as a source described him, he was "desperate." He announced that the interrogators needed to get tougher. The FBI agents, according to one version of events, were so appalled they urged top FBI officials to have Mitchell arrested.

Fearful that they would be implicated, and adamantly opposed to what Mitchell proposed doing, the FBI agents picked up and left. In the following days, reports of deliberate prisoner abuse reached the top rungs of the FBI, causing the Director, Mueller, to bar the Bureau's personnel from participating in the CIA's coercive interrogations. The use of these controversial methods thus deprived the United States of many of its most experienced terrorism experts. It also abandoned the interrogations of the most valuable suspects to intelligence officials with no great interest in prosecuting them, lessening the incentive to play by the rules.

Before the FBI agents left, they relayed to their bosses an interesting exchange about torture they said they had with Mitchell. "We don't do that," they said they had protested. "It's what our enemies do!" Mitchell, they said, denied that he was using torture. Instead, he referred oddly to its being all about countering "resistance."

Mitchell, a retired military psychologist, would seem an odd choice to put on contract in such an immensely sensitive position in America's war on terror. He had, as the FBI discerned, no particular expertise in fighting Islamic terrorism. He also had never been an interrogator. Indeed, according to one colleague who was an interrogator, Mitchell had not even observed an interrogation. But he had extensive experience in designing, testing, implementing, and monitoring torture techniques that were illegal in the United States and elsewhere in the civilized world. Before signing on as a private consultant to the CIA for an undisclosed fee, he had worked as a psychologist assigned to a secretive military training program for pilots and other personnel at high risk of getting captured by enemy forces. It taught these potential captives how to resist torture and other extreme forms of abuse should they have the misfortune to fall into the hands of a dishonorable enemy. The program is known as SERE, an acronym for Survival, Evasion, Resistance, Escape. The theory behind it was that by subjecting U.S. soldiers to the worst treatment the world could mete out, but doing so in a limited and carefully controlled setting, the soldiers could inoculate themselves emotionally, increasing their chances of resisting should they ever be subjected to torture in real life. Psychologists such as Mitchell helped select and train the personnel, then calibrated the torment so that it would be safe but effective.

As such, SERE was a repository of the world's knowledge about torture, the military equivalent, in a sense, of the lethal specimens of obsolete plagues kept in the deep-freeze laboratories of the Centers for Disease Control. SERE was a defensive program, meant to protect American soldiers from torture. But in the CIA's hands after September 11, critics close to the program said, it was "reverse-engineered" into a blueprint for abuse. Mitchell, his partner John Bruce Jessen, and other SERE personnel were by many accounts instrumental to this process, training interrogators and helping to design the harsh CIA protocol for questioning high-value detainees that came to be known as "The Program."

Reached for comment, Mitchell declined to discuss his role. "If that was true," he said about working with the CIA, "I couldn't say anything about it." While he said he couldn't discuss his work on any particular cases, he also stressed that "I don't have anything to hide." The press office at the CIA also declined to publicly confirm Mitchell's relationship with the Agency but said that the Agency's interrogation program was lawful and had produced vital intelligence. In response to a story on *Vanity Fair* magazine's Web site, Mitchell and Jessen released a prepared statement saying, "We are proud of the work we have done for our country. The advice we have provided, and the actions we have taken have been legal and ethical. We resolutely oppose torture. Under no circumstances have we ever endorsed, nor would we endorse, the use of interrogation methods designed to do physical or psychological harm."

The SERE program was a strange choice for the government to pick if it was seeking to learn how to get the truth from detainees. It was founded during the Cold War in an effort to re-create, and therefore understand, the mistreatment that had led thirty-six captured U.S. airmen to give stunningly false confessions during the Korean War.

The most infamous was the confession of the U.S. pilot Frank Schwable in 1953. After the war, U.S. authorities pored over Schwable's experience, hoping to understand how he had been coerced into telling such egregious lies. They discovered that the North Koreans had used a deliberate program of physical and psychological torture. While the physical abuse was bad, Schwable and other former captives described the psychological abuse as worse. It began with two weeks of isolation in which, Schwable said, "your judgment becomes warped . . . You get a feeling of utter, hopeless despair." It was followed by humiliation, including a gambit in which guards barked and growled at Schwable, who was caged, making him feel like a dog. Naked, unbathed, and unshaved, he was demeaned in every way, kept under constant surveillance, forced even to defecate in front of his captors.

Later, in explaining how he broke down and agreed to give his infamous false confession, he noted that he had been spared the ghastly physical torment inflicted on some of his fellow soldiers. But in an eye-opening statement, he suggested that his psychological ordeal may have been worse. "Mine was a more subtle kind of torment," he said. "That kind is a little harder, I am afraid, for the people to understand." Instead of battle scars, all he could point to was the "slow, quiet, and diabolical" destruction of his mind.

Inside the military and CIA, Schwable's account was greeted with alarm. From the start of the Cold War, the CIA had been obsessively studying Stalin's show trials, trying to fathom what secret methods the Communists used to produce such convincing false statements from Soviet political prisoners. In an era when terms like "brainwashing" were current, and Richard Condon's *The Manchurian Candidate* was a bestseller, the CIA secretly tried to match the Communists' methodology, experimenting itself with a variety of psychological and chemical approaches to mind control.

In 2007, the CIA's declassification of long-held secret documents, known as "the Family Jewels," shed new light on the Cold War–era drug experiments. The papers documented experiments on rats and monkeys, as well as the infamous case of Frank R. Olson, an Agency employee who leaped (or some say was pushed) to his death from a hotel window in 1953, nine days after he was unwittingly drugged with LSD. The CIA experimented with substances such as sodium pentothal, as well as hypnosis and electroshock treatment. But most of this in-house research resulted in little more than lawsuits.

There was, however, one promising avenue of research into how to render human subjects pliant. It focused on the surprisingly powerful effects of psychological manipulations, such as extreme sensory deprivation. Many of these behavioral experiments were outsourced to brilliant research scientists at top universities in the United States and Canada. No one produced more significant breakthroughs than Donald Hebb, a psychologist at McGill. According to Alfred McCoy, a history professor at the University of Wisconsin, Madison, who has written extensively on the CIA's experiments in coercing subjects, the

Agency learned from Hebb that "if subjects are confined without light, odors, sound, or any fixed references of time and place, very deep breakdowns can be provoked."

Hebb found that in as few as forty-eight hours some subjects suspended in water tanks—or confined in air-conditioned isolated rooms wearing blacked-out goggles, gloves, and earmuffs—regressed to semipsychotic states. "I had no idea what a potentially vicious weapon this could be," Hebb admitted in an interview.

To extract confessions—and false confessions were the focus of the Agency's research—the CIA concentrated on two discoveries in particular: "self-inflicted pain," a Soviet technique in which merely being forced to stand for long periods of time proved unbearable, and "sensory deprivation." An advantage of the latter technique, McCoy said, was that subjects became so desperate for human interaction that "they bond with the interrogator like a father, or like a drowning man having a lifesaver thrown at him. If you deprive people of all their senses, they'll turn to you like their daddy."

The CIA gathered all it learned about coercive interrogations in what's regarded as the bible of psychological torture, the 1963 *KUBARK Manual,* and its companion, the 1983 *Human Resource Exploitation Training Manual.* These classified documents were never meant to be read by the public, but they were divulged in 1997, after a protracted Freedom of Information lawsuit waged by the *Baltimore Sun.* Their publication stirred recriminations and promises from the Agency to abandon all such morally and ethically offensive human experimentation. McCoy noted that by then the Agency had already discontinued most such work. "After the Cold War, we put away those tools. There was bipartisan reform. We backed away from those dark days," he said.

But after September 11, he said, "under the pressure of the war on terror, they didn't just bring back the old psychological techniques—they perfected them."

During the years that the CIA's mind-control experiments were dormant, however, similar research continued in the military's SERE program. After the Vietnam War, the program was expanded from training Air Force pilots, such as those who had been captured by the North Koreans, to include Special Forces and other elite personnel in the Army and the Navy. By 2001, the flagship program on how to resist torture was run at the Army's John F. Kennedy Special Warfare Center and School at Fort Bragg, North Carolina. Most details of the curriculum were classified. But sources said there were several levels of SERE courses; one, Level C, included a grueling exercise in which trainees endured days of physical and psychological hardship inside a mock prisoner-of-war camp. Trainees were subjected to simulated torture, including waterboarding, sleep deprivation, isolation, bombardment with agonizing sounds, sexual and religious humiliation, and temperature extremes, among other "challenges," as they were called.

A small number of psychologists and other clinicians oversaw the SERE programs. The supervisors discreetly checked on trainees' progress at frequent intervals, keeping extensive charts and records of their behavior and medical status. Numerous experiments aimed at documenting trainees' stress levels were conducted by SERE-affiliated scientists. By analyzing blood and saliva, they charted fluctuations in trainees' level of cortisol, a stress hormone. The data helped the psychologists pinpoint what treatment inspired maximum anxiety.

In general, the best way to stimulate acute anxiety, SERE scientists learned, was to create an environment of radical uncertainty. Trainees were therefore hooded; their sleep patterns were disrupted; they were starved for extended periods; they were stripped of their clothes; and they were subjected to harsh interrogations by officials impersonating enemy captors. Research in social psychology showed that a person's capacity for "self-regulation"—the ability to moderate or control his own behavior—could be substantially undermined in situations of high anxiety. If, for instance, a prisoner of war was trying to avoid revealing secrets to enemy interrogators, he was much less likely to succeed if he was deprived of sleep or was struggling to ignore intense pain.

Many of the program's officials were careful and dedicated public servants. But "some of the folks" associated with the program, an inside source said, got carried away. "They'd play these very aggressive roles, week after week," he said. "It can be very seductive." Although there is no scientific basis for believing that coercive interrogation methods work better than less aggressive ones, the source said that some of the SERE psychologists he knew believed that to get someone to talk "you have to hurt that person." The warrior culture of the Special Forces can be heady and contagious for those working as support staff. The source recalled one SERE psychologist confiding that he felt personally unfulfilled because, unlike the soldiers, he'd never had the opportunity to kill anyone.

Retired Army Colonel Patrick Lang, who was both a Special Forces officer and a Defense Intelligence Agency expert on the Middle East, said that he had attended a SERE school in both the captive role and that of the interrogator, and had found the experience disconcerting: "Once, I was on the other side of the exercise, acting as interrogator," he said. "If you did too much of that stuff, you could really get to like it. You can manipulate people. And most people like power. I've seen some of these doctors and psychologists and psychiatrists who really think they know how to do this. But it's very easy to go too far."

"The idea in SERE," the inside source said, "is to poke and find out what gets an emotional rise out of someone. The underlying theory is that if I can control your emotions, then I can manipulate you. It ties in to sadism," he said. He described Mitchell, whom he knew professionally, as someone who in his opinion enjoyed the work a little too much. "He likes getting reactions out of people. He's interested in being seen as someone who has power over other people's minds," he said.

It's not yet possible to pinpoint exactly how and when the CIA first turned to the SERE program for advice on how to interrogate its own captives. But a well-informed and reliable source who worked closely with the intelligence community after September 11 said that as the Agency struggled to design an interrogation and detention program on the fly, it turned to psychologists in its own scientific division for advice about what might work to "break" terror suspects. Leery about what they saw as potentially unethical and illegal uses of science, many of the Agency's own scientists recoiled. He said their reaction was 'Don't even think about this!' They thought officers could be prosecuted." Like the senior CIA officer who advised Kiriakou not to get involved as an interrogator, many in-house scientists sensed a boundary that the U.S. government shouldn't cross. Some top CIA officers, including R. Scott Shumate, the chief operational psychologist for the CTC from 2001 until 2003, left the Agency, apparently in disagreement over what he believed was a misuse of the SERE techniques. At the CIA, Shumate had reported directly to Cofer Black. Shumate then went to the Pentagon, where he became head of the Behavioral Sciences Directorate within the Counterintelligence Field Activity. He declined to comment, but associates described him as upset in particular about the treatment of Zubayda.

Top counterterrorism officials at the Agency were determined, however, to press on with the coercive techniques. At some point, the source said, a CIA officer who could not be identified, whom a colleague at the

Agency described as "a nobody—a pocket-protector-wearing Joe Molecule" who was "in charge of the shrinks on the science side," turned to the former SERE school psychologists. Having retired from the military and been sidelined from the war on terror, Mitchell and Jessen were eager to get involved. "Mike knew these guys," the source working with the intelligence community recounted, "and when his colleagues were wimps, he said they would fit the bill. They were good-looking, clean-cut, polite Mormons. The pressure was on to take the gloves off. They were prepared to do whatever it takes. The Agency turned to psychologists," he said, "because they wanted some kind of psychological justification for doing what they were doing. They wanted a theoretician to tell them that they could go hard but not seem like brutes."

On March 29, 2002, the day after Zubayda was captured, Mitchell reportedly closed a private consulting firm he'd opened just a few months before. Called Knowledge Works, LLC, the venture was launched with another former SERE psychologist, John Chin. Mitchell's main corporate base became a second-floor suite of offices behind a locked door in Spokane, Washington, doing business under the name Mitchell, Jessen & Associates, not far from the Air Force's SERE school program.

Soon, the former SERE psychologists were training CIA interrogators and advising the CIA on implementing a program that one knowledgeable source describes as "a *Clockwork Orange* kind of approach." As psychologists, they were unusually well-equipped to understand the human psyche. Jonathan Moreno, a professor of biomedical ethics at the University of Virginia and a scholar of state-sponsored experiments on humans, noted, "If you know how to help people who are stressed, then you also know how to stress people in order to get them to talk." A scientific source close to the situation said, "They took good knowledge and used it in a bad way."

Central to Mitchell's thinking, associates said, was the work of one of America's best-known and most successful psychologists, Martin Seligman, the former president of the American Psychological Association and an esteemed professor in the Department of Psychology at the University of Pennsylvania. It was Seligman's experiments with dogs to which Mitchell had referred when defending his approaches to the FBI. In the 1960s, Seligman and colleagues at the University of Pennsylvania pioneered work on a theory he called "Learned Helplessness." He did experiments with dogs in which he used electric shocks to destroy their will to escape from a cage. By shocking a dog repeatedly and randomly, he discovered, he could brutalize it emotionally into a state of complete passivity. The dog had learned helplessness. It could no longer recognize an opportunity to escape, or else was too afraid to take it.

In the spring of 2002, the period during which the CIA was probing what it could do to Zubayda, Seligman was invited by the CIA to speak at the Navy's SERE school in San Diego. Among the organizers was Kirk Hubbard, Director of Behavioral Sciences Research at the CIA until 2005. Neither Hubbard nor Seligman would comment on the special briefing. But in an e-mail Seligman acknowledged that he spoke for three hours. Seligman emphasized that his talk was aimed at helping American soldiers "resist torture," not inflict it. But whether Seligman wanted his discoveries applied as they were or not, Mitchell cited the uses of Learned Helplessness in handling human detainees. According to Steve Kleinman, a reserve Air Force colonel and an experienced interrogator who has known Mitchell professionally for years, "Learned Helplessness was his whole paradigm." Mitchell, he said, "draws a diagram showing what he says is the whole cycle. It starts with isolation. Then they eliminate the prisoner's ability to forecast the future—when their next meal is—when they can go to the bathroom. It creates dread and dependency. It was the KGB model. But the KGB used it to turn people who had turned against the state to confess falsely. The KGB wasn't after intelligence." Kleinman had been a SERE instructor himself, and in his view, the reverse-engineering of the science was morally, legally, and tactically wrong. He described the CIA's reliance on Mitchell as "surreal."

Asked about his theories, Mitchell noted that Seligman was "a brilliant man" and that his experiments were "good science." But through a lawyer, he disputed that Learned Helplessness was the model he used for the CIA interrogation program. Nevertheless, soon after he arrived in the CIA's black site in Thailand, Abu Zubayda found himself naked in a small cage, like a dog.

The extraordinary secrecy surrounding the CIA's program makes it hard to describe with certainty what happened next to Zubayda. But a closely held investigative report written by the International Committee for the Red Cross for the detaining authority, the CIA, which shared it with the President and the Secretary of State, in 2007 described the treatment regime that he underwent, categorically, as "torture" and warned that the abuse constituted war crimes, placing the highest officials in the U.S. government in jeopardy of being prosecuted, sources familiar with the report said. The ICRC was the first and only outside group to gain access to the CIA's fourteen most highly prized detainees. They were held in complete isolation from the outside world for five years before the relief group got to speak to them. While the ICRC would neither confirm nor deny the details, which it does not share with the public or press, other sources familiar with the report say that Abu Zubayda described being kept for prolonged spans of time in a cage that he called "a tiny coffin."

He recounted that the worst treatment he received didn't start until some weeks after he was captured. He believed he was held in one place for six weeks, then moved to a second for two more, and then finally to a third place, where the rough treatment began. His tormentors, he and the other detainees said, never used the word "torture." Instead, they talked about doing "hard time." The credibility of his account is impossible to gauge. He clearly had political and self-serving reasons to exaggerate his mistreatment, and U.S. officials repeatedly stressed that Al Qaeda members were trained to invent accusations of torture. But interestingly, both the timetable he supplied and the euphemisms for torture he described dovetail with the legal maneuvering taking place at the same time in Washington. Additionally, the details of The Program, as described by the detainees, not only are consistent with each other's accounts, despite the fact that they had no occasion to compare notes, they also echo uncannily the ostensible mock torture of the SERE program.

Zubayda's "hard time" began when he was locked into the "tiny coffin" for hours on end, which he described as excruciatingly painful. It was too small for him to stand or stretch out, so small he said he had to double up his limbs in a fetal position. Because of his recently healed injuries, he described this position as particularly agonizing, since it caused his wounds to reopen. He described the box as black, both inside and out, and said that it was covered in towels, which he thought was an effort to constrict the flow of air inside. While locked in the dark interior, he had no way of knowing when, if ever, he would be let out. But he related that most of the sessions lasted less than a day at a time, and were started and stopped during the course of one week. A source familiar with Zubayda's account described the tiny coffin box as "unbearable, most terrible." Article 21 of the Third Geneva Convention—which applies to all prisoners of war—specifically prohibits such forms of cruelty, which are classified as "close confinement."

A CIA source with access to the cable traffic concerning Zubayda's interrogation confirmed Zuabayda's account, saying he was put "in a dog crate—a little cage. They made him stay in it overnight." He said, "They tried it a few times—it was before they got waterboarding authority" from the Justice Department. This suggests that the painful confinement took place prior to the completion of the OLC's torture memo. But interestingly, the CIA source related, "It didn't work." He said, "It pissed him off. He just got more uncooperative." Given that the CIA was awaiting authority to go harder, it seems clear that the lesson learned in Washington from this early experiment was that more force, not less, was needed.

Zubayda told the ICRC that the cell in which he was isolated during this period looked out directly at the "tiny coffin" and another slightly larger cage. These two boxes loomed large in his imagination, even when he was not confined in them, blocking his line of sight as an omnipresent threat.

One unconfirmed account described the CIA interrogation team as building a coffin in which they reportedly threatened to bury Zubayda alive. Mock burials and threats of death are universally regarded as forms of torture. But it may be that the report was referring to the "tiny coffin," rather than a real one. In either case, Zubayda was not literally buried in it, but he was confined in it in a manner that would have been considered a grave breach of the Geneva Conventions had the United States still observed it.

According to this account, in keeping with the Learned Helplessness theory, the CIA interrogators also announced that they planned to become Zubayda's "God." They reportedly took his clothing as punishment, and reduced his human interaction to a single daily visit in which they would say simply, "You know what I want," and then leave.

Accurately or not, Bush Administration officials later described the abuses at Abu Ghraib and Guantánamo as the unauthorized actions of a few ill-trained personnel. By contrast, CIA officials have never denied that the treatment of the high-value detainees was expressly approved by President Bush. The program was closely monitored by CIA lawyers and supervised by the Agency's director and his subordinates in the Counterterrorist Center. Tenet, through a spokesman, denied that he personally reviewed daily dossiers describing the interrogations under way in the black prison sites, as some Agency officials have stated. But according to a deeply involved former Agency officer, "Every single plan was drawn up by interrogators, and then submitted for approval to the highest possible level, meaning the director of the CIA. Any change in the plan—even if an extra day of a certain treatment was added—was signed off on by the Director." A former top CIA lawyer, when asked whether senior administration officials were aware of the harrowing treatment going on inside the black sites, said, "I'm afraid so. You might have thought there was some adult supervision. But you would have been wrong."

Kiriakou made the interrogations sound almost like a game of "Mother, May I?" He said, "It was not up to the individual interrogator to decide 'I'm going to slap him' or 'I'm going to shake him.' Each one of these, though they're minor, had to have the approval of the Deputy Director for Operations," who during most of this period was James Pavitt. "Before you could lay a hand on him, you had to send a cable saying, 'He's uncooperative. Request permission to do X.' And permission would come, saying 'You're allowed to slap him one time in the belly with an open hand . . . or keep him awake for forty-eight hours.'" The program, Kiriakou said, was "extremely deliberate." There was, however, no known instance of the supervisors denying a request to use more force.

The system, which grew to include many more than the top fourteen most-prized prisoners, was remarkable for its mechanistic aura. "It's one of the most sophisticated, refined programs of torture ever," said an outside expert familiar with the protocol. "At every stage, there was a rigid attention to detail. Procedure was adhered to almost to the letter. There was top-down quality control and such a set routine, you get to the point where you know what each detainee is going to say because you've heard it all before. It was almost automated. People were utterly dehumanized. People fell apart. It was the intentional and systematic infliction of great pain, masquerading as a legal process. It was just chilling."

Among the CIA's fourteen highest-value detainees, eleven evidently told the ICRC that they were kept completely naked for prolonged periods of time, including Zubayda. Most said they were doused repeatedly with cold water and kept in frigid temperatures, sometimes, such as in the case of Khalid Sheikh Mohammed, for at least a month.

Sexual humiliation was a regular feature of the SERE program. In addition, the notion that Arabs were particularly vulnerable to it became an article of faith among many conservatives in Washington who were influenced by a book that obtained something of a cult status, *The Arab Mind* by Raphael Patai, a study of Arab culture and psychology first published in 1973. A cultural anthropologist, Patai included a twenty-five-page chapter on Arabs and sex, depicting the culture as crippled by shame and repression. "The segregation of the sexes, the veiling of the women . . . and all the other minute rules that govern and restrict contact between men and women, have the effect of making sex a prime mental preoccupation in the Arab world," Patai wrote. Homosexual activity, "or any indication of homosexual leanings, as with all other expressions of sexuality, is never given any publicity. These are private affairs and remain in private." Bush Administration foreign-policy intellectuals soon held two articles of faith about Arabs, as a source put it, "one, that Arabs only understand force, and two, that the biggest weakness of Arabs is shame and humiliation." Both ideas became mainstays of the interrogation program.

Unexpectedly, perhaps, the most excruciating of the physical treatments for detainees was among the slowest and least dramatic— "long-time standing," the stress position mastered by the Communists that had been studied and copied in the behavioral experiments of the CIA. The detainees told the ICRC that it became extremely painful over time. They described not just standing, but being kept up on their tiptoes with their arms extended out and up over their heads, attached by shackles on their wrists and ankles, for what they described as eight hours at a stretch. During the entire period, they said they were kept stark naked and often cold. This process was repeated every day for two or three months in some cases. Some told the ICRC about having wounds in both their wrists and ankles where the shackles had cut through their skin. "For many, many hours, they were kept there, hurting like crazy," a source familiar with the ICRC report said. "They felt like worms, too, naked, exposed, in front of the world."

In addition to keeping a prisoner awake, the simple act of remaining upright can over time cause significant physical damage. McCoy, the historian, noted in his 2006 book *A Question of Torture* that the Soviets found that making a victim stand for eighteen to twenty-four hours can produce "excruciating pain, as ankles double in size, skin becomes tense and intensely painful, blisters erupt oozing watery serum, heart rates soar, kidneys shut down, and delusions deepen."

One detainee who claimed that he was subjected to stress standing was Tawfiq Bin Attash, also known as Khallad, who was alleged to be one of the masterminds of the attack on the USS *Cole* and involved in the planning of the East African embassy bombings. It was an acutely difficult technique for him, because he had had one leg amputated below the knee following an injury in the Afghan-Soviet War. He had a prosthesis, but he told the ICRC that during the period that he was forced to stand in this stress position, the American captors took his prosthesis away, so that he had to balance himself on one foot, or hang by his arms.

Zubayda also said his interrogators beat him. A source familiar with the details, but not present at the time, said, "They started running the SERE module on him. He had shrapnel in his abdomen. They hit him, and he collapsed."

Six of the fourteen high-value detainees said they were slammed against the walls, according to sources familiar with the ICRC report. Zubayda described being thrust headfirst against a bare concrete wall. In the beginning, he said, he was propelled just by a towel that was wrapped around his neck. This was the method that a top CIA officer ascribed to Israeli advice. Later, however, the interrogators apparently became more technically proficient. Zubayda reported that they used something akin to a dog collar, a thick plastic strip that encircled the prisoners' necks. Evidently, the collar could be attached to a lead, enabling the handler to have better leverage. After one of the early sessions, during which he'd been smashed into the concrete, Zubayda said he found himself waking up in the coffin box. When he was released from it, he said, he discovered that his captors had covered the walls in plywood, apparently to cushion the blows. The occupational hazard of torture is a subject's injury or death. To guard against these, the CIA kept a physician on hand at all times. As a result, the Agency could boast truthfully that none of its fourteen most valued prisoners were killed.

Eleven out of the fourteen also described being subjected to sleep-deprivation regimes. It is unclear how long detainees were kept awake for any given stretch, but in Iraq there were reports of U.S. authorities keeping prisoners awake for as long as ninety-six hours. Some of the CIA's high-value detainees said they were deprived of sleep intermittently for up to three months. They described being bombarded by bright lights and eardrum-shattering sounds twenty-four hours a day for weeks on end. The noise ranged from the Red Hot Chili Peppers, in the case of Abu Zubayda, to rap, chants, and, in one prisoner's description, a tape resembling the soundtrack from a horror movie. In the SERE program, scientists discovered that "noise stress" was often more difficult for trainees to endure than anything else, including waterboarding. SERE personnel found that the most stress-inducing sound for many was a recording of babies crying inconsolably. Evidently, the interrogators brought a certain twisted humor to their DJ duties, searching for sounds they believed would be particularly insufferable. Among their choices were the "meow"s from cat-food commercials, Yoko Ono singing, and Eminem rapping about America.

The effects of sleep deprivation, however, were well known to be serious. Menachem Begin, the Israeli Prime Minister from 1977 to 1982, who was tortured by the KGB as a young man, described it as so difficult to withstand that it led quickly to false confessions. In his book *White Nights: The Story of a Prisoner in Russia,* he wrote, "In the head of the interrogated prisoner, a haze begins to form. His spirit is wearied to death, his legs are unsteady, and he has one sole desire: to sleep. Anyone who has experienced this desire knows that not even hunger and thirst are comparable with it.

"I came across prisoners who signed what they were ordered to sign, only to get what the interrogator promised them. He did not promise them their liberty; he did not promise them food to sate themselves. He promised them—if they signed—uninterrupted sleep! And, having signed, there was nothing in the world that could move them to risk again such nights and such days."

A former CIA officer, knowledgeable and supportive of the terrorist interrogation program, said simply, "Sleep deprivation works. Your electrolyte balance changes. You lose all balance and ability to think rationally. Stuff comes out." But even in the Middle Ages, when it was called *tormentum insomniae,* professional torturers eschewed sleep deprivation, recognizing that the illusions and delusions it caused were more apt to produce false confessions than real ones. Historically, it was the favored choice only of witch hunters, who believed it accurately revealed evidence of pacts with the devil. For decades, it was defined in the United States as an illegal form of torture. An American Bar Association report, published in 1930 and cited in a later U.S. Supreme Court decision, said, "It has been known since 1500 at least that deprivation of sleep is the most effective torture and certain to produce any confession desired." But it became American policy in 2001, and continues to be.

In February 2008, the Bush Administration acknowledged publicly for the first time that it had in fact, as had been previously reported, used what is often considered the most notorious of the U.S.

interrogation tactics—waterboarding—on three high-value terror suspects, including Zubayda. Testifying before Congress, CIA Director Michael Hayden said U.S. government officials had also waterboarded Khalid Sheikh Mohammed and Abd al-Rahim al-Nashiri in 2002 and 2003. The nonprofit group Human Rights Watch and some editorial pages, including that of the *Los Angeles Times,* immediately called for the Justice Department to launch a criminal investigation of top administration officials for authorizing war crimes. "It's torture; it's illegal," the *Los Angeles Times* editorial proclaimed.

As recently as 1983, the Justice Department had in fact prosecuted waterboarding as a crime. Testifying before Congress on behalf of the Bush Administration, acting OLC Director Steven Bradbury argued, however, that in the view of the Bush legal team waterboarding was not torture if "subject to strict safeguards, limitations and conditions." Laying out the theories of OLC's secret legal memos for the first time in public, he calmly explained that "something can be quite distressing or uncomfortable, even frightening, [but] if it doesn't involve severe physical pain, and it doesn't last very long, it may not constitute severe physical suffering. That would be the analysis." As Martin Lederman noted, this interpretation of "severe physical suffering" was "simply made of whole cloth. Well, not even. There's no cloth there at all. It is completely unsupported by, and contrary to, the plain words and structure of the statute."

The Bush Administration's legal arguments were novel, but the use of waterboarding was anything but new. Darius Rejali, in his authoritative and encyclopedic book *Torture and Democracy,* traces variations of the practice running from the Dark Ages on up through the Gestapo in Nazi Germany, the French in the Battle of Algiers, and various Latin American dictatorships, to name just a few. In the midst of the 2008 presidential campaign, John McCain cited this history in an interview with the *New York Times.* As some of his fellow Republican presidential candidates equivocated, he told the paper, "All I can say is that it was used in the Spanish Inquisition, it was used in Pol Pot's genocide in Cambodia, and there are reports that it is being used against Buddhist monks today [in Myanmar]." He added, "It is not a complicated procedure. It is torture."

Sometime in the summer of 2002, in a prison whose location the United States has never disclosed, in the hands of U.S. government employees whose identities remain a secret, Zubayda became the first person ever to be waterboarded at the command of the President of the

United States. The first and most detailed public account of what happened came from Kiriakou, the former CIA officer, in the interview he gave ABC News in December 2007. But Kiriakou was not a firsthand witness. He said he learned about it from internal CIA communications. The version he heard, though, was sharply different from Zubayda's.

Kiriakou maintained that Zubayda was waterboarded only once, after he resisted giving his captors actionable intelligence. "He was able to withstand it for quite some time, by which I mean thirty to thirty-five seconds," Kiriakou said. He noted that he and several colleagues at the Agency had practiced waterboarding each other "to see what it felt like," and that none had lasted more than ten or fifteen seconds. He said he had lasted only five seconds himself. "It's a wholly unpleasant experience," he said. "It's a violent thing to go through. It's not pretty to watch. You're strapped down, your head is immobilized, and it's almost like being shocked. You're gagging, and shouting."

According to the CIA version that Kiriakou heard, almost immediately after being waterboarded, Zubayda announced that "Allah had visited him in the night, and told him to cooperate." Right away, Kiriakou suggested, Zubayda started to give the Agency valuable intelligence that led to the "disruption of dozens of attacks," all of which were planned for outside of the United States. "I think he just didn't want to go through it again," said Kiriakou. He noted, "It was considered a big victory inside the CIA."

Indeed, the harsh SERE-like interrogation methods were described to the top officials back in Washington as unalloyed successes. Mitchell was, according to associates, regarded as a hero. By the summer of 2002, he and Jessen were often seen inside the bull pen of the CTC back in Langley, where one former officer remembers them having permanently assigned seats and desks. Rumors of their brilliant results rippled through the rest of the intelligence community. These miraculous breakthroughs were being reported by the practitioners themselves. But only those who participated in the program had access to what went on in it, which made it difficult for anyone outside to evaluate it. Not until Porter Goss became CIA director in 2004 was the program's effectiveness given any independent review. Then the reviewers' report was kept secret, but the verdict was reportedly mixed. "The fact that there was no effective peer review is one of the reasons they got away with it," Philip Zelikow, who served as Executive Director of the 9/11 Commission and later as an aide to Secretary of State Condoleeza Rice, later said. "The program and their claims were never subjected to any independent analysis. They always went back to the same people who were running the program at the Agency to ask if it was working, and they always said it was."

In contrast to the CIA version, Zubayda claimed that he was not merely waterboarded once. He told the ICRC, according to those familiar with the report, that the CIA waterboarded him at least ten times in a single week, often twice a day. On one day, he claimed, he was waterboarded three times.

His descriptions were consistent with those of the other two high-value detainees who were waterboarded, both of whom claimed to have been put through the procedure multiple times. They all said the waterboarding was done in a very precise way. They were strapped down to a hard surface, placed in leather cuffs, and their feet were elevated. Cloths were put on their faces and water was poured on it. They all felt as if they were drowning. They described being tipped down, then brought back up again, and then tipped down again.

The description was remarkably close to the drill practiced in the U.S. SERE schools. There, a "strapdown" team would lay a partially naked subject on a board and buckle him into leather straps at the feet, hands, legs, chest, and head, so that nothing could move at all. They would tell the subject that when he wanted to "talk," he should shake his boots. Up to two gallons of water were poured in a steady stream from two cups, one in each hand of the interrogator. It was aimed right for the spot between the mouth and nose, above the upper lip. This way, both mouth and nose were filled with water, causing a terrible drowning sensation and gag reflex. In the press, the process has been called "simulated drowning." But Malcolm Nance, a former master instructor at the Navy SERE school who estimated that he had overseen hundreds of waterboarding sessions, as well as having been waterboarded himself, argued that the media didn't really explain the process accurately to the American public. "It's not simulated anything. It's slow-motion suffocation with enough time to contemplate the inevitability of blackout and expiration—usually the person goes into hysterics on the board," he said. "You can feel every drop. Every drop. You start to panic. And as you panic, you start gasping, and as you gasp, your gag reflex is overridden by water. And then you start to choke, and then you start to drown more. Because the water doesn't stop until the interrogator wants to ask you a question. And then, for that second, the water will continue, and you'll get a second to puke and spit up everything that you have, and then you'll have an opportunity to determine whether you're willing to continue with the process." Nance had no doubt that waterboarding was torture, and wrong for U.S. soldiers to use on captives. "Our waterboarders are professional. When the water hits you, you think, 'Oh shit, this is a whole new level of Bad.'"

"Waterboarding works," the former CIA officer who also touted sleep deprivation said. "Drowning is a baseline fear. So is falling. People dream about it. It's human nature. Suffocation is a very scary thing. When you're waterboarded, you're inverted, so it exacerbates the fear. It's not painful, but it scares the shit out of you." (He was waterboarded himself in a training course.) While he had no sympathy for the detainees, the officer was deeply concerned about the impact that these methods had on his colleagues who inflicted them. Experts on torture, such as Rejali, often write of the corrosive and corrupting effect that such animalistic behavior has on discipline, professionalism, and morale. The former officer said that during the "enhanced" interrogations, officers worked in teams, watching each other behind two-way mirrors. Even with this group support, he said, a friend of his who had helped to waterboard Khalid Sheikh Mohammed "has horrible nightmares." He went on, "When you cross over that line of darkness, it's hard to come back. You lose your soul. You can do your best to justify it, but it's well outside the norm. You can't go to that dark a place without it changing you." He said of his friend, "He's a good guy. It really haunts him. You are inflicting something really evil and horrible on somebody."

Without access to solid evidence, it's hard to know which version of Zubayda's treatment was more accurate—the thirty-second waterboarding triumph described by the CIA, or his own account of prolonged and repeated abuse, as told to the ICRC. It's also nearly impossible to settle competing claims about how much valuable intelligence he and other detainees really supplied. Until 2005, an invaluable trove of such documentary evidence existed for the world to see. From the start of Zubayda's capture, the CIA videotaped hundreds of hours of his interrogation, including his waterboarding. The Agency also videotaped the waterboarding of a second high-value detainee, captured later in 2002, Abd al-Rahim al-Nashiri. Top Agency officials have suggested they did so to protect themselves, in case a detainee died, against accusations of carelessness, an explanation that seems less plausible than that they hoped to share the tapes with intelligence experts who were unable to be in the room. The CIA operatives who were involved, however, grew increasingly uneasy that their actions were potentially visible to the entire world. Although the Agency insisted that the Program was legally and politically defensible, it withheld these tapes from both the 9/11 Commission and a federal court judge in the Moussaoui case. And in 2005, on orders from the head of the Clandestine Services, the Agency destroyed them.

The CIA has said that the tapes were the only existing record of what went on in the interrogation chambers—no verbatim transcripts were made. What the tapes would have shown, and why they were destroyed, would become the focus of a criminal investigation by the Justice Department in 2007. But long before then, Zubayda's behavior on film and off had become the talk of the CTC. As one former CIA officer put it, and another confirmed, "He spent all of his time masturbating like a monkey in the zoo. He went at it so much, at some point I heard he injured himself. They had to intervene. He didn't care that they were watching him. I guess he was bored, and mad."

Another source said, "He masturbated constantly. A couple of guards were worried about it. He wasn't brazen about it—he wasn't facing the camera. He'd do it at night, facing the wall, but it was rigged so there was no place for him to not be seen. This was closed circuit. He complained to the interrogator that he would never have the chance to feel a woman's touch again, and lament that he would never have children. He freaked though, at one point, because there was blood in his ejaculate. He saved it for the doctors in a tissue, to show them in the morning. The doctor said not to worry."

Top Bush Administration officials, including the President, have repeatedly argued that the "enhanced" interrogation techniques used on Abu Zubayda yielded valuable results that justified the costs to America's moral authority. In his 2006 defense of "alternative procedures" for high-value detainees, President Bush cited three "vital" pieces of "the puzzle" supplied by Zubayda because of these new methods.

The first was that "Zubayda disclosed Khalid Sheikh Mohammed" as "the mastermind behind the 9/11 attacks, and used the alias Mukhtar."

The second was that "Abu Zubaydah provided information that helped stop a terrorist attack being planned for inside the United States." Bush added dramatically, "Based on the information he provided, the operatives were detained—one while traveling to the United States."

Bush's third claim was this: "The information Zubaydah provided helped lead to the capture of Ramsi bin al Shibh. And together these two terrorists provided information that helped in the planning and execution of the operation that captured Khalid Sheikh Mohammed."

The first claim appears undermined by the 9/11 Commission report. As mentioned earlier, it established authoritatively that in the summer before Al Qaeda attacked, the CIA had already received several reports that Khalid Sheikh Mohammed was involved in terrorist planning against the United States, and specifically, on August 28, 2001, the Agency received a cable reporting that KSM's nickname was "Mukhtar." The Commission noted, "No one made the connection" necessary to unravel the plot in time. Therefore, the information Zubayda gave the Agency on this was redundant. Moreover, Zubayda reportedly told interogators this before he was harshly treated.

The second claim, regarding the detained terrorist on his way to attack the United States, is generally understood to be a reference to Jose Padilla. Yet it has been widely reported, and undisputed, that Zubayda told interrogators about this, too, prior to being harshly treated.

The third claim, concerning the capture of Ramsi Bin Al Shibh, also seems dubious. It is false that Zubayda alerted authorities to Bin Al Shibh's role in Al Qaeda's September 11 plot, initiating the search for him. There were numerous published reports on Bin Al Shibh—Atta's former roommate in Hamburg—before Zubayda's capture. The Associated Press, the *Washington Post,* and the *Daily News,* among others, all carried stories on this prior to Zubayda's capture.

Moreover, two months before Zubayda was captured, Attorney General John Ashcroft played a "martyrdom" video from Bin Al Shibh at a press conference that he said had been recovered from Mohammad Atef's house after an air strike.

If President Bush meant only that Zubayda provided the information that led to Bin Al Shibh's capture, the picture is less clear, but there is still a major contradiction. Bin Al Shibh was not captured until almost a half a year after Zubayda, on September 11, 2002. The time lag makes it seem far more likely that, as Ron Suskind reported, the key information about Bin Al Shibh's location came not from Zubayda but from an Al Jazeera reporter, who indirectly passed it on to the Emir of Qatar in the summer of 2002.

On April 19, 2002, Al Jazeera correspondent Yousri Fouda, a London-based Egyptian, was given a rare, embargoed interview with Bin Al Shibh and Khalid Sheikh Mohammed, who were together at a safe house in Karachi. On camera they openly took credit for the 9/11 attacks—criminally implicating themselves convincingly enough for any jury in the world to convict them. Foudra said he was astounded not only by the frankness of their boastful confessions but also by their seeming imperviousness to the danger of being caught. They permitted him to reveal that they were hiding in the Karachi area, and Mohammed walked out into the open street with him as he left. In June 2002, Fouda told his bosses at Al Jazeera about the remarkable interviews, which he was preparing for a first-anniversary report on the attacks. Among those Fouda confided in was Al Jazeera chairman Sheikh Hamad bin Thamer al-Thani, a cousin of the Emir of Qatar. Unknown to Fouda, the Emir told the CIA all about Fouda's coup right away. In mid-June, Tenet reportedly told his staff at the CIA with great excitement that "my friend the Emir" [of Qatar] "gave us an amazing gift . . . In other words, the fat fuck came through." Tenet had all the details of Fouda's meetings with the terrorists, including the probable location of the building and even the floor where they resided. Soon after, the NSA reportedly pinpointed Bin Al Shibh's suspected apartment by successfully matching his voice from the Al Jazeera interview to his satellite phone. This bit of wizardry apparently led to Bin Al Shibh's capture, along with a number of other suspects, on September 11, 2002.

Both President Bush, in his major address on the subject, and Tenet, in his memoir, curiously omitted any mention of the decisive roles played by Al Jazeera and the Emir of Qatar. Tenet instead, like the President, claimed that "interrogating Abu Zubayda led to Ramsi Bin Al Shibh." One explanation may be that they were protecting a sensitive foreign intelligence source—the Emir. It is also likely that Zubayda did in fact help in some small way to amplify the information they already had learned. But, whatever their motives, it appears the President and the Director of Central Intelligence gave the public misleadingly exaggerated accounts of the effectiveness of the abuse they authorized.

Some might impute dishonest motives to them. But it seems more likely that they fooled not just the public, but also themselves. In the same way that Cheney continued to insist, despite all evidence to the contrary, that Al Qaeda and Saddam Hussein had collaborated on weapons of mass destruction, top Bush Administration officials accepted only the facts that supported their preconceptions. In their use of coercion, they even had a means of manufacturing more such self-justifying evidence.

A former top Bush Administration lawyer, reflecting on the mind-set, said, "They were living in a fantasyland. They were just not welcoming of other views. It was almost like instead of arriving at an opinion, they were writing briefs—one-sided adversarial arguments. If you're sure you're right, you only want to hear what confirms what you think."

The CIA was caught in the middle between its dogmatic political bosses on one side, and the messy, contradictory, nuanced, and often elusive real-world facts on the other, just as it had been in the run-up to the war in Iraq. Under the pressure, Tenet's instinct, as was almost always true, appears again to have been to please the White House under the pressure. Suskind, for instance, reports that the intelligence agency had doubts about Zubayda's value early on, but that Tenet was so anxious not to disappoint Bush, he couldn't quite admit this. "I said he was important," Bush reportedly told Tenet at one of their daily meetings. "You're not going to let me lose face on this, are you?" "No sir, Mr. President," Tenet replied.

To Daniel Coleman, who was back in Washington working on another FBI fusion team helping the CIA to decipher Zubayda's diaries, the terror suspect's marginal value came as no surprise. The diaries were a huge disappointment. Instead of operational intelligence, they contained hundreds of pages of nearly incoherent blather. Zubayda, he said, wrote in three different voices, giving himself three different names, "Hani 1, 2, and 3," each apparently reflecting himself at a different age. There was poetry. There were religious musings. And there was enough sexual content for a CIA briefer to say that all she had learned from the diary was, "Men are pigs."

Coleman suspected that a head wound Zubayda had received during the Afghan war may have rendered him mentally defective. "He had a schizophrenic personality," Coleman said. "They made more of him than he was." There was no way, Coleman believed, that Bin Laden would have entrusted him with major secrets. "They thought he was a big shot, but he was just a hotel clerk," Coleman said. "They thought they knew who he was, but they didn't."

Rather than accepting Zubayda's limitations, Coleman believed, the Agency had tortured him into telling them what they wanted to hear. Zubayda gave up a few useful tidbits, according to the 9/11 Commission, including the name of an Al Qaeda recruiter who was soon captured. Foes of coercion often argue that it doesn't work. Experts suggest this is misleading. Torture works in several ways. It can intimidate enemies, it can elicit false confessions, and it can produce true confessions. Setting aside the moral issues, the problem is recognizing what's true. Zubayda, for instance, reportedly confessed to dozens of half-hatched or entirely imaginary plots to blow up American banks, supermarkets, malls, the Statue of Liberty, the Golden Gate Bridge, the Brooklyn Bridge, and nuclear power plants. Federal law-enforcement officials were dispatched to unlikely locations across the country in an effort to follow these false leads.

"The Agency was putting on a show for the top political people—for the White House—in the daily briefing," Coleman asserted. "Who knows if they really got any intelligence. There's nothing in the way of intelligence that I've seen from the program. It was about face time, and sounding good."

After initially supporting the tormenting of Zubayda, Kiriakou, too, had second thoughts. "At the time, I thought waterboarding was something we needed to do," he said. "But as September 11 passed, I think I've changed my mind. Waterboarding is probably something that we shouldn't be in the business of doing," he concluded, "because as Americans, we're better than that."

For Cofer Black, who had been so anxious to take the gloves off, the new willingness to take more aggressive measures did not seem to bring with it significant career advancement. A colleague said that Black failed to notice in the spring of 2002 that the Bush White House was shifting its focus to the coming war in Iraq. He also overlooked growing jealousy from rivals at the Agency. Black's counterterrorism operation had exploded in size. It rankled some that he seemed intent on spreading his staff's reach globally, even if it meant replicating many of the stations that already existed. Among those whom his expanding empire threatened, according to two sources, was his old friend from their Africa days together, his boss James Pavitt, the head of the entire Operations Division.

"Cofer thought he was at the center of the most important mission," a colleague said. "He was acting wilder and wilder. He said no one could take any money from CTC for Iraq. So he had all this money from Congress, but he wouldn't share it." Instead, the colleague said, Black insisted that he needed more funding and hundreds—even thousands—more people on his staff, and that if he didn't get this, "people were going to die." Everyone expected Black to be dramatic, but this was considered a bit over the top. "He was just fussing and fussing," a colleague recalled. He seemed to divide the world between those who supported his grandiose plans and enemies. "Hey, dude, are you with me or against us?" he asked a startled friend who had assumed that in the Agency they were all on the same side.

The friend said that Black sincerely believed the terrorism situation was so dire, Western civilization hung in the balance. It wasn't an act. His wife told the friend that when Black came home, he would turn off the lights and just sit there in the dark with a glass of something to drink and a cigar, lost in apocalyptic gloom.

Tenet, however, could see the wind shifting in the White House. To staff the coming war in Iraq, essential personnel would have to be taken out of Afghanistan and the fight against Al Qaeda. Tenet could have resisted, as many of his counterterrorism experts wanted. "George had some long nights," John Brennan, his former deputy, said. But again, Tenet sided with his bosses. An assistant, who declined to be named, explained that "Cofer's a terrific field commander—but it was felt at this point that someone a little further from the battlefield, and a bit more of a manager, was needed."

The first clear sign that Black was in trouble came when Tenet assigned three young stars at the Agency to conduct a management study of the CTC. Inevitably, they found flaws. They reported many duplication problems. Black protested, but the office politics were clear. The final blow came when Tenet—in a classic ploy—told Black he had a new assignment for him. Tenet explained that the Agency had a new priority, which he wanted Black to be in charge of: responding to the newly formed 9/11 Commission. Black was deeply upset and hurt, a friend recounted, accusing Tenet of firing him. But Tenet insisted he was not, he just needed Black to spend all of his time preparing for what would inevitably be a grueling investigation.

Tenet appointed Jose Rodriguez Jr., a friend of Pavitt's, to become the new head of the CTC. Other than serving for less than a year as Black's deputy, Rodriguez had no experience or expertise in Islamic extremism. He had spent most of his career in the Directorate of Operations and had a somewhat blemished reputation. The CIA had reprimanded him after he had tried to protect a childhood friend who had become a drug lord, after the friend had been arrested on narcotics charges. Some in the Agency said it sidelined Rodriguez's career, although Rodriguez denies this. It wasn't an auspicious appointment. But a young officer critical of what he saw as Pavitt's tendency toward cronyism, scoffed, "In the Bush Administration, loyalty is the new competence."

By May of 2002, just as his people were taking custody of Zubayda and the tough program he had dreamed of was coming to life, Black left the CTC. Soon after, he retired from the CIA after twenty-eight years. First, he went to the State Department, where his friend, Deputy Secretary of State Richard Armitage, succeeded in getting him appointed the coordinator for counterterrorism. A little over two years later, he moved to the private sector, joining the controversial private security firm Blackwater USA as vice chairman. The move raised some eyebrows and fed into an investigation by the CIA's Inspector General. During Black's tenure, the CTC had hired a number of Blackwater contractors. The State Department, too, gave Blackwater its largest private security contract. The lucrative deals back and forth looked somewhat incestuous, but no wrongdoing was charged. In the private sector, Black nonetheless kept a hand in counterterrorism policy, taking a post as the top terrorism adviser to Mitt Romney's unsuccessful campaign for the Republican presidential nomination in 2007. The echoes of his thinking could be heard in Romney's call to "double Guantánamo" rather than close it down. Long before this, however, the influence of the CIA's extraordinary new methods had already reached the island.

8

THE EXPERIMENT

We're a nation of law. We adhere to laws. We have laws on the books. You might look at these laws, and that might provide comfort for you.

—President George W. Bush, after being asked
if torture was justified, on June 10, 2004

1115: Told detainee a dog is held in higher esteem . . . Began teaching detainee lessons such as stay, come, and bark, to elevate his status to that of a dog. Detainee became agitated . . .
1300: Dog tricks continue . . . Interrogator showed photos of 9-11 victims and told detainee he should bark happy for these people. Interrogator showed photos of Al Qaeda terrorist and told detainee he should growl at these people. A towel was placed on detainee's head like a burka, and interrogator proceeded to give detainee dance lessons.

—Day 28, December 20, 2002,
Interrogation log of Mohammed al-Qahtani

As the first anniversary of September 11 approached and the White House braced for what was considered to be the very real threat of a second major attack on America, frustration practically radiated from the military's prison camp in Guantánamo Bay, Cuba. It had been three-quarters of a year since the first orange-jumpsuit-clad detainees had been unloaded from the war zone in Afghanistan, and the U.S. government had learned almost nothing of importance. In some cases, the government had learned literally nothing at all. When White House staff members had asked to see the prisoners' files, they had been astounded to discover that for some detainees, there were no details of any sort. Not even a name. There was just an assigned prisoner number and a silently uncooperative detainee.

The detainees had been described by Secretary of Defense Rumsfeld as "among the most dangerous, best-trained, and vicious killers on the face of the earth." They would "gnaw through hydraulic lines in the back" of a military plane "to bring it down," in the memorable phrase of General Richard Myers, the Chairman of the Joint Chiefs of Staff. They were all "unlawful combatants," Rumsfeld had declared as they arrived on the island on January 11, 2002, with "no rights under the Geneva Convention." But the decision to sweep away the Geneva Conventions, and with them the Article 5 status hearings formerly required for each prisoner of war, had left the government with an ominous blank slate. In Afghanistan, the military had tried to sort the prisoners, but Michael Gelles, a Navy psychologist involved at the time, described the process as "pure chaos."

The CIA, concerned by the paucity of valuable information emanating from the island, in the late summer of 2002 dispatched a senior intelligence analyst, who was fluent in Arabic and expert on Islamic extremism, to find out what the problem was. The officer, who is now retired, declined to be identified. The report he wrote up from this sensitive, early reconnaissance mission is classified top secret. But after he left the Agency, he described what he found. After spending several hours with each of about two dozen Arabic-speaking detainees, chosen in a random sampling, he concluded that an estimated one-third of the prison camp's population of more than 600 captives at the time, meaning more than 200 individuals, had no connection to terrorism whatsoever. If the intelligence haul was meager, his findings suggested, one reason was that many of the detainees knew little or nothing.

"I wanted to speak to them with no interpreter, just one-on-one," he recalled in an interview. "I just wanted to hear their stories." Some, he believed, were honest with him, others not. Some were involved in "some very nasty stuff." Many, he felt sure, "were just caught in a dragnet. They were not fighters, they were not doing jihad. They should not have been there."

One man was a rich Kuwaiti businessman who took a trip to a different part of the world every year to do charity work. In 2001, the country he chose was Afghanistan. "He wasn't a jihadi, but I told him he should have been arrested for stupidity," the CIA officer recalled. The man was furious with the United States for rounding him up. He mentioned that every year up until then, he had bought himself a new Cadillac, but when he was released, he said, he would never buy another American car. He was switching to Mercedeses.

There was also the pitiful tale of an Iraqi Shiite who had fled from Saddam Hussein. He had escaped to Iran, where he worked in a shoe factory. He was working there alongside many Afghan immigrants when the Iranians expelled them all to Afghanistan. The Taliban then jailed him as an American "spy" for having supported the U.S.-backed opposition to Saddam Hussein. After September 11, when the United States defeated his Taliban jailers, he fled to Pakistan. But, for a $5,000 bounty, the Pakistanis arrested him as a foreign terror suspect and turned him over to U.S. officials, who in turn shipped him to Guantánamo. There, in Guantánamo along with him, was the Taliban member who had accused him of being a U.S. sympathizer. "I could barely keep a straight face, listening to him," the CIA officer recalled.

Beneath the dark tales of human folly and bad luck, he feared, was a potentially toxic political problem. "I was very concerned about the system," he said. By imprisoning innocent Muslims indefinitely, outside the reach of any legal review, he said, "I thought we were going to lose a whole damn generation" in the Arab world. Instead of helping the war on terror, Guantánamo was making the world more dangerous. He said he spoke with Major General Michael Dunlavey, the top military commander in Guantánamo at the time. The CIA officer was further disconcerted to learn that the general agreed with him that easily a third of the Guantánamo detainees were mistakes. Later, Dunlavey raised his estimate to fully half the population. There were mental cases and a few teenagers. One was so demented, he was eating his own feces. When Dunlavey, a reservist who was also a judge in the Court of Common Pleas in Erie, Pennsylvania, took command of the base in March of 2002, he had been so dismayed, he'd personally confronted military officials in Afghanistan about sending too many "Mickey Mouse" prisoners. But he was reportedly told to "please shut up and go home."

A later study undertaken by a team of law students and attorneys at Seton Hall University Law School bolstered the CIA officer's anecdotal impressions. After reviewing 517 of the Guantánamo detainees' cases in depth, they concluded that only 8 percent were alleged to have associated with Al Qaeda. Fifty-five percent were not alleged to have engaged in any hostile act against the United States at all, and the remainder were charged with dubious wrongdoing, including having tried to flee U.S. bombs. The overwhelming majority—all but 5 percent—had been captured by non-U.S. players, many of whom were bounty hunters.

After completing his survey in Guantánamo, the CIA officer wrote up a detailed report describing his findings. He mentioned specific detainees by name, so there was no confusion about whom the United States was wrongly holding. He made clear that he believed that the United States was committing war crimes by holding and questioning innocent people in such inhumane ways.

The CIA analyst's troubling report soon reached the highest-ranking national security lawyer in the White House, Rice's legal counsel, John Bellinger. Immediately distressed, he called the author and brought him in to brief the top terrorism expert on the National Security Council at the time, General John Gordon. The findings were hard to dismiss. The report wasn't written by a bleeding-heart human rights group; it was written by a tough and highly experienced CIA analyst whose career had been spent fighting terrorists. Gordon, too, became alarmed.

Bellinger was in a political minority in the White House, however. His concern for international law and world opinion was ridiculed by the hard-line lawyers of the so-called War Council. Addington particularly disdained Bellinger, according to several sources who watched their constant skirmishes. Addington was a sectarian purist, instinctively challenging and excluding anyone less extreme, and Bellinger epitomized the art of compromise that Addington deplored. Bellinger had discovered it was always 5–1, with himself outnumbered by Addington, Gonzales, Yoo, Haynes, and whichever lawyer was sent by the CIA. Nonetheless, he thought that if they were making mistakes in Guantánamo, potentially incarcerating the wrong people, it couldn't be ignored.

Bellinger asked to see Gonzales about it. The White House Counsel was supposed to be overseeing legal issues involving the detainees. Bellinger mentioned that he thought the question of who was being held in Guantánamo called for a second look.

On the day of the appointed meeting in the early fall of 2002, Bellinger brought Gordon with him. The presence of the retired four-star general, who had also worked as Deputy Director of the CIA, underscored the point that the message was not just being delivered by a squishy scion of the Washington establishment. As they walked into Gonzales's upstairs office at the back of the West Wing, however, they were surprised to find the President's lawyer flanked by Addington and Flanigan. Neither had any official national security role, and no one had warned Bellinger that they would be there. But they did all the talking.

"No, there will be no review. The President has determined that they are ALL enemy combatants. We are not going to revisit it!" Addington said, according to two sources.

"This is a violation of basic notions of American fairness," Gordon and Bellinger argued back. "Isn't that what we're about as a country?"

Addington's response was adamant and imperious. "We are not second-guessing the President's decision. These are 'enemy combatants.' Please use that phrase," he said. "They've all been through a screening process. There's nothing to talk about." The President had made a group-status identification, as far as he was concerned. To Addington, it was a matter of presidential power, not a question of individual guilt or innocence.

Gonzales, as usual, didn't say much. A fellow White House lawyer later related that he studied Gonzales's silences intently for the first few months that they worked together, trying to determine if he was "one of those people who don't talk, because they're so smart they know it all, or one of those people who keep their mouths shut because they haven't got a clue." The lawyer concluded, "He was the latter."

Bellinger left the meeting fuming. He'd been ambushed. He and Gordon had argued that the American public understands that wars are confusing and exceptional things happen. "But the American public will expect some due process," they said. They had gotten nowhere. Rice, at this point, had ceded issues involving detainee policy to the lawyers, so she was of little help. Her deputy, Stephen Hadley, was mildly sympathetic but did nothing about it. The report was sent to the Pentagon. There was even less interest over there. Rumsfeld's disdain for detainee issues became legendary inside the administration.

Early on, President Bush asked the National Security Council to run a "disposition process," to figure out who was in Guantánamo and how they should be handled. It became the PCC—Policy Coordinating Committee on detainee affairs. It was cochaired by Bellinger and Elliott Abrams until 2003, when Abrams, a National Security Council deputy, was reassigned, leaving Bellinger in charge. It was supposed to include top assistants to the Secretaries of Defense, State,

Justice, and the CIA. It met twice a week, on Mondays and Thursdays. But it was soon clear that the Pentagon did not care to be "coordinated." Rumsfeld declared that he reported only to the President. He didn't want the NSC or anyone else telling him what to do with the detainees. One of the representatives from the Pentagon later revealed that his directions were to obfuscate and be as uncooperative as possible.

At one such PCC meeting, a counterterrorism expert from the FBI gave his own assessment of the situation in Guantánamo. It was even more startling than that from the CIA. A source at the meeting recalled that the FBI expert told the assembled Bush legal team that in his view, there were no more than fifty detainees worth holding in Guantánamo. After throwing his energy into the cause, naming names of the wrongly imprisoned and getting them to the top lawyer in the White House, the CIA analyst had only been able to free four captives from Guantánamo, including two men thought to be in their eighties, one of whom was deaf.

Rice, meanwhile, began to raise the subject of Guantánamo during full NSC meetings with the principals, as she became increasingly aware that detainee problems were not just questions for the lawyers but a growing international relations fiasco. Rumsfeld, who evinced little respect for Rice, was often sarcastic and dismissive. He stonewalled suggestions that foreign allies be allowed to visit detainees from their own countries in order to quiet their concerns. "For the first six to nine months, the whole world was excluded," a White House critic said. The exclusion allowed even America's closest ally, Great Britain, to call the notorious prison camp, in the famous phrase of Law Lord Johan Steyn, "a legal black hole." When Rumseld finally relented, he grumbled that he would only allow foreign visits for "intelligence," not consular purposes, and then "they have to pay their own way." Attempts to improve the living conditions for the detainees were a constant irritant to him. Bellinger suggested that the detainees be given something to read, preferably books portraying more positive views of America than most of the jihadis had encountered. "Don't you think you should do something to reeducate these people?" he asked.

"If you want to reeducate people, get the Department of Education!" Rumsfeld shot back. A frustrated former White House official said, "He didn't get it, that defense included their mind-set."

Before long, Rumsfeld simply refused to attend NSC meetings

about Guantánamo. Even Cheney, who had more sway with Rumsfeld than anyone else, having been his ally since the Ford Administration, failed when asked by Rice to help get the Secretary of Defense to deal with the nettlesome topic. In an effort to entrap him, Rice secretly appended the subject onto a meeting about another issue in which Rumsfeld had an interest. "OK, we're switching to detainee issues," she announced, at which point Rumsfeld got up to leave. "Don," she asked, "where are you going?"

"I don't do detainees," he said, walking out.

Rather than heeding the cautionary warnings about detaining the wrong suspects, starting in the summer of 2002 the Department of Defense pushed for greater "flexibility" in Guantánamo to interrogate the detainees more forcefully. It was understandable that in the midst of the confusion and upset surrounding September 11, large and damaging mistakes would be made. But what is less comprehensible is the intransigence, and even belligerence, with which unbiased evidence of error was met months and even years later. Those who shared the goal of defeating terrorism, but saw the administration's extreme response as shortsighted and self-defeating, were shunned and excluded. Meanwhile, the sense of peril inside the top rungs of the administration fed on itself.

"There was tremendous pressure to get results," recalled Colonel Brittain Mallow. "Guantánamo was supposed to be the strategic interrogation center. We were supposed to find Bin Laden. We all expected the next attack. This was our best hope to make a difference—quickly." Mallow, a stiffly correct but deeply thoughtful former military police officer who rose to become the second in command in the Army's detective bureau, earning an advanced degree in Middle East studies and a proficiency in Arabic along the way, became the leader of a unique military task force after September 11, in charge of preparing the criminal cases against detainees for the anticipated military trials. Known as the Criminal Investigative Task Force, or CITF, it was an amalgam of elite military and law-enforcement personnel based in Fort Belvoir in the Washington area.

The CITF worked under the Pentagon's auspices but followed a different chain of command from that of the military interrogators stationed down in Guantánamo, who reported to the Southern Command's Task Force-170. While the CITF was questioning the detainees for evidence of prosecutable crimes, the regular military interrogators were looking for intelligence about ongoing threats. Each had their own mission and their own rules. The CITF was scrupulous in following procedures to gather evidence that could stand up eventually in a legal proceeding. The military interrogators needed only to stop future attacks. It was another version of the "cops" against the "intel" teams. But because they worked so closely together on the same pool of suspects, the CITF had an unusually good vantage point to peer into the most hidden interrogation chambers in Guantánamo, and increasingly what they saw alarmed them.

In the summer of 2002, just as the CIA was secretly subjecting Abu Zubayda to previously criminal mistreatment, the military, too, began to ask the Justice Department for permission to go beyond previous limits. The military's traditional doctrine for acceptable interrogation tactics was spelled out in the *Army Field Manual*, which explicitly forbade torture and other abuse. The field manual warned that coercion produced "unreliable results," including false confessions. The field manual was not legally binding. But the Uniform Code of Military Justice was. It prohibited U.S. forces from engaging in "cruelty," "maltreatment," or "oppression" of prisoners in any way. It also treated both physical assault and threats of injury as felonies, whether they were committed in the course of interrogation or not. But these rules soon became casualties of the paradigm shift in Washington.

Later, when confronted with incontrovertible evidence of criminal behavior such as was captured in the photographs of Abu Ghraib, the Bush Administration steadfastly insisted that it had no policy of military abuse. In the spring of 2005, for instance, Vice Admiral Albert T. Church III released a 368-page report, most of which remains classified, concluding that there was "no link between approved interrogation techniques and detainee abuse." When cruelties did occur, the report claimed, they were rare mishaps, the result of combat stress and insufficient training, or a "breakdown of good order and discipline." The Bush Administration has held this line through some dozen investigations.

But documents and inside accounts from Guantánamo tell a very different story, suggesting that with remarkable speed, the SERE techniques secretly approved only for the CIA's use on Abu Zubayda migrated to America's military interrogators as well. By the fall of 2002, the U.S. military in Guantánamo was subjecting prisoners to treatment that would have been unimaginable, and prosecutable, before

September 11. The trademark techniques of the SERE program soon popped up in Guantánamo and other U.S. military prisons holding suspects from the war on terror around the globe. Hooding, stress positions, sleep deprivation, temperature extremes, and psychological ploys designed to induce humiliation and fear suddenly seemed legion. Michael Gelles, the chief clinical forensic psychologist for the Navy's Criminal Investigative Service, who was assigned to aid the CITF, had a ringside view of this. He explained that the community of military and intelligence experts who have classified clearance to interrogate terrorists is small and ingrown. "It's a community where people communicate with each other, and there's a lot of sharing of information," he said. The extraordinary legal authority granted by the president to the CIA may have been intended only for a handful of exceptional cases. But, said Gelles, the reverse-engineering of SERE techniques was "like a germ. It spread."

The immediate cause for ratcheting up the military's techniques was a twenty-six-year-old Saudi detainee who, by late spring of 2002, had been identified as one of the few held in Guantánamo who were of genuine interest. His name was Mohammed Mani' Ahmad Sha'Lan al-Qahtani, but American officials merely referred to him as "detainee number 063." For months, he claimed to know nothing about Al Qaeda, and the military authorities were clueless about who he was. All that was known was that he had been captured near Tora Bora in Afghanistan in December 2001, which was a suspicious time and place for any Saudi national to be.

Detainee 063 remained anonymous for seven months. He claimed he'd been in Afghanistan to pursue an interest in falconry. But in July 2002, visiting FBI agents ran a routine fingerprint analysis on 063 and discovered that the pattern of whorls on his thumb matched the print of a long-sought Saudi suspect who had made an unsuccessful attempt to get through U.S. customs a month before September 11. The wanted Saudi man had a surly manner, a one-way ticket, and $2,800 in cash—barely enough to pay for a return ticket. When pressed, he had refused to identify where he was staying or who was picking him up at the airport. On August 3, 2001, an astute customs agent in Orlando, Florida, said the man gave him an unsettling feeling. On the grounds that the Saudi might be an illegal immigrant, he refused him entry into America. Through an interpreter, the Saudi vowed menacingly, "I'll be back."

As soon as the identification was made, FBI counterterrorism experts flew to Guantánamo to find out more. They knew already that on the same day that 063 was refused entry, a phone call had been placed from the Orlando Airport to one of the central Al Qaeda telephone numbers they were monitoring, in the United Arab Emirates. The FBI agents then obtained surveillance camera footage for that day of all the airport parking lots and, with meticulous detective work, identified the rental car driven by September 11 ringleader Mohammed Atta, who had apparently come to pick up Qahtani.

Impressive though the police work was, the evidence against 063 was merely circumstantial. It seemed likely that he was the fabled twentieth hijacker, suspected of having been meant to round out the team of four on United Airlines Flight 93. It was the flight on which the passengers had valiantly overpowered the hijackers, crashing in Pennsylvania and thereby sparing its alleged intended destination, the U.S. Capitol. The three other hijacking teams each consisted of five men, fueling theories that one "muscle" man was missing.

Now that the case looked serious, sources said that the FBI sent Ali Soufan, the same agent who had absented himself in disgust from the CIA's mistreatment of Abu Zubayda. Born in Lebanon, Soufan was one of only eight FBI agents who spoke Arabic fluently in 2001. He was also a Muslim who had steeped himself in the details of Islamic extremism, rocketing to the top of the Bureau's terrorism investigations before reaching the age of thirty. An admirer of Khalil Gibran, he was of a philosophic bent and loved to argue religion and politics with terror suspects, drawing them out in the process. He would sit on the floor and drink tea with them, and learn about their families and their concerns. "Ali was phenomenal, and he was making lots of progress on Qahtani," recalled Gelles, who knew Soufan from the *Cole* investigation, which he had worked on, too. "But he wasn't moving fast enough for the intelligence community."

By September, the FBI had reportedly ascertained that Qahtani had in fact intended to join the other hijackers. Qahtani had also reportedly disclosed that he had attended the key Malaysia planning meeting in 2000, along with the two future hijackers who had afterward slipped into America, unknown to the FBI. He also had mentioned a relative living near Chicago whom U.S. officials were subsequently able to identify as Ali Saleh Kahlah al-Marri, an alleged "sleeper cell" agent who was already in U.S. custody as a material witness. Al-Marri was subsequently declared an "enemy combatant" and imprisoned without access to a lawyer in the U.S. naval brig in Charleston, South Carolina.

As Gelles, the Navy psychologist, observed, top Pentagon officials were increasingly desperate for actionable intelligence on pending Al Qaeda attacks. They worried that Qahtani's relative in Chicago may have been part of a planned "second wave." If so, they felt enormous pressure to prevent it quickly, and they doubted that sitting on the floor, drinking tea and praying, was going to get the information fast enough. In April, a terrorist attack had destroyed a synagogue in Tunisia, and in June, the U.S. consulate in Karachi had been attacked. Al Qaeda appeared more threatening than ever. U.S. officials believed the suspect was hiding more, and that tougher measures were called for to make him talk. The military's intelligence experts thought that he had been professionally trained in resistance. They were familiar with a terrorist training book known as the "Manchester Manual" for its place of discovery, which outlined instructions for resistance after capture, including false claims of abuse and torture. They believed Qahtani's refusal to provide more details on future attacks, and about the network he had tried to join in the United States,was part of a well-rehearsed cover-up. Experts on resistance were consulted, which in the military meant SERE personnel.

By late summer, both the FBI agents visiting Guantánamo and the investigators working on the CITF began to hear bizarre and disturbing accounts of late-night interrogations using pounding music, bright strobe lights, extremely painful temperatures, dogs, and other oddities. The head supervisor of the military interrogation teams was a civilian with the Defense Intelligence Agency named Dave Becker. Formerly a U.S. Army interrogator, Becker hailed from a small town in Kansas and, according to a Pentagon adviser, brought with him a "fanatical commitment to a John Wayne kind of outlook. Ball-and-chain stuff was what they believed in. Anything else was considered soft." Neither Becker nor the DIA would comment on his previously unacknowledged role in supervising the most abusive interrogations in Guantánamo. But in a redacted statement to Army investigators, Becker admitted authorizing guards to stop one detainee from shouting by taping the prisoner's mouth shut with duct tape. When he kept shouting, Becker authorized the guards to wrap more tape around his head and beard, "as a control measure," he said, until the prisoner was partially covered, like the "Invisible Man." Other guards flocked in to watch with amusement, the documents show. At around the same time, the FBI and CITF investigators noticed, Qahtani shut down and stopped talking completely.

Bush Administration officials have described the escalation of cruelty in Guantánamo as a bottom-up movement, instigated by frustrated interrogators at the Navy base who were dissatisfied with the answers from Qahtani, among others. Rumsfeld sounded befuddled later when asked by military investigators if he had any inkling that his policies had caused abuse on the base. "My God, you know, did I authorize putting a bra and underwear on this guy's head?" he asked in disbelief.

But documents and interviews suggest that Rumsfeld and others at the highest levels of the Pentagon were closely involved in Qahtani's case from late 2002 on. In a sworn statement to military investigators, Major General Dunlavey, who was the base's commander in Guantánamo until November 8, 2002, described close and constant contact between himself and Rumsfeld. The Secretary of Defense personally chose Dunlavey for the job after interviewing him, and Dunlavey said he was asked to fly up to Washington every week to brief Rumsfeld in person on the intelligence progress in Guantánamo. Dunlavey also noted that although he was initially told he would report through the Southern Command, which in turn would report to the Joint Chiefs of Staff, "the directions changed and I got my marching orders directly from the President of the United States."

The relationship of Dunlavey's successor, Major General Geoffrey Miller, with Rumsfeld was described as equally close. Rumsfeld was "personally involved" in Qahtani's interrogation, according to Lieutenant General Randall Schmidt, an Air Force fighter pilot who interviewed the Secretary of Defense twice in connection with a 2005 Army Inspector General's investigation into abuse in Guantánamo.

In addition, the highest-ranking civilian leaders of the Pentagon, including Rumsfeld's top lawyer, William Haynes, received a stream of information—some of it quite disconcerting—as early as the summer of 2002 about abuse of detainees in Guantánamo, according to several sources who were directly involved. In a series of Pentagon meetings that summer, members of the CITF said they began to raise questions about reports they were hearing concerning potentially criminal mistreatment of detainees down in Guantánamo. The CITF investigators were often in Guantánamo and also had access to computer drives showing the detainees' interrogation logs.

Brittain Mallow, the commander of the task force, recalled raising objections in at least one meeting with Haynes about what was going on. Mallow said that also present was Marshall Billingslea, the acting Assistant Secretary of Defense for Special Operations and Low-Intensity Conflicts. Mallow announced in the meeting that he had forbidden his staff from participating with the military interrogators because he feared their tactics were illegal. It was a signal of very serious wrongdoing. He said he also told Haynes and others at the meeting that coercion was counterproductive and produced unreliable intelligence. "It's immoral, unethical, and it won't get good results," Mallow recalled saying.

"You don't know what you're talking about," Billingslea retorted, according to Mallow. "I've talked to the people overseas and they're getting good results," Mallow recalled Billingslea saying. Mallow took this to be a reference to the CIA. Billingslea was a political appointee whose background was in far-right-wing circles on Capitol Hill, where he had worked for Senator Jesse Helms.

Haynes said little, revealing no point of view as the debate played out in front of him. But Mallow concluded that Haynes knew more about the coercion than he was letting on. "They didn't want to make it known to us, but they told us they had authorization. They also told us we had nothing to say about it. We would say we do [have standing to criticize this], because what you're doing is wrong. There were a lot of e-mails."

It is unclear what legal guidance Haynes sought when weighing the worrisome complaints filtering up from Guantánamo. But according to a former Defense Department lawyer at the time, Haynes spoke frequently with both John Yoo, with whom he played squash, and with Michael Chertoff, who was then the head of the Justice Department's Criminal Division. In discussions about the military's interrogation guidelines, the lawyer heard that Chertoff not only approved questionable details in the treatment of Qahtani, he also had hinted that the Pentagon's tactics were nowhere near the legal line in comparison with the far more aggressive program run by the CIA.

The boasts of miraculous CIA breakthroughs with "enhanced" interrogation techniques clearly had reached the Pentagon. The news arrived at a particularly raw moment in the rivalry between the two bureaucracies. Rumsfeld had already been pushed aside by the CIA when the President gave the Agency the lead role in Afghanistan. He had also lost custody of the most valuable Al Qaeda detainees, whom the Agency had culled from the hordes at Bagram. As soon as the CIA learned of Qahtani's part in the September 11 plot, Tenet started arguing that the CIA should get Qahtani, too. Rumsfeld refused to relinquish him. The custody squabble escalated, growing so bitter, according to a White House source, that Tenet and Rumsfeld squared off on it face-to-face, with Rice having to mediate like a divorce court judge.

The Pentagon won the round, but the source said, "They felt as if they didn't do a better job, they might have to turn Qahtani over to the CIA. They wanted to show they could be successful. That's when the silly stuff started."

Dave Becker, the overseer of much of Qahtani's treatment, who was chief of the "Interrogation Control Element" in Guantánamo until December 2002, also claimed that the problem began at the top. His shifting of blame was, of course, self-serving. But when asked later by investigators with the Department of Defense why he let Qahtani be humiliated and abused, Becker pointed upward in the chain of command. "Many of the aggressive interrogation techniques," he claimed, were "a direct result of the pressure we felt from Washington to obtain intelligence and the lack of policy guidance being issued from Washington."

Most of the military interrogators in Guantánamo were young and inexperienced, with only six weeks of training at the Army's Fort Huachuca, Arizona, interrogation course, where they were taught techniques crafted not for the war on terror, but for the Cold War. "They had miserable, miserable success," Gelles the Navy psychologist said. Having worked on the *Cole* bombing case in 2000 and earlier terrorism cases, he had been grappling with how to unlock Islamic extremists' minds for some time. He believed Arabs were more elliptical and indirect in their way of communicating, requiring more patience and sophisticated cultural sensitivity. He also thought the terror suspects were better understood as criminals and fanatics than as soldiers, so he had little use for the *Army Field Manual*'s approaches, which were geared toward getting tactical information. Military questioners were prompted to ask incessantly, and fruitlessly, "Where is Bin Laden?" The problem, he thought, was that the military "had no understanding of the psychology of the adversary."

Gelles helped to put together what was called a behavioral science consultation team, or BSCT, in order to help guide the CITF in understanding the suspects they were intended to charge. It involved psychologists such as himself, a psychiatrist, as well as other professionals trained in deviant behavior and cultural anthropology. "It was to get into the heads of the suspects," Mallow explained.

When General Dunlavey learned about the approach, he was so enamored of the idea, according to the CITF officials, he copied it, building his own BSCT, or as they were called in the military's jargon, "Biscuit." But unlike Gelles, who believed psychologists had to stay clear of participating inside the interrogation chambers in order not to violate universal codes of medical ethics, Dunlavey soon drafted military psychologists to play direct roles in breaking detainees down. The psychologists were both treating the detainees clinically and advising interrogators on how to manipulate them and exploit their phobias, according to complaints later lodged by some of the detainees' lawyers.

By September, military officials held a series of brainstorming meetings in Guantánamo about how to crack through the resistance of detainees such as Qahtani. One source of ideas was the popular television show *24*. The fictional drama was written by a Hollywood conservative who had no military or intelligence expertise whatsoever. But on Guantánamo, as everywhere else in America, its macho hero, Jack Bauer, who tortured his enemies until they talked, was followed with admiration. On *24*, torture always worked. It saved America on a weekly basis. In conversation with British human rights lawyer Philippe Sands, the top military lawyer in Guantánamo, Diane Beaver, said quite earnestly that Jack Bauer "gave people lots of ideas" as they sought for interrogation models that fall. Beaver explained that even in Guantánamo, "We saw it on cable . . . It was hugely popular."

The other source of wisdom was the military's SERE program, which insiders on the base believed had been the secret of the CIA's ostensible success. By September, Gelles recalled the military command down in Guantánamo saying, "There's this stuff that the CIA does—and it works!"

"We universally thought it was ludicrous," said Mallow. He and the other Criminal Task Force investigators tended to be older and far more experienced than their counterparts on Joint Task Force-170. They knew more not just about the Middle East, but also about how to question terror suspects. They also thought the variations of physical and psychological torture, reenacted in the program under scrupulously controlled circumstances, could become dangerous quickly. A dynamic called "force drift," in which a small amount of force soon leads to more and more, was well documented in the literature on interrogations. "SERE is a training regimen—it's not designed to produce a truthful response," said Mallow. "Without the limits set by training—where do you stop?" he asked. "It just becomes coercion, or whatever you want to call it."

Gelles, who had personal contacts among the military psychologists, called the head psychologist for the Army's SERE program at Fort Bragg, Colonel Louie (Morgan) Banks, and asked, "What is this crap?" Having grown up in the Bronx and bounced around the world from one twisted criminal case to the next, Gelles was blunt and tough. He said Banks sounded concerned about the misuse of the program. But Gelles concluded later, "He was talking out of both sides of his mouth."

In fact, on September 16, Banks cohosted a delegation of Guantánamo interrogators sent by Dunlavey to a SERE conference at Fort Bragg. It was run by the Joint Personnel Recovery Agency, which administers the training program for the military. The visitors were supposed to learn "which SERE techniques might be useful in interrogations in Guantánamo," a military investigation later found. Further confirmation that the Guantánamo interrogators were trained in the totalitarian torture methods came from a reservist named Ted Moss, who followed Becker as the chief of the "Interrogation Control Element" on the island. "My predecessor," he said, "arranged for SERE instructors to teach their techniques to interrogators at GTMO."

Banks, who had a Ph.D. in psychology from the University of Southern Mississippi and was a member of an American Psychological Association's task force on psychological ethics and national security, emphatically denied later that he had advocated the use of the torture-based techniques to break down detainees. When asked about the similarities that emerged between SERE training methods and interrogation practices at Guantánamo, he nonetheless acknowledged that it may have happened after all. "I'm not saying people don't do some stupid things sometimes. Some people who received SERE training may have sometimes done things they shouldn't because they misunderstood what the training was about. I'm not going to tell you it didn't happen. I can't say that someone didn't say, 'Hey, let's try waterboarding' because they'd seen it at SERE."

On their return to Cuba from Fort Bragg, the interrogators' discussions continued. They were brimming with new ideas. The military team drafted a wish list of techniques that they would like to try on hard cases like Qahtani. Beaver, who was one of the few women in attendance during these sessions, surveyed the room full of excited young males growing "glassy eyed," as she put it, about how aggressive they planned to get, and said, "You could almost see their dicks getting hard as they got new ideas."

Into this feverish atmosphere flew a sleek Gulfstream jet filled with some of the most important lawyers in the Bush Administration on September 26, 2002. The group included several members of the War Council from Washington on a road trip to see Guantánamo. The "guy in charge," according to Beaver, seemed to be David Addington. With him were the President's lawyer, Alberto Gonzales, as well as Rumsfeld's top counsel, William J. "Jim" Haynes II, and John Rizzo, a dapper, elfish-looking, white-haired man with manicured fingernails who was then the number-two lawyer at the CIA. Also along were two Justice Department lawyers, Alice Fisher, who became the head of the Criminal Division but was then a top aide to Chertoff, and Patrick Philbin, the close associate of John Yoo in the Office of Legal Counsel. Less well known at the time was an owlish-looking lawyer in the General Counsel's Office at the Pentagon, Jack Goldsmith, who turned forty that day.

During their VIP tour, the Bush legal team surveyed the new prison barracks, Camp Delta. As they inspected the rows of mesh cells, lined up like kennels, some of the detainees stared back with a smoldering hatred the intensity of which Goldsmith said he'd never before experienced in his life. The lawyers also talked with the military officials and observed an interrogation or two. According to Beaver, they already seemed to know all about Qahtani. What to do next with him was the burning question. General Dunlavey said later that Addington asked particularly about Qahtani, wanting to know how the military was "managing" his case. Clearly, Qahtani's controversial interrogation was not the freelance work of amateurs—it was the result of a careful plan unfolded under the watchful eye of the most senior lawyers in the Bush Administration, Cheney's counsel chief among them.

On their way home, the legal delegation stopped in to see two other penitentiaries used in the war on terror. They flew to Charleston, South Carolina, to observe Jose Padilla, the American whom Abu Zubayda had identified as an Al Qaeda operative. After his May 8, 2002, arrest he had been moved to the naval brig. After that, they flew on to

Norfolk, Virginia, where they caught a glimpse of another American citizen incarcerated without charges or access to a lawyer, Yaser Hamdi, who had been captured fighting for the Taliban along with John Walker Lindh. Hamdi, who had dual citizenship with Saudi Arabia, had been held in isolation for some six months. The legal team was only allowed to observe him remotely, by surveillance camera.

There was a theory governing the extreme isolation of both Padilla and Hamdi, which had been articulated by administration lawyers during their court appearances. Its lineage lay in the Cold War behavioral experiments of the CIA, and it explained a lot about the purpose of Guantánamo, too. In Padilla's case, it was articulated by Vice Admiral Lowell Jacoby, Director of the Defense Intelligence Agency, and in Hamdi's case, Colonel Donald Woolfolk, who was then the acting commander of the prison at Guantánamo Bay, had given the court a similar declaration. Both had explained that, foremost, the detention program was aimed at holding the suspects not for punishment or for trial, but rather for gathering intelligence. Woolfolk argued that the loss of this vital information, "in any respect," would prove "crippling to the national security of the United States." Second, the administration believed that in order to succeed in harvesting this intelligence, the detainees had to be kept in "an atmosphere of dependency and trust between subject and interrogator," which required hermetic isolation from any human contact other than with the interrogators. For this reason, neither lawyers nor the Red Cross could be allowed access. Nor could the detainee have communication of any sort with anyone else in the outside world. "Even seemingly minor interruptions can have profound psychological impacts on the delicate subject-interrogator relationship," Jacoby declared.

Hamdi turned twenty-two the day that the Bush legal team visited, sharing his birthday with Goldsmith. As the lawyers viewed Hamdi on the closed-circuit screen, curled in a fetal position in his cell, Goldsmith felt uneasy. Perhaps the connection of their shared birthday, or just the sight on the fuzzy screen of a living person rather than a foreign name, or often just a number, caused a pang of empathy. Like the others, Goldsmith was very conservative. He had no sympathy for Hamdi's pro-Taliban past. Still, he later wrote, "something seemed wrong. It seemed unnecessarily extreme to hold a twenty-two year old foot soldier in a remote wing of a run-down prison in a tiny cell, isolated from almost all human contact and with no access to a lawyer." Goldsmith admitted to thinking, "This is what habeas corpus is for." It was a measure of the Bush Administration, and the terrible time, that he also admitted to being embarrassed for having such a "squishy" sentiment about the bedrock legal procedure for challenging one's imprisonment on which constitutional law had rested since the nobles defeated England's tyrannical King John at Runnymede in 1215.

That fall, Solicitor General Theodore Olson, a leader of the conservative legal movement, had similar misgivings about the sustainability of the administration's extreme position on Padilla and Hamdi. Olson feared, accurately as it turned out, that the Supreme Court would overturn the administration's arguments. But Addington, who made clear that he was representing Vice President Cheney's views, refused to modify the orders to keep these two American suspects in complete isolation, without access to legal counsel, indefinitely. Gonzales sided with Addington, who prevailed.

Goldsmith, meanwhile, was struck with another insight, which would prove as prescient as his concerns about habeas corpus. While the administration could argue that it had the legal authority to impose such frighteningly extreme measures in the war on terror, such legalistic reasoning was a poor substitute for political judgment. Perhaps Cheney and Addington were right that the commander in chief could override every other check and balance in a state of emergency. But that scarcely meant it was wise to do so. Such views were not widely shared among the Bush national security team, which coincidentally was readying another Gulfstream jet that same day—September 26—to fly Maher Arar against his will to Jordan, bound for torture in Syria.

On October 11, 2002, the military officials down in Guantánamo asked Rumsfeld for permission to use the new list of eighteen harsher interrogation techniques they had compiled in their brainstorming sessions. The list bore the distinct imprint of the CIA's Cold War–era *KUBARK Manual* of psychological manipulation, including variations of sensory deprivation such as prolonged isolation, removal of clothing, and hooding, to forms of "no-touch" or "self-imposed" pain, such as shackling in stress positions and forced standing, psychological torment including religious and sexual humiliation, exploitation of the detainee's phobias (such as a fear of dogs) to induce stress, and "scenarios designed to convince the detainee that death or severely painful consequences are imminent for him and/or his family." The

David Addington, Vice President Dick Cheney's chief of staff, in the East Room of the White House. *Photo by Mandel Ngan/AFP/ Getty Images.*

Vice President Dick Cheney, CIA Director George Tenet, President George W. Bush, and White House Chief of Staff Andy Card (from left to right) discuss military action in Iraq in the Oval Office in 2003. *Photo by Eric Draper/The White House/Getty Images.*

J. Cofer Black, the former director of the CIA's Counterterrorist Center and later the State Department, in Manila at the National Intelligence Coordinating Agency in 2003. *Photo by Jay Directo/ AFP/ Getty Images.*

Former Department of Defense General Counsel William Haynes testifies before the Senate Armed Services Committee about the detention and trial of detainees in December 2001. Former Deputy Secretary of Defense Paul Wolfowitz listens. *Photo by Alex Wong/Getty Images.*

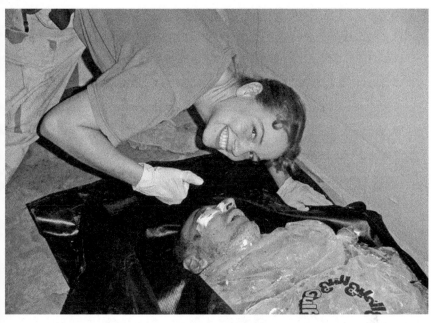

Sabrina Harmon, a soldier in the 372nd Military Police Company, poses in front of the body of Manadel al-Jamadi at Abu Ghraib prison. *Photo via ABC News and Getty Images.*

Maher Arar plays with his children at home in Ottawa in January 2004. The Syrian-born Canadian was deported to and tortured in Syria under the United States's extraordinary rendition program. *Photo by Bill Grimshaw/Getty Images.*

Khaled el-Masri holds a news conference at the National Press Club regarding his case against former CIA director George Tenet in November 2006. *Photo by Chip Somodevilla/Getty Images.*

Senator John McCain at a hospital in Hanoi after his capture by the North Vietnamese in November 1967. He spent more than five years as a prisoner of war, experiencing periods of intense interrogation and torture. *Photo by Getty Images.*

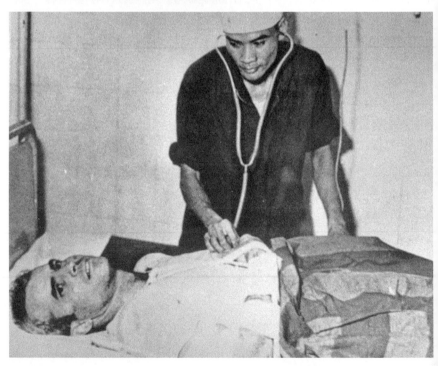

Guantánamo-detainee lawyers Michael Ratner, Thomas Wilner, and Joe Margulies (from left to right) brief the press in Washington in December 2002. *Photo by Stephen Jaffe/AFP/ Getty Images.*

Secretary of Defense Donald Rumsfeld, President George W. Bush, and Vice President Dick Cheney at the Pentagon in December 2006. *Photo by Charles Ommanney/Getty Images.*

Colonel Lawrence Wilkerson, former Chief of Staff to Secretary of State Colin Powell, testifies before the Senate Democratic Policy Committee about the invasion of Iraq in June 2006. *Photo by Chip Somodevilla/ Getty Images.*

John Yoo, professor of law at Boalt Hall, the University of California, speaks at the Heritage Foundation, a conservative think tank, in Washington in February 2006. *Photo by Mandel Ngan/AFP/Getty Images.*

Handcuffs in an interrogation cell in the maximum-security unit of Camp Delta, in Guantánamo Bay. *Photo by Mark Wilson/Getty Images.*

Colonel Steve Kleinman (right) and Brigadier General Joe Shaefer, a retired Air Force officer, both served as interrogators during Operation Desert Storm. *Photo by Sherry Tesler.*

British lawyer Clive Stafford Smith, who specializes in death-penalty and civil-rights cases, has filed lawsuits on behalf of more than 100 Guantánamo detainees. *Photo by Ian Robins.*

(Top left) Alberto Mora, former General Counsel of the U.S. Navy, argued that the Bush Administration's harsh interrogation practices at Guantánamo were wrong. *Photo by Alen MacWeeney for The New Yorker.*

(Top right) Jack Goldsmith, who served under James Comey and John Ashcroft at the Office of Legal Counsel, now teaches at Harvard Law School. *Photo courtesy of Harvard Law School.*

(Bottom) Jim Clemente (center), an FBI agent, receives a Human Rights First award for an episode of the CBS series *Criminal Minds* about legal interrogation methods. He appears with *Criminal Minds'* Andrew Wilder (right) and actor Sam Waterston (left). *Photo by Michael Ian, courtesy of Human Rights First.*

officials also requested permission to use waterboarding and mock executions.

Lieutenant Colonel Diane Beaver, who was then the top legal adviser in Guantánamo and who had helped compile the list, wrote a memo to superiors arguing that these more aggressive approaches were necessary and potentially legal, despite her unease with Guantánamo's atmosphere of overheated machismo. There were two keys to circumventing the criminal codes. The first was the importance of appearing to be acting with a pure "intent." Waterboarding, she wrote, might "be permissible if not done with the specific intent to cause prolonged mental harm, and absent medical evidence that it would." She added, "Caution should be exercised with this method, as foreign courts have already advised about the potential mental harm that this method may cause." The other way to engage in what were normally considered criminal acts, she suggested, was to get immunity from "command authorities," not after the fact, but before a crime had been committed. But without this get-out-of-jail-free card, she warned, some of the physical contact they requested with detainees "will technically constitute an assault under . . . UCMJ."

It was a novel theory. A senior Defense Department official later called Beaver's legal argument inventive. "Normally, you grant immunity after the fact, to someone who has already committed a crime, in exchange for an order to get that person to testify," he said. "I don't know whether we've ever faced the question of immunity in advance before." Nevertheless, the official praised Beaver "for trying to think outside the box. I would credit Diane as raising that as a way to think about it." (Beaver was later promoted to the staff of the Pentagon's Office of General Counsel, where she specialized in detainee issues.)

Beaver's memo was sent first to General James Hill of the U.S. Southern Command. Rather than approving the harsh techniques himself, which would be politically risky, Hill sent the request up the chain of command, in search of "top cover." He wrote to General Richard B. Myers, the Chairman of the Joint Chiefs of Staff, that he was "uncertain whether all the techniques" were "legal." He expressed concern that some of them might violate the federal statute against torture as well as the Uniform Code of Military Justice.

When the request reached Jim Haynes, however, he of course had just returned from Guantánamo, where the top Bush lawyers had discussed the Qahtani case in person with Beaver. His consent wasn't in question. He advised Rumsfeld that all of the techniques were legal. But Haynes added that, in his opinion, waterboarding and mock execution were "not warranted at this time." His later account of his part in authorizing the U.S. military to treat prisoners worse than they had ever been allowed to in the country's history omitted his earlier trip to Guantánamo. In the summer of 2006, during the Senate Judiciary Committee's confirmation hearings on his nomination to the Fourth Circuit Federal Appeals Court, Haynes implied repeatedly that rather than being an instigator, he had been a passive latecomer to the debate on torture, who had merely responded in November to a request from "an aggressive Major General" (Miller) in Guantánamo.

As the paperwork was making its way through a tiny, handpicked channel of Pentagon lawyers, a team of interrogators in Guantánamo went to work on Qahtani. The team was staffed by the Defense Intelligence Agency and supervised by Becker, according to previously secret documents. Gelles, who saw a proposed plan detailing what was in store, recalled saying, "Whoa!"

At this point, a remarkable internal rebellion broke out on the island. It was led not by political opponents of the Bush Administration, nor by human rights activists, but rather by seasoned professional law-enforcement and military men who were appalled at the direction the government was taking. At the helm was Jim Clemente, a thin, intense special agent with distinctively angular features, from the FBI's Behavioral Analysis Unit in Quantico, Virginia. He had been working in Guantánamo since October, and almost from the start had been trying tirelessly to halt what he believed was likely to become the criminal abuse of Qahtani.

Clemente brought unusual credentials to the task. He had a law degree and had previously been a prosecutor in New York. Interestingly, given his attempt to stop mistreatment, his area of expertise prior to September 11 was child sexual abuse. Victimization of the powerless was something he had thought a lot about. He had other talents, too. He was the role model for Mandy Patinkin's part on the television series *Criminal Minds.* And in 2007, after recovering from lymphoma, he collected a human rights award for an episode of the show that he wrote himself. It was about Guantánamo and featured the successful interrogation of a terrorist who was outsmarted by wit, not brawn. Clemente's real-life star turn in Guantánamo didn't go quite as smoothly.

In a series of conversations and meetings in November 2002, Clemente and several other FBI and Criminal Task Force members confronted General Miller, who by then had taken over the military command. They warned him strongly that the cruel and degrading interrogation approaches under contemplation for Qahtani were "potentially illegal."

Clemente and others had already witnessed disturbing scenes on the island. Several had spied Becker's guards wrapping the obstreperous detainee's head in duct tape. They also saw Qahtani "after he had been subjected to intense isolation for three months," according to an e-mail from one agent to his superiors. The agent wrote, "During that time period, the detainee was totally isolated (with the exception of interrogations) in a cell that was totally flooded with light. By November the detainee was evidencing behavior associated with extreme psychological trauma (talking to non-existent people, hearing voices, crouching in a corner of the cell covered in a sheet for hours on end)."

Contemporaneous e-mails from an FBI agent to superiors say, "On a couple of occasions I entered interview rooms to find a detainee chained hand and foot in a fetal position on the floor, with no chair, food or water. Most times they had urinated or defecated on themselves, and had been left there for 18 or 24 hours or more." The agent related that he had visited an "almost unconscious" prisoner in a room where the temperature was "probably well above 100 degrees." There was "a pile of hair next to him," which he seemed to have pulled out.

Clemente sent an e-mail describing a female interrogator "placing lotion in her hand and touching a detainee's . . . lap," at which point the detainee "grimaced in pain." He also reported deliberate uses of extreme temperatures on detainees, quoting an officer saying that General Miller had declared, "If the Torture Statute says 80 degrees is bad, we will set the thermometer at 79.9 degrees."

The tactics used by the military touched off wrenching debates with the FBI agents in which one agent, who cannot be named, accused the military of criminal behavior. "When I became an agent, I swore to uphold the Constitution against all enemies," the agent argued, "both foreign and domestic." The military officer argued that he was defending the country and the Constitution. "Not the same Constitution that I read," said the agent.

In an effort to encourage less coercive treatment, Clemente and the other critics gave Miller's deputy, Lieutenant Commander Jerald

Phifer, an alternative interrogation plan for Qahtani, which they presented at a meeting. Phifer was "enraged" by what he saw "as the FBI obstructing the military's mission," according to a sworn statement from Clemente. "Lead, follow, or get the fuck out of the way!" he shouted. "Then he proceeded to get in my face, and he took the plan and stormed out of the room," the documents show.

A confrontation with General Miller did not go much better. Miller offered to let the others do the interrogations, but they explained that they had a different role and instead suggested they show the military how to do it better. Miller exploded, saying, "If you want to wear the jersey, you've got to be on the team!"

The FBI refused to allow Clemente to discuss his role, so Clemente could not be interviewed. But many of those who were in Guantánamo with him, and who shared his view, regarded him as an unknown hero in America's war on terror, who tried, at great risk to his own career, to steer the government off a disastrous course. But the warnings evidently went unheeded.

As concern mounted, the FBI agents contacted Marion "Spike" Bowman, head of the FBI's national security law section in Washington. Clemente sent Bowman a scathing legal analysis warning that ten of the eighteen interrogation techniques on the military's wish list were unlawful under the U.S. Constitution. He also warned they could violate the U.S. torture statute. "It's possible that those who employ these techniques may be indicted, prosecuted, and possibly convicted if the trier of fact determines that the user had the requisite intent. Under the circumstances, it is recognized that these techniques not be used." Among the techniques he warned against were hooding, twenty-hour interrogation sessions, the use of military dogs to increase fear, the removal of clothing, and stress positions, all of which would become familiar features of military interrogations in Guantánamo, Afghanistan, and Iraq.

Bowman, who had good contacts in the Pentagon, called two lawyers in Haynes's office, expressing concern. But he never heard back from Haynes or the other lawyers there.

How high inside the FBI the message went is unclear. Through a spokesman, Director Mueller declined interview requests. But weeks after Haynes approved the new severe treatment of detainees, at an elegant Washington dinner party attended by a handful of the city's most prominent litigators, there was an interesting moment of awkwardness. Tom Green, one of the best-known defense lawyers in the capital, turned on Tom Wilner, the Washington law partner representing Kuwaiti detainees, and said he couldn't believe that he was defending terrorists down in Guantánamo. According to Wilner, there was an uncomfortable silence at the table as the convivial holiday mood was broken.

Then, Wilner said, Mueller, who was at the table, stood up. He raised his wineglass and said, "I toast Tom Wilner. He's doing what an American should."

By the winter of 2002, Wilner was quite used to being attacked even by otherwise enlightened colleagues in the legal world. Earlier in the year, he had joined forces with the two death-penalty lawyers, Joe Margulies and Clive Stafford Smith, as well as Michael Ratner of the Center for Consitutional Rights, in filing the first civil motion in the federal district court in Washington on behalf of the next of kin of several Guantánamo detainees, asking for some kind of due process. The case, filed as *Shafiq Rasul and others v. George W. Bush,* didn't challenge the Bush Administration's right to detain the captives as enemy combatants. Nor did it demand that they be tried in the regular court system. But it questioned whether the United States could hold the prisoners without a legal process. It asked for some sort of fair hearing to make sure that they were in fact enemy combatants. It also asked for the detainees to get some legal representation in the proposed process, and some access to their family members.

Wilner did not have the typical résumé of a bomb thrower. He was the managing partner for international trade at the staid corporate law firm Shearman & Sterling. He had attended St. Albans School with Al Gore, and been a fraternity brother of George W. Bush at Yale. He was an athlete, an iconoclast, and a Democrat, but scarcely radical. He lived well in Georgetown, sent his children to the best private schools, and had a social network that reached far into Washington's most exclusive salons. His law practice had taken him all over the world, including to the Middle East. He had represented OPEC at one point. He claimed that when he warned the Saudi clients that he was a Jew, they answered, "Of course! We wanted someone smart!" He said he felt at home with fellow Semites of all religious persuasions, and especially liked the Arab headdress, "because no one knows I'm bald."

Following September 11, after a half dozen other establishment law firms had turned them down, a representative for twelve Kuwaiti families, whose sons had disappeared after the United States started taking prisoners in Afghanistan, contacted Wilner. The Kuwaitis didn't know for sure where their relatives were being held, or by whom. The U.S. government wouldn't confirm whether they had custody of them or not. Without hesitation, Wilner said he was interested. After a trip to Kuwait to meet with the families, he informed the partners' committee at his law firm of his intention to represent this small group of accused terrorists believed to be held by the United States in Guantánamo. It set off a crisis inside the firm. A top partner was so furious, he could barely speak to Wilner. Another was in tears. Several protested that they were patriots and wanted nothing to do with it. "Why should we stick our neck in this thing?" was the general feeling, Wilner recalled. "No one wanted to touch it." Even his wife, Jane, was completely against his getting involved, asking, "God—why do you always have to go against everyone else?"

Wilner said he had been "amazed" at the animosity. "This is what lawyers do," he argued. "They defend the rule of law." He said, "All these people knew how terrible the McCarthy Era was, but here they were all caught up in the hysteria. They should have learned from history that justice doesn't threaten society and fairness doesn't make us weaker. It makes us stronger." He said he knew it sounded "corny," but he felt so strongly about it, he offered the firm his resignation. Shearman & Sterling rejected this but told him that on all filings, and public appearances on behalf of the Guantánamo detainees, Wilner was barred from mentioning the firm's name.

The government responded to the suit forcefully. The Justice Department lawyers argued that not only could the detainees have no access to lawyers, they also could not be notified that a case had been filed on their behalf. As the lawsuit wended its way toward the Supreme Court, the defense lawyers had no means of communicating with their clients, nor, like the rest of the world, any idea what was really going on in Guantánamo.

On November 23, Qahtani was brought in shackles to a plywood interrogation booth, where his hood was removed and he was bolted to the floor. For forty-eight of the next fifty-four consecutive days, he was allowed only four hours of sleep a night. "Sleeping and not paying attention will not be tolerated," he was told on day two. Becker, the DIA officer in charge of Qahtani's interrogation plan, explained later that he had decided that four hours of sleep a night was adequate after reading that in the Army Ranger training program, the Special Forces soldiers were kept up for twenty-hour stretches. The Ranger training, like all SERE programs, however, lasted only a few days. It was also voluntarily entered into. But Becker said, "If it was okay to subject our soldiers to twenty hour days, then in our minds it was okay to subject the terrorist to twenty hour days."

Qahtani was also forced to strip naked, wear a leash, and perform dog tricks. He was forced to wear a bra, and thong underwear on his head. He was deprived of the opportunity to use a toilet after having been force-fed liquids intravenously. By day four, he had become so dehydrated that the Navy corpsmen administering an IV was unable to locate a vein in his arm, causing a doctor to be called to implant a shunt in his hand. In anger, Qahtani bit the IV tube in two. Strapped down afterward, he was given three and a half bags of IV fluid, which caused him to moan for a chance to go to the bathroom. He was told he would be allowed to relieve himself only if he talked first.

Interrogator: "Who do you work for?"

Qahtani: "Al-Qaeda."

Interrogator: "Who was your leader?"

Qahtani: "Osama Bin Laden."

Interrogator: "Why did you go to Orlando?"

Qahtani: "I wasn't told the mission."

Interrogator: "Who was with you on the plane?"

Qahtani: "I was by myself."

Dissatisfied with the answers, the unidentified interrogator then told Qahtani, "You're wasting my time." In punishment, when Qahtani asked for the promised access to a toilet, it was denied. He then urinated on himself.

The day after confessing to working for Al Qaeda, he recanted.

As one twenty-hour day blurred into the next, he was ordered to dance with a male interrogator, straddled by a female interrogator in a gambit called "invasion of space by female," forced to undergo an enema, and strip-searched in front of females. He was also shown provocative photos of scantily clad women, some of which were hung around his neck.

Becker, the supervisor, later explained the rationale behind such sexually humiliating antics. He had heard that "devout Muslims can't pray if they feel 'unclean.' Therefore if the detainee was made to feel 'unclean' he would have to stop praying. One way to make a Muslim male 'unclean' is to be touched by a female." An interrogator was sent to the large convenience store that had burgeoned on the base to buy some cheap perfume—rose oil—which she rubbed on the prisoner. He did stop praying. But he was so enraged that he lunged at the woman, striking his mouth on a chair with such force that it chipped his tooth. Becker related that the detainee had to be taken to the hospital.

Qahtani's end of the conversation ran from taunting and accusatory, telling his interrogators they were "animalistic" and that he would give "answers" only if they questioned him "in the right way," to sobbing uncontrollably and asking questions betraying stunning backwardness. Ignorant of science, he wondered whether the sun revolved around the earth and whether it was true that dinosaurs once lived on the planet.

When the logs of his interrogation were published, the Pentagon argued that Qahtani's interrogation was always "humane." An internal investigation strained not to disagree, proclaiming his treatment "degrading" and "abusive" but, ostensibly, not inhumane. Yet the psychological manipulations, packaged under names such as "You're a Failure Approach," read like the hazing rites of a sadistic fraternity. He was moved in shackles to a room with red lights, where he was required to stand as the National Anthem was played. His head and beard were shaved, and he was also given "a birthday party" in which a party hat was placed on his head while the guards sang "God Bless America." The log notes, "Detainee became very angry." He was also shown a "puppet show" that the logs said satirized his involvement with Al Qaeda. He was subjected to loud music and told that his family was in danger. He was also told that his mother and sister were whores and that he was a homosexual. He was forced to observe foraging banana rats outside his cell, whose status was likened to his. He was made to stand so much that his feet and hands swelled and had to be wrapped in bandages and elevated. He was forced repeatedly to view film footage of the September 11 attacks, as well as photos of the victims, some of which were taped to his pants. At one point, he begged to be allowed to commit suicide, asking for a writing implement to scrawl his last will. On and on it went, day after day, week after week, with the log keeping track with the bureaucratic efficiency of a train schedule.

The logs show clearly that a BSCT psychologist participated in the interrogation, and they reveal that after two weeks of sleep deprivation, Qahtani became ill. A doctor, who was apparently a neurological specialist, was summoned from off the island and the coercion stopped, but even then Qahtani was subjected to noise levels that kept him from sleeping. His heart rate dropped. A brain scan was performed. He was given an ultrasound to check for blood clots; none were found. Dr. Stephen Xenakis, a psychiatrist and former brigadier general in the Army medical corps who was not involved in the interrogation, later questioned whether the doctors assigned to his case notified authorities about how ill the treatment was making Qahtani, as is required by virtually every code of medical ethics. Xenakis said, "The clinical picture indicates that the combined effects of the interrogation over December 4–7 contributed to significant physical and metabolic symptoms such that he required close cardiac monitoring. He is evaluated for 'blood clots' . . . which can be fatal." Xenakis asked whether this carefully monitored interrogation, authorized at the top levels of the Pentagon, put "this patient in danger of dying."

According to Dr. Elena Nightingale, a scholar-in-residence of the Institute of Medicine of the National Academy of Sciences, and the co-editor of a 1985 anthology of essays about doctors and torture, *The Breaking of Bodies and Minds,* medical experts are often called on to assist with torture because "people trust and confide in them, which is useful to torturers, and because they have the know-how to keep a person under torture alive, so that more information can be extracted." Dr. Darryl Matthews, a psychiatrist whom the Army brought in as a consultant after many suicide attempts at Guantánamo, and who became a critic of conditions at the prison camp, said, "As psychiatrists, we know how to hurt people better than others. We can figure out what buttons to push. Like a surgeon with a scalpel, we have techniques and we know what the pressure points are."

Leonard Rubenstein, president of Physicians for Human Rights, described the role of psychologists and medical personnel in the Qahtani interrogation as "conduct that's been considered forbidden for thirty years." Psychologists, he said, are subject to the same standards as medical doctors. "Of course they can't participate in coercive interrogations!" he said. "It's clear as day. You can't advise, you can't develop plans, you can't review interrogations, you can't sign off on them, and you can't even be present in the room."

The role of physicians, who take the Hippocratic oath to "do no harm," is ethically complicated in wartime. Doctors are often described as having "dual loyalties," to patients and to country. But at the Nuremberg trials after World War II, revulsion at Nazi atrocities led to the establishment of rules barring medical mistreatment, even for reasons of national security. A section of the 1950 Geneva Convention, for example, states that "no prisoner of war may be subjected to physical mutilation or to medical or scientific experiments of any kind which are not justified by the medical, dental or hospital treatment of the prisoner concerned." In 1962, the United States passed the first law requiring doctors to obtain "informed consent" from patients. And in 1975, the World Medical Association, or WMA, issued the Declaration of Tokyo, which barred medical personnel from participation in either torture or abuse, even as monitors. The American Medical Association is a member of the WMA, which means that U.S. doctors must follow its ethical standards.

In the absence of the Geneva Conventions, however, the rules grew less clear. In 2005, the Pentagon released a new set of formal ethical guidelines, titled "Medical Program Principles and Procedures for the Protection and Treatment of Detainees in the Custody of the Armed Forces of the United States." The document, which was issued by Dr. William Winkenwerder Jr., then the Assistant Secretary of Defense for Health Affairs, stressed the importance of upholding "the humane treatment of detainees." It stated that "health-care personnel charged with the medical care of detainees" cannot participate in interrogations. In this phrase was embedded a troubling loophole, however: Scientific and medical personnel who were not directly responsible for a patient's care were allowed to take part in interrogations. Rubenstein argued that "the Administration basically gave a green light for medical personnel to participate in abuse."

"Non-treating" professionals were allowed to use their skills to "assist the interrogators," as Winkenwerder put it. They belonged to the behavioral science consultation teams, or "Biscuits," which General Miller ardently championed during his command over Guantánamo, which extended from November 8, 2002, until March 2004. "These teams, comprised of operational behavioral psychologists and psychiatrists, are essential in developing integrated interrogation strategies and assessing interrogation intelligence production," Miller explained in an internal report in September 2003.

A confidential report by the International Committee of the Red Cross, parts of which were leaked to the *Washington Post,* charged that doctors consulted detainee medical records to help interrogators, in a "flagrant violation of medical ethics." A spokesman in Guantánamo said that the Red Cross's charges were wrong, but he added that national security concerns might sometimes justify the breaching of a detainee's medical confidentiality.

Exerting psychic stress was, of course, the goal of the interrogation program. By design, the Guantánamo experiment thus tainted not just the lawyers who became complicit but the medical profession as well. Jonathan Moreno, a biomedical ethicist, worried that for doctors, psychiatrists, psychologists, and other members of the scientific community, "Guantánamo is going to haunt us for a long time." He said, "The Hippocratic oath is the oldest ethical code we have. We might abandon our morality about other professions. But the medical profession is sort of the last gasp. If we give that up, we've given up our core values."

By the end of Qahtani's interrogation, the Pentagon proclaimed that it was all worthwhile. A Defense Department spokesman told *Time* magazine that he had become "a valuable source of information." The *New York Times,* too, quoted an unnamed "senior Bush administration official" saying that the harsher techniques used on Qahtani had produced important information about an unspecified "planned attack" and "financial networks used by terrorists."

But Cal Temple, Chief of Intelligence Operations for the DIA, which supervised and manned much of Qahtani's interrogation, later conceded that all they really got from him was a bit of interesting information that was "contextual in nature, confirming in nature. Did it help catch Osama Bin Laden? No."

Brittain Mallow was more dismissive. He said that eventually Qahtani "gave up a few more nuggets." But Mallow and the FBI officials familiar with the case concluded that essentially what the U.S. government got from Qahtani, after all those weeks of bizarre torment, was confirmation of what they had already learned from conventional detective work earlier. "The value of that whole special plan was minimal," said Mallow, who had complete access to the files. "He only knew about the plan for 9/11. He didn't know where Bin Laden was, or about other plans. In fact, it may have worked against our interests," he concluded, "because it was a waste of time."

The final verdict, ironically, may have been rendered by Qahtani's former Al Qaeda commander. A year and a half after Qahtani's interrogation, when the CIA captured Khalid Sheikh Mohammed, they asked him about the twentieth hijacker. Mohammed, who had organized the September 11 attacks, had no means of checking his testimony with that of Qahtani. Mohammed was snidely condescending about Qahtani, describing him as "too much of an unsophisticated Bedouin," an "extremely simple man" who had no understanding of the Western world. He had not known what a visa was and had trouble with codes. After Qahtani failed to talk his way past U.S. customs, Mohammed said, he had "no further use or patience for him." He said Qahtani knew he was bound for a suicide operation in the United States, but beyond that "did not know the specifics of the operation." He had been a last-minute addition who joined the plot "very late." He was brought in near the end as muscle, to round out the numbers on the hijack teams. Mohammed said that Qahtani flew to Florida un-accompanied and was given "very limited information about his points of contact" in the United States. He had not been told who was going to meet him at the airport. In other words, the gap-ridden story that Qahtani had told his interrogators, which caused them to disbe-lieve him and push him to the point of medical emergency and, in the view of some colleagues, criminal excess, had been true from the start.

9

THE MEMO

Crime is contagious. If the government becomes a lawbreaker, it breeds con-
tempt for the law; it invites every man to become a law unto himself . . .
To declare that the government may commit crimes in order to secure the
conviction of a private criminal—would bring terrible retribution.

—Justice Louis Brandeis,
Olmstead v. United States, 1928

On December 17, 2002, Alberto Mora first learned there was
a problem at Guantánamo when David Brant, the head of
the Navy's criminal investigations, walked unannounced
into his office at the Pentagon with a startling accusation of wrongdoing. "We think people are being abused by the interrogators in
Guantánamo in unlawful ways," Brant said, "and it seems to have
been approved at a higher level. Do you want to hear more?"

Mora—whose status in the Pentagon was equivalent to that of a
four-star general—was at the time the General Counsel of the United
States Navy. He was a courtly and engaging man, with neatly
trimmed silver hair, warm brown eyes, and the ability to both listen
well and to lead. Politically he was a conservative who admired President Reagan. He had served in both the first and the second Bush
Administrations as a political appointee. He strongly supported the
administration's war on terror, including the invasion of Iraq, which
at that moment was gaining unstoppable momentum. He was not a
military man himself, but he had come to revere the Navy.

During his first days as a civilian appointee at the Pentagon, he later said, he had found himself staring, mystified, at a large and not particularly distinguished painting that hung in the marble staircase leading to the office of the Secretary of Defense. It depicted an Air Force officer and his wife and children, kneeling in church as beams of colored sunlight filtered through stained-glass windows, dappling their bowed heads. It was almost embarrassingly kitschy. As he passed it on his way through the maze of hallways, he often wondered why of all the department's invaluable collection of heroic art, which included any number of scenes of far more memorable bravery, this one had been chosen for such a choice spot.

As he told the story, it took quite some time before he noticed and read the small plaque beneath the painting. Its words were transformative for Mora, making him suddenly comprehend a quietly eloquent kind of courage that he felt all around him in the building. The inscription was from the Bible—Isaiah, chapter 6, verse 8—in which God asks the question: "Whom shall I send? And who will go for us?" Isaiah answers: "Here I am. Send me!"

Mora took two lessons from the painting after that. It taught him that a soldier's courage is tested not just when facing death on the battlefield but in thousands of smaller moments, including when a citizen hears and answers the nation's call and says, "Send me," leaving the safety of his life and family behind. The second meaning he read into it was that American military power must be exercised in the service of principles and values. For some, such as the family in the painting, these were religious values, but for all American soldiers, he believed, this meant a devotion to the U.S. Constitution and the ideas it represented. Without such higher purpose, the exercise of power could easily become illegitimate. These thoughts animated his work as the Navy's most senior civilian lawyer.

As Mora's musings on the painting suggested, he had a thoughtful, philosophic bent. He wasn't ponderous. In fact, his mind and his words moved unusually quickly. But he was someone for whom abstractions had concrete meaning.

When Dave Brant walked into Mora's office that day, he was taking a gamble, because he didn't know Mora that well. By the time Brant walked in, it had become clear to him that the abuse in Guantánamo had been sanctioned in some way by people near or at the top of the military chain of command, which meant that anyone who questioned the order risked charges of insubordination. Brant was the head of the Naval Criminal Investigative Service, the internal police department for the Navy. It didn't report directly through the same channels that the Guantánamo interrogators did, but at the apex of the Pentagon they all had the same commanders—Secretary of Defense Rumsfeld and President Bush.

Brant had reported to Mora before, but never on anything quite so sensitive as that day. "I wasn't sure how he would react," said Brant, a tall, thin man with a mustache and a slightly doleful air. Brant had already conveyed the allegations about Guantánamo to Army leaders, since they had command authority over the military interrogators, and to the Air Force, too. But he said that nobody seemed to care. Therefore, he wasn't hopeful when he went to Mora's office that afternoon.

It was just fifteen months after the September 11 attacks, and as Mora recalled, the mood in the Pentagon was bellicose. "The mentality was that we lost three thousand Americans, and we could lose a lot more unless something was done," he said. "It was believed that some of the Guantánamo detainees had knowledge of other 9/11-like operations that were under way, or would be executed in the future. The gloves had to come off. The U.S. had to get tougher." Rumsfeld said at one point, "I need responsibility to prosecute the war, and the President said, 'You got it.'"

Mora had been inside the Pentagon himself on September 11 and recalled the jetliner crashing into the building one facet over. He said that it "felt jarring, like a large safe had been dropped overhead." From the parking lot, he watched the Pentagon burn. The next day, he said, he looked around a room full of top military leaders and was struck by the thought that "these guys were going to be the tip of the spear." The massive amount of military might represented by the officers in that room had filled him with pride.

As the head of the NCIS, Brant oversaw the agents from his organization who were working with the FBI at Guantánamo in the Criminal Investigative Task Force. Unlike the group of interrogators run by Army Intelligence, most of his agents, such as Brittain Mallow, the task force head, had experience and training in law enforcement. Brant, who was a civilian, himself held an advanced degree in criminology and had worked as a policeman in Miami in the 1970s.

Brant had heard a number of disturbing reports from Mallow and others by then. They believed that the military interrogators seemed poorly trained and were dangerously frustrated by their lack of success. Brant had been told that the interrogators were engaging in escalating levels of physical and psychological abuse. Speaking of the tactics that he had heard about, Brant said, "Repugnant would be a good term to describe them."

Much of Brant's information had been supplied by Michael Gelles, the NCIS psychologist, who worked with the CITF and had computer access to the Army's interrogation logs at Guantánamo. As a result of the widening rift between the two teams, Major General Miller had begun to refuse to share any information that his interrogators got from detainees with the Task Force agents. They found him petulant and unprofessional. But they had secretly penetrated a shared computer hard drive, hacking into Qahtani's interrogation logs, among others. The Army general apparently had no idea. What they read, in Gelles's view, was shocking. His opinion about the seriousness of the problem had carried great weight with Brant, who respected the psychologist's judgment hugely. Gelles was "phenomenal at unlocking the minds of everyone from child abusers to terrorists," Brant said.

The logs detailed, for example, that the day before Brant dropped in on Mora, Mohammed al-Qahtani had been forced to pick up trash from the floor of the interrogation chamber while his hands were cuffed and he was being called a pig. Three days earlier, on December 13, the logs said that "in order to escalate the detainee's emotions, a mask was made from an MRE box with a smiley face on it, and placed on detainee's head for a few moments. A latex glove was inflated and labeled the 'sissy slap' glove. This glove was touched to the detainee's face periodically, after explaining the terminology to him. The mask was placed back on detainee's head. While wearing the mask, the team began dance instructions with the detainee." The logs also showed that Qahtani was going day after day and week after week with only four hours of sleep a day, a situation that led his interrogators to dump water on his head and force him to stand at repeated intervals through the hours, in order to keep him from nodding off.

Brant told Mora that he had come because he didn't want his team of investigators to "in any way observe, condone, or participate in any level of physical or in-depth psychological abuse. No slapping, deprivation of water, heat, dogs, psychological abuse. It was pretty basic, black and white, to me," he recalled saying. Later, he explained, "I didn't know or care what the rules were that had been set by the Department of Defense at that point. We were going to do what was morally, ethically, and legally permissible."

Declassified e-mails and orders obtained by the American Civil Liberties Union document Brant's position, showing that by then he had ordered all CITF personnel to "stand clear and report" any abusive interrogation tactics. There was no doubt in Brant's mind, regardless of the legal advice from the lawyers in the Pentagon's Office of General Counsel, that the Army's interrogation of Qahtani was unlawful. If an NCIS agent had engaged in such abuse, he said, "we would have relieved, removed, and taken internal disciplinary action against the individual—let alone whether outside charges would have been brought."

Brant also feared that such methods would taint the cases his agents needed to make against the detainees, undermining any attempts to prosecute them in a court of law—or even in the anticipated military commissions. Additionally, he doubted the reliability of forced confessions. And really, the bottom line for him was that, as he put it tersely, "it just ain't right."

When Brant came to Mora, he had finally found a lawyer who cared not just about the letter but also the spirit of the law. Unlike the officials at the Army and Air Force, Mora was "rocked" when he was told about the abuse, Gelles said. The psychologist saw Mora, in contrast to the other Pentagon bureaucrats, as "visionary about this. He quickly grasped the fact that these techniques in the hands of people with this little training spelled disaster." Thus, when Brant asked Mora if he wanted to hear more about the situation, Mora later recalled, "I responded that I felt I had to."

Mora was a well-liked and successful figure at the Pentagon. Born in Boston in 1952, he was the son of a Hungarian mother, Klara, and a Cuban father, Lidio, both of whom left behind Communist regimes for America. Klara's father, who had been a lawyer in Hungary, joined her in exile just before the Soviet Union took control. From the time Alberto was a small boy, Klara Mora recalled, he heard from his grandfather the message that "the law is sacred." For the Moras, injustice and abuse were not merely theoretical concepts. One of Mora's greatuncles had been interned in a Nazi concentration camp, and another was hanged after having been tortured. Mora's first memory, as a young child, was of playing on the floor in his mother's bedroom and watching her crying as she listened to a report on the radio declaring that the 1956 anti-Communist uprising in Hungary had been crushed. "People who went through things like this tend to have very strong views about the rule of law, totalitarianism, and America," Mora said.

At the time, Mora's family was living in Cuba. His father, a Harvard-trained physician, had taken his wife and infant son there in 1952. When Castro seized power seven years later, the family barely escaped detention after a servant informed the authorities that they planned to flee to America. In the ensuing panic, Alberto obtained an emergency passport from the American embassy in Havana. "This was my first brush with the government," he said. "When I swore an oath of allegiance to the American government, part of the oath involved taking up arms to defend the country. And I was thinking, 'This is a serious thing for me, to be an eight-year-old boy, raising my hand before the American vice-consul and taking the oath of allegiance.'" Cuban customs officials, seeing Alberto's American passport, threatened not to let him board a ship. At the last minute, one of his father's colleagues, who had been put in charge of the port, allowed Alberto's emigration.

Mora's family settled in Jackson, Mississippi, where his father taught at the state medical school and Mora attended a Catholic school. For the most part, Jackson was "a wonderful place," Mora recalled, although it was also "very conservative." Racism was rampant, and everyone, including Mora, backed Barry Goldwater in the 1964 election. Mora had never met anyone who opposed the Vietnam War until he enrolled at Swarthmore College, a school that he chose after reading an SAT-preparation booklet that described it as small and especially rigorous. He also had never met a feminist before going to hear Kate Millett speak at Bryn Mawr during his freshman year; her talk infuriated him. After growing up in the South among friends who played sports, drank beer, and had a good time, he found the Northeastern liberal elite curiously "nerdish." The girls had thrown away their skirts—if they'd ever had them, he joked—and there were no parties. Yet he loved the intellectual environment. "You just had these intense discussions," he recalled. "I reveled in it." Mora said that he was the only person among his friends who wasn't a conscientious objector to the war.

Mora graduated in 1974 with honors and joined the State Department, working in Portugal; in 1979, he entered law school in Miami. Finding litigation work more "a living than a life," Mora said, he was happy to get an appointment as General Counsel of the U.S. Information Agency in the first Bush Administration. During the Clinton years, he was appointed to a Republican seat on the Broadcasting Board of Governors, where he was an advocate for Radio Martí, the American news operation aimed at Cuba. He also practiced international law in several private firms. When George W. Bush was elected, Mora—with the backing of former Defense Secretary Frank Carlucci, whom he had befriended in Portugal—was appointed General Counsel of the Navy. He expected to spend most of his time there streamlining the budget.

The day after Mora's first meeting with Brant, they met again and Brant showed him parts of the transcript of Qahtani's interrogation. Mora was shocked when Brant told him that the abuse wasn't "rogue activity" but was "rumored to have been authorized at a high level in Washington." The mood in the room, Mora recalled, was one of "dismay." He added, "I was under the opinion that the interrogation activities described would be unlawful and unworthy of the military services." Mora said, "I was appalled by the whole thing. It was clearly abusive and assaultive. It was also clear it would get worse. It could lead to creep, where if the violence didn't work well, they would double it," as psychological studies like the Zimbardo experiment at Stanford, in which students guarding mock prisoners became abusive, had shown. In Mora's view, the state-sanctioned cruelty was also "clearly contrary to everything we were ever taught about American values."

Looking back, Mora believed that the media had focused too narrowly on allegations of U.S.-sanctioned torture. Waterboarding, in particular, was covered as the sine qua non of criminality. As he saw it, the authorization of cruelty was equally pernicious. "To my mind, there's no moral or practical distinction," he said. "If cruelty is no longer declared unlawful, but instead is applied as a matter of policy, it alters the fundamental relationship of man to government. It destroys the whole notion of individual rights. The Constitution recognizes that man has an inherent right, not bestowed by the state or laws, to personal dignity, including the right to be free of cruelty. It applies to all human beings, not just in America—even those designated as 'unlawful enemy combatants.' If you make this exception, the whole Constitution crumbles. It's a transformative issue."

Mora said that he did not fear reprisal for stating his opposition to the administration's emerging policy. "It never crossed my mind," he said. "Besides, my mother would have killed me if I hadn't spoken up. No Hungarian after Communism, or Cuban after Castro, is not aware that human rights are incompatible with cruelty." He added, "The debate here isn't only how to protect the country. It's how to protect our values."

After the second meeting with Brant, Mora called his friend Steven Morello, the General Counsel of the Army, and asked him if he knew anything about the abuse of prisoners at Guantánamo. Mora said that Morello answered, "I know a lot about it. Come on down."

In Morello's office, Mora saw what he later referred to as "the package"—the collection of secret military documents that traced the origins of the coercive interrogation policy at Guantánamo. It began on October 11, 2002, with the request by JTF-170's commander, Major General Michael Dunlavey, for permission to make interrogations more aggressive. "The same techniques have become less effective over time," he explained. "I believe that the methods and techniques delineated in the accompanying memoranda will enhance our efforts to extract information." This was accompanied by Diane Beaver's acrobatic leaps over the many legal hurdles contained in U.S. and international law, and the set of requested techniques.

The paper trail continued as Major General Miller assumed command of Guantánamo Bay, and, on the assumption that prisoners like Qahtani had been trained by Al Qaeda to resist questioning, he too pushed his superiors hard for more flexibility in interrogations.

On December 2, there was the final green light from Secretary of Defense Rumsfeld, following the recommendation of his legal counsel, Jim Haynes. Rumsfeld formally approved three categories of incrementally harsher treatment. Documents suggest there was a fourth category that disappeared after the FBI agents in Guantánamo successfully opposed it. It would have permitted the military—not just the CIA—to oversee renditions of noncompliant prisoners "temporarily or permanently" to third countries, such as "Egypt and Jordan," that could "employ interrogation techniques allowing them to obtain the requisite information." Clemente had sent a memo warning that rendition to torture violated U.S. laws and that aiding and abetting such renditions in any manner could be construed as a criminal conspiracy.

Rumsfeld approved most of the requested other three categories, including the use of "hooding," "exploitation of phobias," "stress positions," "deprivation of light and auditory stimuli," and other coercive tactics ordinarily forbidden by the *Army Field Manual.* (As Haynes had suggested, he reserved judgment on "waterboarding" and death threats.)

As Morello fanned these documents out on his desk, behind the carefully closed door of his office, he told Mora, "We tried to stop it." But he said he couldn't. He was told to shut up. He was so nervous about the whole thing, he made Mora promise not to let on where he had seen the documents.

On close inspection, it was clear that these documents had been kept in an unusually narrow circle. They were missing the initials indicating the approval of the Chairman of the Joint Chiefs of Staff, General Richard Myers, among others. "This was not the way this should have come about," Myers later said. He blamed what he called "intrigue" that was "probably occurring between Jim Haynes, White House general counsel, and Justice." The document was also missing the "buck slip," as it was called, showing that it had been read and signed off on by the required circle of officials. Instead, as it reached Rumsfeld, it had just a note from Haynes saying, "Good to go." The process had been short-circuited; several of the military lawyers, who might have known better, but objected more, had been cut out. "Everything was close hold," another lawyer involved in the process said. "That's how Jim Haynes operated." As Mora put it dryly, "He was not a sharer."

As he examined the "package," Mora grew ashen-faced. He was not impressed with the analyses submitted by Lieutenant Colonel Beaver, floating her theory that interrogators could get "permission, or immunity" from higher authorities "in advance" to violate various laws, including the Uniform Code of Military Justice. Her brief, he said, "was a wholly inadequate analysis of the law." It held that "cruel, inhuman, or degrading treatment could be inflicted on the Guantánamo detainees with near impunity"; in his view, such acts were unlawful. Rumsfeld's December 2 memo approving these "counter-resistance" techniques, Mora believed, "was fatally grounded on these serious failures of legal analysis."

Of course, Mora did not know at the time that the Justice Department had espoused similar and even more extreme theories in the Bybee/Yoo torture memo, granting new powers to the CIA, all of which Gonzales had signed off on four months earlier. Nor did he realize that David Addington and Alberto Gonzales, among others, had discussed the issue of Qahtani's interrogation with Beaver in person, down in Guantánamo, before she wrote her memo that fall. Addington, in particular, had shown an interest in Qahtani.

The problem that leapt out at Mora, that had been unaddressed by the others, was that the legal authorities had drawn no "bright line," as he put it, to prohibit the combination of these techniques. It defined no limits for their use. He believed that such rhetorical laxity "could produce effects reaching the level of torture," which he knew was prohibited, without exception, under both U.S. and international law. Mora took his concerns to Gordon England, the Secretary of the Navy, who later became the Deputy Secretary of Defense. Then, on December 20, with England's authorization, Mora went to Haynes. They met in Haynes's office, an elegant suite behind vaultlike metal doors sealed with a massive, circular combination lock.

In confronting Haynes, Mora was engaging not just the Pentagon but also the Vice President's office. Haynes, an ultracautious political appointee who constantly reminded those who worked for him to send no e-mails, write no memos, and leave no other paper trail that could be traced to his fingerprints, was a protégé of David Addington. In 1989, when Cheney was named Secretary of Defense by George H. W. Bush, he hired Addington as a special assistant and eventually appointed him to be his general counsel. Once Addington reached the Pentagon, he in turn hired Haynes as his special assistant and soon promoted him to General Counsel of the Army. Haynes's résumé was shallow, but his deference to Addington ran deep.

After the 2000 election, Haynes had confessed his worry to a former colleague that he had very few connections in the new Bush crowd. Addington and Cheney were his only sponsors. They, of course, were all he needed. Haynes was soon given Addington's old job as the top lawyer at the Pentagon. But Haynes's dependence on his patrons left the Pentagon's legal process under the control of the Office of the Vice President to an unusual degree.

"Haynes became General Counsel to the Army just three years after the Army General Counsel Internship program," a top Pentagon lawyer said. "He got there because Addington put him there. As a result, he was very compliant." He noted, "Addington basically had his say-so with every high-level attorney in the administration." What everyone who dealt with him knew, of course, was that, as the Pentagon lawyer put it, "Addington was just a stand-in for Cheney."

Haynes rarely discussed his alliance with Cheney's office, but his colleagues, as one of them put it, noticed that "stuff moved back and forth fast" between the two power centers. Haynes was not considered to be a particularly ideological thinker, but he was seen as loyal when it came to serving the agenda of Cheney and Addington. In October 2002, almost three months before his meeting with Mora, Haynes gave a speech at the conservative Federalist Society disparaging critics who accused the Pentagon of mistreating detainees. A year later, President Bush nominated him to the Federal Appeals Court in Virginia. His nomination was one of several that were stalled by Senate

Democrats. But the presidential nomination and elongated confirmation process served to make Haynes still more indebted to the White House.

In his meeting with Haynes, Mora argued that whatever its intent had been, what Rumsfeld's memo permitted was "torture."

"No it isn't," Haynes replied.

Mora asked Haynes to think about the techniques more carefully. What did "deprivation of light and auditory stimuli" mean? Could a prisoner be locked in a completely dark cell? If so, could he be kept there for a month? Longer? Until he went blind? What, precisely, did the authority to exploit phobias permit? Could a detainee be held in a coffin? What about using dogs? Rats? How far could an interrogator push this? Until a man went insane?

Mora drew Haynes's attention to a comment that Rumsfeld had added to the bottom of his December 2 memo, in which he asked why detainees could only be forced to stand for four hours a day, when he himself often stood "for 8–10 hours a day." Mora said that he understood that the comment was meant to be jocular. But he feared that it could become an argument for the defense in any prosecution of terror suspects. It also could be read as encouragement to disregard the limits established in the memo. (Colonel Lawrence Wilkerson, the retired military officer who was a chief of staff to former Secretary of State Powell, had a similar reaction when he saw Rumsfeld's scrawled aside. "It said, 'Carte blanche, guys,'" Wilkerson asserted. "That's what started them down the slope. You'll have My Lais then. Once you pull this thread, the whole fabric unravels.")

Increasingly, the lawyers inside the CIA were facing similar questions about what the limits were, although Mora had no knowledge of this. After the Bybee/Yoo torture memo had been issued, giving CIA interrogators a green light to walk up to the edge of torture, they began to pepper the General Counsel's office, one of the CIA lawyers later told the *New York Times*. "We were getting asked about combinations—'Can we do this and this at the same time?'" recalled Paul C. Kelbaugh, a veteran intelligence lawyer who was Deputy Legal Counsel at the CIA's Counterterrorist Center from 2001 to 2003. Interrogators, he said, were worried that even approved techniques might cross the legal line when combined for painful, multiplying effect. He recalled agency officers asking: "These approved techniques, say, withholding food, and 50-degree temperature—can they be combined?" Or "Do I have to do the less extreme before the more extreme?"

A still-classified list of allowable techniques accompanied the broader legal authorization given by the Office of Legal Counsel. But according to a knowledgeable source, nowhere in either directive were there any limits imposed.

Haynes said little during the meeting with Mora, but Mora left the room certain that Haynes would realize he had been too hasty and would get Rumsfeld to revoke the inflammatory December 2 memo. "My feeling was it was just a blunder," Mora said. The next day, he left Washington for a two-week Christmas holiday.

The authorization of harsh interrogation methods that Mora had seen was, of course, no aberration. Some critics later faulted Mora for being naive. "They didn't want serious legal advice," said one former Justice Department lawyer. "They *liked* the answers they were getting," said another.

It was not until the first Bybee/Yoo torture memo leaked out in the spring of 2004 that the public could see that legalizing cruelty had been the Bush Administration's deliberate policy. But while Mora was on Christmas vacation, the public got an early hint. On December 26, the *Washington Post* published a story, by Dana Priest and Barton Gellman, alleging that CIA personnel were mistreating prisoners at the Bagram military base in Afghanistan. Kenneth Roth, the Director of Human Rights Watch, was quoted in the story warning that if this was true, U.S. officials who knew about it could be criminally liable under the doctrine of command responsibility. The specific allegations closely paralleled what Mora had seen authorized at Guantánamo. The story described a "brass-knuckled quest for information" that included "stress and duress" interrogation techniques. Citing "Americans with direct knowledge and others who have witnessed the treatment," the paper reported that "captives are often 'softened up' by MPs and U.S. Army Special Forces troops who beat them up and confine them in tiny rooms."

Mora was disturbed by what he read. He would have been more so if he had learned about several far more dire situations in Afghanistan that had yet to surface in the press. Mora had no idea that senior military and intelligence officials were grappling with three homicides in Afghanistan at the same time that Haynes was authorizing tougher tactics in Guantánamo. In December, two Afghan prisoners held by the U.S. military at Bagram Air Base were beaten to death by their interrogators. One of these, a falsely accused taxi driver named Dilawar, who officials later conceded had been innocent, was hit so often with a "common peroneal strike"—a blow to the soft tissue and sensitive nerves just above the knee—a coroner later testified that the tissue in his legs had "basically been pulpified." A third prisoner, meanwhile, had died of hypothermia under the auspices of the CIA in the notorious prison known as the "Salt Pit," also in Afghanistan. He died after local guards left him wet, naked, and chained in a freezing cell overnight. The CIA supervisor, who was young and inexperienced, apparently ordered him buried in an unmarked grave. Later, when the Justice Department weighed filing criminal charges, the CIA said that it was the Afghans who had run the prison, on foreign property, so the CIA had no legal liability and the U.S. government no jurisdiction. The prisoner was never publicly identified; he just "disappeared from the face of the earth," a U.S. government official said.

President Bush's tone during this period pointed to the tough tactics, even if the public had no access to any details. On December 3, shortly after the Al Qaeda suspect Abd al-Rahim al-Nashiri was abducted to Thailand, where the CIA waterboarded him and subjected him to other forms of coercion, Bush hinted at the administration's extralegal success. "Let me just put it to you this way. He no longer has the capacity to do what he did in the past," Bush told a jubilant crowd at a state fairgrounds in Shreveport, Louisiana. "He's out of action."

As it turned out, Nashiri was the last of the CIA's high-value detainees to be videotaped while undergoing "enhanced" interrogation, according to Agency officials. News of the death of the unidentified CIA prisoner in Afghanistan sent a surge of worry through the officers manning the black site detention program. By the end of 2002, the Agency had changed its policy about keeping such evidence on film. The videotapes remained, however, in a vault overseas.

At this point, the Bush Administration's policies toward terrorism were almost beyond challenge in the political arena. A measure of the pro-administration mood occurred inside the *New York Times*, where Carlotta Gall, a British stringer based in Afghanistan, filed a story on February 5, 2003, about the deaths of Dilawar and another Afghan detainee. It sat for a month, according to Eric Umansky, who wrote about the American coverage of the war on terror in the *Columbia Journalism Review*, finally appearing a little over a month before the U.S. invasion of Iraq. "I very rarely have to wait long for a story to run," Gall said. "If it's an investigation, occasionally as long as a week."

Her story, Umansky found, was at the center of an editorial fight. Her piece was "the real deal. It referred to a homicide. Detainees had been killed in custody. I mean, you can't get much clearer than that," Roger Cohen, then the *Times*'s foreign editor, told him. "I pitched it, I don't know, four times at page-one meetings, with increasing urgency and frustration. I laid awake at night over this story. And I don't fully understand to this day what happened. It was a really scarring thing. My single greatest frustration as foreign editor was my inability to get that story on page one."

Doug Frantz, who was then the *Times*'s investigative editor, said that Howell Raines, then the *Times*'s top editor, and his deputies "insisted that it was improbable; it was just hard to get their mind around." Eventually, the paper finally ran the story, buried on page fourteen. "If it had run on the front page, it would have sent a strong signal not just to the Bush Administration but to other news organizations," Frantz said. Gall concluded there had been a reluctance to "believe bad things of Americans" that had chilled the pursuit of truth even inside the most esteemed daily newspaper in the country.

It was in this political atmosphere that Mora attempted to take on the most powerful figures in the Bush Administration. Upon returning to work on January 6, 2003, Mora, who knew nothing of the clandestine detention program or the proliferating secret legal memos, was upset to learn from Brant that the abuse at Guantánamo had not stopped. In fact, Brant told him, it was getting worse. Qahtani had been forcibly shaved, force-fed intravenously, and ordered to bark like a dog. He'd been forced to listen to pop music at an earsplitting volume, deprived of more sleep, and kept in a painfully cold room. His hands had been shackled to his sides so that he couldn't pray. It was around this time that he had begged to be allowed to commit suicide.

Suspecting by then that such abuse was a deliberate policy, Mora widened his internal campaign in the hope of building a constituency against it. In the next few days, his arguments reached many of the Pentagon's top figures: Deputy Secretary of Defense Paul Wolfowitz; Captain Jane Dalton, the legal adviser to the Joint Chiefs of Staff; Victoria Clarke, who was then the Pentagon spokeswoman; and Rumsfeld himself.

Later, Rumsfeld would insist that any abuse in Guantánamo was unrelated to his department's policies. "What took place at Guantánamo is a matter of public record today, and the investigations turned up nothing that suggested that there was any policy in the department other than humane treatment," Rumsfeld said in January 2006. But Mora's determined campaign demonstrates otherwise. Almost from the start of the administration's war on terror the White House, the Justice Department, and the Department of Defense, intent upon having greater flexibility, ignored sustained and strenuous warnings from some of its own top lawyers that the government was embarking on a course that was both inhumane and unlawful.

On January 9, 2003, Mora had a second meeting with Jim Haynes. According to Mora, when he told Haynes how disappointed he was that nothing had been done to end the abuse at Guantánamo, Haynes defended the tough new tactics. He told Mora that "U.S. officials believe the techniques are necessary to obtain information," and that the interrogations might prevent future attacks against the United States and save American lives. Haynes didn't specify which "U.S. officials" he was referring to. But a close aide to Rumsfeld later said that "Jim talked to Addington about it." Addington's view, this official said, was that these techniques were "vetted and accepted." Also, Addington had convinced Haynes that without these measures they wouldn't get the information. "Everyone knew that the interrogation process in Guantánamo was dysfunctional," the Rumsfeld aide said. "It wasn't exactly a secret in the building."

In an effort to appear reasonable, Mora told Haynes that he wasn't "an absolutist" about torture. He could imagine "ticking bomb" scenarios in which it might be moral—though still not legal—to torture a suspect. But, he asked Haynes, how many lives had to be saved to justify torture? Thousands? Hundreds? What about one child? Where do you draw the line? To decide this question, shouldn't there be a public debate?

Mora said he doubted that Guantánamo presented such an urgent ethical scenario in any event, since most of the detainees had been held there for more than a year. Mora also warned Haynes that the legal opinions the administration was counting on to protect itself might not withstand scrutiny—such as the notion that Guantánamo was beyond the reach of U.S. courts.

If the Pentagon's theories of indemnity didn't hold up in the courts, Mora warned, criminal charges ranging from assault to war crimes could conceivably be filed against administration officials. He added that the interrogation policies could threaten Rumsfeld's tenure and could even damage the presidency. "Protect your client!" he said.

Haynes, again, didn't say much in response. He furrowed his brow. But soon afterward, at a meeting of top Pentagon officials, he mentioned Mora's concerns to Secretary Rumsfeld. A former administration official disclosed that Rumsfeld was unconcerned; he once more joked that he himself stood eight hours a day, and exclaimed, "Torture? That's not torture!" ("His attitude was 'What's the big deal?' " the former official said.) A subordinate delicately pointed out to Rumsfeld that while he often stood for hours it was because he chose to do so, and he could sit down when he wanted. Victoria Clarke, the Pentagon spokeswoman, also argued that prisoner abuse was bad from a public-relations perspective. (Clarke declined to discuss her conversations with administration officials, other than to say that she regarded Mora as "a very thoughtful guy, who I believed had a lot of important things to say.") But Rumsfeld had a saying among his family and close friends: "I have plenty of advisers, but I only listen to one of them—the one I take a shower with every morning."

By mid-January, the situation at Guantánamo had not changed. Qahtani's "enhanced" interrogation was in its seventh week and other detainees were also being subjected to extreme treatment. Mora continued to push for reform, but a former Pentagon colleague told me that "people were beginning to roll their eyes. It was like 'Yeah, we've already heard this.' "

On January 15, Mora took a step guaranteed to antagonize Haynes, given his phobia about putting anything controversial in writing. Mora delivered an unsigned draft memo to Haynes and said that he planned to "sign it out" that afternoon—making it an official document—unless the harsh interrogation techniques were suspended. Mora's draft memo described U.S. interrogations in Guantánamo as "at a minimum cruel and unusual treatment, and, at worst, torture." The word "torture" was right there, in black and white, above the signature of the most senior lawyer in the U.S. Navy. It would jump off the page to any congressional investigator or news reporter. It would remain there in the Bush Administration's record for future historians.

By the end of the day, Haynes called Mora with good news. Rumsfeld was suspending his authorization of the disputed interrogation techniques. The Defense Secretary also was authorizing a special "working group" of a few dozen lawyers, from all branches of the armed services, including Mora, to develop new interrogation guidelines.

Mora, elated, went home to his wife and son, with whom he had felt bound not to discuss his battle. He and the other lawyers in the working group began to meet and debate the constitutionality and effectiveness of various interrogation techniques. He felt that "no one would ever learn about the best thing I'd ever done in my life."

A week later, Mora was shown the draft of an eighty-one-page classified document that negated almost every argument he had made. Haynes had outflanked him. He had solicited a separate, overarching opinion from the Office of Legal Counsel at the Justice Department on the legality of harsh military interrogations—effectively superseding the working group.

There was only one copy of the opinion and it was kept in the office of the Air Force's general counsel, Mary Walker, whom Rumsfeld had appointed to head the working group. While Walker sat at her desk, Mora looked at the document with mounting disbelief; at first, he thought he had misread it. There was no language prohibiting the cruel, degrading, and inhumane treatment of detainees. The opinion was sophisticated but, he thought, displayed "catastrophically poor legal reasoning." In his view, it approached the level of the notorious Supreme Court decision in *Korematsu v. United States* in 1944, which upheld the government's internment of citizens of Japanese descent during the Second World War.

The author of the opinion was John Yoo. He and Haynes had become buddies. In addition to taking day trips together with the other members of the War Council to see Guantánamo, naval ships, and other war-related destinations, and meeting every few weeks together in the secretive group, they were also regular racquetball partners. A Justice Department lawyer who knew them both well said that it was widely believed that Yoo issued legal opinions orally to the Pentagon while the two ambitious lawyers challenged each other in sports matches.

Mora and many other lawyers believed that the legal questions were difficult and that there were in fact gaps in the law, making unclear what rules applied to foreign terror suspects held by the United States outside of U.S. borders. Many academics believed that Congress needed to craft a new legal framework to deal with the problem. But the Bush Administration had cut Congress out. When Senator Carl Levin, chairman of the Armed Services Committee and a member of the Senate Intelligence Committee, demanded to see the legal memos underlying the Bush policies on interrogation, he was rebuffed. "It's totally inexcusable, the administration is getting away with just saying no," he complained, "there's no claim of executive privilege, or national security—we've offered to keep it classified. It's just bullshit. They just don't want us to know what they've done."

As he reviewed the memo, Mora thought that Gonzales's abdication, in particular, was appalling. "They advised that the United States can apply cruelty without any legal restraints? It was astounding at so many levels," he said.

Yoo's March 2003 opinion, which was directed to Haynes and prepared specifically for the working group, declared that federal laws prohibiting assault, maiming, and other crimes did not apply to the military interrogators in Guantánamo. The sum effect of the pages and pages of arguments was that Guantánamo was, for all intents and purposes, a law-free zone.

Yoo wrote, "As we have made clear in other opinions involving the war against Al Qaeda, the Nation's right to self-defense has been triggered by the events of September 11. If a government defendant were to harm an enemy combatant during an interrogation in a manner that might arguably violate a criminal prohibition," he wrote, "he would be doing so in order to prevent further attacks on the United States . . . in that case we believe that he could argue that the executive branch's constitutional authority to protect the nation from attack justified his actions."

He suggested that interrogators could claim a "national and international version of the right to self-defense." Mistreatment of prisoners would not "shock the conscience" of the court, or violate constitutional prohibitions against "cruel and unusual" punishment, unless malice or sadism could be proven. Among the practices the memo discussed as arguably legal were gouging a prisoner's eyes out, dousing him with "scalding water, corrosive acid, or caustic substance," or "slitting an ear, nose, or lip, or disabling a tongue or limb." Biting, too, was considered. All of these forms of assault and maiming would ordinarily be criminal, but in times of war, Yoo wrote, the laws were trumped by the powers of the commander in chief.

Evidently, Yoo had not reached these conclusions entirely on his own. The memo noted that the "Criminal Division concurs in our conclusion" that federal criminal laws didn't apply to the military during wartime. The Justice Department's Criminal Division was led at the time by Chertoff, the future head of the Department of Homeland Security, whom, like Haynes, the White House had just nominated to a federal judgeship.

Eugene Fidell, a respected military law expert, later called Yoo's final version of the legal memo, which was dated March 14, 2003, "a monument to executive supremacy and the imperial presidency."

Mora believed that Yoo's opinion was "profoundly in error." He believed that it "was clearly at variance with applicable law." He noted, "If everything is permissible, and almost nothing is prohibited, it makes a mockery of the law."

A few days after reading Yoo's opinion, Mora sent an e-mail to Mary Walker saying that the document was not only "fundamentally in error" but "dangerous," because it had the weight of law. When the Office of Legal Counsel issues an opinion on a policy matter, it typically requires the intervention of the attorney general or the president to reverse it.

Walker wrote back, "I disagree, and I believe D.O.D. G.C."—Haynes, the Pentagon's general counsel—"disagrees."

On February 6, Mora invited Yoo to his office in the Pentagon to discuss the opinion. Mora asked him, "Are you saying the President has the authority to order torture?"

"Yes," Yoo replied.

"I don't think so," Mora said.

"I'm not talking policy," Yoo said. "I'm just talking about the law."

"Well, where are we going to have the policy discussion, then?" Mora asked.

Yoo, according to Mora, replied that he didn't know; maybe, he suggested, it would take place inside the Pentagon, where the defense-policy experts were.

In an e-mail, Yoo said that he recalled discussing only how the policy issues should be debated, and where. Torture, he said, was not an option under consideration.

But Mora knew that there would be no such policy discussion; as the administration saw it, the question would be settled by Yoo's opinion. The policy set by the President was to be as aggressive as the laws allowed. This left policy in the thrall of the lawyers. Indeed, Mora soon realized that, under the supervision of Mary Walker, a draft working-group report was being written to conform with Yoo's arguments. Mora noticed that the contributions from the working group "began to be rejected if they did not conform to the OLC guidance."

The draft working-group report noted that the Uniform Code of Military Justice barred "maltreatment" but said, "Legal doctrine could render specific conduct, otherwise criminal, not unlawful." In an echo of the torture memo, it also declared that interrogators could be found guilty of torture only if their "specific intent" was to inflict "severe physical pain or suffering" as evidenced by "prolonged mental harm." Even then, it said, the commander in chief could order torture if it was a military necessity: "Congress may no more regulate the President's ability to detain and interrogate enemy combatants than it may regulate his ability to direct troop movements on the battlefield."

A few days after his meeting with Yoo, Mora confronted Haynes again. He told him that the draft working-group report was "deeply flawed." It should be locked in a drawer, he said, and "never let out to see the light of day again." He advised Haynes not to allow Rumsfeld to approve it.

Mora was not alone in protesting. The senior uniformed lawyers for Army, Navy, Air Force, and Marines, known as the "TJAGs," who had also been tapped to participate in the working-group process, all sent extraordinary memos of dissent to Haynes. The JAG corps, however, was a particularly intense dislike of Addington's. From his days as a politically appointed Pentagon lawyer he had done all he could to weaken the power of the independent military lawyers, whose judgments he regarded as illegitimate interference in the powers of the executive branch. Dismissing their views was for him "a religious issue," a former Bush Administration lawyer noted.

The Defense Department promptly classified them as secret. In 2005, Senator Lindsey Graham, a Republican of South Carolina, who had been a military judge advocate general himself, publicly revealed the passionate memos. He noted that the authors were "not from the ACLU. These are not from people who are soft on terrorism, who want to coddle foreign terrorists. These are all professional military lawyers who have dedicated their lives, with 20-plus year careers, to serving the men and women in uniform and protecting their Nation. They were giving a warning shot across the bow of the policymakers that there are certain corners you cannot afford to cut because you will wind up meeting yourself."

The memos from the uniformed lawyers to the politically appointed general counsel were brimming with barely concealed disbelief at the direction the Justice Department was proposing for soldiers to take.

In one such dissent, Air Force Major General Jack Rives wrote:

> [T]he use of the more extreme interrogation techniques simply
> is not how the U.S. armed forces have operated in recent
> history. We have taken the legal and moral "high-road" in the

conduct of our military operations regardless of how others may operate. Our forces are trained in this legal and moral mindset beginning the day they enter active duty.

Rives also warned that the Justice Department's radical and idiosyncratic interpretation of the law "puts the interrogators and the chain of command at risk of criminal accusations abroad."

Another of the military lawyers, Rear Admiral Michael F. Lohr, the Navy's chief lawyer, wrote on February 6, 2003, conceding that detainees at Guantánamo Bay might not qualify for international protections, but asked nonetheless, "Will the American people find we have missed the forest for the trees by condoning practices that, while technically legal, are inconsistent with our most fundamental values?"

The senior-ranking uniformed Army lawyer, Major General Thomas Romig, argued that the Justice Department's approach "will open us to international criticism that the 'U.S. is a law unto itself.'"

In the spring of 2003, Mora waited for the final working-group report to emerge, planning to file a strong dissent. But the report never appeared. Mora assumed that the draft, based on Yoo's ideas, had not been finalized. He also thought, therefore, that Rumsfeld's suspension of the harsh techniques was still in effect, as Haynes had indicated, before the working group was put together.

Mora's assumptions about this continued in June, when press accounts asserted that the United States was subjecting detainees to "stress and duress" techniques, including beatings and food deprivation. Senator Patrick Leahy, Democrat of Vermont, wrote to Secretary of State Condoleezza Rice asking for a clear statement of the administration's detainee policy. Rice stuck Haynes with answering the letter, to his annoyance. He wrote a letter back to Leahy, which was subsequently released to the press, saying that the Pentagon's policy was never to engage in torture or cruel, inhumane, or degrading treatment—just the sort of statement Mora was hoping for. He took Haynes's letter to be "the happy culmination of the long debates in the Pentagon." He sent an appreciative note to Haynes saying that he was glad to be on his team.

On April 28, 2004, ten months later, the first pictures from Abu Ghraib became public. Mora said, "I felt saddened and dismayed. Everything we had warned against in Guantánamo had happened—but in a different setting. I was stunned."

He was further taken aback when he learned, while watching Senate hearings on Abu Ghraib on C-SPAN, that Rumsfeld had signed the working-group report—the draft based on Yoo's opinion—a year earlier, without the knowledge of Mora or any other internal legal critics. Rumsfeld's signature gave it the weight of a military order. "This was the first I'd heard of it!" Mora said.

The Air Force's deputy general counsel, Daniel Ramos, told him that the final working-group report had been "briefed" to General Miller, the commander of Guantánamo, and General James Hill, the head of the Southern Command, months earlier.

The final working-group report, it turned out, included a list of thirty-five possible interrogation methods. On April 16, 2003, the Pentagon issued a memorandum to the U.S. Southern Command approving twenty-four of them for use at Guantánamo, including isolation and what it called "fear up harsh," which meant "significantly increasing the fear level in a detainee." A Defense Department official who asked not to be named, but who spoke for Rumsfeld and Haynes, stressed, "It should be noted that there were strong advocates for the approval of the full range of thirty-five techniques," but he noted that Haynes was not among them. The techniques not adopted included nudity; the exploitation of "aversions," such as a fear of dogs; and slaps to the face and stomach. Thus, as the Pentagon told the story, Rumsfeld and Haynes had exercised great restraint, stopping far short of authorizing the torture that John Yoo had sanctioned. Yet these forms of torture were no longer prohibited by binding law—their use was a discretionary issue resting solely on the whim of a handful of powerful officials.

The same unidentified senior official at the Pentagon acknowledged that in addition to giving General Miller the restricted list of approved techniques, the Pentagon also gave the Guantánamo commander an oral briefing about the Justice Department's legal theories. The general was not shown Yoo's legal memo authorizing the circumvention of the laws, but the Pentagon official said he was briefed on it.

The fact that all of this had been going on without Mora's knowledge, or that of the other members of the working group, "was astounding," Mora said. "Obviously, it meant that the working-group report hadn't been abandoned, and that some version of it had gotten into the generals' possession."

Evidently, the Pentagon had pursued a secret detention policy, hidden not just from the public but from its own high-ranking opponents in the building. There was one version, enunciated in Haynes's letter to Leahy, aimed at critics. And there was another, secretly giving the operations officers legal indemnity to engage in cruel interrogations and, when the commander in chief deemed it necessary, torture. Legal critics within the administration had been allowed to think that they were engaged in a meaningful process, but their deliberations appeared to have been largely an academic exercise or, worse, a charade. "It seems that there was a two-track program here," said Martin Lederman, the Georgetown Law School professor who was formerly a lawyer with the Office of Legal Counsel. "Otherwise, why would they share the final working-group report with Hill and Miller but not with the lawyers who were its ostensible authors?"

Lederman said that he regarded Mora as heroic for raising crucial objections to the administration's interrogation policy. But he added that Mora was unrealistic if he thought that, by offering legal warnings, he could persuade the leaders of the administration to change its course. "It appears that they weren't asking to be warned," Lederman said.

The senior Defense Department official, speaking for Rumsfeld and Haynes, defended as an act of necessary caution the decision not to inform Mora and other legal advisers of the new official policy. The interrogation techniques authorized in the signed report, he explained, were approved only for Guantánamo and the Pentagon needed to prevent the practices from spreading to other battlefronts. "If someone wants to criticize us for being too careful, I accept that criticism willingly, because we were doing what we could to limit the focus of that report . . . to Guantánamo," the official said.

But Mora said that the Pentagon's contention that it couldn't risk sharing the report with its authors "doesn't make any sense." He explained, "We'd seen everything already." The real reason for their exclusion, he speculated, was to avoid dissent. "It would have put them in a bind," he said. "And it would have created a paper trail."

In fact, techniques that had been approved for use only at Guantánamo quickly migrated elsewhere. Four months after Haynes's office briefed General Miller on the working-group report, the Pentagon sent him to Iraq to advise officials there on interrogating Iraqi detainees. Miller arrived with a group of Guantánamo interrogators known as the Tiger Team. Later, he supervised all U.S.-run prisons in Iraq, including Abu Ghraib.

The Bush Administration continued to insist, even in 2008, that there was no connection between the thirty-five techniques listed in its working-group report and the outbreak of identical abusive techniques in Iraq and elsewhere. The administration also argued that John Yoo's memos were never more than academic exercises, since torture was never contemplated for use. But somehow, even though the exploitation of "aversions," including fear of dogs, was ostensibly prohibited in Iraq, military dogs were soon there. So were leashes—not just for canines.

Mora, who left the Bush Administration to become the general counsel for Wal-Mart's international operations, felt that he had witnessed both a moral and a legal tragedy. On July 7, 2004, he finished writing an extraordinary twenty-two-page memo chronicling his wide-ranging and persistent efforts in the winter of 2002 to push the Pentagon back from an official policy of cruelty. The memo, which he prepared for Vice Admiral Albert Church, who led a Pentagon investigation into abuses at the U.S. detention facility at Guantánamo, was marked secret and kept from public view. In Mora's view, the administration's legal response to September 11 was flawed from the start, triggering a series of subsequent errors that were all but impossible to correct. "The determination that Geneva didn't apply was a legal and policy mistake," he said. "But very few lawyers could argue to the contrary once the decision had been made."

Mora went on, "It seemed odd to me that the actors weren't more troubled by what they were doing." Many administration lawyers, he said, appeared to be unaware of history. "I wondered if they were even familiar with the Nuremberg trials—or with the laws of war, or with the Geneva conventions. They cut many of the experts on those areas out. The State Department wasn't just on the back of the bus—it was left off the bus." Mora understood that "people were afraid that more 9/11s would happen, so getting the information became the overriding objective. But there was a failure to look more broadly at the ramifications. For as long as these policies were in effect our government had adopted what only can be labeled as a policy of cruelty," he said. "Cruelty disfigures our national character. It is incompatible with our constitutional order, with our laws, and with our most prized values. . . . Where cruelty exists, law does not."

Having known Haynes and many of the others personally, Mora regarded their choices as less nefarious than tragic. "These were enormously hardworking, patriotic individuals," he said. "When you put together the pieces, it's all so sad. To preserve flexibility, they were willing to throw away our values."

Elsewhere in the world, as Mora predicted, the controversy grew. In 2006, the United Nations Human Rights Commission called for the United States to shut down the detention center at Guantánamo, where it said some practices "must be assessed as amounting to torture." The U.N. report described "the confusion with regard to authorized and unauthorized interrogation techniques" as "particularly alarming."

Dave Brant, who also left the administration to work in the private sector in 2006, said that before the Abu Ghraib story broke, "We'd sit around and say, you know what's going to happen. You've got guys who've been pumping gas in Nebraska or a cop on a beat in New York City suddenly thrown together in the war in Iraq, face to face with a terrorist, and you know it's a ticket for problems. It's just going to happen. It was inevitable."

10

A DEADLY INTERROGATION

The United States is committed to the world-wide elimination of torture and we are leading this fight by example. I call on all governments to join with the United States and the community of law-abiding nations in prohibiting, investigating, and prosecuting all acts of torture and in undertaking to prevent other cruel and unusual punishment. . . . Nowhere should the midnight knock foreshadow a nightmare of state-commissioned crime. The suffering of torture victims must end, and the United States calls on all governments to assume this great mission.

—Statement of President George W. Bush
on the United Nations International Day in
Support of Victims of Torture, June 26, 2003

The last night in the life of Manadel al-Jamadi, whose iced corpse became one of the more harrowing images of the Abu Ghraib scandal, began at home—a small apartment in a middle-class neighborhood on the outskirts of Baghdad. It ended before dawn in a cell in Abu Ghraib, the notorious Iraqi prison in which Saddam Hussein had tortured his political enemies. By the time that Jamadi entered the prison, sometime after four in the morning on November 4, 2003, Abu Ghraib was under American control. Jamadi, who was unarmed, was in the custody of the CIA. As they walked him in to be interrogated, he was alert and talking, answering questions in Arabic and English. An hour later, he was dead. An autopsy performed by military pathologists classified his death a homicide. What transpired during the last hours of his life remains a national security secret, closely guarded by the CIA. Five years later, there had been no public investigation of the CIA officers involved, nor any indication that anyone had been held to account for the killing. Under the new legal paradigm, it was unlikely there ever would be.

The death of one more Iraqi, in the midst of a bloody war in which thousands died on all sides, could easily be dismissed as insignificant. It's doubtful that Jamadi's loss was mourned anywhere in America. He may well have been guilty of plotting against U.S. forces in Iraq. Formerly an officer in Saddam Hussein's military, he was suspected of having a role in the October 27, 2003, bombing of the International Committee of the Red Cross Headquarters in Baghdad, an act of inhuman terrorism that killed a dozen innocent people. But whether he was guilty or innocent—and no one really knows for sure because he died before the United States could learn anything useful from him— Jamadi's death posed an unwelcome question going to the heart of the Bush Administration's secret interrogation protocol: Could the CIA legally kill a defenseless prisoner?

The events leading to Jamadi's unsolved homicide began months before he entered Abu Ghraib. Although no public hearing or trial would ever identify the clandestine officers who were responsible, a paper trail of internal documents led almost as directly to Washington as Iraq.

In the capital by the late summer of 2003, the realization was dawning on some inside the administration that the war in Iraq was turning from the predicted "cakewalk" into a horror show. In August, the number of terrorist bombings in Baghdad reached new records. American soldiers were getting killed in alarming numbers by planted roadside bombs. The military was increasingly baffled and battered, seemingly unable to stop the insurrection. Terrorists were attacking symbols of the U.S. occupation with new ferocity that summer, killing at least ten people in the bombing of the Jordanian embassy and at least twenty-three more with a massive truck bomb detonated at the United Nations Headquarters in Iraq. Among the dead was Sergio Vieira de Mello, the internationally admired head of the UN mission, who had devoted his career to peace.

Secretary of Defense Donald Rumsfeld's public posture was to be dismissive of the insurgents. On August 25, less than a week after the UN bombing, he described them as "dead-enders," adding, "There are some today who are surprised that there are still pockets of resistance in Iraq, and they suggest that this represents some sort of failure on the part of the Coalition. But this is not the case." The insurgents, he said, were just final remnants of the fallen government, like the deluded loyalists who "fought on during and after the defeat of the Nazi regime in Germany."

In private meetings inside the Pentagon and the White House, however, Rumsfeld and other top officials were in a rage over the military's apparent powerlessness to stop what was fast becoming a full-fledged insurgency. Rumsfeld was described as "pounding on the tables," demanding to know why the military had not yet found Saddam Hussein. He was similarly furious about the military's inability to locate any of Saddam Hussein's alleged weapons of mass destruction, the ostensible threat that had justified the preemptive war. Inadequate intelligence on the insurgents was the final affront. Despite a massive effort, the U.S. military and intelligence communities were having next to no success in penetrating the increasingly lethal Iraqi opposition.

At about this time, a troubling internal report commissioned by the military and obtained by *The New Yorker* correspondent Seymour Hersh traced the insurgency to deep-seated political problems in Iraq. In particular, it blamed the dysfunctional occupation authority set up by the Bush Administration. "Politically, the U.S. has failed to date," the report warned. "Insurgencies can be fixed or ameliorated by dealing with what caused them in the first place. The disaster that is the reconstruction of Iraq has been the key cause of the insurgency. There is no legitimate government, and it behooves the Coalition Provisional Authority to absorb the sad but unvarnished fact that most Iraqis do not see the Governing Council"—the Iraqi body appointed by the CPA—"as the legitimate authority. Indeed, they know that the true power is the CPA."

The report made clear that the military's failure to quell the insurgency had more to do with misunderstanding the political dynamics than being too soft on the Iraqis. Yet Rumsfeld and his staff responded by focusing on ways to make interrogations tougher. In an intelligence briefing at the Pentagon with Stephen Cambone, the Undersecretary of Defense for Intelligence, and his military assistant, Army Lieutenant General William G. (Jerry) Boykin, and other senior officers, Rumsfeld loudly disparaged the quality of the information coming from U.S.-held prisoners in Iraq. What he wanted, he told his staff, was the kind of intelligence being gathered from the detainees in Guantánamo. Boykin, an evangelical Christian who became controversial for equating the Muslim world with Satan, was also perturbed. He was a hardliner, prone to describing America as "having too soft an underbelly." Sometimes he made a stroking motion with his hand, as if touching the country's underside, and said, "She's soft—too soft." Greater force, the group seemed to think, was the answer.

At this point, the new, extreme interrogation rules that Rumsfeld had secretly authorized in April, in the Pentagon's Working Group Report, had been in place in Guantánamo for several months, and Rumsfeld made clear that he liked the results they were producing. In Iraq, however, the military was following a very different approach. Iraq was an occupied state, and so all citizens of the country were ostensibly protected by the Geneva Conventions. The military was supposed to be questioning prisoners under the traditional rules spelled out in the *Army Field Manual.* But after discussing the problems besetting Iraq, Rumsfeld issued an oral order that would have momentous consequences for the way the world viewed American power abroad. He wanted Major General Geoffrey Miller, the commander in Guantánamo, to "Gitmoize" Iraq, as Army Reserve Brigadier General Janis Karpinski, who oversaw the detention facilities there, later described it.

On August 31, 2003, Miller, whose experience prior to Guantánamo lay in the area of artillery, not detention or intelligence, arrived in Baghdad with his seventeen-person "tiger team." The members were handpicked by Miller, culled entirely from his staff in Guantánamo Bay. Their mission was to advise the senior commander of U.S. forces in Iraq, Lieutenant General Ricardo Sanchez, on how to get better intelligence. Miller and his team stayed ten days. By early September, Miller had in place a classified plan, which promised almost instant results. As he wrote, "a significant improvement in actionable intelligence will be realized within 30 days."

Miller's concept was a change in policy that would place military intelligence officers in charge of prison operations in Iraq, blending the functions of interrogation and detention. Miller also recommended that interrogations be centralized at Abu Ghraib so that intelligence could be processed more efficiently. And in a break with traditional military doctrine, Miller advocated using ordinary military police officers who worked as guards in the prison to participate in the interrogation process, even though they had not been trained for this. The guards, he wrote, "must be actively engaged in setting the conditions for successful exploitation of the internees." Miller also recommended using military dogs for interrogation.

Karpinski later said she tried to dissuade Miller from using his Guantánamo experience as the baseline for Iraq. She warned him that the situation in Iraq was very different. "At Guantánamo, they had 800 MPs for 640 prisoners," or more than a guard for each inmate, Karpinski said she pointed out. "At Abu Ghraib, we had about 300 MPs for about 6,600 prisoners." The facility was jammed to the point of rioting. No one had time to supervise individual interrogation plans. Another key difference was that unlike the prisoners in Guantánamo, those in Iraq were supposed to be covered by the Geneva Conventions. Furthermore, the prisoners were not all suspected terrorists; many were petty criminals, ignorant of useful intelligence. Many more had been mistakenly swept up in raids. But Karpinski said that Miller made clear he was not there to listen. "He said, 'Look, we can do this my way or we can do this the hard way,'" Karpinski later recalled.

By September 14, Sanchez had put in place a new policy, modeled on Guantánamo Bay but modified, he said, for a theater of war where the Geneva Conventions applied. The threshold for treatment, he noted, was that interrogations needed to be "humane." But exceptionally tough tactics could be allowed if the commander sanctioned it. Among the techniques that were available with Sanchez's personal approval were "stress positions," military dogs, and "environmental manipulation"—the blanket term covering sleep deprivation, exposure to uncomfortable temperatures, and bombardment by noise and light.

Sanchez didn't wait long to authorize the harsher tactics. He approved the first instance of detainee isolation on September 15 and the first instances of military interrogators removing detainees' clothing on September 16. Military dogs appeared in Abu Ghraib's interrogation chambers soon after. According to an internal Pentagon document, known as the Fay-Jones report, "Abusing detainees with dogs started almost immediately after the dogs arrived at Abu Ghraib." Low-ranking military personnel such as Sergeant Javal Davis would recall that they had been told by intelligence interrogators to do things like "loosen this guy up" and "make sure this guy gets the treatment." In a tell-all memoir, Sanchez later charged the Bush Administration with "gross negligence" and "dereliction of duty" for sweeping away the Geneva Conventions and providing no guidance to the armed forces in their place. By doing so, he said, "The civilian leaders at the highest levels of our government . . . unleashed the hounds of Hell, and no one seemed to have the moral courage to get the animals back in their cage."

To handle the hard-core leaders of the growing insurgency, Rumsfeld reportedly pushed the limits further still. He and Cambone expanded to Iraq a top-secret, highly compartmentalized program set up in the first few weeks after September 11 to combat high-value terrorism targets. Its code name was reportedly "Copper Green," but its description in the Pentagon's jargon was "Special Access Program"—a military program so secret fewer than 200 carefully selected officials had a complete understanding of its scope.

The SAP, which was run out of a secret office in the Pentagon, was Rumsfeld's answer to the CIA death squads envisioned by Cofer Black. It authorized commando teams composed of combat-hardened soldiers from the elite Special Forces—the Navy SEALs, Army Rangers, and the Army's Delta Force—to work closely with the CIA's paramilitary operatives in hunting, killing, or capturing and interrogating suspected Al Qaeda figures anywhere in the world. To foster complete secrecy, the members of the squads were given aliases, dead mail drops, and unmarked clothing. They worked in a loose structure outside the Pentagon's usually rigid chain of command. At a moment's notice, this rapid deployment force was ready to cross borders without visas, using its own aircraft. The commandos reportedly had legal authorization, in advance when necessary, to use lethal force.

A prisoner died in the custody of one of these task forces in Afghanistan in the beginning of March 2003. A military investigation found that in Afghanistan the Special Forces interrogators were modeling their treatment of prisoners on the SERE training they had received. The unit, the "20th Special Force Group," had forced detainees to kneel outside in wet clothing. The prisoners were kicked and punched in the kidneys, nose, and knees if they moved, according to the documents.

As the insurgency grew, the Pentagon redeployed some of these unconventional squads from the war on terror to Iraq, where they were tasked with providing tactical intelligence support to the main invasion forces. Instead of rounding up Al Qaeda, they were hunting for insurgents. But while the targets shifted, the tactics remained as aggressive as ever. "The rules," a source told Seymour Hersh, who first wrote about the program, were "'Grab whom you must. Do what you want.'"

At the CIA's Baghdad station, a young and relatively inexperienced station chief took over in July 2003. Faced with the expanding counterinsurgency mission, he asked supervisors in Langley for better legal guidance on the interrogation rules governing the Agency's officers in Iraq. He also asked for on-site legal advisers to help out with the growing challenge. But according to *New York Times* reporter James Risen, CIA headquarters refused to give the Baghdad station the resources it needed. The station chief specifically asked headquarters for written guidelines on how to conduct detainee interrogations, but none were forthcoming. The friction escalated to the point where the two sides were yelling at each other during long-distance videoconferences. Rather than sending the requested help, however, the CIA brass dressed the Baghdad station down for its insubordination. Tenet's deputies didn't deliver the sought-after interrogation guidelines until after the Abu Ghraib scandal became public, in April 2004.

At the same time, the size of the CIA's Baghdad station was expanding so rapidly, the station chief could barely keep up with its supervision. It more than tripled from 70 or 80 people in July to some 300 by the end of the year. Yet amid all of this expansion, headquarters didn't send the Baghdad station the requested lawyer who could advise on the laws controlling interrogation and detention until January 2004—two months after Jamadi died. The station was short on another form of expertise as well—only four officers spoke Arabic, even though as of midsummer, the Agency had agreed to take a lead role in extracting intelligence from local high-value detainees.

Some of these prisoners were held by Agency personnel in highly unconventional circumstances. Among the most legally troubling was the Agency's practice of abducting and holding prisoners in secret, off the books. Known as "ghost" detainees, these disappeared persons were unregistered with the International Committee of the Red Cross or any other outside authority. The Agency reportedly sent a handful of this population—six to eight—outside of Iraq for interrogation in other countries with approval from the highest levels in Washington. Perhaps this was rationalized as another form of extraordinary rendition. But unlike the terror suspects renditioned from elsewhere in the world, those taken from Iraq during this period of American occupation were supposed to be protected by international law, making their secret removal to other countries potentially serious, prosecutable war crimes.

One such suspect, an Iraqi member of the terrorist group Al Ansar identified as Hiwa Abdul Rahman Rashul, was captured by Kurdish soldiers in the summer of 2003 and taken outside of Iraq for interrogation by the CIA. Another detainee was "lost" for seven months in the system, according to the *Washington Post*. Tenet had asked Rumsfeld not to give the prisoner a number and to keep him hidden from the International Committee of the Red Cross.

The lawlessness and cruelty on the ground in Iraq clearly stemmed from the policies at the top of the Bush Administration. Another indication of this appeared in August 2003. In a little-noticed development, supervisors from the Joint Personnel Recovery Agency, the military entity that monitored and oversaw all SERE training, paid an unusual visit to the battlefront. Since SERE was designed as a training course to help captured U.S. soldiers resist torture, the deployment of the JPRA officials in this way was highly unusual and outside the organization's stated mission. It soon emerged that the officials had not come to help U.S. soldiers resist abuse. They had come to teach them how to inflict it. Just as SERE training had seeped into Guantánamo and the CIA's black sites, it was formally imported during this period into Iraq.

According to an internal investigation conducted later by the Pentagon's deputy inspector general for intelligence, the decision to send SERE instructors to Iraq originated with the Joint Chiefs of Staff, whose operations commander was frustrated at the lack of progress being made by what was called the "Iraq Survey Group," the Iraq-based U.S. task force charged with locating weapons of mass destruction and Saddam Hussein. As it turned out, the Iraq Survey Group resisted the SERE officers' advice to get tougher. The Inspector General's report notes that they "disagreed with what they described as the 'hard-line approach' that the assessment team recommended."

But while the Iraq Survey Group rejected Washington's pressure to use SERE techniques, another task force based in Iraq was excited at the prospect. The Pentagon report found that in September 2003, with the encouragement of the U.S. Joint Forces Command, SERE advisers were sent to aid one of the special new secretive commando teams in Iraq, known as "Joint Task Force 20" or "TF-20." The task force's commander, the report showed, did not call on SERE to help protect his soldiers, but rather asked the SERE officials to "provide advice and assistance to the task force interrogation mission." Within months of the JPRA delegation's visit, TF-20 developed a reputation for uncontrolled brutality. A confidential report to the commanding authorities in Iraq written by Colonel Stuart Herrington, an expert on counterintelligence and interrogation, at the end of 2003 warned the military leadership that the task force, which had about 1,000 Special Forces soldiers working with CIA counterparts, was abusing prisoners in ways that could be construed as illegal. It was a platoon from this task force that kicked in Jamadi's door three months later.

Air Force Reserve Colonel Steve Kleinman risked a twenty-two-year career as a commissioned officer in the U.S. Air Force to try to stop it. Kleinman was thin and fit, with sharply chiseled features, green eyes, and a military haircut. He had spent his whole career in the area of human intelligence. In 2003, he became the senior intelligence officer for survival training in the Department of Defense. The assignment brought him to the JPRA's headquarters at Fairchild Air Force Base in Spokane, Washington, from which SERE training was administered. Although he was surrounded by SERE instructors, Kleinman was surprised to find that he was the only officer there with any real-life experience questioning foreign prisoners. While they were teaching in simulated conditions of capture and torture, he had served as a military interrogator in two previous campaigns, in Panama and the first Gulf War. He regarded survival training as "noble." But when he was sent to Iraq in the fall of 2003 as part of the SERE delegation advising on interrogation, he said, "It was a life-changing event for me."

Kleinman declined to provide details about whom he worked with in Iraq, some of which were classified. But other sources and documents make clear that he was sent in to advise TF-20. The first stop was Camp Cropper, the military's central booking facility near the Baghdad International Airport. So many Iraqi prisoners were being brought in that Kleinman asked where they would all be housed. "When they told me Abu Ghraib," he said, "I laughed. I couldn't believe it. The place was a symbol of Saddam's abuses. They should have turned it into a school, or a hospital, or just blown it up." Instead, he said, "As soon as they stood it up, Abu Ghraib became the repository for our mistakes." Rejecting Rumsfeld's argument that the only problem was a handful of wayward soldiers, he said, "It was not a few rotten apples. It was the Zimbardo experiment writ large."

Kleinman thought he had been brought to Iraq to identify problems in the task force's interrogation program. The Special Forces commanders in Washington were dissatisfied and wanted better intelligence. After a cursory look, the problem seemed obvious to him. "I couldn't believe the lack of professionalism. Interrogation is both an art and a science, but what they were doing was neither," he said. Many of the interrogators lacked training, and those who had attended the Army's course on interrogation in Fort Huachuca—often years earlier—had been taught the wrong methods for an insurgency. "They were asking the wrong questions. They were trained on a Cold War model," Kleinman said, designed for combat in which one organized force faced another. "So when they asked insurgents for their chain of command," he said, many truthfully didn't know. Insurgencies have cellular structures without formal commands. "But these guys didn't believe them," said Kleinman. "They thought they needed more force."

Instead of wanting his analysis, Kleinman soon learned, the JPRA wanted him to share his SERE techniques. He said the attitude was "Hey, we have a real live interrogator who also knows SERE—show us!" Kleinman refused. "It was an unlawful order, and an unlawful act." He reminded his commander that the SERE techniques were designed to re-create illegal abuse outlawed by the Geneva Conventions. He pointed out that the task force, and all U.S. personnel in Iraq, were obliged to treat captured insurgents within the bounds of the Geneva Conventions.

But according to an internal military investigation, the JPRA commander, Randy Moulton, argued that the Geneva Conventions were moot. "These people would never observe them if it was us," he argued. The investigative report by the Inspector General says that Moulton believed that the Iraqi insurgents were not enemy prisoners of war covered by the Geneva Conventions, but "designated unlawful combatants" against whom SERE techniques could be used. The report says further that the top commander in the U.S. Joint Forces, overseeing special operations, agreed and gave "verbal approval" to try to use the SERE techniques.

For bucking these direct orders from the top rungs of the Pentagon to inflict illegal levels of cruelty on the prisoners, Kleinman said he soon found himself "the least popular officer in the whole country. I got into serious arguments with many people. They *wanted* to do these things. They were itching to. It was about revenge, not interrogation. And they thought I was coddling terrorists." He said some of the Special Forces operatives soon started getting up whenever he sat down near them in the mess hall. One Ranger stood over him while sharpening a knife in his face and warned, "It wouldn't be good for your health to sleep too soundly."

Two years later, Kleinman was exonerated by the Department of Defense's investigation. He was thanked for upholding the law by the Inspector General at the Joint Forces command and promoted to full colonel. His commander at JPRA, the administrators of the SERE program, soon retired. The report chastised the JPRA for reverse-engineering its resistance training into a curriculum for abuse, noting that the SERE program was "not appropriate to use in training interrogators." But a senior civilian at the JPRA, Chris Wirts, described by colleagues as an extensively tattooed former SERE instructor with a shaved head, who was particularly avid about exporting SERE techniques into the war on terror remained.

The CIA, meanwhile, became so concerned about the questionable tactics of the joint task forces that it withdrew its officers from participating in joint interrogations in Iraq.

That fall of 2003, the conditions were ripe for abuse. Cruel and unusual treatment of detainees was commonplace. Kleinman said, "The information coming from Secretary Rumsfeld was confusing—there was no clarity. You could see it all over."

What was clear, however, was that as the insurgency in Iraq grew, the Justice Department's legal memos from Washington, separating CIA from military, and law-free zones like Guantánamo from those where international law applied, were all but meaningless in a geographically unbounded war where fighters of different training and experience were thrown together. Enlisted soldiers, bound by the Uniform Code of Military Justice and following the decades-old rules spelled out by the *Army Field Manual,* found themselves fighting and interrogating Iraqi insurgents side by side with hardened unconventional warriors claiming not to be bound by the same rules. Bush and Cheney's lawyers had created a recipe for confusion and lawbreaking. In such a fog, it was hard to tell who had committed the crime of killing Jamadi. The only clues he could provide were those that could be deduced from the physical damage to his corpse.

According to hundreds of pages of internal military and CIA records, a platoon of Navy SEALs working for Task Force 20 arrived at Jamadi's house that night with a clear goal: They were going to either capture or kill the suspected Saddam Hussein loyalist. The SEALs had arrived at his three-story apartment in a convoy of Humvees and SUVs with the windows blacked out. They had expected to blow the apartment's front door open, but Jamadi opened it instead and was soon on the floor fighting ferociously from room to room with one of the SEALs. As fists flew, the SEAL tried to regain his balance by reaching for a heavy stove in the kitchen. Instead, it toppled down, striking Jamadi in the head and chest. At this point, the SEAL was able to subdue Jamadi, who was considerably taller than him. As the Iraqi's wife and children watched, the soldier tied Jamadi's hands in plastic flexicuffs so tightly that later a military policeman would have trouble cutting them off.

The SEAL team had located Jamadi with the help of the CIA, which itself had been tipped off by an Iraqi agent. The Americans suspected Jamadi of hiding as much as two tons of explosives and teaching other insurgents how to shoot mortars and launch other attacks. The Task Force's mission was to get enough information to prevent him and his network from carrying out any further terrorist attacks.

The melee in Jamadi's house created a heightened emotional pitch. Some of the SEALs said later they had never encountered tougher resistance. By the time they dragged Jamadi to a waiting Humvee, he was treated, in the words of a CIA security agent who was riding shotgun that night, "like a bag of potatoes." National Public Radio reporter John McChesney aired a detailed account reconstructed from court and other documents in which he quoted the guard as exclaiming to the others, "Did you see that? Did you see that?" Two SEALs had flipped Jamadi head over heels into the floor of the Humvee, where they then straddled him. Under his bloody hood, he already had a black eye and a cut on his face.

What happened next was painstakingly dissected by investigators for both the CIA and Pentagon after Jamadi's death, as each organization tried to isolate which blow, by which outfit, may have killed the detainee.

Jamadi was driven first to an Army base for debriefing, where the SEALs punched, kicked, and struck him with their rifle muzzles for some twenty minutes. Then they moved him to a secret interrogation center in a nearby Navy camp at Baghdad International Airport known as "The Romper Room." One of its memorable features was a rope noose hanging from the ceiling.

Contemporaneous accounts describe TF-20 and its successors, TF-121 and TF 6-26, as taking detainees for interrogation to Camp Nama, a secret compound off a dusty road in front of the airport. There U.S. personnel questioned prisoners in five interrogation rooms ranging in degrees of coerciveness from an Oriental-carpeted room in which tea was served and respect was shown, known as "the soft room," to the "black room," in which eighteen-inch hooks hung from the ceiling and speakers blasted detainees, who were beaten and kept in agonizing stress positions.

The task forces operated in complete secrecy, so little was known about them by the American public, particularly before the photographs from Abu Ghraib emerged. Pentagon officials repeatedly denied rumors of abuse. But human rights groups such as the American Civil Liberties Union and Human Rights Watch, and journalists at the *New York Times* and *Washington Post* later pieced together revealing accounts and documents. Among the findings was that the walls at Camp Nama were posted with placards warning against leaving telltale marks on the detainees, with the motto "No Blood, No Foul." Soldiers stationed there told human rights workers that they witnessed detainees being stripped, beaten, covered in mud, drenched in freezing water, and made to stand all night in front of air conditioners. One was made to drink urine. Several, including the mother of a six-month-old infant, were locked up away from their husbands and children as hostages, to be traded for suspects in the family.

While the CIA reportedly barred its agents from participating with the joint task forces in interrogations after August 2003, the Agency had an operations center next door to Camp Nama and continued to work closely with the commandos, meeting twice a day with interrogators and their supervisors to analyze fresh intelligence.

The CIA's prohibition against participating in interrogations, however, did not stop a CIA interrogator from being present that November night in the Romper Room with Jamadi. A former CIA polygrapher named Mark Swanner, who had been with the Agency since the 1980s, now working in Iraq as an interrogator, played a key role. According to one eyewitness, Jamadi seemed to go limp, as if passing out, on his way into the room. There, several witnesses said, he was stripped, seated, and drenched in cold water. One of the SEALs said that after Jamadi was handcuffed a CIA interrogator rammed "his arm up against the detainee's chest, pressing on him with all his weight." A witness said the CIA interrogator leaned into Jamadi's face and yelled, "I'm going to barbecue you if you don't tell me the information."

One witness recalled Jamadi moaning, "I'm dying, I'm dying." Others didn't recall those words. The same witness said that the CIA interrogator replied, "I don't care. You'll be wishing you were dying."

After an hour and a half of fruitless interrogation during which

Jamadi denied having any explosives, the SEALs "body-slammed" Jamadi into the back of a Humvee, witnesses said, before delivering him to Abu Ghraib for interrogation in the custody of the CIA.

By the time that Jamadi arrived at Abu Ghraib, it was clear that the CIA was playing outside everyone else's rules. The August 2004 report by Major General George Fay concluded that "CIA detention and interrogation practices led to a loss of accountability, abuse, reduced interagency cooperation and an unhealthy mystique that further poisoned the atmosphere at Abu Ghraib."

Karpinski, the former commander of the 800th Military Police Brigade, which oversaw the administration of Abu Ghraib during that period, was not certain herself what the CIA was doing there. "I thought most of the civilians there were interpreters, but there were some civilians I didn't know," she said. "I called them disappearing ghosts. . . . They were always bringing in somebody for interrogation, or waiting to collect somebody going out."

Walter Diaz, a military policeman, was on guard duty at Abu Ghraib the morning that Jamadi was delivered to the prison. He said, "The OGA"—"other government agencies," initials commonly used to protect the identity of the CIA—"would bring in people all the time to interview them. We had one wing, Tier One Alpha, reserved for the OGA. They'd have maybe twenty people there at a time." He went on, "They were their prisoners. They'd get into a room and lock it up. We, as soldiers, didn't get involved. We'd lock the door for them and leave. We didn't know what they were doing." But, he recalled, "We heard a lot of screaming."

Considering this level of secrecy, it's doubtful that any details would have emerged about the CIA's role in Jamadi's death had it not been for a strange and tangential chain of events. Three months after Jamadi died, Jeffrey Hopper, a Navy SEAL who had been assigned to carry out joint operations with the CIA in Baghdad, was accused of stealing another SEAL's body armor. Hopper, who had been nicknamed Klepto by the unit, was expelled from the Special Forces. When he was dismissed, he told authorities that he knew of far worse offenses committed by other SEALs, and he cited the abuse of several prisoners, including Jamadi. His accusations formed the basis of multiple charges against several SEALs, which led to the court-martial of Lieutenant Andrew Ledford, the commander of the platoon that captured Jamadi, for, among other things, allowing his troops to assault the prisoner. In May of 2005, Ledford was acquitted of any wrongdoing; but during the hearings, which were open, a number of troubling facts spilled out, hinting at the CIA's role in Jamadi's death.

By late spring of 2004, the SEALs' reputations had been tarnished by the exposure of their rough treatment, but they were cleared of the gravest abuse charges. The question of who was responsible for Jamadi's death remained unanswered. Milt Silverman, one of the defense attorneys, asked, "Who killed Jamadi? I know it wasn't any of the SEALs. . . . That's why their cases got dismissed." Frank Spinner, a civilian lawyer who represented Ledford, said, "There's a stronger case against the CIA than there is against Ledford. But the military's being hung out to dry while the CIA skates. I want a public accounting, whether in a trial, a hearing before a congressional committee, or a public report. There's got to be something more meaningful than sticking the case in a Justice Department drawer."

Spinner and several of the other defense lawyers learned more about the CIA's role in Jamadi's death than they were supposed to know, owing to a classification error made by the Agency. The CIA sent hundreds of pages of material on Jamadi's death to the Navy; much of it was classified and all of it was marked unclassified. The pages were passed on to the civilian lawyers, who read them carefully. The Agency, after realizing its mistake, demanded that the lawyers return the classified material and subsequently sealed virtually all the court records relating to the case. Some of the CIA documents, however, were seen by a source familiar with the case, who shared their contents.

What they showed was that Jamadi arrived at Abu Ghraib around 4:30 in the morning, naked from the waist down, according to an eyewitness, Jason Kenner, an MP with the 372nd Military Police Company. In a statement to CIA investigators, Kenner recalled that Jamadi had been stripped of his pants, underpants, socks, and shoes, arriving in only a purple T-shirt and a purple jacket, and with a green plastic sandbag completely covering his head. He was shivering from the cold. Nevertheless, Kenner told CIA investigators, "The prisoner did not appear to be in distress." Kenner replaced Jamadi's plastic flexicuffs with steel handcuffs and secured his hands behind his back.

Staff Sergeant Mark Nagy, a reservist in the 372nd Military Police Company, was also on duty at Abu Ghraib when Jamadi arrived. According to the classified internal documents, he told CIA investigators that Jamadi seemed "lucid," noting that he was "talking during intake." Nagy said that Jamadi was "not combative" when he was placed in a holding cell and that he "responded to commands." In Nagy's opinion, there was "no need to get physical with him."

Kenner told the investigators that "minutes" after Jamadi was placed in the holding cell, an "interrogator" began "yelling at him, trying to find where some weapons were."

For most of the time that Jamadi was being interrogated at Abu Ghraib, there were only two people in the room with him. One was an Arabic-speaking translator for the CIA, working on a private contract, who has been identified in military-court papers only as "Clint C." He was given immunity against criminal prosecution in exchange for his cooperation. The other person was Mark Swanner. Both Swanner and his lawyer declined to be interviewed. A visit to his home address in northern Virginia suggested only that he seemed to lead a quintessentially middle-class suburban life, living in a colonial-style house with a front porch and swimming pool on a cul-de-sac. To some extent Swanner, like the abusive soldiers at Abu Ghraib, was a victim himself of circumstance. Poorly trained, placed in an unclear legal framework, and facing enormous pressure to help save American lives, he was only one of many responsible for what happened next.

Kenner said that he could see Jamadi through the open door of the holding cell, "in a seated position like a scared child." The yelling went on, he said, for five or ten minutes. At some point, Kenner said, Swanner and his translator "removed the prisoner's jacket and shirt," leaving him naked. He added that he saw no injuries or bruises. Soon afterward, the MPs were told by Swanner and the translator to "take the prisoner to Tier One," the agency's interrogation wing. The MPs dressed Jamadi in a standard-issue orange jumpsuit, keeping the sandbag over his head, and walked him to the shower room there for interrogation. Kenner said that Jamadi put up "no resistance."

On the way, Nagy noticed that Jamadi was "groaning and breathing heavily, as if he was out of breath." Walter Diaz, the MP who had been on guard duty at the prison, told CIA investigators that Jamadi showed "no distress or complaints on the way to the shower room." But he said that he, too, noticed that Jamadi was having "breathing problems." An autopsy showed that Jamadi had six fractured ribs; it is unclear when they were broken. The CIA officials in charge of Jamadi did not give him even a cursory medical exam, although the Geneva Conventions require that prisoners receive "medical attention."

"Jamadi was basically a 'ghost prisoner,' " a former investigator on the case, who declined to be named, said. "He wasn't checked into the facility. People like this, they just bring 'em in, and use the facility for interrogations. The lower-ranking enlisted guys there just followed the orders from OGA. There was no booking process."

According to Kenner's testimony, when the group reached the shower room Swanner told the MPs that "he did not want the prisoner to sit and he wanted him shackled to the wall." There was a barred window on one wall. Kenner and Nagy, using a pair of leg shackles, attached Jamadi's arms, which had been placed behind his back, to the bars on the window behind him.

The Associated Press quoted an expert who described the position in which Jamadi died as a form of torture known as "Palestinian hanging," in which a prisoner whose hands are secured behind his back is suspended by his arms. (The technique has allegedly been used in the Israeli-Palestinian conflict.) The MPs' sworn accounts to investigators suggest that, at least at first, Jamadi was able to stand up without pain: Autopsy records show that he was five feet ten and, as Diaz explained, the window was about five feet off the ground. The accounts concur that, while Jamadi was able to stand without discomfort, he couldn't kneel or sit without hanging painfully from his arms. Once he was secured, the MPs left him alone in the room with Swanner and the translator.

Less than an hour later, Diaz said, he was walking past the shower room when Swanner came out and asked for help, reportedly saying, "This guy doesn't want to cooperate." According to National Public Radio, one of the CIA men told investigators that he called for medical help, but there is no available record of a doctor having been summoned. When Diaz entered the shower room, he said, he was surprised to see that Jamadi's knees had buckled and that he was almost kneeling. Swanner, he said, wanted the soldiers to reposition Jamadi so that he would have to stand more erectly. Diaz called for additional help from two other soldiers in his company, Sergeant Jeffery Frost and Dennis Stevanus. But after they had succeeded in making Jamadi stand for a moment, as requested, by hitching his handcuffs higher up the window, Jamadi collapsed again. Diaz said, "At first I was, like, 'This guy's drunk.' He just dropped down to where his hands were, like, coming out of his handcuffs. He looked weird. I was thinking, 'He's got to be hurting.' All of his weight was on his hands and wrists—it looked like he was about to mess up his sockets."

Swanner, whom Diaz described as a "kind of shabby-looking, overweight white guy," who was wearing black clothing, was apparently less concerned. "He was saying, 'He's just playing dead,'" Diaz recalled. "He thought he was faking. He wasn't worried at all." While Jamadi hung from his arms, Diaz told me, Swanner "just kept talking and talking at him. But there was no answer."

Frost told CIA investigators that Swanner claimed that the prisoner was just "playing possum." But as Frost lifted Jamadi upright by his jumpsuit, noticing that it was digging into his crotch, he thought, 'This prisoner is pretty good at playing possum." When Jamadi's body went slack again, Frost recalled commenting that he "had never seen anyone's arms positioned like that, and he was surprised they didn't just pop out of their sockets."

Diaz, sensing that something was wrong, lifted Jamadi's hood. His face was badly bruised. Diaz placed a finger in front of Jamadi's open eyes, which didn't move or blink, and deduced that he was dead. When the men lowered Jamadi to the floor, Frost told investigators, "Blood came gushing out of his nose and mouth, as if a faucet had been turned on."

Swanner, who had seemed so unperturbed, suddenly appeared "surprised" and "dumbfounded," according to Frost. He began talking about how Jamadi had fought and resisted the entire way to the prison. He also made calls on his cell phone. Within minutes, Diaz said, four or five additional CIA officers, also dressed in black, arrived on the scene.

Later that morning, Colonel Thomas M. Pappas, the commander of military intelligence at the prison, was overheard saying, "I am not going down for this alone."

CIA personnel ordered that Jamadi's body be kept in the shower room until the next morning. The corpse was packed in ice and bound with tape, apparently in an attempt to slow its decomposition. The ice was already melting when Specialist Sabrina Harman posed for pictures while stooping over the corpse, smiling and giving the thumbs-up sign. The next day, a medic inserted an IV in Jamadi's arm, put the body on a stretcher, and took it out of the prison as if Jamadi were merely ill, ostensibly so as to "not upset the other detainees." A military-intelligence officer later recounted that a local taxi driver was paid to take away Jamadi's body. CIA officials took with them the bloodied hood that had covered Jamadi's head; it was later thrown away. "They destroyed evidence, and failed to preserve the scene of the crime," Spinner, the lawyer for one of the Navy SEALs, said.

Before leaving, Frost told investigators, Swanner confided that he "did not get any information out of the prisoner."

The next day, Swanner gave a statement to Army investigators, stressing that he hadn't laid a hand on Jamadi and hadn't done anything wrong. "Clint C.," the translator, also said that Swanner hadn't beaten Jamadi. "I don't think anybody intended the guy to die," a former investigator on the case, who asked not to be identified, said. But he believed that the decision to shackle Jamadi to the window reflected an intent to cause suffering. The CIA, he said, "put him in that position to get him to talk. They took it that pain equals cooperation." Intent, as John Yoo had emphasized, was central to assessing criminality in war crimes and torture cases.

The autopsy, performed by military pathologists five days later, classified Jamadi's death as a homicide, saying that the cause of death was "compromised respiration" and "blunt force injuries" to Jamadi's head and torso. But apparently the pathologists were unaware that Jamadi had been shackled to a high window. When a description of Jamadi's position was shared with two of the country's most prominent medical examiners—both of whom volunteered to review the autopsy report free, at the request of a lawyer representing one of the SEALs—their conclusion was different.

One of those examiners, Dr. Michael Baden, who was the chief forensic pathologist for the New York State Police, said, "What struck me was that Jamadi was alive and well when he walked into the prison. The SEALs were accused of causing head injuries before he arrived, but he had no significant head injuries—certainly no brain injuries that would have caused death." Jamadi's bruises, he said, were no doubt painful, but they were not life-threatening. Baden went on, "He also had injuries to his ribs. You don't die from broken ribs. But if he had been hung up in this way and had broken ribs, that's different." In his judgment, "asphyxia is what he died from—as in a crucifixion."

Baden, who had inspected a plastic bag of the type that was placed over Jamadi's head, said that the bag "could have impaired his breath, but he couldn't have died from that alone." Of greater concern, he thought, was Jamadi's position. "If his hands were pulled up five feet—that's to his neck. That's pretty tough. That would put a lot of tension on his rib muscles, which are needed for breathing. It's not only painful—it can hinder the diaphragm from going up and down, and the rib cage from expanding. The muscles tire, and the breathing function is impaired, so there's less oxygen entering the bloodstream." A person in such a state would first lose consciousness, he said, and eventually would die. The hood, he suggested, would likely have compounded the problem, because the interrogators "can't see his face if he's turning blue. We see a lot about a patient's condition by looking at his face. By putting that goddamn hood on, they can't see if he's conscious." It also "doesn't permit them to know when he died." The bottom line, Baden said, is that Jamadi "didn't die as a result of any injury he got before getting to the prison."

Dr. Cyril Wecht, a medical doctor and a lawyer who was the coroner of Allegheny County, Pennsylvania, and a former president of the American Academy of Forensic Sciences, independently reached the same conclusion. The interpretation put forward by the military pathologists, he said, "didn't fit with their own report." Instead, Wecht believed that Jamadi "died of compromised respiration" and that "the position the body was in would have been the cause of death." He added, "Mind you, I'm not a critic of the Iraq war. But I don't think we should reduce ourselves to the insurgents' barbaric levels."

Walter Diaz said in a later interview, "Someone should be charged. If Jamadi was already handcuffed, there was no reason to treat the guy the way they did—the way they hung him." Diaz said he didn't know if Swanner had intended to torture Jamadi or the death was accidental. But he was troubled by the government's inaction and by what he saw as the Agency's attempt at a cover-up. "They tried to blame the SEALs. The CIA had a big role in this. But you know the CIA—who's going to go against them?"

In fact, unlike the military, which subjected itself to a dozen internal investigations in the aftermath of the Abu Ghraib scandal, and punished more than 200 soldiers for wrongdoing, the CIA underwent no public accountability process. After September 11, the Agency was implicated in at least four deaths of prisoners in its custody, including that of Jamadi. The CIA's inspector general had referred at least eight cases involving potentially criminal misconduct to the Justice Department for possible prosecution. But the only case that went forward to trial involved David Passaro, a low-level contractor—not an Agency employee, who had beaten an Afghan prisoner to death in 2003. "Is the CIA capable of addressing an illegal killing by its own hands?" asked Thomas Powers, the author of two books about the Agency. "My guess is not."

It appeared that in the view of the Bush Administration, the killing of Jamadi broke no laws. The CIA's inspector general launched an investigation of the homicide and eventually made a criminal referral to the Justice Department, after finding "the possibility of criminality" in the Agency's conduct. But the referral went nowhere. Former CIA Inspector General Fred Hitz, a lecturer in public and international affairs at Princeton University, said, "I think they're just playing stall ball. They want this case to disappear off the screen." Given that both Attorney Generals John Ashcroft and Alberto Gonzales, as well as the head of the Criminal Division, Michael Chertoff, had signed off on the CIA's secret interrogation and detention program, a prosecution would have risked exposure and blame. As John Sifton, a lawyer for Human Rights Watch, concluded, "It's hard to imagine the current leadership pursuing these guys, because the Justice Department is centrally implicated in crafting the policies that led to the abuse."

Jeffrey Smith, a former general counsel of the CIA who handled numerous national security cases in his private practice, said it was possible that the Office of Legal Counsel's memos had succeeded in indemnifying CIA interrogators such as Swanner even in cases of homicide. The lawyers may have opened too many loopholes, Smith said, "making prosecution somehow too hard to do." Smith added, "But even under the expanded definition of torture, I don't see how someone beaten with his hands bound, who then died while hanging—how that could be legal. I'd be embarrassed if anyone argued that it was."

Unknown to all but a handful of officers, on January 13, 2004, Specialist Joseph Darby was disturbed enough by the photos he'd been given of the abuse inside Abu Ghraib that he delivered them to investigators in the Criminal Division. Soon after, General Antonio Taguba was assigned to investigate further. By statute, he could only probe those lower than himself in rank, guaranteeing that those above him in the chain of command would escape blame. As he gathered evidence for what would become a devastating report, however, conditions inside the U.S. military prisons remained hidden. Even the defense lawyers for the detainees in Guantánamo knew next to nothing about the conditions there. On March 9, 2004, however, Shafiq Rasul and Asif Iqbal, the two British citizens who had been the earliest clients of Joe Margulies, were released from Guantánamo. Neither was ever charged with a crime. After they returned home to England, they gave a fantastical-sounding account of their mistreatment. They described so many bizarre experiences in the hands of the U.S.

military—painfully long interrogations while squatting with wrists shackled between their legs, solitary confinement until they feared they would lose their minds, loud music, strobe lights, and snarling dogs—even Michael Ratner, the leftist civil liberties lawyer from the Center for Constitutional Rights who represented them with Margulies, admitted later that he had doubts. "They said they were tortured. I didn't believe it," he said.

Then, on April 28, 2004, the CBS News show *60 Minutes II* aired the first graphic photos taken by American soldiers tormenting detainees in Abu Ghraib. Senator Richard Durbin, a Democrat from Illinois, was serving on the Senate Intelligence Committee when the story broke. Soon after, he forced himself over to a secure room in the U.S. Capitol to see the full set of classified photographs, many of which were shot around the time Jamadi died. The photos depicted American soldiers grinning and giving thumbs-up signs as naked and hooded Iraqi prisoners were forced to perform simulated sex acts, wear leashes, pile into human pyramids, cower in front of vicious-looking dogs, and, in one iconic image, stand hooded with arms outstretched on a box and electrical wires attached. Among them was the image of Jamadi's battered corpse, with American soldiers giddily cavorting over it. The snapshot of Jamadi in death did more damage to America than he could have dreamed of in life. Durbin was deeply shaken.

"You can't imagine what it's like to go to a closed room where you have a classified briefing, and stand shoulder to shoulder with your colleagues in the Senate, and see hundreds and hundreds of slides like those, most of which have never been publicly disclosed. I had a sick feeling when I left." He added, "It was then that I began to have suspicions that something significant was happening at the highest levels of the government when it came to torture policy."

Durbin had no doubt that the behavior was criminal. He wanted to see prosecutions. He planned to introduce legislation affirming that the CIA was covered by U.S. laws banning torture as well as cruel, inhuman, and degrading treatment. He wondered how much of what he was seeing had been authorized. "The world was very simple before 9/11. We knew what the law was, and I understood it to apply to everyone in the government," he said. But as the details of the Bush Administration's secret interrogation and detention program started to surface, he began to think, "There is real uncertainty. There is a shadow over our nation that needs lifting."

At almost precisely the same moment, the Supreme Court entered the picture. On April 28, 2004, the day the Abu Ghraib photos reached the world, the nine justices heard the consolidated case of Hamdi and Padilla. These were the two U.S. citizens held as enemy combatants whom Jack Goldsmith and the other lawyers from the Bush Administration had observed in military brigs a year and a half earlier. They were still being held in extreme isolation, without charges or judicial review. Their defense counsel argued that they needed to be given some legal process in which they could challenge their detention. Deputy Solicitor General Paul Clement, however, argued for the government that the executive branch had the authority to detain them indefinitely, until the end of hostilities, in conditions of the President's choosing.

In a strikingly perceptive string of questions, the justices asked Clement what would prevent the President from ordering torture. He assured them that it was unthinkable, because the United States would court-martial any soldier for such an "atrocity" against a "harmless, detained enemy combatant." Clement added, "I wouldn't want there to be misunderstanding about this. It's also the judgment of those involved that the last thing you want to do is torture somebody, or try to do something along those lines."

Justice Ruth Bader Ginsburg pushed him further. "Suppose the executive says that mild torture will help get this information?" she asked. "It's an executive command. Some systems do that to get information."

Clement retorted, "Well, our executive doesn't."

Eight hours later, CBS News broadcast the photos from Abu Ghraib. The images became instantly viral. The coverage on Al Jazeera and other Middle Eastern media outlets was particularly intense. The court, like the rest of the world, could see the results of the executive branch's unfettered exercise of power. Justice Ginsburg's fears were realized.

As the images of sadistic abuse in Abu Ghraib flickered across the television screen in the corner of Gonzales's White House office, he turned the volume down. The President's lawyer didn't need the sound on to understand what the story meant. "This is going to kill us," he said.

11

BLOWBACK

He who does battle with monsters needs to watch out lest he in the process becomes a monster himself. And if you stare too long into the abyss, the abyss will stare right back at you.

—Friedrich Nietzsche, *Beyond Good and Evil*

By happenstance, Jack Goldsmith was in Alberto Gonzales's office late in April 2004, when he saw the television coverage of Abu Ghraib for the first time. As the images flashed by of American soldiers taunting naked, hooded prisoners, Goldsmith was deeply shaken. He wondered, "Was I indirectly responsible for the abuses? Could I have done something to stop them?"

For months, Goldsmith had been beset by doubts. He had been fighting a secret war, issue by issue, hidden from the public's view, against what he saw as the most excessive and indefensible of the Bush team's legal opinions. The unexpected struggle had begun as soon as he walked into the Justice Department's Office of Legal Counsel, to which the Senate confirmed him as chief, replacing Jay Bybee, on October 6, 2003. In almost every respect, he was an unlikely renegade.

Goldsmith had been the White House's second choice to run the small but critical legal office. Originally, David Addington and Gonzales had picked their ally John Yoo, who was the Deputy Director of the office. But in a surprisingly defiant move, Attorney General John Ashcroft blackballed Yoo. As with many Washington fights, the opposition had as much to do with self-interest as ideology. Yoo's habit of working directly with the White House lawyers without bothering to consult with his boss had infuriated Ashcroft. In a rare defeat for Addington, Ashcroft convinced Andrew Card, the White House Chief of Staff, that Yoo was "a loose cannon," not competent to run the OLC. Soon after being denied the promotion, Yoo announced his intention to leave the Bush Administration and return to teaching law at the University of California in Berkeley. Also exiting in mid-2003 was another charter member of the hawkish War Council, Tim Flanigan.

Goldsmith was expected to hew to the same hard-right political line. As a law professor at the University of Chicago, he had won a reputation for brilliant but extremely conservative stances against the growing reach of international law. He and Yoo were friends and collaborators, having written a piece in the *Wall Street Journal,* for instance, in 1999, arguing that human rights treaties were not binding on the United States unless Congress had independently voted to confirm them as law. They had taken a similarly hard line in arguing in another article that President Bush had the right to withdraw from the Anti-Ballistic Missile Treaty unilaterally. Goldsmith had also been a strong supporter of the Bush Administration's military commissions, which few other academics supported.

Before getting the OLC job, Goldsmith had served in the Pentagon as a lawyer in the office of General Counsel William Haynes. His opposition to the International Criminal Court and to other legal efforts by human rights lawyers had won him attention and praise in the administration. But he was nonetheless surprised to be drafted for the top OLC position in the summer of 2003. The twenty-two-lawyer office was known as a launch pad for high-profile legal careers, and the top job was a sought-after plum. Yet Goldsmith's White House interview had been perfunctory. The only skeptical questions Gonzales's aides had asked when vetting him concerned a political donation he had made to a Democrat. He allayed suspicions by explaining that he was a loyal and conservative Republican but the Democrat was a personal friend.

Had the screening committee been more astute, however, Goldsmith's résumé might have set off one other alarm. Unlike most of the top politically appointed lawyers in the Bush Administration, he had not worked on *Bush v. Gore,* the legal brawl over Bush's 2000 election. The fight was a litmus test of partisan fervor. Goldsmith lacked this. Reagan had inspired him as he grew up in the South, the son of Miss

Teenage Arkansas and a series of stepfathers. But Goldsmith wasn't a political activist as much as a conservative legal theorist. The danger in this distinction, for the ideologues in the administration, was that he had independent principles, including a deep respect for law as something more than the means to a political end.

Goldsmith hadn't formally assumed his new job at the Justice Department before his principles placed him in a bind. As he awaited Senate confirmation in the summer of 2003, he received an urgent phone call from Patrick Philbin, the deputy at OLC who was handling national security matters after Yoo's departure. There was a desperate need for legal guidance. Senior officials had to know right away if it was legal to move Iraqi terror suspects outside the country for interrogation. Goldsmith didn't know what had prompted the question. He was obliged to say he really wasn't sure what the answer was. By the time he was confirmed and had assumed the OLC job in the first week of October, the question was boiling over in urgency. Gonzales called him about it within two hours on his first day, giving him until the end of the week to come up with an answer.

Goldsmith didn't know that in Iraq the CIA had begun to seize "ghost prisoners" like Jamadi, moving some outside the country for especially harsh interrogations. The Fourth Geneva Convention, which spells out the responsibilities of an occupying power such as America then was in Iraq, prohibits the forced transfer of prisoners outside of the occupied country. But there was vast confusion on the ground in Iraq about to whom these laws applied. General Ricardo Sanchez seemed to think all Iraqis fell under the Geneva Conventions. But Addington and Gonzales believed that some Iraqi fighters—those who could be classified as terrorists—didn't deserve these legal protections. They wanted insurgents to be treated as harshly as Al Qaeda terror suspects. A line from John Yoo in the Pentagon's Working Group Report seemed to back up this idiosyncratic view. Yoo advised that no part of the Geneva Conventions protected "unlawful combatants," including the Fourth Convention.

As the insurgency grew and the joint U.S. task forces in Iraq devolved into unruly commandos, however, Scott Muller, the General Counsel at the CIA, and Philbin, the deputy at the OLC, had grown worried. They had read the law and believed that the Fourth Geneva Convention *was* binding. All Iraqis were covered. Even local terrorists had to be treated humanely. None of them could be moved outside of Iraq. To do so would qualify as a "grave breach" of the law, which could be punishable under U.S. war crimes statutes—torture, in particular, carried a potential death sentence.

The answer to Gonzales's question would affect thousands of U.S. soldiers and CIA officers in Iraq who were unsure whether they were breaking the laws. When the issue erupted publicly later, various administration figures, including Yoo, insisted that they had always made it clear that all Iraqis were covered by international law. But on the ground, confusion was rampant. One soldier, Captain Ian Fishback, a West Point graduate with the 82nd Airborne Division, who served tours of duty in both Afghanistan and Iraq, said that he tried for seventeen months to get clear legal guidance, while witnessing a wide variety of abuses that would ordinarily be illegal under military and international law. "Death threats, beatings, broken bones, murder, exposure to elements, extreme forced physical exertion, hostage-taking, stripping, sleep deprivation and degrading treatment" were commonplace in Iraq, he said. But because the command authorities—beginning with President Bush—cast the fight in Iraq as part of the global war against terrorism, he said, no one knew which laws applied.

As Goldsmith read through the pertinent laws of war, he could see that the questions were complicated. Spies and saboteurs, who might include the insurgents, forfeited some legal protections. Still, it seemed like grotesque neglect to leave those in the war zone in a climate of such legal uncertainty. By the end of the week, Goldsmith concluded that Addington and Gonzales were wrong. Goldsmith first told Ashcroft, who was surprised by his opinion but backed it. Ashcroft had already received a call from George Tenet at the CIA, who had apparently heard about the dispute and had argued for maximum "flexibility" in dealing with Iraqi insurgents.

The next step was telling Addington. "They're going to be really mad," Patrick Philbin, the deputy at OLC, warned as the two conservative Ivy League legal stars drove toward the White House. Philbin added ominously, "They've never been told 'No.'"

They soon found themselves in Gonzales's office, seated on a couch like miscreants facing the school principal, as Gonzales and Addington took turns berating them from their respective wing chairs. Gonzales was typically low key, assuming the approach of a disappointed father. "I don't see how terrorists who violate the laws of war can get the protections of the laws of war," he said, looking puzzled. Addington was less restrained. "The President has already decided that terrorists do not receive Geneva Convention protections!" he shouted furiously. Addington, who was over six feet tall, seemed to grow bigger and redder as his anger rose. Goldsmith felt him looking down on everyone else, figuratively and literally. "You cannot question that decision," Addington said with unconcealed condescension.

In other administrations, the vice president's legal counsel would have been unlikely to have any say on the subject at all. Ordinarily, the State Department has the authority to interpret treaties such as the Geneva Conventions. The State Department's lawyers are the experts. But soon after September 11, Gonzales and Addington had usurped this role, giving the awesome responsibility to Yoo at the Justice Department instead. Gonzales obtained a presidential letter requiring his permission before any major international legal question was shared with the State Department. Both Rice and Powell had protested but lost. Effectively, the experts were cut out and Yoo was put in. "It was ridiculous," a colleague acknowledged, "he was just a deputy in the Office of Legal Counsel—he was smart—but he couldn't interpret treaties!" Predictably, the result was error-prone legal decisions whose preordained conclusions were dictated by Addington. It seemed unlikely in Goldsmith's inauspicious White House meeting, for instance, that either Gonzales or Addington had read the Fourth Geneva Convention.

The visit was short. On the way back to the Justice Department, Goldsmith reflected on the advice that Walter Dellinger, a Democratic predecessor in the Office of Legal Counsel, had given him. Your obligation as a government lawyer serving not just the President but the public, Dellinger warned, "is to tell them 'no' even when they don't want to hear it." Dellinger, a law professor and prominent Supreme Court litigator, promised archly, "They'll respect you more in the morning." But after defying Addington, Goldsmith wasn't so sure.

As Assistant Attorney General, Office of Legal Counsel, Goldsmith's interpretation of law, however, was the last word. Within days, the CIA had received the order to repatriate the Iraqi prisoner in question. It caused great consternation among the operatives who had moved him. "It was a huge pain in the ass," said one of them.

Goldsmith's opinion that Geneva's rules covered all Iraqis also had the effect of heightening the legal peril for those involved in killing Jamadi. His ruling was issued in mid-October. Jamadi was killed less than a month later, after the new ruling was in effect. Under the clear new legal order, anything short of "humane" treatment of Iraqi prisoners was unlawful. The killing was a serious war crime.

There were other repercussions, too. Within a week of Goldsmith's opinion, the Central Command's General Sanchez revised his interrogation policy, removing several of the harshest techniques. It was the beginning of a long effort to reform intelligence gathering by the Special Forces in Iraq.

The "ghost detainee" dispute was just the first round of an escalating internecine struggle waged by Goldsmith that fall. It was not a battle he wanted to fight, since many of those on the other side were personal friends and political allies. But he felt he had no choice. Looking back, he would realize how naive he had been. At first, he had little idea of the size and scope of the secret infrastructure that he was imperiling. Bit by bit, however, the enormity of it became abundantly clear.

About six weeks after Goldsmith took over at OLC, his deputy, Philbin, brought him a short stack of worrisome papers to read inside the Justice Department's ultrasecure, electronically impenetrable command center, referred to as the SCIF for Sensitive Compartmentalized Information Facility. Philbin was a hard-core conservative on issues of national security and presidential power, but he warned Goldsmith that even in his view the opinions were pretty far "out there."

As Goldsmith read, he grew increasingly alarmed. He asked to see more. Soon he had read through both of the key legal memos authorizing "enhanced" interrogations. There was the August 1, 2002, Bybee/Yoo torture memo written for the CIA. Accompanying it was the list of techniques, including waterboarding. Also in the stack was the March 14, 2003, legal memo to the Pentagon Working Group, written during the interrogation of Qahtani.

At that moment—nearly half a year before the Abu Ghraib photos surfaced—Goldsmith had very little idea what was going on inside America's detention sites for terror suspects. The memos clinically parsing the legal boundaries of permissible pain were fairly bloodless and sterile on one level, but astonishing on another. The idea of torture scared and repelled him. He knew very little about it, other than what everyone knew, which was that it was among the last nearly universal moral taboos, forbidden by every major religion and civilized government. But Yoo's bureaucratic nit-picking about ways around the torture ban was weirdly numbing. On paper, the techniques didn't look so bad. Also, Goldsmith worried that perhaps the national security experts had reason to take these aggressive steps. He didn't want to be the one second-guessing them, especially in the event of another attack. Bit by bit, Goldsmith convinced himself that it would be best to set aside his personal qualms. The moral trade-offs between torture and security were so difficult, he saw them as policy questions for the President. His job as a lawyer, he told himself, was simply to provide legal analysis. His political and moral opinions were irrelevant. He hadn't yet realized that it was the lawyers, however, who were defining the counterterrorism policy, since the elected officials wanted to do everything that the law could possibly be said to allow.

Goldsmith set aside the big moral questions and instead focused in on the law. But he found the two interrogation memos highly disconcerting from this standpoint as well. They were quite similar. Both had clearly been written to circumvent the 1994 torture ban. Both displayed what New York University law professor Stephen Gillers, a specialist in legal ethics, called "the veneer of serious scholarship (abundant footnotes, many citations, long dense paragraphs) to create an aura of legitimacy for near-death interrogation tactics and unrestrained executive power." But beneath the surface, both of Yoo's interrogation opinions had the same flaw. As Goldsmith wrote in his account, *The Terror Presidency,* Yoo's assertions of absolute power for the commander in chief in dictating the treatment of wartime captives "had no foundation." It was so extreme it would mean the Uniform Code of Military Justice, and all laws written by Congress regulating warfare, were illegitimate. In Goldsmith's view, Yoo's legal guidance had "no basis in prior OLC opinions, or in judicial opinions, or in any other source of law." Yoo's adamant assertions—which were guiding the United States government in prosecuting a global war—were simply unsubstantiated.

Many of the smaller details of the torture opinion were equally shoddy. Yoo turned out to have based his broad definition of allowable pain—anything less than the "pain accompanying serious physical injury such as organ failure, impairment of bodily function, or death"— not on torture cases but rather on a document defining thresholds for public health benefits. It sounded authoritative, but it was garbled and inapposite. On top of this, the torture memo's arguments concerning executive power were, in Goldsmith's view, "cursory and one-sided." The tone was "tendentious" and "lacking [in] caution." But the memo had one obvious attraction: It told Bush and Cheney what they wanted to hear. The opinion opened so many loopholes in the torture ban that Goldsmith could see why the CIA referred to it as "the golden shield" against criminal prosecution. The more Goldsmith read, the more concerned he grew that he would have to do what was nearly unthinkable in the Office of Legal Counsel—retract his friend John Yoo's legal opinions. By custom, the OLC acted somewhat like the Supreme Court, overturning as few prior opinions as possible in order to create legal consistency and clarity within the executive branch. To do otherwise would create terrible disruption. The military and CIA programs would be instantly cast under a legal cloud. The interrogators who had thought themselves safe might face prosecution. So might their bosses—in theory, at least. Withdrawing legal authority like this simply wasn't done. But by early December 2003, Goldsmith decided he had to revoke the interrogation opinions. By then, however, he had seen enough of Addington to know it wasn't going to be easy.

A few weeks after Philbin brought him the troubling legal memos, Goldsmith found himself in a meeting on another subject with Addington inside the Justice Department's SCIF. A few senior lawyers from the National Security Agency had come to discuss the ultrasecret Terrorist Surveillance Program, or TSP, that the Bush Administration had initiated after September 11. Addington was the chief author of the program. But the NSA lawyers were worried that their agency's actions might not be legal. The program seemed in direct conflict with the Foreign Intelligence Surveillance Act, the post-Watergate regulation requiring the government to obtain warrants from a special FISA court before engaging in domestic spying. When one of the NSA lawyers asked to examine the legal analysis on which the program rested, however, Addington, a witness said, "basically ripped the guy's head off."

"You don't need access," Addington said, raising his voice. "The President decides who sees what, not you!" The message, a participant said, was "None of your fucking business!"

It was not until this moment that Goldsmith, who was just a bystander, realized that the NSA lawyers had been barred from seeing the legal foundation for their own agency's program.

This restrictive control was ostensibly imposed to prevent leaks. But in time, Goldsmith concluded, the extreme secrecy served another purpose. It enabled the Vice President's office to implement policies that were highly questionable and unlikely to survive open debate. "After 9/11 they and other top officials in the administration dealt with FISA the way they dealt with other laws they didn't like," he wrote. "They blew right through them in secret, based on flimsy legal opinions that they guarded closely so that no one could question the legal basis for the operations."

In fact, Goldsmith soon found, the legal work for the domestic spying program, which had been done principally by Yoo, was riddled with huge errors. The OLC hadn't had the necessary legal expertise to sort out the NSA program properly. It was a very complicated area of law. After studying it further, Goldsmith thought the program's legality was dubious at best. Putting it on "a proper legal footing," he wrote, ". . . was by far the hardest challenge I faced in government."

Addington did all he could to impede reform. He clearly detested the FISA Court, which had been set up to monitor domestic surveillance after Nixon's illegal wiretaps on political enemies. It was exactly the sort of curb on executive power that he reviled.

Addington had been heard to mutter, "We're one bomb away from getting rid of that obnoxious court." When Goldsmith signaled his intention to rein in the domestic surveillance program, Addington warned him in no uncertain terms that he might have "the blood of a hundred thousand" Americans on his hands. The pressure was awful. But try as Goldsmith did to interpret the law to make the spying program legal, he knew it wasn't.

Complicating Goldsmith's efforts to push the Bush Administration's secret programs back inside the law was their reputed success. On the other side of the globe, in an undisclosed location, the CIA's clandestine efforts were more than justifying themselves in the eyes of the administration's top officials. Khalid Sheikh Mohammed, the primary architect of the September 11 attacks, had been captured in March 2003 by the CIA and was, according to a former Agency official knowledgeable about the case, "singing like a bird." Mohammed had led the Agency to a string of other terrorists, including Hambali, whose real name was Riduan Isamuddin, the head of the Southeast Asian affiliate of Al Qaeda, Jemaah Islamiyah. Hambali was believed to have masterminded the lethal bombing of a Bali nightclub in 2002 that had killed over 200 people. By August, Hambali had been captured, and he reportedly gave information leading to the revelation that Al Qaeda had been in the process of producing high-grade anthrax. Plans for various U.S. targets, including New York businesses and train stations, had also reportedly been captured. This information was old by the time it reached the United States, dating back to before September 11. The Malaysian scientist who had been developing the anthrax had been in custody before Khalid Sheikh Mohammed, since December 2001, raising questions about why the capture of Mohammed was so essential to establish this threat. But in any case, it predictably triggered renewed fears in the White House, where Bush and Cheney hammered the Agency for more details and chastised the FBI for doing too little to root out domestic sleeper cells.

In a heated National Security Council meeting at the end of the summer of 2003, Bush put FBI Director Robert Mueller on the spot about why the FBI hadn't rounded up more terrorists inside America. "If they don't commit a crime, it would be difficult to identify and isolate" possible suspects, Mueller explained. Cheney, who had joined the meeting by video from one of his undisclosed locations, scolded the FBI Director for showing the "same mentality" that had enabled the September 11 attacks. "That's just not good enough," Cheney continued. "We're hearing this too much from the FBI."

In contrast, the CIA was boasting that its "enhanced interrogations" were producing staggering amounts of vital intelligence. Tenet also wrote that "what [they] gave us was worth more than CIA, NSA, the FBI and our military operations had achieved collectively." He described Khalid Sheikh Mohammed as practically playing a consulting role to the Agency, providing key names, filling in gaps, and confessing to multiple crimes, including the grisly murder of Daniel Pearl, a talented young reporter for the *Wall Street Journal* who had been kidnapped and beheaded in Karachi, Pakistan, in early 2002. "Of all the terrorist takedowns," Tenet later wrote, "none was more important or memorable than the capture in Pakistan of Khalid Sheikh Mohammed, whom everyone in our business referred to simply as 'KSM.' No person other than perhaps Usama Bin Ladin was more responsible for the attacks of 9/11 . . . [or] more deserved to be brought to justice."

The U.S. government had been tracking Khalid Sheikh Mohammed since 1993, but Mohammed, a Sunni extremist from the Baluchistan region of Pakistan who had studied at two colleges in North Carolina, had displayed a knack for escaping American law enforcement. Finally, in the early months of 2003, U.S. authorities paid a $25 million reward to a Pakistani informant for information that led to Mohammed's capture. Just as in Zubayda's case, it was the lure of money, not the threat of pain, that produced the breakthrough. U.S. officials closed in on Mohammed at 4 A.M. on March 1, waking him up in a borrowed apartment in Rawalpindi, Pakistan. The officials hung back as Pakistani authorities handcuffed and hooded him and took him to a safe house. The CIA happily transmitted his mug shot, showing a pudgy, unkempt man with matted hair and a slept-in-looking undershirt, to news organizations around the world. A videotape obtained by *60 Minutes* showed Mohammed a day or so later, apparently in Pakistani custody, complaining of a head cold. An American voice could be heard in the background. This was the last image to be seen of him in public. By March 4, he had begun a long trek through a series of secret CIA black prisons.

According to Tenet, Mohammed told his captors that he wouldn't talk until he was given a lawyer. "Had that happened, I am confident that we would have obtained none of the information he had in his head about imminent threats against the American people," Tenet wrote in his memoir. Why Tenet was so sure of this was never made clear. A number of terror suspects in the era before September 11 gave voluminous confessions even after having been read their Miranda rights. Mohammed's nephew, Ramzi Yousef, for example, famously told the U.S. agents who had taken him into custody in Pakistan so much during a plane ride to America, where he was to stand trial, that they had to take turns taking notes to keep up. He was subsequently convicted and sentenced to serve the rest of his life in a U.S. maximum-security prison. "These guys are egomaniacs," a former federal prosecutor close to that case said. "They love to talk!"

The capture of Mohammed was unquestionably a breakthrough for America's counterterrorism campaign, bolstering the CIA's standing. But the CIA's subsequent treatment of Mohammed and the other detainees had begun to stir soul-searching and regret among some inside the Agency. By the time Mohammed was taken into custody, in the spring of 2003, the clandestine program was both more routinized and more controversial in the Agency. Some insiders feared that the network of CIA prisons had spawned a corrosive new subculture, eating away at the ideals that America's intelligence service had been created to protect. "Brutalization became bureaucratized," said one former CIA officer. "I mean, were there career paths in this now? What are the criteria for evaluation and promotion? That's how bureaucracies work. Do you really want to be building these skill sets?" There was also a growing unease about legal exposure. Among the few CIA officials who knew the full details of the detention and interrogation program, there was a tense debate developing about where to draw the line in terms of treatment. John Brennan, Tenet's former chief of staff, said, "It all comes down to individual moral barometers." Waterboarding, in particular, troubled many officials from both a moral and a legal perspective.

Mohammed's interrogation, in particular, raised broader questions about torture. Soon after Mohammed was arrested, two sources said, his American captors told him, "We're not going to kill you. But we're going to take you to the very brink of death and back." They came close enough to make officials in Langley call a halt to the interrogation several weeks after it began, fearing that the combined effect of all the techniques they subjected Mohammed to crossed the criminal line. "We leaned in pretty hard on KSM," Paul Kelbaugh, a CIA lawyer, acknowledged in an interview with the *New York Times.* "We were getting good information, and then they were told: 'Slow it down. It may not be correct. Wait for some legal clarification.'"

"There were some horrible moments," said another former CIA officer, who declined to provide details. "Things went too far. It was awful. Awful."

By the time Mohammed was captured, according to Agency officers involved in the program, the CIA's interrogation protocol was ostensibly more systematic than it had been for Abu Zubayda. "The CIA's interrogations were very, very regimented," said Robert Grenier, the former chief of the Counterterrorist Center, and "very meticulous."

Prisoners such as Mohammed were transported to secret prisons— Afghanistan was apparently the first stop in his case—by teams of black-masked commandos attached to the CTC's paramilitary Special Operations group. A former member of a CIA transport team described the "takeout" of prisoners as a carefully choreographed twenty-minute routine, during which a suspect was hog-tied, stripped naked, photographed, hooded, sedated with anal suppositories, placed in diapers, and transported by plane to a secret location.

The cavity searches and the frequent use of suppositories were likened to "sodomy" by an official involved in an investigation by the Council of Europe, the agency that effectively polices the European Convention on Human Rights. He believed, "It was used to absolutely strip the detainee of any dignity. It breaks down someone's sense of impenetrability. The interrogation became a process not just of getting information but of utterly subordinating the detainee through humiliation." A former CIA officer who favored the program confirmed this supposition, on background, saying that the agency frequently photographed the prisoners naked "because it's demoralizing." The photos were also part of the CIA's quality-control process. They were passed back to case officers for review.

A secret government document, which was originally written for use in Guantánamo, gave further credence to the Bush Administration's official use of forced nakedness as a psychological weapon. "In addition to degradation of the detainee, stripping can be used to demonstrate the omnipotence of the captor or to debilitate the detainee," it said. The document advised interrogators to "tear clothing from detainees by firmly pulling downward against buttoned buttons and seams. Tearing motions shall be downward to prevent pulling the detainee off balance."

According to his own account, the CIA kept Mohammed naked for more than a month, during which time he said he was questioned by an unusual number of female handlers, perhaps as an additional humiliation. Despite the CIA's insistence on the professionalism of its interrogation program, according to two well-informed Agency sources, one particularly overzealous female officer had to be reprimanded for her role. After Mohammed was captured, the woman, who headed the Al Qaeda unit in the CTC, was so excited she flew at government expense to the black site where Mohammed was held so that she could personally watch him being waterboarded. The CIA declined to discuss the matter, to make the officer available for comment, or to allow her to be named, because of a sensitive assignment she was subsequently given. Coworkers described her, however, as the same hard-driving, redheaded former Soviet analyst who had been in the Bin Laden Unit during Michael Scheuer's supervision, who was reviled by some male colleagues for what they regarded as her aggression. Coworkers said she had no legitimate reason to be present during Mohammed's interrogation. She was not an interrogator. "She thought it would be cool to be in the room," a former colleague said. But ironically, her presence during Mohammed's ordeal, sources said, seemed to anger and strengthen his resolve, helping him to hold out longer against the harsh tactics used against him. Afterward, two sources said, word leaked out about her jaunt and superiors at the CIA scolded her for treating the painful interrogation as a show. "She got in some trouble. They told her, 'It's not supposed to be entertainment,'" the former colleague disclosed.

Mohammed, meanwhile, alleged that he was beaten incessantly, attached to a dog leash, and yanked in such a way that he was propelled into the walls of his cell. Sources said that he also claimed to have been forced to stand shackled in a stress position for eight hours a day, during which he was suspended from the ceiling by his arms, his toes barely touching the ground. The pressure on his wrists evidently became exceedingly painful. Many other detainees held by the CIA in Afghanistan around the same time gave notably consistent accounts of their treatment, though they had no opportunity to collude. Ramzi Kassem, who taught at Yale Law School, said that a Yemeni client of his, Sanad al-Kazimi, who was eventually moved to Guantánamo, alleged that he had received similar treatment in a pitch-black facility that detainees called the "Dark Prison," near Kabul Airport. Kazimi claimed to have been suspended by his arms for long periods, causing his legs to swell painfully. "It's so traumatic, he can barely speak of it," Kassem said. "He breaks down in tears." Kazimi also claimed that, while hanging, he was beaten with electric cables.

Mohammed described being chained naked to a metal ring in his cell wall for prolonged periods in a painful crouch. Several other detainees who were confined in the Dark Prison described identical treatment. Mohammed also claimed that he was kept alternately in suffocating heat and in a painfully cold room, where he was doused with ice water.

Some detainees held by the CIA claimed that their cells were bombarded with deafening sound twenty-four hours a day for weeks and even months. Usually the sounds were music, but a detainee named Moazzam Begg described hearing hysterical female screams from an unseen woman who he was led to believe was his wife. Another detainee, Binyam Mohamed, who was later transferred to Guantánamo, told his lawyer, Clive Stafford Smith, that he found the psychological torture more intolerable than the physical abuse that he said he had been previously subjected to in Morocco, where, he said, local intelligence agents had sliced his penis with a razor blade. "The CIA worked people day and night for months," Smith quoted his client as saying. "Plenty lost their minds. I could hear people knocking their heads against the walls and doors, screaming their heads off."

Kassem said his Yemeni client told him that during his incarceration in the Dark Prison he attempted suicide three times by ramming his head into the walls. "He did it until he lost consciousness," Kassem said. "Then they stitched him back up. So he did it again. The next time, he woke up, he was chained, and they'd given him tranquilizers. He asked to go to the bathroom, and then he did it again." This last time, Kazimi was given more tranquilizers and chained in a more confining manner. The Bybee/Yoo torture memo had authorized the use of drugs on detainees, without their consent, so long as it did not "profoundly disrupt" the personality.

"They were torturing people," said a former CIA official with extensive knowledge of the CIA's program. "No question. They did disgusting things to people. Their attitude was, 'Laws? Like who the fuck cares?'" It was the simultaneous use of multiple forms of coercion for extended periods that made the treatment of Mohammed and other CIA detainees "especially abusive," according to those who read the Red Cross report on it. Mohammed was subjected not just to waterboarding but to hundreds of different techniques in just a two-week period soon after his capture, according to one account. A former U.S. official, with access to details of the interrogation program, stressed that few outsiders truly understood the overwhelming power of the program. Critics have focused on specific techniques, such as waterboarding. But, he said, "What mattered was things done in combination. It can look antiseptic on a piece of paper, when it's a legal checklist. It seems clinical. It doesn't sound so much. You have to have the imagination to visualize it graphically, and in combinations, over time, to understand how this all would work in reality. The totality is just staggering." Senator Carl Levin, the chairman of the Senate Armed Services Committee, came to a similar conclusion, arguing in an interview that "there's a point where it's torture. You can put someone in a refrigerator and it's torture. Everything is a matter of degree."

While the prisons in Afghanistan were primitive, a later CIA facility to which Mohammed was transferred was troubling in a different way. Designed exclusively for the highest-value detainees, it was sleeker and more Orwellian. The special facility appears to have been in Eastern Europe, probably Poland, according to a source who studied the details closely, although the Polish government denied this. After examining flight records and interviewing numerous inside sources, Dick Marty, a Swiss prosecutor who led the investigation by the Council of Europe, concluded in 2006, "It is now clear—although we are still far from having established the whole truth—that authorities in several European countries actively participated with the CIA in these unlawful activities."

The newer prison, according to well-informed sources, was far more high-tech than the prisons in Afghanistan, and more intensely focused on psychological torment. The cells had hydraulic doors and air-conditioning. Multiple cameras in each cell provided video surveillance of the detainees. In some ways, the circumstances were better: The detainees were given bottled water. Without confirming the existence of any black sites, Robert Grenier, the former CIA counterterrorism chief, said, "The agency's techniques became less aggressive as they learned the art of interrogation," which, he added, "IS an art."

Mohammed described being kept in a prolonged state of sensory deprivation, during which every point of reference was erased. In an echo of the CIA's mind-control experiments, he was kept naked except for goggles and earmuffs. The Council of Europe's report described a four-month isolation regime as typical. The prisoners had no exposure to natural light, making it impossible for them to tell if it was night or day. They interacted only with masked, silent guards. In an interview, Mohammed al-Asad, a detainee held at what was most likely a different Eastern European black site from that holding Mohammed, said white noise was piped in constantly, although during electrical outages he could hear people crying. Mohammed said he had no idea where he was, although at one point he apparently glimpsed Polish writing on a water bottle.

Meals were delivered sporadically, to ensure that the prisoners remained temporally disoriented. The food was largely tasteless and barely enough to live on. Mohammed claimed to have lost some forty pounds in his first month. American officials who saw him later confirmed that he appeared physically transformed. Experts on the CIA program said that the administering of food was part of its psychological arsenal. Sometimes portions were smaller than the day before, for no apparent reason. "It was all part of the conditioning," the official involved in the Council of Europe inquiry said. "It's all calibrated to develop dependency."

A CIA source said that Mohammed was subjected to waterboarding only after interrogators determined that he was hiding information from them. But Mohammed claimed that even after he started cooperating, he was waterboarded numerous times. Footnotes to the 9/11 Commission report indicate that by April 17, 2003—a month and a half after he was captured—Mohammed had already started providing substantial information on Al Qaeda. Nonetheless, he was kept in isolation for years.

During the most intense phases of his interrogation, Mohammed described being interrogated by three men, all of whom seemed to him to be about sixty-five years old. One had an accent that seemed Arab—possibly Moroccan. Another seemed South American. And the third seemed Eastern European. They were all very strong, and seemed to be the bosses of the prison and guards. He called them "emirs." When they were happy with what he told them, they gave him candies.

Concern about cruelty was not the only worry beginning to roil some at the CIA during this period. While Tenet continued to assure the White House that Mohammed's interrogation in particular had been a gold mine of invaluable intelligence, a few officers began to question the reliability of his coerced confessions. Some also feared that the torturous methods used by the Agency would undermine eventual efforts to convict him in any legitimate court. Mohammed claimed responsibility for so many crimes that his testimony began to seem inherently dubious. In addition to confessing to the Pearl murder, he said that he had hatched plans to assassinate President Clinton, President Carter, and Pope John Paul II. CIA cables carrying Mohammed's interrogation transcripts back to Washington were prefaced with the warning that "the detainee has been known to withhold information or deliberately mislead."

After Mohammed had been interrogated for some time, a top Agency official asked for a few choice revelations from his confession that he could share with officers from an allied foreign intelligence agency. To his surprise, he was told by top CIA officials that there really was nothing "solid" enough to pass on. Although few outside of the CIA knew it, Mohammed had recanted substantial portions of his initial confessions.

Mohammed brazenly boasted later about his ability to mislead the United States. He claimed that the false information he fabricated caused the U.S. Department of Homeland Security to issue urgent terrorist threat alerts on several occasions, for no real reason. He just wanted the interrogators to stop, he said, so he told them whatever they seemed to want to hear.

The reliability of Mohammed's coerced confessions was a particularly painful problem in the Daniel Pearl case. In the fall of 2003, Condoleezza Rice called Pearl's young widow, Mariane, with the confidential news that Mohammed had confessed to personally killing her husband. But many of the federal officials who knew the most about Mohammed were deeply skeptical. It was possible, of course.

But they noted that Mohammed had "no history of killing with his own hands. He'd be happy to commit mass murder from afar," said one government expert, but to behead someone, which required horrific psychological and physical force, was inconsistent with his history. "He was just a little dough-boy," said one doubter. "It wasn't his style." Another government official involved in the case worried that Mohammed's confession was fabricated in order to cover up the real murderer. In Pakistan, a different suspect, an Islamic terrorist named Ahmed Omar Saeed Sheikh, had already been charged and convicted and was awaiting sentencing for the kidnap and murder.

Judea Pearl, Daniel's father, was dubious. "Something's fishy," he said. "He could say he killed Jesus—he had nothing to lose." Mariane Pearl was also disconcerted, and increasingly uncomfortable with the CIA's secretive extralegal methods, which made it difficult to know for sure how much weight to give to the confession. She was relying on the Bush Administration to bring justice in her husband's case, so she was careful with her words. But she noted, "You need a procedure that will get the truth. An intelligence agency is not supposed to be above the law." Five years after Mohammed's capture, he had yet to be tried for any crime, and many legal experts questioned whether he could be, given the torture that he could claim to have undergone. Bruce Riedel, who was a CIA analyst for twenty-nine years before joining the Brookings Institution, asked, "What are you going to do with KSM in the long run? I don't think anyone has an answer. If you took him to any real American court, I think any judge would say there's no admissible evidence. It would be thrown out."

The problems stemming from the legally dubious program were bigger than Mohammed's case. Later, as more was learned about the CIA's unorthodox methods, critics such as Senator Carl Levin feared that the CIA's secret program would undermine the public's trust in American justice and make it impossible to prosecute the entire top echelon of Al Qaeda leaders in captivity. "Is that what we want?" asked Levin. "A guy as dangerous as KSM, and half the world wonders if they can believe him? Statements that can't be believed, because people think they rely on torture?"

The CIA's treatment of detainees was also a concern of the 9/11 Commission during this period. Among the only outsiders to see the summaries of Khalid Sheikh Mohammed's confessions in "real time," as they were being extracted from him, was Philip Zelikow, the

Executive Director of the bipartisan Commission. He and a staff of laser-bright legal experts were tasked by Congress and the President with piecing together the story of the 9/11 plot shard by shard, in order to create the first and fullest possible historic record of one of the greatest crimes in American history. Zelikow asked the CIA for permission to interview Mohammed and other high-value detainees, in order to document their roles. The CIA refused. At first, the Agency argued that any outside interference would disrupt the psychological dynamics required for interrogation. This was the same argument the administration had made concerning Padilla and Hamdi—outside contact would give the detainee hope, destroying the desired state of helplessness and dependency.

Zelikow, whose training as both a historian and a lawyer made him unusually attuned to the value of unfiltered primary source material, kept pushing. He proposed that he be allowed to submit questions and observe Mohammed answering them through a two-way mirror or a remote surveillance camera. His concern was that some of the accounts he had seen from Mohammed and other detainees were contradictory and lacking convincing detail. "There were problems from our perspective," he said. "There were internal and unexplained inconsistencies. There were cases where people were talking about things that were ripe for further examination. And there were other puzzling things," he said. Zelikow wanted to know more about the interrogators' questions and training, too. But the CIA again refused his request for more information. There would be no access, no remote access, no observation, and no information on where Mohammed and the other detainees were being held, or under what conditions. The CIA also refused to let Zelikow's team talk directly to the interrogators.

In a meeting on December 23, 2003, Zelikow demanded that the CIA at the very least provide any and all documents responsive to its requests, even if the Commission had not specifically asked for them. Tenet replied by alluding to several documents he thought would be helpful. But in an omission that would later become part of a criminal investigation, neither Tenet nor anyone else from the CIA in the meeting mentioned that, in fact, the Agency had in its possession at that point hundreds of hours of videotapes of the interrogations of Abu Zubayda and Abd al-Rahim al-Nashiri, both of whom were waterboarded. These tapes would clearly have been of interest to Zelikow. In 2008, when the Commission's chairmen, Thomas Kean and Lee Hamilton, found out that the CIA had withheld the relevant videotapes and later destroyed them, they accused the CIA of "obstruction," a federal crime.

The fight over the Commission's access to the detainees built to a head on January 21, 2004. Kean and Hamilton faced off against Tenet, Rumsfeld, and Gonzales in a White House meeting. Tenet and Gonzales "took a very hard line," said Zelikow. They were adamant. Afterward, Zelikow argued for the Commission to defy the CIA and issue a subpoena. "You can imagine how explosive this would have been," said Zelikow. "It would have been a dramatic and very, very difficult confrontation on all sides. But we thought the matter was important enough." The Commission took a vote, but the majority of members opposed getting into a public confrontation with the CIA.

Zelikow and his assistants continued to pass questions back and forth to the detainees through the CIA's mysterious channels. An analysis by NBC News later showed that the Commission relied on more than 100 interrogation reports produced by the CIA. Additional questions posed by the Commission spurred some thirty extra interrogation sessions, NBC reported, raising the question of whether the Commission's work was both based on torture and unwittingly complicit in it.

No one on the Commission, however, knew exactly why its members were being kept away. But the CIA's extreme secrecy raised Zelikow's suspicions. He talked it over with a CIA veteran, who was equally concerned. "We inferred that the interrogations were being conducted under highly unusual circumstances," he said. He also thought it odd that the FBI, which had whole teams of experienced investigators assigned to each of the 9/11 flights, was not involved in the CIA's interrogations. "Why not include some of these people?" he wondered. He asked the FBI, but, he said, "They didn't want to tell me." The FBI's determined absence, he said, was another clue that something was very wrong. "It was the dog that didn't bark," he said.

In July 2004, the 9/11 Commission issued its final report, along with twenty-four recommendations. One called on the United States to make clear that as a matter of policy, all detainees, including those held by the CIA, would be handled in the humane fashion outlined in the Geneva Conventions. Commission members, who suspected the CIA of prisoner abuse, considered the issue key to winning the world's hearts and minds in the larger war against terrorism. The White

House adopted twenty-two of the twenty-four recommendations. The call for "humane treatment" was one of the two that the Bush Administration explicitly rejected.

In December 2003, all that Goldsmith knew for sure about the CIA's program was that his bosses in the administration considered the "enhanced" interrogations of terror suspects to be the single most effective tool in the war on terror. Nevertheless, by then Goldsmith had independently become convinced that he had to withdraw John Yoo's torture memos. The question, though, was how? The secret program had been approved by the President, the Vice President, the Attorney General, and the National Security Council. The congressional leadership, too, had signed off on it, although some members of Congress complained later that the CIA had never explained graphically enough how torturous its methods were. (The line that the Bush Administration used to reassure Democratic members of Congress, in particular, was that the CIA was doing nothing to its detainees beyond what the U.S. military did in its own training program—a reference to the SERE exercises.) Taking on so many powerful interests in the midst of the war on terror was a daunting challenge. Goldsmith was barely forty, and he had been in the Justice Department for a little over two months.

After discussing it with Philbin, Goldsmith decided that it would be best to tackle the torture memos one at a time, starting first with the one written only for the Defense Department. It would be less of a confrontation, because it didn't involve dealing with the White House. Because the Pentagon memo was addressed to Jim Haynes, Goldsmith decided he wouldn't even tell the White House about his decision. (The CIA memo had been addressed to Gonzales, making a White House confrontation unavoidable.) During the slow week between Christmas and New Year's, Goldsmith called his former boss, Haynes. "Jim, I've got bad news . . . ," he began.

Goldsmith told Haynes that the twenty-four techniques that had been approved for military interrogations by Rumsfeld were still fine, but that the legal opinion that had authorized the military to use torture, and lesser cruelty if military necessity so required, could no longer be relied upon. Haynes, of course, had had this conversation before, with Mora, almost precisely a year earlier, and had used the legal memo to say that Mora was wrong.

Goldsmith recalled that there was a long silence, after which Haynes replied, "Okay." Haynes asked what was wrong with the original opinion, but he didn't argue. The whole conversation lasted fewer than five minutes.

Fixing the CIA torture memo would prove quite a bit more challenging. In preparation, Goldsmith began researching.

During that same holiday week, in Skopje, Macedonia, unknown to Goldsmith, a related drama involving the CIA's secret interrogation program was playing out. Khaled el-Masri, a barely employed car salesman from Ulm, in southern Germany, was stopped and separated from fellow passengers on a tourist bus by border guards at the Tabanovce border crossing between Serbia and Macedonia. Apparently, his name was similar to that of a wanted Al Qaeda leader. Masri had left his wife and four young sons behind for a breather from family life. He and his wife had been arguing, and in a huff he had taken off on his own for a cheap round-trip package holiday in Macedonia. Although he was a Muslim of Lebanese descent, he was by 2003 a German citizen whose children were all born in the country. His brandnew German passport, however, was confiscated by the border guards. Unfamiliar with a redesigned version just issued by Germany, they believed it to be a forgery. They took him into a windowless room and started asking him bizarre questions about being a terrorist.

For thirteen days, the Macedonian authorities held him at gunpoint in a nice hotel room across from the zoo, just a stone's throw from the American embassy. Masri begged them to call his wife, to let her know where he was, and to call the German embassy, which could vouch for his good citizenship. Only after he began a hunger strike did they promise to let him go home.

Masri had no inkling of it, but he was causing great excitement inside the Skopje station of the CIA, where a young officer who was in charge for the holiday saw the case as a chance to score a counterterrorism coup. "Everyone wanted to play the game," a former Agency official said.

Back in Langley, the head of the Al Qaeda Unit, the same harddriving woman who had been scolded for her voyeuristic trip to watch the waterboarding of Khalid Sheikh Mohammed, agitated for the CIA to take custody of Masri. She had no proof, but she argued that he was probably a terrorist. Having been in the Bin Laden Unit that failed to connect the dots before September 11, she was doubly determined to let no terrorist slip through the cracks again. She wanted Masri rendered to one of the CIA's black site prisons in Afghanistan for interrogation. Doubters in the Agency suggested they should wait for German officials to establish first whether his passport was in fact a forgery. They pointed out that there was no evidence he was anything more than a tourist. But the Al Qaeda Unit's chief was skeptical about the Germans' trustworthiness because she regarded them all as soft on terrorism, according to a colleague. Complicating matters further, most of the government officials there were off on Christmas break. By the time the Berlin station looked at any of the paperwork, Masri was already on his way to Afghanistan.

Masri thought, however, that he was heading home. When the Macedonians brought him to the airport, he was surprised to be blindfolded and led into a small room. There, he later said, he was beaten by a new set of captors who proceeded to slice his clothes off him with what felt like knives. He could hear the sound of camera shutters clicking. When they adjusted the blindfold, he saw a team of black-masked men—one of the CIA's "takedown" teams. After putting plugs in his ears and a hood over his head, the team dragged him aboard a waiting Boeing business jet, injected him with a sedative, and flew him to Afghanistan. The CIA held him there, without evidence or charges, and without word to his family or anyone else outside, for the next 149 days.

Masri's nightmarish tour through the secret underworld of America's war on terror became public in January 2005, when the *New York Times* published a front-page story alleging that the CIA had falsely imprisoned him in a case of mistaken identity. Less well known, however, was that almost from the first moment that the CIA took custody of him, some Agency officials suspected that Masri was innocent. Yet for months they subjected him to unsparing abuse anyway. The CIA has maintained that its secret program was "careful," "legal," and "professional." But without any procedure for independent judicial review, or any accountability for imprisoning an innocent victim, once a mistake was made there was little incentive to correct it.

Almost from the start, the rendition team had a strange feeling about Masri. He wasn't acting like a terrorist. By the time their flight reached Afghanistan, the head of the rendition team sent word to the CIA station chief in Kabul that he thought something wasn't right. The Kabul station chief was incensed and sent a cable to the CTC accusing Langley of having sent him an innocent person. But the CTC officials sent back word that the head of the Al Qaeda Unit wanted Masri held and interrogated. She thought he seemed suspicious.

Over a cup of coffee during a visit to America two years after he was released, Masri's eyes still grew red-rimmed and welled with tears as he described his prison in Afghanistan as a filthy hole, with walls scribbled on in Pashtun and Arabic. He was given no bed, only a coarse and dirty blanket on the floor. At night, it was too cold to sleep. He said, "The water was putrid. If you took a sip, you could taste it for hours. You could smell a foul smell from it three meters away."

On his first night, he said, he was stripped. On the second, he was roughed up in an interrogation room by a half-dozen English-speaking masked men, one of whom warned him, "You're in a country where no one knows about you. There's no rule of law. If you die, you will be buried here. No one will ever know."

During the day, the guards were Afghan, but at night, he said, it became clear that the prison "was managed and run by the Americans. It was not a secret. They introduced themselves as Americans." He added, "When anything came up, they said they couldn't make a decision. They said, 'We will have to pass it on to Washington.'"

There were frequent checkups from someone he believed to be an American doctor, who Masri said took blood and urine samples and checked vital signs. An Agency source said Masri was also subjected to enemas. Yet the doctor did nothing to stop the abuse. Masri choked up as he recalled the plight of a Tanzanian in a neighboring cell. The man seemed "psychologically at the end," he said. "I could hear him ramming his head against the wall in despair. I tried to calm him down. I asked the doctor, 'Will you take care of this human being?'" But, he said, the doctor refused to help. Masri also said that he was told that guards had "locked the Tanzanian in a suitcase for long periods of time—a foul-smelling suitcase that made him vomit."

As Masri wasted away, being fed rotten chicken bones and suffering from chronic diarrhea, the chief of station in Kabul was saying, "I want this guy out"—but in Washington, the head of the Al Qaeda Unit kept insisting she had "a gut feeling he's bad. She can't admit a mistake," a former colleague said. The "Techs," meanwhile, in Germany had after several weeks thoroughly analyzed Masri's passport. They called the CTC with bad news: There was nothing wrong with it. It was legitimate.

The head of the Al Qaeda Unit still wanted Masri held. "She just looked in her crystal ball and it said that he was bad," said another former colleague at the CIA in disgust. "If you're going to unleash the beast," he said of the CIA's terrible powers, "you better be damn sure of your target."

After this had gone on for several months, some of those in the Agency who knew that Masri's passport was legitimate started to lobby for his release. One CIA official said he came in every morning and asked, "Is that guy still locked up in the Salt Pit?"

But the Al Qaeda Unit leader was still saying she had suspicions about him. She argued, a source said, that Masri "had phone calls to people who were bad. Or to people who knew people who were bad."

"But is he a terrorist?" the others would ask. If not, they argued, the CIA had to let him out of the Afghan prison. "It wasn't exactly the Hilton," one noted.

By late March, the Al Qaeda Unit chief agreed to release him, but only if the German intelligence services would promise to follow him once he was free. "They were still claiming he was bad," a CIA source recalled. She was told that if Masri wasn't a terrorist, they couldn't put him on a watch list. He was a German citizen. There were no charges against him. They couldn't just tap his phone for no reason and follow him around. The Al Qaeda Unit head again was reluctant to let him out.

Meanwhile, Masri—who had already lost sixty pounds—had gone on a hunger strike and was in such dire shape he was being force-fed through a tube stuck down his nose.

Finally, to break the stalemate, a lawyer for CTC surreptitiously alerted a lawyer for the European Division—which had an interest in Masri because of his German citizenship—that he was innocent. Together, the CIA lawyers schemed about how to get Masri released.

A senior officer in the European Division then took the bad news to Jose Rodriguez, who at the time was the head of the CTC. Rodriguez was skeptical. He had heard that Masri was a tremendous catch. But Rodriguez was told at that point, "It's the wrong Khaled el-Masri."

James Pavitt, Chief of Clandestine Operations in the Agency, was also told about the problem at this point. Yet for months after these senior CIA officials were warned that the Agency was holding an innocent man in dire circumstances, the situation continued. "I call it the 'Home Alone Syndrome,'" said a former CIA officer of the lax supervision and absent oversight.

Eventually, two officers in the European Division drew up a plan to release Masri in what they called a "reverse rendition." The idea was to drive him around in circles for a few hours and then let him go. But the Al Qaeda Unit chief was still arguing that he was a terrorist. She had an unusual amount of clout in the Agency. She was smart and tough. And her trump card was that she sometimes personally briefed President Bush.

Finally, the dispute over Masri reached Tenet. A meeting took place to resolve it. Rodriguez, Pavitt, the European Division officials, and the Bin Laden Unit head were all there. After each made their arguments, Tenet looked stunned. "Are you telling me we've got an innocent guy stuck in prison in Afghanistan? Oh shit! Just tell me—please—we haven't used 'enhanced' interrogation techniques on him, have we?"

His dismay was obvious. The group started hatching a plan to release Masri. The problem was how to let him go without blowing the cover of the secret prison program. One notion they discussed was giving Masri a large quantity of cash. Pavitt, according to two sources, chuckled and said, "At least the guy will earn more money in five months than he ever could have any other way!"

Soon after, Tenet went to the White House to tell Rice about the German citizen the Agency was imprisoning by mistake. Her demeanor was described as "very flat, as always." After hearing the story, she just said slowly, "Okay."

Tenet then explained the CIA's plan to release Masri—with cash—but without any explanation to anyone. They would just cover the whole thing up. Tenet suggested that no one needed to tell the German government what had happened.

"No," Rice said. "Your plan won't work. We have to tell the Germans. We can't put the President in the position of telling a lie to our allies."

When consulted, Secretary of State Colin Powell's deputy, Richard Armitage, felt the same way. One of the CIA officers involved thought that under the circumstances all of these scruples were rather absurd. "For guys who are basically running 'Kidnap Inc.,'" he said, "they sure were pretty squeamish."

At the end of May 2004, the U.S. Ambassador to Germany, Daniel Coats, briefed Otto Schily, the German Interior Minister, about the Masri mistake, as Rice had insisted. According to a well-informed source, Schily was extremely unhappy. He made clear that he would have preferred not to have known. "Why are you telling me this?" he asked irately. "My secretary is here—taking notes! Now there's a record! It will get out—it will become a German political issue. I'll have to face investigations—I'll have to testify in front of the Bundestag! Why didn't you just let him go, give him some money, and keep it quiet?"

The CIA, meanwhile, had flown Masri to Tirana, Albania, driven him blindfolded down a long, winding, potholed road, handed him back his possessions, and dropped him near the border with Serbia and Macedonia, where he was told to start walking and not look back. At the end of a path, three waiting men handed him a picnic lunch and drove him to the Tirana Airport, from which he flew home. He had lost so much weight, and looked so haunted and aged, the airport authorities accused him of using someone else's passport. When he arrived at his apartment, it was deserted and ransacked. His wife and sons, he learned later, had assumed themselves abandoned and moved in with his in-laws in Lebanon.

Asked if the treatment he got was torture or, as American officials have said, something less, Masri repeated the word. "Torture? I'm not sure what torture is. I'm not a lawyer. But it is my belief that I was tortured. Whoever says that's not torture should just have it done to them. They should feel it in their own mind and body. The whole time, I was in fear for my life. I was deadly afraid of what might happen next."

A former top Agency official declined to discuss the details of the Masri case, but he said in defense of the aggressive head of the Al Qaeda Unit, whose hunch had driven the mistaken rendition, "General Patton wasn't popular either, but sometimes it takes a tough person to win a war."

As Goldsmith was weighing how to withdraw the CIA's torture memo and replace it with a more restrictive version, a massive top-secret report detailing serious and mounting problems inside the Agency's program landed on his desk. Signs of trouble in the detention program had drawn the scrutiny of the Intelligence Agency's Inspector General, John Helgerson. By the end of 2003, he had begun an investigation, which some insiders believed might end with criminal charges for abusive interrogations. The Agency's internal watchdog was looking into at least three deaths of CIA-held prisoners in Afghanistan and Iraq. He had serious questions about the Agency's mistreatment of dozens more, including Khalid Sheikh Mohammed. And according to two former Agency officers, the Inspector General was investigating "seven or eight other cases like Masri" in which the CIA had apparently abducted and jailed the wrong people in its black prison sites. None of these other cases have become public.

The 2004 Inspector General's report, known as a "special review," was tens of thousands of pages long and as thick as two Manhattan phone books. It contained information, according to one source, that was simply "sickening." The behavior it described, another knowledgeable source said, raised concerns not just about the detainees but also about the Americans who had inflicted the abuse, some of whom seemed to have become frighteningly dehumanized. The source said, "You couldn't read the documents without wondering, 'Why didn't someone say, "Stop!"'"

Goldsmith was required to review the report in order to settle a sharp dispute that its findings had provoked between the Inspector General, Helgerson, who was not a lawyer, and the CIA's General Counsel, Scott Muller, who was. After spending months investigating the Agency's interrogation practices, the special review had concluded that the CIA's techniques constituted cruel, inhuman, and degrading treatment, in violation of the international Convention Against Torture. But Muller insisted that every single action taken by the CIA toward its detainees had been declared legal by John Yoo. With Yoo gone, it fell to Goldsmith to figure out exactly what the OLC had given the CIA a green light to do and what, in fact, the CIA had done.

As Goldsmith absorbed the details, the report transformed the antiseptic list of authorized interrogation techniques, which he had previously seen, into a Technicolor horror show. Goldsmith declined to be interviewed about the classified report for legal reasons, but according to those who dealt with him, the report caused him to question the whole program. The CIA interrogations seemed very different when described by participants than they had when approved on a simple menu of options. Goldsmith had been comfortable with the military's approach, but he wasn't at all sure whether the CIA's tactics were legal. Waterboarding, in particular, sounded quick and relatively harmless in theory. But according to someone familiar with the report, the way it had been actually used was "horrible."

Vice President Cheney, however, did not share this view. His reaction to this first, carefully documented in-house study concluding that the CIA's secret program was most likely criminal was to summon the Inspector General to his office for a private chat. Cheney's involvement was unusual. The Inspector General is supposed to function as an independent overseer, free from political pressure, but Cheney summoned the CIA Inspector General more than once to his office, an informed CIA source said. "Cheney loomed over everything," said the former CIA official. "The whole IG's Office was completely politicized. They were working hand in glove with the White House." Helgerson, the source said, "is very astute. It wouldn't take more than the flicker of an eyelash for him to understand what they wanted." Fred Hitz, a former Inspector General at the CIA, said that Cheney's interference was unlike anything he had experienced in earlier administrations. "I never got a call like that. It's not par for the course," he said.

Before he could deal with torture, however, Goldsmith was thrust into the center of another extraordinary drama, this over the Terrorist Surveillance Program (TSP). In early March, the program, which needed regular renewal, was set to expire. Goldsmith had concluded it was illegal, so he had convinced Ashcroft not to recertify it. In taking this bold stance, Goldsmith had strong support from Philbin and also from a former federal prosecutor who had joined the top ranks of the Justice Department in December, Deputy Attorney General James Comey. The nonpolitical, career legal experts who dealt with the wiretapping laws at the Justice Department also sided with Goldsmith.

But shortly after Ashcroft agreed to let the program lapse, he was rushed to the hospital, where he underwent surgery for gallstone pancreatitis. His condition was critical enough that he transferred his legal powers to Comey. A week later, on March 9, 2004, just two days before the TSP was set to lapse, Goldsmith and Comey went to the White House to explain in person, as they had been signaling for weeks, that the program was illegal and so they planned to let it lapse. Cheney and Addington were outraged. Addington insisted that it was FISA law that was unconstitutional and there was no need for the President to abide by it. "His attitude," said a former administration source, "was cite the Commander in Chief's powers, and ignore the statutes." According to a different source who was involved at the time, John Yoo's opinion authorizing the surveillance program— which has never been made public—simply gave no analysis of the key provisions in FISA law. "It was such a weak, sloppy opinion, it just didn't address the law at all," he said. Comey was so underwhelmed by Yoo's legal justification for the NSA program that he argued "no lawyer" would buy it. Addington, incensed, replied that he was a lawyer and he found it thoroughly convincing. Comey reportedly shot back, "No good lawyer," according to another participant.

The next night, March 10, hours before the TSP was set to lapse, Comey was on his way home when he received a frantic call from Ashcroft's wife. She had forbidden visitors to see her husband because he was so ill. But President Bush himself had called her at the hospital to say that Gonzales and White House Chief of Staff Andrew Card were coming over. Comey suspected that the White House team was trying to subvert the law by strong-arming Ashcroft, in his enfeebled state, into renewing the TSP. Alarmed, Comey reached Robert Mueller, the FBI Director, who supported him, as well as Goldsmith and Philbin. They all sped to the hospital—Comey got his driver to use the car's siren—hoping to beat the White House officials to Ashcroft's bedside, in order to stop him from being bullied into renewing the illegal program.

After bounding up the hospital stairs, Comey reached Ashcroft first but found him alarmingly weakened. He was in intensive care, lying in a hospital bed, looking deathly. Mueller hadn't arrived yet, but he had called the FBI security guards watching over Ashcroft and told them to bar the White House officials from removing Comey from the room, under any circumstances. Goldsmith and Philbin arrived soon after, joining Comey at Aschroft's side. A few minutes later, Card and Gonzales walked through the door carrying an envelope. In it was the order that the White House wanted Ashcroft to sign, reauthorizing the TSP.

"How are you, General?" asked Gonzales, paying no attention to the other unexpected visitors.

"Not well," Ashcroft replied. He had already been briefed by Comey and was coherent enough to grasp what Gonzales was up to.

Gonzales didn't engage in small talk. He quickly pulled out the draft order and asked Ashcroft to sign it. Ashcroft lifted his head off the pillows and delivered a strong denunciation of the TSP's legal framework. Then, spent, he sank back into the pillows, from which he wearily added that whatever he thought was irrelevant anyway, because, he said, turning to Comey, "He's the Attorney General."

Defeated, Gonzales and Card got up to go. "Be well" is all Card said on the way out. As they left, according to Goldsmith, Mrs. Ashcroft stuck out her tongue at them.

"It was just despicable," said one of Ashcroft's top aides. "I thought I had just witnessed an effort to take advantage of a very sick man," said Comey.

Moments later, Card reached Comey by phone and ordered him to the White House. "After what I just witnessed," Comey said, "I will not meet with you without a witness, and I intend that witness to be the Solicitor General of the United States," Theodore Olson.

Late that evening, Comey and Olson headed to the White House to meet with Card. When they got to the West Wing, however, Card refused to allow Olson into his office. After arguing a few minutes, Gonzales appeared and brought Olson in with him. Comey stressed that if the White House didn't accept his judgment, he and a raft of other top Justice Department figures, including Goldsmith, were planning to resign.

Two days later, however, Bush asked Comey and Mueller to speak with him privately in his study, one by one, after the daily national security briefing. Comey told Bush that his staff was disserving him. Afterward, Mueller disappeared into the study for fifteen minutes. By the time they emerged, Bush had changed his mind and authorized Goldsmith to try to fix the program so that it would be legal. What Mueller said remains unknown, but a confidant of his said the FBI Director told Bush that he personally planned to resign if the TSP was renewed, because he had sworn to uphold the law. "Mueller and Comey were probably the first lawyers to tell the President that the program was illegal," the confidant said. He noted that once Bush was given the facts, he chose a more cautious approach. "I tend to think no one had ever told him the truth before," said the confidant, "and part of the reason they fought so hard was that they were afraid to tell the President the bad news."

After the confrontation over the NSA program, Goldsmith was becoming a pariah at the White House. He was smart and tough enough to hold his own in arguments with Addington, and it seemed that in a perverse way Addington respected him, but the two argued ferociously. The tension built further when Goldsmith and the CIA's General Counsel, Scott Muller, started to ask questions in White House meetings about the advisability of the CIA's rough interrogation techniques. Both Muller and Goldsmith had been affected by the documented abuses in the Inspector General's report. "Scott started asking, 'Is this the right thing to do? Do we want to be doing this as a nation? Are these the kind of people we want to be?'" a participant recalled. "Maybe we can't control this stuff, so maybe we shouldn't do it," Goldsmith chimed in. John Bellinger, the top legal adviser to Rice, had also grown increasingly critical, questioning not only the legality and morality of the CIA's program, but also its reliability. "How do we know these confessions are true?" he asked.

Addington pounced on the doubters, deriding them as squishy. "You can't imagine what the dynamic was like in the White House," said another former administration lawyer. "Basically anything less than being as macho as Addington was seen as a sign of weakness. The mood was, 'You can't be sentimental. You have to be cold-eyed.' It resulted in these supposed neo-realists doing unnecessarily self-destructive things."

Then, on April 28, the Abu Ghraib story broke. Panic spread through the administration, from the top of the Pentagon through the CIA and on through the White House. One obvious lesson was that pictures—the actual incontrovertible visual proof of abuse—had a power that no written or oral description could match. At the CIA, where hundreds of hours of videotapes of two U.S.-held Muslim detainees being strapped down and waterboarded were sitting in a safe, the immediate reaction, one administration source involved at the time said, was "Uh-oh. A lightbulb went on."

On May 24, Muller met at the White House with Addington, Gonzales, and Bellinger to discuss the fallout from both the Inspector General's report and Abu Ghraib. He mentioned the CIA's videotapes and said the Agency wanted to destroy them. According to CIA notes taken at the time, the consensus of the group was that the CIA should not destroy the tapes. Addingon's attitude, a participant said, was along the lines of "Don't bring this into the White House!" The explosiveness of even talking about destroying potential evidence was clear to all.

Less than a month later, on June 8, an even more damaging story for top Bush Administration officials broke: Someone leaked the August 2002 Yoo/Bybee torture memo to the *Wall Street Journal* and the *Washington Post.* The papers published devastating stories linking the scandalous abuses in Abu Ghraib to the Bush Administration's stunning legal policy authorizing everything short of near-death. Amid the public firestorm, even those who had known of the CIA and military interrogation programs for years acted shocked.

After reading the torture memo itself for the first time in the newspapers, Rice and Powell confronted Gonzales together and furiously insisted that there be "no more secret opinions on international and national security law." Their righteous anger seemed somewhat undercut by reports that Tenet had provided graphic details of specific coercive interrogations during Principals Committee meetings while both were present. And while they directed their frustration at Gonzales, neither had the temerity to confront Cheney, who clearly was the true source of these policies.

Meanwhile, as some of the former defenders of "enhanced" interrogations looked for political cover, Addington angrily defended the program, insisting that they had to stand by it because to do anything less would expose the CIA to criminal charges.

Goldsmith was caught in a terrible predicament. He still had not had enough time to research the torture laws in order to figure out what techniques would be legally acceptable. He hadn't wanted to withdraw the torture memo without offering a replacement. But suddenly the administration was being bombarded with questions from the press about its position on the leaked memo. Goldsmith had already withdrawn the nearly identical memo to the Defense Department five months earlier. It made no sense to defend the CIA memo, but he wasn't ready yet to yank it. Under huge pressure, he helped prepare Ashcroft for public testimony defending the memo. But days later, he indicated to Addington and Gonzales that he planned to withdraw it.

"There was a series of extremely dramatic meetings in Gonzales's office," a participant recalled. "Addington was pounding the table," he said. Bellinger was arguing that the CIA torture memo had to be withdrawn immediately, and that it could be done in twenty-four hours. Goldsmith was caught in the middle. Addington was pushing for him to reconfirm the memo. But Goldsmith was saying, "It's flawed. I can't."

Addington retorted angrily, "There are a whole bunch more of these—what about them? If you withdraw it, what about the others?"

"I haven't even read them—I don't know," Goldsmith replied. "How can I vouch for them if I haven't read them?"

"I haven't seen them all either," said Bellinger. "Neither has the State Department. Neither have others at Justice. How can Jack vouch for them if he hasn't read them? He should read them."

"Addington," said a participant, "was getting extremely upset. He saw the underpinnings of his whole thing beginning to crumble. He demanded to know, 'How long is this going to take?'"

"I don't know. I don't know what I'll think of the memos," Goldsmith said. "I haven't read them. I just don't know how long it will take. I just don't know." Goldsmith, an observer said, "just said it over and over. He was controlled, but very emotional. I thought he'd have a nervous breakdown on the spot."

Addington, meanwhile, was practically shaking, demanding to know, "How long is this going to take?" He gave Goldsmith no more than a week. Then, according to one account, he "stormed out of the meeting."

The pressure on Goldsmith was intense. At about this point, he decided, he had to quit. Addington had gone out of his way to humiliate Goldsmith in front of several other administration lawyers, pulling a three-by-five card from his jacket pocket with a list of other OLC decisions and asking snidely which ones he planned to overturn next, since "you have already withdrawn so many that the President and others have been relying on."

During the week that he deliberated, Goldsmith twice called James Comey, in whom he had huge faith, for advice. Comey was traveling at the time, but in a series of late-night phone calls, the two worked out a plan. They were both so paranoid by then about the powerful backlash they had provoked inside the administration that they actually thought they might be in physical danger. Goldsmith and Comey, who knew more about the domestic surveillance program than practically anyone else in America, also feared that their communications were being monitored. To foil possible surveillance, they talked in codes. Together they devised the strategy of timing the withdrawal of the torture memo to Goldsmith's resignation letter. If the White House refused Goldsmith's advice to withdraw the torture memo, they knew, Goldsmith's resignation would look as if he quit in protest. The threat was implicit that he could go public, setting off another political storm.

On June 14, Goldsmith informed Ashcroft that he planned to withdraw the CIA legal memo. On June 16, he offered Ashcroft his letter of resignation. Goldsmith still had not had time to draft a replacement memo. That process would take his successor six months. Meanwhile, the CIA was plunged into a precarious state of legal liability. "I had done the unthinkable," Goldsmith later wrote. He had withdrawn the "Golden Shield."

12

COVER-UP

"This country does not believe in torture. . . ."

—George Bush at a press conference, March 16, 2005

Dan Levin had long wanted to run the prestigious Office of Legal Counsel. Soon after being appointed on an interim basis to take over after Jack Goldsmith's hasty departure, however, Levin found it was not exactly the sort of lofty public service position that he had envisioned during the long nights that he studied at Harvard, obtaining one of the highest grade point averages in the class of 1978, or afterward at the University of Chicago Law School, where he honed his conservative political views. Levin had methodically built a strong foundation for a distinguished government legal career. He had accumulated a series of powerful Republican mentors while serving stints as an Assistant United States Attorney, then as the Chief of Staff to William Barr, the Attorney General during the first Bush presidency, and the Chief of Staff to Robert Mueller, the FBI Director during the second. Levin was tall and thin, with a courteous, almost apologetic manner. Few would have predicted that his promising trajectory would all come to this: In the late summer of 2004, on the fifth floor of the million square feet of limestone that formed the U.S. Department of Justice, in a hushed room just down the hall from Attorney General Ashcroft, Levin was hunched over the *American Heritage Dictionary of the English Language.* His career now rested on the meaning of the word "severe" as it was conjoined with "pain."

Levin had inherited from Goldsmith the dauntingly distasteful task of defining the outer limits of suffering that the United States government could legally inflict on prisoners in the war on terror. It actually was a tough legal question, even for an exceptionally bright and hardworking lawyer like himself. Levin was known for his long hours. He was often the first person in the office, greeting the cleaning crews as they finished their night shift. When a trusted Bush Administration aide had been needed to prepare the overnight FBI threat report for the President's Daily Briefing, Levin was chosen to come into the Justice Department at four-thirty in the morning to cull the raw intelligence data coming in over the transom. Before dawn, he stapled the most important hair-raising items together into the reports that were among the very first things that Cheney and Bush read every morning.

Long hours and disturbing subject matter weren't new to Levin. What made his new assignment so difficult, beyond the unpleasantness of the task at hand, was the uncertainty surrounding the laws. He was a precise and scholarly lawyer and his sense of responsibility was keen. The memo he had been tasked to personally prepare, which would replace John Yoo and Jay Bybee's infamous torture memo, would guide the covert war against terrorism, shaping America's impact all around the globe. As he explored the case law, however, Levin was uneasy. It only took a few seconds to see that there was next to nothing to go on. Elsewhere in the world, there were plenty of torture cases that served as precedents, but America had virtually no history in this area of the law. There had never been a Supreme Court ruling on it. The United States had always officially recognized the Geneva Conventions, so there had been no occasion to even indirectly address torture. Without these rules, Levin was left with the untested words in the Convention Against Torture, which the United States signed in 1988 and ratified in 1994. It prohibited "cruel, inhuman and degrading treatment," but the Bush legal team had concluded these lesser categories didn't apply to the CIA. For intelligence officers holding prisoners abroad, the line that couldn't be crossed was "the intentional infliction of severe pain or suffering, whether physical or mental." But what did that mean? There was no thermometer for pain.

Levin went to the dictionary, but it wasn't much help. What was the difference between "suffering" and "pain"? There must be one, or else the treaty wouldn't have banned them separately. They didn't teach this in law school. Nor was it an area of Justice Department expertise. Was a broken leg more painful than a migraine headache? If you couldn't hit someone with a seven-pound hammer, would a two-pound hammer be okay? It seemed to Levin, he told colleagues, that it depended on the person. If severe pain was a crime, was moderate pain legal? Measuring "mental suffering" was even harder. Who knew what that meant? In order for mental suffering to reach the threshold of torture under the U.S. statute, it would have to "profoundly disrupt the personality" and cause harm of "prolonged duration." But wouldn't that vary, depending upon one's personality? For many, being forced to walk naked through the public square would cause "severe mental pain or suffering." Rape, too, might. But neither was explicitly banned under the 1994 law.

It was clear that whatever Levin decided, he was sure to be criticized. If he narrowed the wide latitude that John Yoo had given the White House, the hawks such as Addington would be furious. But if he didn't, the public, which would likely learn of his decision, someday might hold it up in shame.

Critics of torture within the administration, such as Richard Armitage, the Deputy Secretary of State, who served three tours of combat duty during the Vietnam War, later made the matter sound simple. As Armitage put it after he left office, "If you were twisting yourselves into knots because you're fearful that you may be avoiding some war crimes, then you're probably tripping too closely to the edge." Waterboarding in particular, Armitage said, was so obviously torture, "I'm ashamed we're even having this conversation."

By the time that Levin came into the debate, however, the administration had already gone so far that it would take a bold and principled renunciation of torture and all lesser forms of abuse from the top to turn back. On top of ideological rigidity, and President Bush's well-known resistance to self-criticism, another element was impeding change. As the detainees' months of secret suffering turned into years, and the potential legal exposure grew more serious, the administration's resistance to reform was increasingly self-protective. The CIA was particularly worried about crimes that its officers may have committed. If Levin were to rule that waterboarding was torture, as it had been defined for centuries before September 11, it might place anyone who had participated in the program in legal jeopardy. Those who had directly authorized the policy, including Cheney and Gonzales, were also theoretically at risk. Like Goldsmith before him, Levin was caught between the law and the administration's practices. It was hard for an honorable lawyer to square the two.

Desperate to be correct, and woefully short of reliable information, Levin arrived at a remarkable plan of action that likely no other government lawyer in the country's history had tried. As an assistant U.S. attorney on murder cases, he had found it immensely useful to go to the scene of the crime. Only then had he fully grasped the details. To determine what torture was, he decided, he would have to conduct similar on-site, empirical research. Levin felt he had an obligation to subject himself to some of the CIA's most controversial interrogation techniques. The Agency's experts swore that these methods were safe and ultimately harmless. They also insisted that coercion had saved American lives, so it needed to continue.

To test this, Levin decided, he would find out for himself. If he felt the pain was "severe," it didn't necessarily mean everyone else would. He knew, too, that he would never be able to simulate the mind-set of an unwilling victim. But certainly, it would help him understand a bit more about whether America had gone too far. It would also make it hard for critics to suggest he hadn't tried hard enough to figure it out.

Soon after taking over the Office of Legal Counsel, therefore, Levin started making arrangements with the CIA to have himself waterboarded at a local military base. There, the distinguished officer of the Justice Department would have himself strapped down to a board while water was forced into his nose, mouth, and lungs until he gagged and cried out for it to stop. Levin also would go on to put himself through other CIA interrogation techniques, including uncomfortable "stress positions" and "open-handed slapping." He might have tried the program of sleep deprivation if he had been able to give his empirical research more time. But reading he had done showed that some victims lasted as long as a dozen days without sleep. That was too much time out of the office. The same apparently held true for isolation. Extremes of heat and cold and close confinement were, apparently, not part of the CIA's program by then, so were not contemplated.

Levin declined to comment, because these and other details of the CIA's interrogation program are classified. But according to those familiar with his conclusions, the ordeal proved useful if unusual. It created one problem, however. Levin's firsthand experience put him at variance with the Bush Administration's conclusions. His own experimentation with stress positions, for instance, made obvious that when it came to avoiding torture, limits were everything. Waterboarding in particular, Levin found, could definitely be classified as illegal torture unless, in his view, it was strictly limited in terms of time and severity and was closely monitored in a very professional way. He told others that while being waterboarded he found the strong sensation of drowning to be terrifying. It could be deeply scarring, easily causing "prolonged mental pain" or "severe suffering"—the legal description of torture. Levin's views were not as categorical as those of human rights activists, most of whom would argue that waterboarding was torture, no matter how it was done. He seemed to think it could be done legally, if held to a brief enough bout. But his opinions concerning the potential criminal liability were also distinctly out of line with those of the White House. As autumn came, Levin began incorporating these findings into the replacement memo that he was drafting.

None of these conclusions, he knew, would be welcomed by his bosses. Levin had purposely told only a few colleagues about his experiments, none of whom were in the White House. His attitude of open-minded inquiry, fact-gathering, and consultation with experts in other agencies was at complete odds with the rigid doctrinal approach favored by Addington. It was just a matter of time before the two collided. So Levin kept working away quietly. Meanwhile, the White House hard-liners were confronted with a growing number of other signs that their extreme policies were unlawful, unsustainable, and increasingly destructive to America's reputation and interests. The question, however, was whether they would turn back.

In a stunning rebuke to Bush and Cheney's grandiose position on executive power, on June 28, 2004, the Supreme Court ruled in favor of the lawyers for the Guantánamo detainees in two separate landmark cases. In the Rasul case (*Rasul v. Bush*), which had originated two and a half years earlier with the long-shot efforts of the unlikely team of Joe Margulies, Tom Wilner, Clive Stafford Smith, and Michael Ratner, the Court ruled 6–3 that Guantánamo Bay was not beyond the reach of U.S. law. That same day, the Court also ruled, in an 8–1 upset for the Bush Administration in the Hamdi case (*Hamdi v. Rumsfeld*), that the executive branch could not hold prisoners indefinitely without charges—due process entitled them to a lawyer and the right to challenge their detention in front of a "neutral decision-maker."

The rash, secretly crafted decisions made by the knot of like-minded lawyers around Cheney in the days just after September 11, giving all power to the commander in chief to designate by himself who was an enemy combatant, what rules the military commissions would follow, and the conditions in which the detainees could be held, were all debunked by the court. Addington had confided to Goldsmith at an earlier point that "we're going to push and push and push until some larger force makes us stop." For almost three years, there had been virtually no checks on the executive branch's power. The lower courts had equivocated, and Congress had all but abdicated. Two months to the day after the Abu Ghraib photos were first seen in America, however, the consequences of the administration's go-it-alone approach had triggered a backlash from the Supreme Court; for the moment, it seemed that Addington had finally met his "larger force."

The Rasul case had been argued by neither Margulies nor Wilner, though both would have loved to have been the lead attorney. But in an attempt at a more politically neutral choice, they had drafted a lifelong Republican, retired federal judge John Gibbons, to argue the case. In doing so, they hoped to communicate to the court that the argument transcended partisan affiliation. As a former member of the judicial branch, Gibbons also carried added authority as he argued against the Bush Administration's assertion that no court had the right to intervene in the White House's treatment of foreign prisoners. "What is at stake in this case," he told the justices, "is the federal courts' ability to uphold the law." The Bush White House, he said, had created "a lawless enclave insulating the executive branch from any judicial scrutiny, now or in the future."

Six of the justices agreed, granting the Guantánamo inmates the right to challenge the correctness of their detention in federal court. It had taken years, but the Court had shattered the legal fib that Guantánamo was not under U.S. control—that it existed in some kind of legal black hole. As Justice Anthony Kennedy, the all-important swing vote, wrote in a concurring opinion, regardless of other technicalities, Guantánamo is "a place that belongs to the United States." As such, the court decreed that the detainees must be given a chance to challenge their imprisonment in the U.S. courts.

The Supreme Court's verdict in the second detainee case, that of

Yaser Hamdi, the young American prisoner whom Jack Goldsmith and the other administration lawyers had watched on closed circuit in the naval brig in Norfolk two years earlier, was an even more decisive defeat for the Bush lawyers. Justice Sandra Day O'Connor accepted the argument that the President had the power to imprison detainees in the war on terror, but she famously scolded the White House for providing the prisoners with no legal process at all. "A state of war is not a blank check," she emphasized, and the commander in chief's powers were not an excuse to "turn our system of checks and balances on their head."

Most surprisingly, Justice Antonin Scalia, the Court's most outspokenly conservative member, not only voted against the Bush Administration, he also thundered, "Indefinite imprisonment at the will of the Executive" strikes at "the very core of liberty."

The Supreme Court's opinions were lauded on editorial pages all over the world. Typical was the *Los Angeles Times*'s declaration that "It's Called Democracy." The editorial said, "It's hard to see what is left of American freedom if the government has the authority to make anyone on its soil—citizen or non-citizen—disappear and then rule that no one can do anything about it."

Inside the White House, the Supreme Court's rulings utterly stunned Addington. A fellow administration lawyer noted that while Addington had a prodigious command of relevant case law, he had a completely tin ear when it came to understanding the politics of the Supreme Court or, for that matter, politics in general. For more than a year, Ted Olson, the Solicitor General, along with some of the White House lawyers, had been arguing with Addington, in fruitless attempts to convince him to soften some of the hard edges of his extreme legal positions in order to buy some support from Congress and the Courts. The moderates in the administration argued that by building more political consensus, the administration could win more legitimacy for its policies. Addington accused them of being defeatist and unnecessarily yielding the president's powers.

Olson had been particularly worried about his ability to convince the Supreme Court that Hamdi—a U.S. citizen—had absolutely no right to legal counsel. Associate White House Counsel Bradford Berenson, who had clerked for Justice Kennedy, agreed with Olson that the Court would never go along with granting the president the sole power to imprison an Americn citizen indefinitely. But despite Olson and Berenson's intimate knowledge of the Supreme Court, Addington wouldn't budge. He had been swayed by Cheney, who in turn had been influenced by the CIA's arguments that any outside contact might jeopardize the psychological control necessary to interrogate terror suspects. In a heated meeting, Addington accused Berenson of trying to throw away the president's powers for nothing. Berenson retorted that it was Addington who exhibited "know-nothingness."

Addington's absolutism prevailed inside the White House but failed abjectly in front of the Supreme Court. Ten days after the decisive defeats for the government, Olson, who was the most prominent conservative lawyer in the Bush Administration, followed through on his previous vow to resign from his post as Solicitor General.

Such losses might have served as important warning signs to a more flexible administration. But rather than adjusting its course, the Bush White House dug in deeper. Addington, a former colleague said, treated the Supreme Court's opinions as little more than a "slap on the wrist." The lawyers for the Bush Administration soon revealed their new position, which was that while the Guantánamo detainees could *seek* relief in the U.S. courts—as the Supreme Court had insisted—they had no right to actually be *given* any relief because they were foreigners. As Margulies, the Guantánamo defense attorney, put it, "Before *Rasul,* the government argued that the doors of the courthouse were closed to the prisoners; now it argued that the doors were open, but the building was empty."

Margulies soon discovered that the Supreme Court's ruling that the Guantánamo detainees were all entitled to lawyers was also going to be honored as little as possible by the administration. After the Court's rulings, he and a growing number of other volunteer defense lawyers asked the administration to give them a list of the Guantánamo detainees' names so that they could match them up with lawyers. But the administration refused. "How are we supposed to get them lawyers then?" Margulies asked. The Justice Department's representative said he didn't know. "Can we go down and see them?" Margulies asked. The answer was "Not if you don't represent them." The lawyers then asked, "Well, how are we supposed to represent them if we don't know who's there?" It went round and round.

Meanwhile, however, Clive Stafford Smith, the gangly British death-penalty lawyer who lived in New Orleans, had begun an extraordinary trek around the world in an attempt to gather the names of missing persons who may have been detained in Guantánamo. Working from a tentative list compiled by the *Washington Post,* and snippets gathered from foreign newspapers, he traveled to countries such as Bahrain and Jordan, where he held press conferences, hoping to attract "next-of-kin" who could retain him on behalf of a detainee. "Not having all of the names was a huge problem," Stafford Smith said. "It was incredibly hard work and very expensive, too." By the end of 2004, he had over nine hundred names, even though there were only 800 detainees. The Arab names, some of which were spelled in multiple ways, caused endless confusion. What mattered most, though, was that he had gathered sixty-two authorizations to represent specific detainees. It was less than 10 percent of the total population in Guantánamo, but Stafford Smith soon had an epiphany about how to reach the rest. Since the administration wouldn't give the lawyers the other detainees' names, Stafford Smith passed forms out to those he had already identified, authorizing them to act as "next-of-kin" for the others. These "next-of-kin" jotted down the names of every other detainee they knew. "I got the next three hundred authorizations very quickly," he chuckled.

Despite the obstacles that kept being thrown in his way, Stafford Smith was optimistic that in the end, if they could just get a case in front of a real court, his side would win. He had a theory about Guantánamo, which was that "If we could just open it up, they'd shut it down—because its only purpose was to keep the truth from the world."

The subsequent handling of the Hamdi case seemed to illustrate Stafford Smith's point. After the Supreme Court ruled that Hamdi, who had dual U.S. and Saudi citizenship, was entitled to challenge his detention in an ordinary U.S. court hearing, the Bush Administration instead quietly released him. Having argued for more than two years that Hamdi was too dangerous to be allowed to have any human contact other than with his captors, on October 12, 2004, the government let him return home to Saudi Arabia, where he was set free. The Bush Administration never presented any evidence against him. Like hundreds of detainees later freed from Guantánamo without a court hearing, Hamdi spent years in prison without ever having the opportunity to contest his status as an enemy combatant before an impartial judge. Critics suspected the Bush Administration knew that its case could never have survived the scrutiny of an open court.

As the legal pressure built against the White House's detention and interrogation policies outside, an unseen reform effort was under way inside, too. Even while John Kerry, the Democratic nominee for the presidency in the summer of 2004, cautiously avoided any mention of Abu Ghraib, evidently for fear of appearing anti-military, a few brave staffers spoke up in White House meetings. John Bellinger III, the top lawyer at the NSC, asked repeatedly what the administration's "End Game" was for the CIA prisoners in particular. Addington argued before the election that any move that the White House might make to resolve the prisoners' fates would be dismissed as a cheaply political "October Surprise," so they had to wait at least until November to address such concerns. After the election, Bellinger confronted Addington, saying, "Okay, now we've won—what are we going to do with these people?" The answer, another White House lawyer sympathetic to Bellinger said, was that "Cheney's people decided to gum it to death." They created an interagency group at the deputy level, to study detainee issues. It was a vehicle, the lawyer said, to "slow roll everything."

As these meetings droned on, Bellinger argued hard for transferring the CIA's "high-value detainees" such as Abu Zubayda and Khalid Sheikh Mohammed from the secret black prisons to Guantánamo, where they could be prosecuted in front of the proposed military commissions. "It will give some legitimacy to the program," he stressed. He pointed out that the public and the Supreme Court were more likely to support Guantánamo if they saw it holding serious terrorists rather than just an Australian kangaroo skinner like David Hicks, or Salim Hamdan, whom an administration lawyer described as "some two-bit driver for Bin Laden." Bellinger also pushed repeatedly for the administration to adopt at least the minimum treatment standards for wartime prisoners spelled out in the Geneva Conventions just as a matter of policy—not as binding law. Bellinger argued that the Geneva standards were clear and universally understood, and they would restore order and consistency to the treatment of detainees. If the rules were adopted just as a policy matter, not as a matter of law, it would cost the administration nothing.

But in a series of White House meetings between 2004 and 2006, other participants said that Cheney, Gonzales, and Addington, in particular, raised one objection after another. Their arguments were presented in terms of protecting the country from future terrorist attacks, but opponents began to suspect that they were just as concerned about protecting themselves from future legal repercussions.

"Their theory was that if you adopt rules, people will accuse you of violating them," a former White House official said. "There would be a risk. It all fit in with the War Crimes Act," he said, noting that it criminalizes violations of Common Article Three of the Geneva Conventions. Their fear, he said, was that "We'd be saying our people were committing prosecutable war crimes."

Cheney argued that as soon as the administration released a single CIA prisoner, the whole clandestine program would be revealed. "People will ask where they've been and 'What have you been doing with them?'" he said in one White House meeting, according to a participant. Cheney also argued that it would mean they could no longer continue the program, which he was convinced the country needed. As he saw it, the prisoners were not people with rights so much as exploitable intelligence resources. If they were moved out of the dark, he warned, "They'll all get lawyers." Once that happened, he reasoned, the government would no longer be able to continue to interrogate them freely. "These people have intelligence value," Cheney argued, according to another participant. "It's important to ask them questions. We just don't know what could happen." The observer said, "He plays on the President's fears. He'd remind him that the welfare of the whole country rests on him."

Cheney's chief of staff, I. Lewis "Scooter" Libby, was particularly opposed to changing course, an administration observer said. "He said the detention system was working fine as it was. Legally, he said, there was nothing wrong with the CIA's secret program, or almost nothing. "Ninety-nine percent of what we do is legal," Libby said with a chuckle at one such White House meeting, to the amazement of another administration lawyer who took the comment as an admission that Cheney's staff realized that some part of what they were condoning was illegal.

On December 30, 2004, one week before Alberto Gonzales was scheduled to face Senate confirmation hearings on his nomination to replace John Ashcroft as Attorney General, the administration posted a document on the Justice Department's Web site that sounded like a ringing denunciation of torture. The rhetoric was partly aimed at helping Gonzales, who was sure to face skeptical questions about his role in advising Bush to discard the Geneva Conventions. Bush and other top administration officials had expressed outrage at the lawlessness exhibited by low-level U.S. troops at Abu Ghraib and had vowed to hold the perpetrators accountable. Rumsfeld had assured Congress, "What we believe in . . . is making sure when wrongdoing or scandal occur that they are not covered up, but exposed, investigated and publicly disclosed—and the guilty brought to justice."

Despite such calls for accountability, not a single administration investigation had questioned the top policy-makers in the war on terror. Bush's promotion of Gonzales, whose legal advice had so muddied the laws of war, could only be helped by the Justice Department's new anti-torture declaration.

The document was Dan Levin's long-awaited legal memo replacing the notorious torture guidance that had been written by John Yoo. Its opening line declared unequivocally, "Torture is abhorrent both to American law and values and to international norms." In tone and scope, Levin's revised memo was vastly more careful than the one it replaced. Levin had excised all claims to the commander in chief's authority to ignore laws such as the ban on torture. It also cut many of the legal defenses that Yoo had suggested could be used against charges of torture. In place of the earlier unbounded assertions of executive power was a tightly worded advisory opinion. In contrast to the August 1, 2002, memo enabling the CIA to all but kill Abu Zubayda and Khalid Sheikh Mohammed, Levin specifically rejected Yoo's extreme definition of torture as needing pain equivalent to that accompanying organ failure or "even death."

In almost every way, the new interpretation seemed a step toward restoring America's laws and values. But on closer reading, the revised memo included two oddly contradictory lines. One was yet another description of torture that seemed specifically written to legalize waterboarding so long as the severe pain it produced was not of "extended duration."

The other curiosity was a single footnote—evidently written to reassure the CIA—suggesting that although the earlier legal guidance was being withdrawn, nothing that the government had previously authorized would be considered criminal under the new interpretation of the laws. The footnote had a contorted, forced quality. Although few knew it, there was a reason why.

By the time that Levin issued the new interrogation guidance, it had been made clear to him that he would not be chosen to get the top OLC job beyond his temporary, acting status. "Dan was seen as too independent," a colleague said, "too much like Jack Goldsmith. He was a total law-and-order conservative, but they wanted someone they could control."

Levin, it turned out, had challenged Addington about the legality of the NSA program, even after Goldsmith's departure. His independent research into torture, and his insistence upon consulting with other government lawyers, including those at the State Department and CIA, had also drawn the ire of secretive staff in the Vice President's office.

Tensions had escalated toward an extraordinary, private showdown. Gonzales, who was awaiting confirmation as Attorney General, made clear to Levin that unless he included language in his new legal memo declaring that nothing the Bush Administration had done in earlier interrogations was illegal, the Justice Department would not accept his opinion. In essence Levin, the top legal adviser to the executive branch, was being virtually extorted for a written legal pardon. Levin was worried that unless he gave Gonzales what he wanted, the Bush Administration would scrap his memo, abandoning the whole effort to reform interrogation practices. Under these extraordinary circumstances, Levin agreed to put in the cryptic footnote whitewashing previous practices. He reasoned that if he wrote it carefully enough, it would accurately reflect his thinking.

Levin refused, however, to give the administration carte blanche. He had heard rumors that his predecessor, John Yoo, had orally approved especially questionable CIA practices, including the use of mind-altering drugs and mock-burials. Levin wasn't sure if this was true, but he knew these tactics were completely illegal, and he didn't want his name on any document condoning them. So he worded the footnote in a contorted manner meant to exclude any oral advice given to the CIA by the Justice Department. He also tried to draw a distinction between what had previously been authorized and what had previously been done, condoning only the earlier legal advice but not abusive interrogations that might have exceeded the previous limits.

The footnote was nonetheless a victory for Cheney. It also delighted John Yoo, who cited it in a later memoir as proof that his torture memo had been right all along. Thanks to Levin's footnote, he wrote, "in the real world of interrogation policy nothing had changed."

With the help of the legal cover provided by Levin's memo, Gonzales was confirmed as Attorney General in February 2005. His confirmation survived despite his admission for the first time in public that under the Bush legal team's idiosyncratic interpretation, the CIA was exempt from international prohibitions against cruel, inhumane, or degrading treatment of foreign prisoners held abroad.

Soon after, Levin became one more in the procession of highly credentialed conservative lawyers cast aside by the Bush Administration after warning top officials that their tactics in the war on terror were less than legal. Before leaving the OLC, however, Levin gave a last piece of unsolicited advice to Gonzales. By then it was clear that Steven Bradbury, another ambitious young conservative lawyer, who had clerked for Supreme Court Justice Clarence Thomas, was eager to take over the OLC. "Don't pick him," Levin told Gonzales. "He wants the job too much. He won't give you any independent advice." As far as the White House was concerned, there was no more perfect recommendation.

Having been burned twice, as they saw it, by Justice Department lawyers who refused to rubber-stamp their plans, White House officials, including the new White House Counsel, Harriet Miers, this time set out to keep Bradbury on a shorter leash. Instead of nominating him for the job outright, they gave it to him only "on probation." His promotion to permanent status depended upon what sort of legal advice he gave. A former senior administration official said, "The White House held the nomination over him, because they wanted a particular work product out of him."

The OLC, with its tremendous authority to issue "golden shields" to the executive branch against prosecution, was designed to exercise independent judgment. But according to another former administration official, a conservative lawyer who was troubled by the leverage over the office that was exerted by the White House, "They didn't care if the opinions would stand scrutiny. They just wanted to check a box saying, 'OLC says it's legal.' They wanted lawyers who would tell them that whatever they wanted to do was okay."

With Ashcroft gone, Gonzales running the Justice Department, and Miers now taking his place as the top lawyer in the White House, observers noticed that Addington and Cheney's influence over legal policy only expanded. Attorney General Gonzales, who owed his professional ascent almost entirely to Bush, seemed intimidated by the Vice President and his staff. Even before his confirmation as Attorney General in February 2005, Gonzales caved in to Addington on an important personnel decision, his choice of Deputy Solicitor General. Gonzales had backed the longtime Justice Department aide Patrick Philbin. But Addington thought that Philbin had been out of line in questioning the legality of the NSA program. Gonzales backed down, candidly admitting to a colleague that he just "couldn't afford" to pick a fight with Addington.

Soon after Gonzales took over the Justice Department, the torture question was revisited. Bradbury began work on yet another secret interrogation memo, which Levin hadn't had time to finish himself. Levin's publicly released opinion calling torture "abhorrent" may have given critics the impression that the Bush Administration had rejected cruelty and coercion. But behind closed doors, Bradbury began crafting a very different secret memo authorizing the CIA to undertake more sadistic interrogations than ever before. For the first time, the U.S. government explicitly legalized the infliction of several different coercive techniques at the same time. It was exactly this combination of multiple forms of pain that had so worried the CIA Inspector General's office, as well as a handful of other top administration officials who knew of the severity of its effects and had been repelled.

When Bradbury finished his opinion in the late spring of 2005, it expanded the CIA's legal latitude so that interrogators could use ten or fifteen different techniques at once, including waterboarding, head and belly slapping, sensory deprivation, sleep deprivation, temperature extremes, and stress positions, among others, according to sources familiar with the still-secret document. Gone, sources said, were the careful limits that had been imposed by Levin.

The White House was so pleased with Bradbury's work that the day after he completed his opinion legalizing the cruelest treatment of U.S.-held prisoners in history, President Bush sent his name forward to the FBI to begin work on a background check, so that Bradbury could be formally nominated to run the OLC. Evidently, the White House had received the "work product" it wanted; Bradbury had passed his probation.

From one corner of the Justice Department, however, there was high-level concern. Deputy Attorney General James Comey, the second-in-command in the department, refused to concur with Bradbury's legal advice. He told colleagues that in his view, any one of the forms of physical and mental coercion that Bradbury had authorized could inflict severe pain and physical suffering on its own, and that combining them was breathtakingly irresponsible and a recipe for real problems. Comey was a staunch Republican who had served as the U.S. Attorney for the Southern District of New York. He also, however, had evinced an independent streak during his confirmation hearings, assuring Congress, "I don't care about politics. I don't care about expediency. I don't care about friendship. I care about doing the right thing."

In the strongest terms, Comey warned Gonzales against approving Bradbury's memo. He told colleagues that if Gonzales adopted these debased standards, someday it would come back to "haunt" both Gonzales and the U.S. Department of Justice.

"It's wrong, and you shouldn't do it," the Deputy Attorney General said. Comey himself declined to comment, but several former colleagues described his extraordinary exchanges. To Comey's surprise, Attorney General Gonzales said that he agreed with Comey that the legalization of such cruelty was "wrong." Gonzales admitted, however, that he was under tremendous pressure from the Vice President to go along with it.

Although the Attorney General, who was nominally the most powerful law-enforcement officer in the U.S. government, apparently believed that his department's interrogation opinion was legally flawed and morally wrong, he nonetheless approved it anyway because Cheney, who was not a lawyer, told him to.

Afterward, Gonzales asked Comey if he had received all the "process" he felt was necessary. Comey told colleagues that he replied, "I thought I did—and that the attorney general of the United States agreed with me. But now he's changed his mind."

Having lost the legal battle, Comey made one last play to right what he saw as the country's tragically wrong course. In the late spring of 2005, Comey went to the Attorney General and said in essence, "OK—I get it that you won't accept my interpretation of the law." He then argued, "Just because you think you *can* do these things, it doesn't mean you should." The point, which was echoed also by Bellinger and Philip Zelikow, who by this point were both providing legal counsel to Condoleezza Rice at the State Department, was that tiptoeing along the outer edges of criminal law wasn't necessarily the best policy. As Zelikow later put it, "There's a gap between what's right, and what's legal." Again, surprisingly, Attorney General Gonzales claimed to agree with the criticism. However, Vice President Cheney once again overpowered him.

Soon after, in the late spring of 2005, Gonzales attended a Principals Committee meeting on the topic of detention policy. Comey prepped Gonzales for the debate, arming him with all kinds of arguments against torture and cruelty as U.S. policy. But Gonzales returned from the meeting dejected and defeated. He told a subordinate that not a single cabinet member in attendance had any second thoughts about the CIA's secret program. Cheney was adamant about it. Gonzales claimed that Rice, too, took a surprisingly hard line (although others disputed this assertion). Her position, according to the Attorney General, was that if the Justice Department said these harsh practices were legal, and the CIA said they worked, she was on board. The question of whether it was smart, and right, and in the interests of America's long-term foreign-policy goals, Gonzales suggested, was not deemed worth talking about by fellow members of the Bush cabinet. Gonzales went along.

As Attorney General, Ashcroft had backed up the Justice Department lawyers when they tried to stop the Bush Administration from breaking laws in the instance of the Terrorist Surveillance Program. Comey had been in the midst of that rebellion. (He had been taken aback, he told colleagues, when General Michael Hayden, who at the time was the Director of the NSA, had "read him in" to the program with a disconcerting welcome, saying, "I'm glad you're joining me, because now I won't have to be lonely, sitting all by myself at the witness table in the John Kerry administration.") Unlike Ashcroft, when Gonzales was faced with allegations of lawlessness at the highest levels of the administration, he deferred, particularly to the wishes of Vice President Cheney.

Soon after Comey left the administration to become the general counsel to Lockheed Martin. Before he left, though, he fired two parting shots. One was his appointment of his friend Patrick Fitzgerald, a fellow prosecutor with a reputation for relentlessness, to investigate the role played by the Vice President's staff in leaking the name of undercover CIA agent Valerie Plame. The investigation would end in Libby's criminal conviction.

Comey's other last word was an impassioned farewell speech in August 2005, lauding unnamed colleagues who had fought the good fight with him, on still-secret issues "of consequence almost beyond my imagination." He said their loyalty "to the law . . . would shock people who are cynical about Washington." They had been "committed to getting it right, and doing the right thing, whatever the price." He mentioned no names, and he specified no issues, but he noted, "These people know who they are. Some of them did pay a price for their commitment to right, but they wouldn't have it any other way."

Despite Gonzales's restoration of the CIA's "golden shield," top intelligence officials were increasingly nervous that their abusive treatment of detainees was illegal. A new guard was taking over at the intelligence agency. In June 2004, Tenet had stepped down as Director, just as the 9/11 Commission was on the verge of issuing its withering history of the Agency's missteps. Porter Goss, a former CIA officer and member of the House Intelligence Committee, became the new Director. Jose Rodriguez Jr., the officer whose reputation had been tarnished by his attempts to help an accused drug lord, was promoted to run the entire clandestine service. Taking over as head of the Counterterrorist Center was a particularly unusual choice: a Shiite Muslim convert with a Muslim wife. The top lawyer at the Agency was replaced as well. John Rizzo, a cagy veteran of the legal office known for his professionally manicured fingernails and equally polished interpretations of the law, replaced Scott Muller, who, according to one friend "practically had a breakdown" from the psychic pressure by the time he left.

As the new group at the CIA was taking over, the drumbeat of criticism over the administration's detention and interrogation policies was quickening. In May 2005, *Newsweek* magazine reported that guards in Guantánamo had thrown a Koran in a toilet, sparking riots in the Muslim world. *Newsweek* backed down from the story, but other revelations flooded out. The *New York Times* published a harrowing account on May 20 detailing how an innocent Afghan prisoner had been beaten so badly by U.S. soldiers at the U.S. facility at Bagram Air Base, an autopsy showed that before dying, his legs were "pulpified." On May 24, Irene Khan, the Secretary General of Amnesty International, denounced Guantánamo as "the gulag of our times." Bush called the accusation "absurd." But international opinion was souring against the Bush Administration's policies. The international goodwill that had flowed toward America after the terrorist attacks was running out.

On May 29, *New York Times* columnist Thomas Friedman, a bellwether of Washington punditry, who had supported the administration's war in Iraq, denounced Guantánamo for "inflaming sentiments against the U.S. all over the world and providing recruitment energy on the Internet for those who will do us ill." Friedman decried Guantánamo as "worse than an embarrassment . . . [it is] becoming the anti–Statue of Liberty." He called for the detainees to be prosecuted if they could be, and if not, he said, they should be let go. As for the prison camp, he said, "Just shut it down and plow it under."

Several weeks later, *Time* magazine published the explosive excerpts from the secret logs of Qahtani's interrogation in Guantánamo, provoking international outrage at his sadistic treatment, and bipartisan criticism in Congress. Three days later, Congress held its first hearings on Guantánamo.

Richard Durbin, a minority member of the Senate Judiciary Committee, proved how tricky the political terrain still was, however, when he likened the Bush Administration's treatment of detainees to the sort of abuse more befitting the Nazis. His comments were denounced as unpatriotic and anti-military by critics, including fellow Democrat Richard Daley, the mayor of Chicago in Durbin's home state of Illinois, whose son was serving in Iraq. Before the firestorm died down, Durbin was forced to apologize tearfully from the well of the Senate.

But the attack on Durbin didn't quell the increasing disquiet in Congress. Further rattling the CIA was a request in May 2005 from Senator Jay Rockefeller, the ranking Democrat on the Senate Intelligence Committee, to see over a hundred documents referred to in the earlier Inspector General's report on detention inside the black prison sites—the one that had so upset Goldsmith. Among the items Rockefeller specifically sought was a legal analysis of the CIA's interrogation videotapes. Rockefeller wanted to know if the intelligence agency's top lawyer believed that the waterboarding of Zubayda and Khalid Sheikh Mohammed, as captured on the secret videotapes, was entirely legal. The CIA refused to provide the requested documents to Rockefeller. But the Democratic senator's mention of the videotapes undoubtedly sent a shiver through the Agency, as did a second request he made for these documents to Goss in September 2005.

Ratcheting up the pressure on the CIA further, in May 2005, the federal judge presiding over the September 11 conspiracy trial of Zacarias Moussaoui, Leonie Brinkema, ordered the Justice Department prosecutors to tell her of the existence of any videotapes of terror suspects in U.S. custody, including Zubayda. The government objected to the order from the judge. But she showed no signs of dropping the matter.

At that same moment, top CIA officials knew that an extraordinarily damaging story was unfolding in Italy. On June 25, 2005, anyone reading the front page of the *New York Times* or the *Washington Post* learned about what came to be known inside the Agency as the "Italian Job." The day before, an Italian judge in Milan issued arrest warrants for thirteen CIA agents on charges of kidnapping, stemming from the CIA's 2003 rendition of an Islamic cleric known as "Abu Omar." Italy had given the Muslim cleric asylum, but the American operation had snatched him and flown him to Egypt, where he claimed he had been brutally tortured. The Italian indictment named, among others, the CIA's Milan station chief, Robert Seldon Lady, who had worked under diplomatic cover. The court papers were an unmitigated fiasco for the CIA, laying bare some of the Agency's darkest secrets, and exposing incredibly sloppy tradecraft showing that the CIA officers had left hundreds of embarrassing credit card bills and cell phone records all along the way. Among other juicy details, the Italian police uncovered nearly $145,000 in luxury hotel bills run up by the CIA crew. Under Italian law, the accused, if convicted, could face as much as four years in prison. As the summer wore on, the list of accused CIA officers grew to twenty-two. Meanwhile, the court records transformed the subject of CIA renditions from the realm of journalistic conjecture into a certified international legal imbroglio. Worse still for the CIA, the European backdrop to the rendition triggered a series of governmental inquiries by the European allies who, unlike the United States, regarded breaches of the Convention Against Torture as serious, prosecutable war crimes.

With the cover on the CIA's clandestine program unraveling and public opposition rising, John Maguire, a former officer in the clandestine service, said that by 2005 there was "a high level of anxiety about political retribution" inside the CIA. Officers involved in the interrogations had started seeking out lawyers and liability insurance. "Several guys," he said, "expected to be thrown under a bus."

The sense of peril inside the CIA during the summer of 2005 became more acute with the growing activism of the one member of Congress who had the strongest moral authority to take on the administration about torture: Senator John McCain of Arizona. For more than a year, a handful of Democrats had been waging a hopeless battle against the Bush Administration on this and related issues, but without a voting majority, their efforts had foundered. In addition, they had been too vulnerable to attacks on their patriotism. McCain was a Republican and a decorated Vietnam War hero who had been tortured for five years as a POW. No one had more standing to oppose the administration on this subject.

A Navy fighter pilot whose plane had been shot down in 1967, McCain had been kept in solitary confinement in a Vietnamese dungeon for two and a half years. His staff wasn't sure how he would react to the issue of torturing detainees. He might think that what the U.S.-held detainees went through was nothing compared with having been tied up in ropes in such a way that his bones were broken. But his staff found that starting with the photographs of Abu Ghraib, as one put it, "It was like an order of magnitude how disgusted he was. He was so personally pained by it. As soon as he saw that stuff, he saw how dangerous it would be."

The Senate staff member described what bothered McCain. "Everyone was approaching him as a torture-ee. He didn't want people to say that was the only reason he cared." McCain didn't want people thinking that he was grandstanding or somehow exploiting his own experience. He also didn't want to speak publicly about his belief that the Bush Administration's policies could cost the life of his son, who was serving in the military in Iraq. He didn't like talking about personal matters.

The question, though, said his aide, "was how to get beyond the coffee clatch of just a few other guys in the Senate." On the Republican side, McCain had support from fellow war veterans Lindsey Graham, a military reserve lawyer who represented South Carolina, and John Warner of Virginia, Chairman of the Armed Services Committee, on which they all served. Among the Democrats, Richard Durbin, Carl Levin, Ted Kennedy, Representative Ed Markey, and Patrick Leahy had all been outspoken. But beyond that, few in Congress wanted to run the political risk of opposing the administration on an issue that could make them appear to be pro-terrorism.

For months, human rights groups had been begging McCain to step in. Despite his huge stature on military matters, even he had felt politically intimidated, saying he needed more "cover." Elisa Massimino, a lawyer—and military brat herself—with the nonprofit organization Human Rights First, was instrumental in paving the way for McCain to come forward. She quietly put together a stunning coalition of retired military dignitaries, including the hugely respected former Chairman of the Joint Chiefs of Staff, General John Vessey, a four-star World War II veteran who had commanded the U.S. forces in Korea, to support the restoration of the Geneva standards in the treatment of prisoners. She ushered these military figures in to see McCain and other sympathetic members of Congress.

After joining forces with McCain, Senator Graham called over to the Pentagon to ask for a meeting with Rumsfeld about detainee treatment. According to a well-informed Senate aide, however, Graham was told, "Don't bother. Rumsfeld's not worth meeting with. On this subject, Cheney is the power player."

Meanwhile, after a series of moribund interagency meetings at the White House in which Addington angrily insisted that everything the administration had done was right so there was no need for change, a small group of reform-minded lawyers inside the Bush Administration decided that if the festering issues of Guantánamo and the CIA's black prisons were ever to be seriously addressed, it would take the bureaucratic equivalent of dynamite.

Over the weekend of June 11, 2005, in a huge office in the E-Ring of the Pentagon, the would-be reformers worked in secrecy on a laptop, where they wouldn't be detected by their superiors. They wanted a solid, uninterrupted block of time to compose a radical plan of action. They called it "The Big Bang." It was a proposal to shut down the secret detention and interrogation program. The group planned to call on the President to announce the new policies in just thirty days.

They were formidable players. In the room was Zelikow, the former Executive Director of the 9/11 Commission, who by then had joined Rice at the State Department as her counselor. Professorial and formal, he brought a deep knowledge of international history and also a little-known past as an expert on law cases dealing with "cruel and unusual punishment." He knew enough about the Eighth Amendment to think that the Bush Administration was seriously wrong in its belief that its interrogation practices did not violate this constitutional standard.

Joining Zelikow was a young, boyish-looking lawyer named Matthew Waxman, who had clerked for Justice David Souter during *Bush v. Gore.* Waxman had a knack for quick, clear analysis, and the kind of earnest, friendly demeanor that attracted mentors. Rumsfeld had asked Waxman to become his deputy assistant secretary of defense for detainee issues after the Abu Ghraib scandal. It was just one more in a string of disaster assignments that Waxman had fallen into— which in addition to *Bush v. Gore* had included joining the staff of the Bush National Security Council the month before September 11. Waxman joked that if he ever wrote a memoir, he would have to title it *Shit Storm.*

The meeting took place in the office of the third participant, Gordon England, Deputy Defense Secretary and former Secretary of the Navy, who had previously been the president of Lockheed. A fourth member of the group, Bellinger, was unable to attend that day, but his ideas infused the cabal. The group had decided that the only way to get past Cheney was to convince both the Secretary of Defense and the Secretary of State to endorse a proposal, which then could be shown to the President. Bush, they reasoned, had professed an interest in closing Guantánamo down, but had never been presented with a concrete proposal to do so.

They hoped to draft the proposal that weekend and then take it to Rumsfeld and Rice. If these cabinet secretaries signed on, they could submit it directly to the President, regardless of Cheney's views. Obviously, it meant going outside of prescribed channels and running a political risk. But they saw no other hope.

The proposal they drafted that day was remarkable. It noted that after five years, the time had come for reform, including the eventual closing of the CIA's secret prisons and Guantánamo. It admitted, "The dilemmas are not easy." Captured terrorists may have information, they noted, that could save lives. They also didn't fit easily into the existing criminal justice system. What they proposed was "a new international system for handling captured combatants in a new kind of global conflict."

Among the changes they called for was an outside review to assess whether the claims of success from the interrogators who used coercion were truly accurate. They warned that the CIA was relying on a false sense of security if it believed its secret program could be forever "walled off" from the world. "That wall will inevitably be broken through," they said, "and it would be better if the administration did it."

They also called for America to return to treatment standards for all prisoners that met those laid out under international law. "We are not doing this for them, we are doing this for us," they wrote. "There is a risk that some intelligence may be lost." But it went on, "As in prior wars, this risk should be accepted as necessary to maintain the integrity of our common-found values." They also called for an admission that abuses had occurred and for investigations to hold those in power accountable. The ICRC should be allowed to meet with all U.S.-held detainees, they wrote. Guantánamo should be closed.

Finally, they called for the CIA's prisoners to be prosecuted, even if it meant exposing the egregious secret conditions in which they had been held. "It's a fact. It must be faced," they wrote. "Better to face it now, in this administration," they warned, than under a more hostile, later administration.

The architects of the Big Bang left the E-Ring intending that Zelikow would pass their proposal to Rice, while England would give it to Rumsfeld. The State Department component went well. Rice was said to be impressed with the draft. Rumsfeld, however, was another story. He was furious with England for sending the paper to the Secretary of State without his prior sign-off, or that of Jim Haynes, the Pentagon's General Counsel. Stephen Cambone, Undersecretary of Defense for Intelligence, and Douglas Feith, Undersecretary of Defense for Policy, were also furious when they learned they had been bypassed. "They claimed it was a process issue," said a source, "but really they didn't like the substance."

Rice pushed the proposal forward, sharing it with Steven Hadley, the National Security Adviser, who scheduled a meeting of the Principals to discuss it. Rumsfeld angrily demanded that the meeting be canceled. In the end, the meeting on detainee matters was held, but because of Rumsfeld's objections, the paper was not allowed to be part of the discussion.

It appears to be this meeting that Gonzales described to a subordinate, claiming that none of the cabinet members but he wanted to make any changes in detainee policy, despite his desire to move past cruel practices. It's not how another participant saw it. According to a second source, Rice was the only cabinet officer favoring serious reform. Gonzales in particular followed Cheney's lead, opposing any change.

The Big Bang proposal reached Bush, two sources said, proving that as of the summer of 2005, he knew there were senior officials inside his administration, including a deputy defense secretary, who thought the war on terror was being undermined by his detention policies, and that Guantánamo needed to be closed. If he read the report, he also knew there were credible allegations of CIA abuse and calls for accountability. Nonetheless, said one of its sponsors, "The Big Bang just died on the vine."

Controlling Congress was slightly harder. On July 24, 2005, McCain introduced an amendment to the Defense Department's budget prohibiting military interrogators from using more force than allowed by the traditional limits in the *Army Field Manual,* even if the commander in chief ordered it. The proposed bill also prohibited other U.S. personnel—including the CIA—from engaging in torture and other forms of cruel, inhuman, and degrading treatment of U.S.-held prisoners anywhere in the world.

Cheney personally went up to Congress to lobby against McCain's proposed torture ban. He met three times with McCain. What transpired has never been told. But according to a well-informed congressional official, "With Cheney, it was all about how to stop the next terrorist attack. Will this help or hurt it?" He was "absolutely convinced" that the CIA wouldn't be able to get the information any other way, he said. When McCain asked for evidence that coercion worked, "They would just say, 'We can't tell you—but trust us.'" All that Cheney and other defenders of the program pointed to were a handful of specific cases. There was no scientific study or larger analysis. Moreover, the CIA experts admitted that much of the information they got was unreliable.

"The administration's position was relentlessly short-term and narrow," said the congressional official. McCain liked to travel, and everywhere he went in any country, he had noticed, torture and Abu Ghraib would come up. He believed it was making it harder to get foreign cooperation. It was also radicalizing the Muslim population. Cheney, however, told McCain that the terrorists hated America and would try to attack regardless of U.S. policies. Torture, as he saw it, was just an excuse. Cheney also made clear to McCain that, as the official put it, "he wasn't worried about winning popularity contests."

By the fall, with the assistance of Human Rights First, more than a dozen generals, including former Secretary of State Colin Powell, who was also a former Chairman of the Joint Chiefs of Staff, signed a passionate letter to Congress urging them to pass McCain's legislation. Their petition blamed administration policies for creating confusion that resulted in abuse, and criticized the administration for leaving service members "to take the blame when things went wrong."

On October 5, 2005, Bush threatened to exercise his veto power—the first veto of his presidency—to kill the McCain bill if it passed. Hours later, the Senate overwhelmingly approved the measure by a margin of 90–9, which included 46 of the 55 Republican members.

The haggling continued into November as Cheney returned to Capitol Hill to stave off a version of the legislation involving the House of Representatives. Cheney personally made the case for a CIA exemption from such conduct codes, earning the sobriquet "Vice President for Torture" on the *Washington Post*'s editorial page.

"I don't know how you could possibly agree to legitimizing an agent of the government engaging in torture," McCain countered. In private, McCain accused Cheney of trying to create a "secret police," with different rules from everyone else. He also argued that if the United States gave the CIA exemptions to torture, then the United States wouldn't be able to protest when Americans fell into the hands of other countries' brutal secret police. "It didn't go well," the official said of Cheney's effort to dissuade McCain.

On November 2, as these arguments were raging, the *Washington Post* published a stunning exposé by reporter Dana Priest describing the CIA's global network of secret black prison sites, some of which, the paper disclosed, were based in former Soviet states in Eastern Europe. The news ignited an international furor. In Washington, the Bush Administration's response was to blame the messenger and announce a leak investigation into how Priest got the story.

The next day, November 3, Judge Brinkema, who was still presiding over the Moussaoui trial, issued a modified order to the government to produce any video- or audiotapes of U.S. interrogations of terror suspects. Eleven days later, amid the damning newspaper revelations and the clamorous public debate about CIA torture in Congress, the Bush Administration told the judge it had no such tapes. Senior CIA officials "absolutely knew it was a lie," said a former CIA source with no specific knowledge of the machinations, but who was knowledgeable about the Agency's inner workings.

Sometime during that month, Jose Rodriguez Jr., the head of the CIA's clandestine operations, ordered subordinates to destroy the tapes. Depending on the circumstances, the act was potentially a serious felony. The cliché after the Watergate scandal in Washington was that typically cover-ups were worse than the original crime, but in this instance, law professor Martin Lederman speculated, "They must have thought the crime was worse than the cover-up."

In a prepared statement, CIA Director Michael Hayden later called the CIA's actions "in line with the law." Several former Agency officials doubted this. One former CIA officer said the tapes "definitely would have shocked the conscience of the country—the impact would have been unmanageable." Another said there was no doubt "they were evidence." John Gannon, a former CIA deputy director, told the *New York Times* that he believed that if the tapes had survived to be seen by the public, they would have settled the debate over the CIA's "enhanced" interrogation methods. "To a spectator it would look like torture," he said. "And torture is wrong."

Addington found a more ingenious way to erase the unwelcome intrusions into the CIA's secret program. Just before Bush signed McCain's Detainee Treatment Act into law, on December 30, 2005, Addington unsheathed the red pen he kept in his pocket and eviscerated the compromise language that had been worked out between Congress and the White House. In its place, he wrote a presidential "signing statement" suggesting that Bush would only enforce the new law "in a manner consistent with" his constitutional role as commander in chief. It was one of hundreds of similar notes he had insinuated into the legislative record, reserving the President's right to ignore Congress.

Bellinger, who had worked hard to forge the compromise with Congress, was apoplectic. Yet Addington's signing statement, symbolically thumbing its nose at Congress, prevailed. To placate Bellinger, a second, more conciliatory presidential statement was eventually added.

Although Cheney suggested he had lost the fight to McCain, his aides kept fighting. A new, secret legal memo commissioned by the White House from Steven Bradbury at the OLC provided a stealthy means of undercutting McCain's intent. On its face, McCain's Detainee Treatment Act seemed to prohibit all abuse—allowing only humane treatment of prisoners by all officials of the U.S. government, including the CIA. But Bradbury argued that none of the CIA's interrogation techniques were cruel, inhumane, or degrading. Not even waterboarding. His secret opinion nullified McCain's public victory.

The gimmick Bradbury relied upon was a Supreme Court ruling that mistreatment had to "shock the conscience" of a court in order to meet the constitutional definition of "cruel and unusual punishment." With Bradbury's memo in hand, the Bush Administration could argue with a straight face that many courts would not be shocked by the abusive treatment of terror suspects, so therefore waterboarding and other forms of near-death techniques were not necessarily "inhumane." It all depended upon the circumstances. McCain didn't know it, but his effort to clarify the rules for U.S. personnel had been clouded by the Justice Department in a whole new way. The State Department's legal team argued heatedly that Bradbury was wrong, and that the CIA's practices were criminal after McCain's legislation. No minds were changed, but the tough and incessant arguments made the CIA more nervous by the day.

Meanwhile, Matthew Waxman, the young Deputy Assistant Secretary of Defense whom Rumsfeld had assigned to oversee detainee issues, had a memorable firsthand confrontation with Addington. Waxman had helped organize a Pentagon meeting in which an impressive array of military figures, including the civilian secretaries of the Army, Air Force, and Navy, along with the highest-ranking military officers in each branch of the services, all came out in support of returning to Geneva's standards of treatment as a matter of military policy. Included in the meeting were two opponents, however—Stephen Cambone and Jim Haynes, General Counsel to the Pentagon.

It took no time before word of the rebellion reached Cheney's office. Soon after, Waxman, who was traveling abroad at the time, was summoned to meet in the White House with Addington. When Waxman arrived, a colleague later related, Scooter Libby, the Vice President's chief of staff, was there, too. The two took turns berating him for having the audacity to reopen the question of adherence to the Geneva Conventions. They insisted that the President had decided that question categorically and in perpetuity.

Waxman tried to argue that Guantánamo, Abu Ghraib, and other instances of U.S. human rights abuse were undermining America in the war on terror. But Cheney's aides scoffed at him. The only people who believed that, they said, were political enemies—Democrats— and the *New York Times*—who would always be against Bush anyway. The phrase that rang in Waxman's head as he left the manicured White House lawn was Addington's vituperative denunciation. "What you're doing," Addington boomed, while physically towering over Waxman, "is an abomination!"

Waxman was shaken and depressed. It was as if these issues were theological creeds for Addington and Cheney—not policy issues that could be discussed with reason.

In retrospect, it seemed bizarre that the Vice President's chief of staff and lawyer were calling the shots on such vital military matters. Waxman had been asked by the Secretary of Defense, in whose department he served, to take on these issues. The Vice President and his staff had no place in the chain of military command. Addington talked endlessly about the President's prerogatives. But the Vice President dominated the entire national security apparatus. The President, whose powers he was constantly touting, was all but invisible on these issues. "Addington spoke authoritatively about what the President decided in 2002, but he wrote the document, and it was probably his decision," a former White House official said later.

After his searing confrontation with Addington, Waxman departed from the Pentagon, first to the State Department, and later from the administration altogether.

On June 29, 2006, less than a year after Addington called the effort to revive the Geneva Conventions an "abomination," the Supreme Court ruled emphatically that the Bush Administration had to abide by these laws in its war on terror. The Supreme Court's ruling in *Hamdan v. Rumsfeld* rejected the Bush Administration's radical legal theories even more soundly than the earlier decisions. Yale Law School Dean Harold Koh called it "a stunning rebuke to the extreme theory of executive power that has been put forward for the past five years." The Court ruled that the president, even in war, was bound by laws and treaties, including the Geneva Conventions. He had no right to unilaterally appoint military commissions using his own rules.

The judgment had numerous ramifications, not the least of which was that if Geneva's rules applied to terror suspects, the CIA's "enhanced interrogations" were potentially war crimes. People could be prosecuted.

Addington was outraged. What he did next shocked several colleagues. Rather than complying with the Supreme Court's judgment, Addington had the legislation drafted to overturn the Court. It would say simply that the Geneva Conventions did not give terror suspects access to U.S. courts and that the president had the authority to try them in military commissions. The Republicans in Congress could ram it through. Then no one in the administration would need to worry about war crimes prosecutions.

Harriet Miers, the White House Counsel, who was strongly influenced by Addington, went along with the plan, as did Attorney General Gonzales. The proposed piece of legislation was drafted, reversing the Court. The constitutional crisis grew so heated that Bellinger, the highest-ranking lawyer in the State Department, threatened to resign if the President supported legislation superseding the Supreme Court. Waxman, who was also at the State Department by then, was ready to resign, too.

Rice intervened, making a personal plea to Bush, saying, according to a witness, "Mr. President, you can't reverse the court!" Karen Hughes, who at the time was running the Office of Public Liaison at the State Department, also threw herself into stopping the President from undoing the *Hamdan* ruling. In the end, Bush sided with Rice and Hughes, saying, "I accept the decision."

Cheney and his staff, however, didn't stop fighting. They went on to work closely with Congress to restore virtually every aspect of the earlier executive power they had exercised over the detainees, including sole control over the military commissions. Congress ratified most of the White House's wishes in what came to be known as the Military Commissions Act—which McCain voted for—despite his earlier reform efforts.

Particularly important to Cheney, according to a congressional insider familiar with the negotiations, was the issue of retroactive "immunity" from future criminal prosecution. "They kept talking about how they had to have immunity for the young guys at the CIA who had taken on the terrorists," said the congressional source. "But their draft of the [immunity] legislation covered the policy-makers, all the way up to Cheney. It wasn't just the young guys in the trenches they were worried about."

After the *Hamdan* ruling, there were growing calls from within the CIA to move the remaining high-value detainees out of the black sites and to Cuba. The CIA feared the prisoners were too much of a legal liability. In a series of impassioned meetings chaired by President Bush during the summer of 2006, Rice supported the plan, saying, "Now's the time. We have to do it on this president's watch. We should try them under this President." Cheney strongly resisted, in part, according to a former senior official involved in the discussions, because he "worried about what would come to light." Gonzales, too, was adamantly opposed. He warned the other top officials about the risk that administration officials faced of being prosecuted for war crimes. "He was scaring everyone," a participant in one such meeting said.

Once the CIA shifted sides, saying it wanted to move the prisoners out, however, Bush agreed. "He had grown uneasy with the identity of America on these issues," the same official claimed, although there is no record that Bush ever objected to the methods employed by the CIA in its black sites or insisted on any outside review of the CIA's claims that their approach was working. For his part, Robert Grenier, the head of the Counterterrorist Center, like many people in the CIA, was relieved. "There has to be some sense of due process," he said. "We can't just make people disappear."

Bellinger and Waxman were ecstatic, thinking finally they were on the verge of restoring the country's values and laws. They prepared an eloquent draft of what they hoped would be the presidential address in which Bush would finally acknowledge, and at the same time end, the clandestine global detention and interrogation program.

On September 6, 2006, in front of a somber East Room audience composed in part of family members of the victims of September 11, 2001, Bush delivered an extraordinary, thirty-seven-minute address. Standing in front of a cluster of American flags, flanked by Cheney, Gonzales, and Michael Hayden, who by then was the Director of the CIA, and framed by a bust of Lincoln, who had established that "military necessity shall not permit of cruelty," Bush admitted for the first time that America had been holding secret prisoners for years, without charges and outside the reach of authorities, and subjecting them to "an alternative set of procedures." He announced that he had emptied the black sites and transferred these suspects to Guantánamo Bay.

As he went on, however, Bush defended the program as "one of the most vital tools in our war against terror," insisting that everything about the program had been legal. The President noted that he could not reveal exactly what the government had done to the prisoners, because it would "help the terrorists." But he assured the world that his administration's calibrated program of torment was highly effective. He rattled off the details of several cases, including those of Abu Zubayda and Khalid Sheikh Mohammed, never revealing that both said they had given false information under torture. He never mentioned the name of Ibn al-Shaykh al-Libi, whose fabrications under torture had helped sell the war in Iraq.

As he watched the President's address, Waxman's hopes sank. "We wanted this to be about change," he said. "We wanted it to have the President saying he was committed to closing Guantánamo. But instead of turning the page, they laminated it."

Karen Hughes was also distressed, according to colleagues who spoke with her. In her liaison position at the State Department, she had seen firsthand the damage that the torture issue had done to America's moral standing in the world. After reading one of several euphemisms that Bush's speech used to avoid calling the CIA's interrogation techniques torture, she told a confidant, "Yuck! Special procedures? It sounds scary!"

It turned out that the speech had gone through many drafts. An earlier version had included a clarionlike call to close down the CIA's secret prison program for good. This had survived edits and rewrites until Vice President Cheney held a short, private meeting with President Bush. Afterward, the President made no more promises to end America's experiment with secret detention.

The same day as the Bush address, across the Potomac River, Lieutenant General John Kimmons presented a new interrogation manual for the Army. A year after Addington had squelched efforts by Waxman and others at the Pentagon to restore the standards of the Geneva Conventions, the uniformed military officers had finally prevailed.

Kimmons made no effort to paper over the military's disdain for the Bush Administration's program of prisoner abuse. "No good intelligence is going to come from abusive practices," he said. "I think history tells us that. I think the empirical evidence of the past five hard years tells us that . . . any piece of intelligence which is obtained under duress through the use of abusive techniques would be of questionable credibility . . . nothing good will come from them."

At a press conference soon after, on September 15, 2006, President Bush expressed puzzlement over what the Supreme Court meant when it ruled that the United States government must abide by the Geneva Conventions, laws that America itself had drafted and led the world in adopting sixty years before. Mocking the language of the Conventions, he asked, "What does that mean? 'Outrages upon human dignity'?"

AFTERWORD

A lady asked Dr. {Benjamin} Franklin, "Well Doctor, what have we got, a republic or a monarchy?"

"A republic," replied the Doctor, "if you can keep it."

—Papers of Dr. James McHenry, describing the scene as they left the Federal Convention of 1787 in Philadelphia

Seven years after Al Qaeda's attacks on America, as the Bush Administration slips into history, it is clear that what began on September 11, 2001, as a battle for America's security became, and continues to be, a battle for the country's soul.

In looking back, one of the most remarkable features of this struggle is that almost from the start, and at almost every turn along the way, the Bush Administration was warned that the short-term benefits of its extralegal approach to fighting terrorism would have tragically destructive long-term consequences both for the rule of law and America's interests in the world. These warnings came not just from political opponents, but also from experienced allies, including the British Intelligence Service, the experts in the traditionally conservative military and the FBI, and perhaps most surprisingly, from a series of loyal Republican lawyers inside the administration itself. The number of patriotic critics inside the administration and out who threw themselves into trying to head off what they saw as a terrible departure from America's ideals, often at an enormous price to their own careers, is both humbling and reassuring.

Instead of heeding this well-intentioned dissent, however, the Bush

Administration invoked the fear flowing from the attacks on September 11 to institute a policy of deliberate cruelty that would have been unthinkable on September 10. President Bush, Vice President Cheney, and a small handful of trusted advisers sought and obtained dubious legal opinions enabling them to circumvent American laws and traditions. In the name of protecting national security, the executive branch sanctioned coerced confessions, extrajudicial detention, and other violations of individuals' liberties that had been prohibited since the country's founding. They turned the Justice Department's Office of Legal Counsel into a political instrument, which they used to expand their own executive power at the expense of long-standing checks and balances. When warned that these policies were unlawful and counterproductive, they ignored the experts and made decisions outside of ordinary bureaucratic channels, and often outside of the public's view. Rather than risking the possibility of congressional opposition, they classified vital interpretations of law as top secret. No one knows to this day how many more secret opinions the Bush Justice Department has produced. Far from tempering these policies over time, they marginalized and penalized those who challenged their idées fixes. Because the subject matter was shrouded in claims of national security, however, much of the internal dissent remained hidden.

Throughout this period, President Bush and Vice President Cheney have continued to insist that they never authorized or condoned "torture," which they acknowledge is criminal under U.S. law. But their semantic parsing of the term began to seem increasingly disingenuous as details from the secret detention and interrogation program surfaced, piece by piece. By the last year of the Bush presidency, many of the administration's own top authorities, including Director of National Intelligence Mike McConnell and former Secretary of Homeland Security Tom Ridge, as well as the former CIA officer involved in Abu Zubayda's capture, John Kiriakou, acknowledged that as far as they were concerned, waterboarding was torture.

Such extreme measures were perhaps understandable in the panic-filled days and weeks immediately after September 11, falling into place among other historic infringements of civil liberties during times of dire national security crisis. Yet seven years later, the Bush Administration's counterterrorism policies remained largely frozen in place. There had been some alterations and improvements. But the legal framework survives despite nearly universal bipartisan acceptance outside of the Bush Administration that Guantánamo should be shut down, that the military commission process was hopelessly flawed, and that the human rights violations at Abu Ghraib and elsewhere were not the work of a few "rotten apples" on the bottom, but rather the result of irresponsible leadership at the top. In fact torture, which was reviled as a depraved vestige of primitive cultures before September 11, seemed in danger of becoming normalized.

Through four congressional election cycles and two presidential campaigns, there has been surprisingly little intelligent debate about the Bush Administration's approach to terrorism. Top administration officials continue to insist that their program is legal and effective; while critics complain, they rarely provide their own proposals for a better system. Since the Democratic Party gained control of Congress in 2006, there have been stirrings toward investigation and reform. But in July 2007, a bill to close Guantánamo was defeated when the Senate voted overwhelmingly (94–3) against transferring the detainees to prisons in the United States. Clearly, the fear of appearing "soft" on terrorism still haunts elected officials.

The presidential election of 2008 may prove a turning point. In a hopeful sign of change, both parties' presidential nominees have taken strong, principled stands against torture, promising to close loopholes that secretly sanction it, and bring the country's detention and interrogation policy back in line with its core constitutional values. Yet neither candidate had put forward a coherent alternative by May 2008. The Bush Administration's "New Paradigm" remains intact, allowing the administration to claim all of the powers that flow from war, while allocating detainees almost none of the rights that either the military or criminal justice system confers.

Senator John McCain's opposition to torture surely runs as deep as that of any politician in America. He captured the essence of the issue eloquently in a simple declaration in 2005 that "It's not about them, it's about us." Yet in a nod to the conservative base of his party, even McCain has feinted to the right, siding with the Bush White House in early 2008 against proposed legislation that would limit CIA officers to the humane interrogation techniques allowed by the military.

An obvious reason for the political caution is fear. By the measure that matters most, the Bush Administration can point to its record in fighting terrorism as a success. There have been no additional terrorist attacks in America since September 11, 2001. No rival wants to be accused of breaking this streak.

Yet it is hard to know if the Bush Administration's success represents the vanquishing of new credible threats, or rather the absence of any. As former Secretary of Defense Donald Rumsfeld himself acknowledged in 2003, "Today we lack metrics to know if we are winning or losing the global war on terror." During the Bush years, it's been almost impossible to tell. In the absence of government transparency and independent analysis, the public has been asked to simply take the President's word on faith that inhumane treatment has been necessary to stop attacks and save lives.

Increasingly, however, those with access to the inner workings of the Bush Administration's counterterrorism program have begun to question those claims. In March 2008, after President Bush announced his intention to veto legislation requiring the CIA to abide by the same interrogation rules as the military, Senator Jay Rockefeller, Chairman of the Senate Intelligence Committee, challenged the administration's entire rationale. Rockefeller's criticism over the years was muted, at best, and so his bold rebuke was particularly noteworthy. "As Chairman of the Senate Intelligence Committee," a statement he released said, "I have heard nothing to suggest that information obtained from enhanced interrogation techniques has prevented an imminent terrorist attack. And I have heard nothing that makes me think the information obtained from these techniques could not have been obtained through traditional interrogation methods used by military and law enforcement interrogators. On the other hand, I do know that coercive interrogations can lead detainees to provide false information in order to make the interrogation stop."

In other words, according to one of the few U.S. officials with full access to the details, the drastic "ticking time bomb" threat used to justify what many Americans would otherwise consider indefensible tactics, had never actually occurred, other than on the TV sets of those watching Fox-TV's terrorism fantasy show *24.*

Rockefeller asserted that the Bush Administration's approach was not only unnecessary, it was also undermining the security that it claimed to safeguard. "The CIA's program damages our national security by weakening our legal and moral authority, and by providing al Qaeda and other terrorist groups a recruiting and motivational tool," he said. "By continuing this interrogation program, the President is sacrificing our strategic advantage for questionable tactical gain."

Doubt has begun to emerge from within the administration itself, too. In 2006, a scientific advisory group to the U.S. intelligence agencies produced an exhaustive report on interrogation called "Educing Information," which concluded that there was no scientific proof whatsoever that harsh techniques worked. In fact, several of the experts involved in the study described the infliction of physical and psychological cruelty as outmoded, amateurish, and unreliable.

In confidential interviews, several of those with inside information about the NSA's controversial Terrorist Surveillance Program have expressed similar disenchantment. As one of these former officials says of the ultrasecret program so furiously defended by David Addington, "It's produced nothing."

While the Bush Administration can point proudly to its record of no terrorist attacks on America since 2001, its progress in bringing the perpetrators of the attacks to justice is less impressive. The administration certainly could claim a number of top Al Qaeda scalps. Yet as of May 2008, both Osama Bin Laden and Ayman al-Zawahiri remained at large. The government's own statistics, meanwhile, showed that both the number of terrorist attacks and the estimation of the threat posed by Al Qaeda were growing. According to the most recent National Intelligence Estimate, issued in April 2006, "A large body of all-source reporting indicates that activists identifying themselves as jihadists, although still a small percentage of Muslims, are increasing in both numbers and geographical distribution." The report noted carefully, "If this trend continues, threats to U.S. interests at home and abroad will become more diverse, leading to increasing attacks worldwide."

The war in Iraq, the Israeli-Palestinian conflict, and the deteriorating security situations in Afghanistan and Pakistan have all reportedly contributed to the radicalization of the Muslim world. But according to one former official who traveled extensively through the Middle East, no subject was described by Muslims he spoke with as more deeply disturbing than America's abuse of the detainees. Eric Haseltine, the former top adviser on science and technology to the Director of National Intelligence, worries that prisoner abuse has profoundly hurt what he defines as the most important battle in the war on terror—the struggle to win the support of the next generation of Arab youth. "I came away from my many visits to the Middle East convinced there is a widespread belief that if *America* abuses prisoners then there can be no true freedom for anyone," he said. "It seemed to me that our greatest sin in the eyes of Muslims was not invading the Middle East, or even our support of Israel: our greatest sin was robbing Muslims of hope."

By many estimates, by the end of the Bush years, America's reputation as a lead defender of democracy and human rights was in tatters. According to the Pew Global Attitudes Project, in June 2006, public opinion in two countries in the world supported the U.S. war on terror—India and Russia. Meanwhile, corrupt and repressive states, including Egypt, Sudan, and Zimbabwe, have all justified their own brutality by citing America's example. Egyptian president-for-life Hosni Mubarak declared that the U.S. treatment of detainees proved that "We were right from the beginning in using all means, including military tribunals, to combat terrorism." Even the most dependable of U.S. allies, including Germany, Denmark, and the European Union, by 2008 had all accused the United States of violating internationally accepted standards for humane treatment and due process. Canada went so far as to place America on its official list of rogue countries that torture.

The Bush Administration's controversial anti-terrorism program had other unwelcome consequences as well. Seven years after the attacks of September 11, not a single terror suspect held outside of the U.S. criminal court system has been tried. Of the 759 detainees acknowledged to have been held in Guantánamo, approximately 340 remained there, only a handful of whom had been charged. Among these, not a single "enemy combatant" had yet had the opportunity to cross-examine the government or see the evidence on which he was being held.

The military commission process was clearly plagued by problems to the point of dysfunction. One stalwart official after another has stepped forward with astounding accusations of impropriety. In a sworn statement in the spring of 2008, for example, the former top prosecutor in the Office of Military Commissions disclosed that the Pentagon had pressured him to time "sexy" prosecutions for political advantage, and to use evidence against the detainees that he considered tainted by torture. After resigning in protest, the prosecutor, Air Force Colonel Morris Davis, also disclosed that when he suggested to Jim Haynes, the General Counsel at the Pentagon, that a few acquittals might enhance Guantánamo's reputation for fair treatment, as had been true of the war crimes trials of the Nazis in Nuremberg, Haynes was horrified. "We can't have acquittals! We've got to have convictions!" he quoted the top Pentagon lawyer as saying. "If we've been holding these guys for so long, how can we explain letting them get off?"

As the FBI and other early critics had warned, the administration's use of coercion to force confessions has created legal havoc. Impassioned disputes over the admissibility of evidence obtained through torture have crippled the administration's efforts to prosecute many detainees. In May 2008, the Pentagon announced that it was dismissing charges against Mohammed al-Qahtani, the Saudi suspected of having been the "20th hijacker" apparently because the inhumane treatment to which he had been subjected during his long interrogation in Guantánamo, all of which had been authorized by Rumsfeld, had destroyed the credibility of his confession, hopelessly tainting the case. In one particularly poignant case in 2004, suspicions of torture caused a Marine Corps prosecutor to reluctantly drop charges against Mohamedou Ould Slahi, an alleged Al Qaeda leader in Guantánamo who was accused of helping the Hamburg cell that planned the September 11 attacks. The prosecutor, Lieutenant Colonel Stuart Couch, had enlisted specifically because he had wanted to help bring justice for a friend who had been the co-pilot of United Flight 175, the second plane that Al Qaeda hijacked into the World Trade Center. After he pieced together the record of torture techniques to which Slahi had been subjected, however, Couch, who is a devout Christian, could no longer continue the case in good conscience. "Here was somebody I thought was connected to 9/11," Couch told the *Wall Street Journal,* "but in our zeal to get information, we had compromised our ability to prosecute him."

In February 2008, the Bush Administration announced its intention to bring capital murder charges against six detainees it said were linked to the September 11 attacks, including Khalid Sheikh Mohammed. But the taint of torture loomed over these prosecutions, too. Notably missing from the list of the accused were Abu Zubayda and Abd al-Rahim al-Nashiri, the two detainees whose waterboarding sessions had been videotaped by the CIA. The CIA's destruction of the videotapes, which was under criminal investigation by an outside counsel by May 2008, clearly jeopardized any future prosecution of these two figures, whom the administration had previously described as key Al Qaeda leaders.

Despite Bush's vows to hold the perpetrators accountable after Abu Ghraib, as of the spring of 2008 no senior Bush Administration official had been prosecuted or removed from office in connection with the abuse of prisoners. By then, the non-governmental organization Human Rights Watch estimated that more than 600 U.S. military and civilian personnel were involved in abusing more than 460 detainees. President Bush sporadically mentioned a wish to close Guantánamo, but since September 2006, six new detainees were sent there, including two from unspecified CIA black sites. At the same time, Puli-Charki, an American prison outside of Kabul, Afghanistan, was being expanded. If Bush or Cheney regretted the uncounted deaths, disappearances, and torment of prisoners in their administration's custody, or the false intelligence and contaminated prosecutions that these tactics produced, they didn't express it.

After some dozen internal investigations, mostly by the military, a number of low-ranking enlisted soldiers and officers were convicted or disciplined for prisoner abuse. But by design, the investigations were focused downward in the chain of command, not up to those who set the policy. As Major General Antonio Taguba told *The New Yorker,* his investigation of Abu Ghraib was limited to the military police below, not those above him. "I was legally prevented from further investigation into higher authority," he said. "I was limited to a box."

The CIA, meanwhile, quietly investigated seven or more allegedly mistaken renditions of innocent victims, and sent several homicide cases resulting from prisoner abuse to the Justice Department for possible criminal prosecution, but not a single officer was charged. Instead, President Bush gave George Tenet, who presided over the creation of the CIA's interrogation and detention program, the Medal of Freedom. The female officer who pushed to keep Khaled El-Masri imprisoned in Afghanistan after his mistaken rendition was promoted to a top post handling sensitive matters in the Middle East. Masri, meanwhile, was denied the opportunity to bring a civil suit against the U.S. government for his false imprisonment because the Bush Administration succeeded in arguing that simply addressing the subject of rendition in a U.S. court would violate national security. Back in Germany, he was reportedly beset by emotional problems.

By the last year of the Bush presidency, growing numbers of former administration insiders had abandoned the government with the conviction that in waging the war against terrorism, America had lost its way. Many had fought valiantly to right what they saw as a dangerously wrong turn. With Bush, Cheney, and Addington still firmly in power, it was hard to declare their efforts a success. Still, with change in the air, there was a sense that history might be on their side. Jack Goldsmith moved to Boston to teach law at Harvard, where he was ironically greeted with protests because of his association with the Bush Administration's torture policies. Matthew Waxman moved to New York, where he, too, began to teach law, in his case at Columbia. Alberto Mora left the administration as a pariah in the eyes of some Pentagon colleagues but was given the John F. Kennedy Foundation's Profiles in Courage Award in 2006 for speaking out. Most of the FBI agents who opposed "enhanced" interrogation techniques retired and joined private security firms, taking vast amounts of wisdom about Islamic terrorism with them.

In Charlottesville, Virginia, Phillip Zelikow, who returned to teaching history at the University of Virginia, tried to take stock. In time, he predicted, the Bush Administration's descent into torture would be seen as akin to Roosevelt's internment of Japanese Americans during World War II. It happened, he believed, in much the same way, for many of the same reasons. As he put it, "Fear and anxiety were exploited by zealots and fools."

As for our common defense, we reject as false the choice between our safety and our ideals. Our Founding Fathers, faced with perils we can scarcely imagine, drafted a charter to assure the rule of law and the rights of man, a charter expanded by the blood of generations. Those ideals still light the world, and we will not give them up for expedience's sake.

—Barack Obama, Inaugural Address, January 20, 2009

The first edition of *The Dark Side* was shipped off to the printer in the spring of 2008 with a huge unanswered question hanging over the country. Democratic candidate Barack Obama and Republican John McCain were locked in a close fight for the presidency, and it wasn't clear who would win. Uncertain, too, was whether the Bush Administration's approach to fighting terrorism—with its assertions of law-free zones and rights-free suspects, as well as its extraordinary claims of presidential authority to ignore domestic and international laws in the name of national security—would be an aberration, or the start of a whole "new normal."

At a candlelit dinner with friends at a country inn over the summer, the betting was that it might take fifty years for the pendulum to swing back. Or, some suggested, it never would. The memory of a time when America's commitment to the rule of law was not subsumed by the war on terror might grow dim, and then be lost altogether, like Pericles's Greece or the Roman Republic.

In the dwindling weeks of the presidential campaign, though, there was a small, but remarkable harbinger that America's ideals might be renewable after all, and sooner rather than later. Defenders of the Bush record tried but failed to get the usual political traction from the kind of fear-inducing rhetoric about terrorism that had all but silenced opponents in the past. At her debut at the Republican National Convention in St. Paul, Minnesota, Sarah Palin, the governor of Alaska and John McCain's running mate, reprised the tough talk of the Bush Administration. She derisively mocked Obama for ostensibly wanting to coddle terrorists. While Al Qaeda agents were still plotting to "inflict catastrophic harm on America," she said, Obama was "worried that someone won't read them their rights." The familiar trope of worldly Republicans mocking naive Democrats for their belief in taking the high road in fighting evil had the wished-for effect in the convention hall. Palin's performance was praised by most observers as masterful. For a brief period, her popularity soared nationwide. But her words drew an unexpected response from her opponent. Rather than shying away from the fight about due process and the proper balance between liberty and national security, as most Democrats had before, Obama took Palin on.

"My position has always been clear," he replied at a campaign stop in Michigan soon afterward. U.S.-held terror suspects deserved American justice, Obama argued. In particular, he said they had the right to challenge their detention in some form of a habeas corpus hearing. This, he noted, was "the foundation of American law." Sounding like the former constitutional law professor he had once been, he explained the principle simply. "If the government grabs you, then you have the right to at least ask, 'Why was I grabbed?' And say, 'Maybe you've got the wrong person.' We don't always catch the right person," he explained. "We may think it's Mohammed-the-terrorist, but it might be Mohammed-the-cab-driver. You might think it's Barack-the-bomb-thrower, but it might be Barack-the-guy-running-for-president."

In other circumstances Obama's explication of America's most basic legal principles might have seemed pedantic. But after seven years of denial from the most powerful legal officials in the land, it constituted a political breakthrough, pushing the public to reconsider how many core beliefs had been sacrificed during the Bush years. At the time, polls showed that the majority of Americans still favored locking up terror suspects in the military detention camp in Guantánamo Bay, Cuba, indefinitely, regardless of their rights. But Obama had at last joined the debate. "The reason you have this principle is not to be soft on terrorism," he pointed out. "It's because that's who we are.

That's what we're protecting. Don't mock the Constitution!" he implored the crowd. "Don't make fun of it! Don't suggest that it's not American to abide by what the Founding Fathers set up. It's worked pretty well for over two hundred years!"

Obama's ease at defending legal truths that had been deemed too politically costly to acknowledge during most of the previous seven years was noteworthy. But even more so was the reaction of the crowd that day. It rose to its feet and cheered. Emboldened, Obama let down his guard long enough to reveal a glimpse of his contempt for the legal antics of his opponents. The *Washington Post* reported that, shaking his head dismissively, he muttered, "These people!"

In truth, Obama's position had evolved over the course of the campaign. In the beginning, according to an adviser, Obama and his political aides hadn't fully grasped the scope of the Bush Administration's legal breeches or the seriousness with which military officials, among others, viewed the issue. Shortly before the January 3, 2008, Iowa caucus, Obama was confronted by a handful of former high-ranking military officers who opposed the Bush Administration's legalization of abusive interrogations. Sickened by the photographs of Abu Ghraib and other such scandals, and disheartened by what they regarded as the dishonorable, illegal, and dangerous degradation of military standards, the officers had formed an unlikely alliance with human rights advocates and had begun lobbying the candidates of both parties to close the loopholes Bush had opened for torture.

A participant, who declined to be named because the meeting was off the record, later said that Obama seemed "very excited" that day in Iowa, "because he had just gotten polls showing that he was ahead." But at that early stage, Obama didn't seem particularly "comfortable" with the military officers. They lectured him about the importance of being commander in chief. In particular, they warned him that every word he uttered would be taken as an order by everyone from the highest-ranking officers down to the lowliest private. So, they emphasized, any wiggle room he allowed for abusive interrogations would send a green light to every soldier. Obama "asked smart questions, but didn't seem inspired by it. He totally understood the effect that Abu Ghraib had on America's reputation," said the participant. But in general, "he was very businesslike. He didn't flatter the officers," as most of the other candidates had. "But," in retrospect, the participant said, "it started an education process."

Almost a year later, during the transition period after the election but before Obama took office, several retired officers from the same group met again in a closed-door session, this time with his nominee for attorney general, Eric Holder, and Greg Craig, a Washington criminal lawyer with an interest in human rights, who by then was slated to become Obama's White House counsel. Improbably, perhaps, the two top Obama Administration lawyers were particularly taken with former four-star Marine General Charles "Chuck" Krulak, a deeply conservative Republican from a fabled military family. Krulak insisted that ending the Bush Administration's coercive interrogation and detention regime was "right for America and right for the world," a participant recalled, and promised that if the Obama Administration did what he described as "the right thing," which he acknowledged would not be politically easy, he would personally "fly cover" for them.

On January 22, 2009, the second full day of the Obama presidency, sixteen retired generals and flag officers from the same group did just that. Told just days before that they were needed at the White House, most of them dropped what they were doing, and flew to the capital from as far away as California. In one of his first acts in office, Obama had prepared three remarkable executive orders aimed at restoring the rule of law in the fight against terrorism. As he signed these from the large wooden desk that George Bush had turned over to him just days before, a phalanx of square-jawed, impressively titled military men, stood behind him, literally covering his back.

With the stroke of his pen, Obama swept away many of the most egregious excesses that had characterized George Bush's war on terror. He ordered the military prison camp in Guantánamo Bay, Cuba, where the detainees had been denied any recognizable form of justice, to be closed within the year. Meanwhile, he suspended the military commissions and ordered that a cabinet-level task force spend the next few months studying alternatives. He also prohibited the CIA from running any future secret "black site" prisons overseas. And he decreed that, from then on, the International Committee for the Red Cross must have access to all detainees in U.S. custody—ending seven years of stonewalling by the CIA.

In perhaps the most dramatic repudiation of the Bush legal regime, Obama nullified every one of the legal memoranda on interrogation policy that had been issued by the executive branch during the previous seven years. Gone in a matter of minutes were the John Yoo memos, the Jack Goldsmith replacements, the Daniel Levin footnotes, and Steven Bradbury's equivocations. David Addington's dictates were replaced by an unambiguous order that all U.S.-held prisoners abroad would from that moment on be under the protection of the Geneva Conventions, thereby outlawing any cruel, inhuman, or degrading treatment. In addition, both military and CIA interrogations would have to hew to the standards set out in the *Army Field Manual.* "We intend to win this fight," Obama said, but he added, "We are going to win it on our own terms."

These decisions were the result of intense deliberation. During the transition period, Obama's legal, intelligence, and national security advisers had gone to Langley for two long unpublicized sessions with current and former intelligence community members. They debated whether a ban on brutal interrogation practices would hurt America's ability to gather intelligence. In an effort to be abundantly cautious, Obama's advisers asked the bipartisan intelligence veterans to prepare a cost–benefit analysis. After seven years of justifications for harsh interrogation tactics from the most powerful officials in the country, the conclusions of this secret exercise were quite startling: "There was unanimity among Obama's expert advisers," Craig, the White House Counsel said, "that to change the practices would not in any material way affect the collection of intelligence."

The sharp turn in direction was evident in many of the personnel decisions of the new president as well. Nowhere was the contrast more visible than at the Justice Department. Obama's choice to head the small but influential Office of Legal Counsel, whose lawyers had produced the "torture memo" and other notorious opinions, was one of the most outspoken critics of the Bush Administration's legal distortions in the country. Dawn Johnsen, a law professor at Indiana University, had unabashedly described the memos written by her predecessors as an "outrage." Before taking over the office, she wrote that "when the government acts lawlessly and devises bogus constitutional arguments for outlandishly expansive presidential power," it would be a mistake to categorize it as anything less. Before taking office, she called on the country to "condemn our nation's past transgressions and reject Bush's corruption of our American ideals."

Joining Johnsen as her principal deputy, and so literally taking the job that John Yoo held before, was Harvard Law Professor David Barron. There was a certain amount of poetic justice to the choice. Barron had been besting Yoo since college, where they were both in the same class at Harvard and where Barron had beaten Yoo out to become editor of the *Harvard Crimson*. As a professor at Harvard Law School, Barron also had coauthored the definitive rebuttal to Yoo's claims of virtually unlimited executive powers for the commander in chief during war times. The other coauthor of this devastating critique was Georgetown Law Professor Marty Lederman, who joined the Obama Administration's Office of Legal Counsel, too, as another top deputy.

Change was plainly evident at the top of the Justice Department as well. Holder finally gave a straightforward answer when asked point blank during his Senate confirmation hearings, whether waterboarding was torture. After seven years of definitional denial, Holder simply answered yes. Holder paid a price in Republican votes for his candor. Some Republican senators also tried to extract a pledge from him that he would commit in advance never to prosecute anyone in the Bush Administration for abuses committed in the name of fighting terrorism, a deal Holder refused to make.

Obama picked Leon Panetta, a former Democratic congressman from California, and one-time chief of staff to President Clinton, to lead the CIA. Before taking over the spy agency, Panetta had written an impassioned essay for the *Washington Monthly* titled, "No Torture. No Exceptions." His point of view during his confirmation hearing before the Senate Intelligence Committee was equally clear. Where his predecessors in the Bush Administration had insisted they had tortured no one, while also acknowledging that they had waterboarded detainees, Panetta said outright, "I believe that waterboarding is torture and it's wrong." Asked whether the president could authorize the agency to resume using such extralegal methods if he were in the midst of a national crisis, Panetta replied: "Nobody is above the law." Panetta also had a strong retort for former Vice President Cheney, who had criticized Obama's plans to close the prison at Guantánamo Bay and his ban on abusive interrogation methods as foolishly risking the nation's security. "I was disappointed by those comments," Panetta said. "The implication is that somehow this country is more vulnerable to attack because the president of this country wants to abide by the law and the Constitution."

Cheney's comments on Guantánamo were part of an extraordinary set of exit interviews given by departing members of the Bush Administration, in which they essentially laid out the case for the prosecution against themselves. In an astounding admission, Susan Crawford, a lifelong Republican, former U.S. judge on the Court of Appeals for the Armed Forces, and the top Bush Administration official in charge of deciding what criminal charges to bring against the detainees in Guantánamo, publicly and unequivocally declared that the U.S. military had tortured Mohammed al-Qahtani, the suspected twentieth highjacker. "His treatment met the legal definition of torture," Crawford told the *Washington Post*'s Bob Woodward. "And that's why I did not refer the case" for prosecution. "And unfortunately what this has done, I think, has tainted everything going forward."

Just the week before, Cheney had dismissed allegations of torture as the ravings of "left-wing Democrats." But now the charge was being leveled in the most serious way, by one of the highest-ranking political appointees in his administration. Significantly, Qahtani was not among the three CIA detainees who had been waterboarded. The abuses he had been subjected to were no different from those suffered by hundreds of other U.S.-held prisoners. These techniques might not in and of themselves appear to constitute torture, but in combination over a long enough period of time, Crawford said, the impact was indisputably criminal. "You think of torture, you think of some horrendous physical act done to an individual," Crawford said. "This was not any one particular act; this was just a combination of things that had a medical impact on him, that hurt his health. It was abusive and uncalled for. And coercive. Clearly coercive."

Crawford's acknowledgment that torture in Guantánamo had forced her to drop charges against one of the most serious suspects in U.S. custody, laid bare the fallacy of Bush's approach. As the Qahtani case showed, it had produced neither intelligence nor a conviction. Rather, it had created an unsolvable problem, which was what now to do with Qahtani.

Crawford's declaration also had the effect of exposing top U.S. officials to serious criminal charges. Not just any officials. The entire chain of military command, straight up to former Secretary of Defense Donald Rumsfeld, had authorized and followed Qahtani's interrogation closely. The President and Vice President too could be implicated. As Gitanjali Gutierrez, Qahtani's defense lawyer said, "There's a really clear paper trail here. No one disputes what happened. The only dispute has been about the definition." And after years of denial and obfuscation, Crawford had essentially called the President and Vice President's bluff.

Nonetheless, as if inhabiting an alternative legal universe as he exited the White House, Bush provided new details of his hands-on involvement in authorizing the cruel treatment of detainees. He described how he had personally decided in favor of waterboarding Khalid Sheikh Mohammed. His words illustrated exactly how the inner circle of his White House had operated. First they decided on a course of abusive treatment, or, as he put it to Fox News's Brit Hume, "I asked what tools are available for us to find information from him, and they gave me a list." Then underlings were asked to come up with legal justifications, or as Bush told CNN's Larry King, "I got legal opinions that said whatever we're going to do is legal."

As Cheney made the final rounds of Washington media outlets, he too offered fascinating new admissions, bolstering suspicions that he had been the single-minded driving force behind the most aggressive aspects of the Bush Administration's counterterrorism policy. For the first time, Cheney publicly confirmed what unnamed sources had indicated earlier: That he had been cognizant not only of the grim details of the secret interrogation and detention program, he had actively played a major role in putting it in place. "I was aware of the program, certainly," Cheney admitted in an interview with ABC's Charles Gibson, "and involved in helping get the process cleared as the Agency in effect came and wanted to know what they could and couldn't do. They talked to me as well as others, to explain what they wanted to do, and I supported it."

Cheney elaborated further in an interview with the *Washington Times*, explaining that he had himself given the go-ahead for the use of "enhanced interrogations" on dozens of detainees suspected of terrorism and approved the waterboarding of three. "I signed off on it; others did, as well, too," Cheney said. More audaciously, Cheney also told interviewers, "I feel very good about what we did. I think it was the right thing to do." He added that he would "do exactly the same thing again," and claimed, "It would have been unethical or immoral not to." After leaving office, Cheney was no less vocal. In a breach with traditional protocol calling for former officials to refrain from attacking their successors immediately after an election, Cheney virtually accused Obama of putting the country at dire risk. In January 2009, he warned that a catastrophic nuclear or biological terror attack on America would occur unless Obama kept the Bush policies in place. Echoing Palin's words at the Republican Convention, he chided the Obama Administration as "more concerned about reading the rights to an Al Qaeda terrorist then they are with protecting the United States."

Cheney's words practically dared the Obama Administration for response. Officially, Obama professed to have no interest in "witch hunts" or unnecessary, backward-looking attempts to lay blame on the previous administration. But a top adviser acknowledged that, "Dick Cheney is inviting an investigation every time he opens his mouth to say he did this to save lives." He explained, "It's a dangerous assertion to make, if it's not true. The government has to be authoritative on this," he said. "We're almost obliged to settle it." What form that might take, and who might lead the effort, remained in flux.

Meanwhile, much else remained to be done. Obama's executive orders set up two cabinet-level task forces to review interrogation and detention issues further. The possibility for backsliding remained. Obama's aides said he was not necessarily averse to allowing the CIA to use different interrogation techniques from the military. He also wasn't categorically opposed to all renditions, so long as they didn't result in torture. Many of the toughest issues—including what to do with the remaining 240 or so detainees in Guantánamo—were, as one top adviser put it, "kicked down the road." To the distress of defenders of civil liberties and human rights, Obama and his legal team said that among the possibilities they were weighing were new forms of preventive detention for terror suspects, possibly including the creation of a national security court that could hold terror suspects without charges. Craig said that it was "hard to imagine Barack Obama as the first president to introduce a preventive detention law." But he didn't rule it out.

In the early weeks of the administration, there were other causes for concern among the civil libertarians, including a surprise decision by the Obama Justice Department to defend a position taken by the Bush Administration in front of the Ninth Circuit in California. The case involved Jeppesen, the division of Boeing that handled the flight planning for the CIA's renditions. The American Civil Liberties Union had sued the company on behalf of five former detainees who said they had been brutalized during the rendition process, including Binyam Mohammed, a British citizen who said he had been excruciatingly tortured in Morocco by interrogators wielding scalpels and hot, stinging liquid. Mohammed's allegations were well known. Yet first the Bush Administration, and now the Obama Administration, argued that the case could not go forward because it might reveal national security secrets. Human rights lawyer Scott Horton described the Obama Justice Department's position as a betrayal of the "promises of transparency and accountability" made by Obama during the campaign.

Despite such disappointments, it was clear that few political reversals in modern Washington were swifter or more decisive than Obama's repudiation of George Bush's approach to the war on terror. In the course of an election, a peaceful revolt had taken place. It was the culmination of the efforts of many people of both parties who had refused to believe that it was necessary, or even possible, to prevail by sacrificing the country's soul. Shortly before the January 22, 2009 signing ceremony for the executive orders dismantling much of the previous administration's legal framework, Obama took time to talk with the military officers who were gathered in the Roosevelt Room. Two of the officers had sons serving in Iraq and Afghanistan. One of these, Major General Paul Eaton, couldn't have been clearer. "Torture," he said, "is the tool of the lazy, the stupid, and the pseudo-tough. It's also perhaps the greatest recruiting tool that the terrorists have." The feeling in the room that day, according to retired Rear Admiral John Hutson, "was joy, perhaps, that the country was getting back on track."

Jane Mayer
Chevy Chase, Maryland
February 2009

CAST OF KEY CHARACTERS

Bush Administration, White House Officials

President George W. Bush

Vice President Richard Cheney

David Addington Chief of staff and legal counsel to Vice President Cheney.

John Bellinger III Condoleezza Rice's top legal counsel, first at the National Security Council, then at the State Department.

Bradford Berenson Associate White House counsel to President Bush from 2001 to 2003.

Richard Clarke Head of counterterrorism at the National Security Council under President Clinton and President Bush; resigned in March 2003.

Timothy Flanigan Associate White House counsel.

Alberto Gonzales Served as White House Counsel from 2001 until 2005, and as Attorney General from 2005 until 2007.

I. Lewis "Scooter" Libby Vice President Cheney's chief of staff until his indictment on charges of perjury in 2005.

Condoleezza Rice National Security Adviser from 2001 to 2005, then Secretary of State until the end of the Bush Administration.

Karl Rove White House political director and deputy chief of staff to President Bush until August 2007.

State Department Officials

Richard Armitage Deputy Secretary of State under Colin Powell from 2001 to 2005.

Colin Powell Secretary of State from 2001 to 2005.

William Taft IV Chief legal adviser.

Lawrence Wilkerson Retired Air Force colonel and chief of staff to former Secretary of State Colin Powell from 2002 to 2005.

Defense Department and Military Figures

Diane Beaver Top military lawyer in Guantánamo in 2002.

General Michael Dunlavey The top military commander at Guantánamo from its opening until 2002.

Michael Gelles Chief clinical forensic psychologist for the U.S. Navy's Criminal Investigative Service.

William J. "Jim" Haynes III General counsel to the United States Department of Defense.

Steve Kleinman Air Force colonel and an experienced interrogator and SERE expert.

Brittain Mallow Commander of the Criminal Investigative Task Force at Guantánamo Bay from 2002 until 2005.

Major General Geoffrey Miller Commander of Joint Task Force Guantánamo beginning in November 2002 and adviser on interrogations in Iraq in 2003.

Alberto J. Mora Former general counsel of the U.S. Navy.

Donald Rumsfeld Secretary of Defense from 2001 to 2006.

Johnny "Mike" Spann CIA officer who interrogated John Walker Lindh in Afghanistan. Spann died during a subsequent firefight, becoming the first casualty of the war on terror.

Matthew Waxman Lawyer working as assistant to Condoleezza Rice on the National Security Counsel from 2001 until 2004, and Deputy Assistant Secretary of Defense for detainee affairs from 2004 to 2005.

Central Intelligence Agency Figures

J. Cofer Black Served as the head of the CIA's Counterterrorist Center from 1999 to 2002 and the State Department's coordinator for counterterrorism from 2002 to 2004.

John Brennan Served as CIA chief of staff from 1999 until March 2001, then became Deputy Director of the CIA until March 2003 and Director of the National Counterterrorism Center until 2005. Also an adviser on counterterrorism to President Barack Obama.

Tyler Drumheller A twenty-five-year CIA veteran; Chief of European Operations until 2005.

Porter Goss Director of the CIA after George Tenet stepped down from 2004 until 2006.

General Michael Hayden Director of the National Security Agency from 1999 to 2005 and Director of the CIA from 2006 to the end of the Bush Administration. In 2008, acknowledged CIA waterboarded three prisoners.

John Bruce Jessen Military psychologist in the SERE program, who advised the CIA on interrogation protocols. He later became a business partner and CIA contractor with James Mitchell.

John Kiriakou A former CIA officer and the first U.S. official to admit to the use of waterboarding as an interrogation technique. Aided in the capture of Abu Zubayda.

James Mitchell Retired military psychologist, hired as consultant to the CIA on interrogation techniques.

James Pavitt Deputy Director for Operations for the CIA from 1999 until 2004.

Jose Rodriguez Jr. The head of the Counterterrorism Center from 2002 until 2004 and Deputy Director for Operations from 2004 until 2008. Authorized the destruction of CIA interrogation videotapes, including that of Abu Zubayda's waterboarding.

Michael Scheuer Chief of Alec Station, the CIA Bin Laden Unit, from 1996 to 1999 and a CIA adviser from 2001 to 2004.

George Tenet Director of Central Intelligence during the Clinton and Bush administrations, from 1997 until 2004.

Justice Department and FBI Figures

John Ashcroft Attorney General from January 2001 to February 2005.

Steven Bradbury Head of the Office of Legal Counsel from 2005 to 2009.

Jay Bybee Head of the Office of Legal Counsel from 2001 to 2003. Signed the August 1, 2002 "torture memo."

Michael Chertoff Head of the Justice Department's Criminal Division from 2001 until 2003; Secretary of Homeland Security from 2005 until the end of the Bush Administration.

James Clemente Member of the FBI's Behavioral Analysis Unit in Quantico, tried to stop abuse in Guantánamo.

Jack Cloonan Former FBI agent, expert on Islamic terrorism.

Daniel Coleman Former FBI agent, expert on Islamic terrorism.

James Comey Deputy Attorney General from December 2003 through August 2005.

Jack Goldsmith Head of the Office of Legal Counsel from 2003 to 2005.

Martin Lederman Lawyer in the Clinton Administration's Office of Legal Counsel who stayed on under Bush until 2002, before leaving to become a professor at Georgetown Law School.

Dan Levin Acting head of the Office of Legal Counsel, 2004 to 2005

Robert Mueller Director of the FBI since 2001.

Ali Soufan Former FBI agent, expert in Islamic terrorism. At the time of 9/11, Soufan was one of eight Arabic-speaking agents.

John Yoo Lawyer in the Office of Legal Counsel from 2001 to 2003.

Members of Congress and Others

Richard Dearlove Chief of MI6, Britain's Intelligence Agency.

Richard Durbin Democratic senator from Illinois and Democratic Party Whip.

Carl Levin Democratic senator from Michigan, chairman of the Armed Services Committee.

John McCain Republican senator from Arizona.

Philip Zelikow Executive Director of the bipartisan commission on the 9/11 attacks. Later, counselor to Secretary of State Condoleezza Rice.

Outside Lawyers

Joe Margulies Death penalty and human rights lawyer who defended Guantánamo detainees' rights to legal process.

Dick Marty Swiss prosecutor who led the investigation by the Council of Europe that found fourteen European countries colluded with the CIA to create secret prisons for enemy combatants.

Michael Ratner Head of the Center for Constitutional Rights. Early defense lawyer for Guantánamo detainees along with Joe Margulies and Clive Stafford Smith.

Clive Stafford Smith British death penalty and human rights lawyer. Filed lawsuits on behalf of more than one hundred Guantánamo detainees.

Tom Wilner Washington-based corporate law partner, who represents Kuwaiti citizens detained in Guantánamo.

Detainees and Others

Maher Arar Canadian engineer apprehended by the U.S. government at JFK Airport in New York, rendered to Syria for coercive interrogation. Later released without charge.

Mamdouh Habib Egyptian-born citizen of Australia, detained and coercively interrogated in Pakistan, rendered by the United States to Egypt for further coercive interrogation. After six months, flown to Guantánamo via Afghanistan. Released without charges.

Yaser Hamdi A dual U.S.-Saudi citizen captured in Afghanistan in 2001, fighting with the Taliban. Detained for three years without charge in U.S. consolidated naval brigs in Norfolk, Virginia and Charleston, South Carolina. Released without charge to Saudi Arabia after the Supreme Court declared his right to legal process in June 2004, in exchange for relinquishing U.S. citizenship.

Nawaf al-Hazmi Hijacker on American Airlines Flight 77, which crashed into the Pentagon. The CIA learned in early 2000 that Hazmi, who they suspected of being an Al Qaeda terrorist, had entered the United States, along with his associate Khalid al-Mihdhar, but the CIA lost track of them and failed to notify the FBI of his presence.

David Hicks Australian who trained in Al Qaeda–linked camps and served with the Taliban in Afghanistan, where he was turned over to the United States in December 2001. Detained in Guantánamo. The first to be tried by military commission, he pleaded guilty to a single count of "material support for terrorism" in 2006. Transferred to Australian custody where he served a nine-month sentence and was released in December 2007.

Manadel al-Jamadi Former Iraqi military officer captured and interrogated to death by Navy SEALs and the CIA in November 2003.

Ibn al-Shaykh al-Libi Chief of Al Qaeda's Khalden training camp. He was captured in December 2001 by the Pakistanis, turned over to the FBI who interrogated him at Bagram Air Base, but seized and rendered to Egypt by the CIA. Under coercive interrogation in Egypt, he fabricated details linking Saddam Hussein to Al Qaeda. Colin Powell cited this intelligence in his February 2003 speech justifying going to war in Iraq. A year later, al-Libi recanted, admitting he had made false statements.

John Walker Lindh Californian captured in Afghanistan in late 2001, fighting alongside the Taliban. After entering a guilty plea, sentenced by a U.S. court to twenty years in prison.

Khaled el-Masri German car salesman mistakenly identified as an Al Qaeda operative, detained by Macedonian authorities at the request of the CIA. Rendered to Afghanistan and brutally interrogated. Released after 149 days without charge.

Khalid al-Mihdhar Saudi national, assisted in the hijacking of American Airlines Flight 77, with Hazmi, with whom he slipped into the United States in early 2000.

Khalid Sheikh Mohammed According to the 9/11 Commission report, the "principal architect" of the attacks. Captured in Pakistan in March 2003 and taken into CIA custody and subjected to waterboarding at a black site prison, before transfer in 2006 to Guantánamo.

Zacarias Moussaoui French citizen and Al Qaeda co-conspirator arrested in August 2001 in Minnesota. After pleading guilty in a U.S. court, sentenced to life in prison.

Jose Padilla United States citizen originally accused of planning a "dirty bomb" attack, and detained in the U.S. consolidated naval brig in Charleston as an "enemy combatant." Later transferred to the criminal court system without "dirty bomb" charges. He was convicted of criminal conspiracy. Sentenced to seventeen years in prison.

Mohammed al-Qahtani, "Detainee 063" Saudi national captured near Tora Bora in December 2001. Attempted to enter the United States before 9/11 allegedly to be the twentieth hijacker. Held in Guantánamo. Convening authority Susan Crawford declined to prosecute him in May 2008 because she acknowledged he had been tortured.

Abd al-Rahim al-Nashiri Al Qaeda leader in the Gulf region, suspected of planning the USS *Cole* bombing, captured and waterboarded by the CIA.

Ramzi bin al-Shibh Yemeni Al Qaeda leader who helped plan 9/11 attacks, captured on September 11, 2002; interrogated and detained by CIA, later transferred to Guantánamo.

Abu Zubayda The CIA's first "high value" detainee, captured in Pakistan in March 2002. CIA operatives waterboarded him and destroyed the videotapes of his interrogation. Eventually transferred to Guantánamo.

ACKNOWLEDGMENTS

This book could not have been written without the encouragement and thoughtful contributions of many more people than I could possibly name. Some need to remain anonymous, but you know who you are, and I thank you. Others, undoubtedly, I have forgotten to add, and to you, I apologize. Much of the work for this book was done at *The New Yorker* magazine, where I am privileged to have the brilliant editorial guidance of David Remnick, Daniel Zalewski, and Dorothy Wickenden. They are cherished colleagues and friends. I also owe a debt of gratitude to Ed Hirsch and the John Simon Guggenheim Memorial Foundation, which has generously funded much of the research for this book.

It was Bill Thomas, the editor-in-chief at Doubleday who had the imagination and dexterity to turn a sheaf of *New Yorker* stories into a book, and it was my endlessly supportive agent, Sloan Harris, co-director of the Literary Department at ICM who made it happen. Thanks also go to Melissa Danaczko and Kathy Trager at Doubleday, for their generous editorial and legal assistance.

This book was written quickly, and inevitably there will be errors, but there would have been many more without the tireless work and dedication of three wonderful research assistants. Julie Tate has redefined what it means to do editorial research—her expertise in this subject, and resourcefulness in digging to the bottom of the darkest secrets—is unparalleled. Her professionalism is awe-inspiring. I am also deeply indebted to Katherine Hawkins, a meticulous lawyer and scholar, whose sharp eye and encyclopedic knowledge of the legal practices of the Bush Administration's war on terror improved the manuscript immeasurably. I also want to thank *The New Yorker*'s overqualified news aide, Annie Lowrey, whose unflappable cheer and uncomplaining hard work held everyone together.

There are long-suffering victims of every obsession, and in this case, no one had to sacrifice more than my husband and daughter, Bill and Kate Hamilton. They selflessly encouraged me to take on this book, even though it meant they had to carry on without my help for much of a year, while enduring more talk of torture than most families could stand. Their humor, love, and irreverence have sustained me. Marrying Bill and having Kate have been the happiest achievements of my life.

The list of others I would like to thank is long, reflecting an amazing community of bright and generous friends and colleagues, among them: Jill Abramson, David Barron, Peter Baker, Robert Baer, Rand Beers, Mark Benjamin, Bradford Berenson, Peter Bergen, Sidney Blumenthal, David Bowker, Phillip Carter, Steve Clemmons, Jack Cloonan, Andrew Cockburn, David Cole, Dan Coleman, Steve Coll, David Danzig, Amy Davidson, Walter Dellinger, Sen. Richard Durbin, Alexander Dryer, Robert Fein, Yosri Fouda, Glenn Frankel, Jeff Gerth, Alex Gibney, Jeffrey Goldberg, Jamie Gorelick, Karen Greenberg, Stephen Grey, Sue Halpern, Hossam el-Hamalawy, Margaret Hamburg, Laura Handman, Seymour Hersh, Stephen Holmes, Beth Horowitz, Sari Horwitz, Scott Horton, David Ignatius, Michael Isikoff, Mark Jacobson, Michiko Kakutani, Michael Kazin, Charles Kaiser, Colonel Steve Kleinman, Sanford Levinson, Marty Lederman, Joe Lelyveld, Senator Carl Levin, Anthony Lewis, Tom Malinowski, Jim Margolin, Elissa Massimino, Joe Margulies, Joanne Mariner, Georg Mascolo, Mary McCarthy, Alfred McCoy, Tara McKelvey, Brent Mickum, Steven Miles, Alberto Mora, Steve Mufson, Deborah Pearlstein, Dana Priest, Todd Purdum, John Radsan, Darius Rejali, Michael Ratner, David Remes, Philippe Sands, Jill Savitt, Bill Schultz, Amrit Singh, John Sifton, Clive Stafford Smith, Ron Suskind, Will Taft IV, Eric Umanksy, Don Van Natta Jr., Steven Watt, Colonel Lawrence Wilkerson, Tom Wilner, Senator Ron Wyden, Bob Woodward, Lawrence Wright, Daniel Zalewski, Joe Zogby.

ENDNOTES

1 *practicing for doomsday*: James Mann, "The Armageddon Plan," *The Atlantic Monthly*, March, 2004, pp. 71–74.
3 *America's best-informed national security leaders*: Bob Woodward, *Bush at War* (New York: Simon & Schuster, 2002), p. 248.
3 *the CIA had compiled a list of likely targets*: George Tenet, *At the Center of the Storm* (New York: HarperCollins, 2007), p. 188. *Topping the list was the White House*: Woodward, *Bush at War*, p. 270.
4 *additional anthrax traces* and *every citizen . . . should be vaccinated against smallpox*: Jacob Weisberg, *The Bush Tragedy* (New York: Random House, 2008), pp. 190–94; Weisberg, "Fishing For a Way to Change the World," *Newsweek*, January 28, 2008, p. 31.
4 *subterranean bunker*: Barton Gellman, "In U.S., Terrorism's Peril Undiminished," *Washington Post*, December 24, 2002.
5 *"Led Zeppelin music"*: James Baker quoted in Jack L. Goldsmith, *The Terror Presidency* (New York: Norton, 2007), p. 72.
5 *"an obsession"*: James Comey quoted in Goldsmith, *The Terror Presidency*, p. 72.
5 *biochemical survival suit*: Todd Purdum, "A Face Only a President Could Love," *Vanity Fair*, June 2006, p. 129.
6 *"Cheney was traumatized"*: Lawrence Wilkerson interview with the author.
7 *"materialistic, hedonistic"* and *"didn't feel threatened"*: Woodward, *Bush at War*, p. 39.
11 *"We're fucked!"*: Former CIA officer interview with the author.
12 *"Without any coercion at all"*: Former FBI agent interview with the author. *The number . . . in Yemen*: Lawrence Wright, *The Looming Tower* (New York: Knopf, 2006), p. 277.
13 *"We have a plan to attack the U.S."*: Saudi detainee quoted in Wright, *The Looming Tower*, p. 279.
13 *one of the future 9/11 hijackers*: Wright, *The Looming Tower*, p. 343.
13 *"something more nefarious was at foot"*: The National Commission on Terrorist Attacks Upon the United States, *The 9/11 Commission Report* (New York: Norton, 2004), p. 181.
15 *"nothing more was done"*: The National Commission on Terrorist Attacks, *The 9/11 Commission Report*, p. 182.
15 *"action" requiring immediate follow-up*: Tenet, *At the Center of the Storm*, p. 197.

16 *two Al Qaeda suspects had come to America*: Lawrence Wright, "The Spymaster," *The New Yorker*, January 21, 2008, p. 45.

16 *"prescribed channels"* and *"intended or actual travel"*: The Office of the Inspector General, *The OIG Report on CIA Accountability*, June, 2005, p. 14. Available at http://www.mideastweb.org/cia_911_oig.htm.

16 *"It just didn't get done"*: Former CIA official interview with the author.

19 *Clinton reportedly authorized the Agency . . . to kill Bin Laden*: In *The Commission*, Philip Shenon describes contradictory testimony from George Tenet and Sandy Berger, complicating the picture of Clinton's willingness to assassinate Bin Laden. See Shenon, *The Commission* (New York: Twelve, 2008), pp. 357–58.

20 *"rid-me-of-this . . ."*: J. Cofer Black quoted in Steve Coll, *Ghost Wars* (New York: Penguin, 2004), p. 466.

20 *Tenet himself never advised . . . the use of lethal force*: Woodward, *Bush at War*, p. 318.

20 *"How would the U.S. government explain it"*: Tenet, *At the Center of the Storm*, p. 143.

20 *Clarke argued that the administration "urgently need{ed}" to "roll back" Al Qaeda*: Richard A. Clarke, "Presidential Policy Initiative/Review—the *Al-Qida* Network," memorandum to Condoleezza Rice, January 25, 2001, reproduced by the National Security Archive of the George Washington University. Available at www.gwu.edu/~nsarchiv/NSAEBB/NSAEBB147/index.htm. See also Tenet, *At the Center of the Storm*, p. 143, and Coll, *Ghost Wars*, p. 543.

21 *Rice scheduled no cabinet meeting*: Coll, *Ghost Wars*, p. 543.

21 *"He had a reputation for coloring outside the lines"*: Former administration official interview with the author.

21 *"the most immediate and serious threat"*: Tenet, *At the Center of the Storm,* p. 144.

22 *the Blue Sky Memo was sent back to the CIA*: Tenet, *At the Center of the Storm,* p. 144.

22 *"bi-polar mood swings"* and *"masterful passive-aggressive behavior"*: The National Commission on Terrorist Attacks, *The 9/11 Commission Report*, pp. 212–13.

22 *"This country needs to go on a war footing"*: Black quoted in Tenet, *At the Center of the Storm*, p. 153.

22 *"attack within the United States itself"*: Black quoted in Woodward, *State of Denial* (New York: Simon & Schuster, 2006), p. 51.

22 *"the brush off"* and *"they were not getting through to her"*: Woodward, *State of Denial*, p. 51.

23 *"we did not have . . . information about any specific ongoing plot"*: Tenet, *At the Center of the Storm*, p. 159.

23 *"You've covered your ass now"*: George W. Bush quoted in Ron Suskind, *The One Percent Doctrine* (New York: Simon & Schuster, 2006), p. 2.

23 *"I don't want to hear about that anymore!"*: John Ashcroft quoted in Shenon, *The Commission*, p. 247.

24 *"a terrorist wants to learn to fly. They chuckle about it"*: Official of 9/11 Commission interview with the author.

24 *"Are we serious about dealing with the al Qida [sic] threat"*: The National Commission on Terrorist Attacks, *The 9/11 Commission Report*, note 247, p. 212.

24 *"Tenet said he opposed using the Predator"*: Richard Clarke interview with the author. *"It sounds terrible"*: Roger Cressey interview with the author.

25 *"People are working their butts off"*: Tenet quoted in Woodward, *Bush at War*, p. 90.

25 *"We cannot be second-guessing our team"*: Bush quoted in Suskind, *The One Percent Doctrine*, p. 16.

25 *"He was like a puppy-dog, wagging his tail"*: Former CIA officer interview with the author.

25 *"His greatest wish was to hold onto his job"*: Former CIA officer interview with the author.

26 *"There's no need to punish people for legitimate differences"*: Foreign Ambassador interview with the author.

26 *"The new Pakistani general, he's just been elected"*: Bush quoted in Glen Johnson, "Bush Fails Quiz on Foreign Affairs," Associated Press, November 4, 1999.

27 *"Oh! I thought you said some band"*: Bush quoted in Coll, *Ghost Wars*, p. 538.

27 *he received more than forty Presidential Daily Briefings*: Shenon, *The Commission*, p. 151.

27 *"Cheney was the detail guy"*: Former CIA officer interview with the author.

29 *"an affirmation of the special relationship"*: Tenet, *At the Center of the Storm*, p. 174.

29 *a catered dinner in a private dining room*: Dinner participant interview with the author.

29 *then they were directed to send a few choice body parts back to Langley*: Black discounts this anecdote, saying he does not remember this.

30 *barbaric language*: Black said he had no recollection of this.

31 *"Whatever it takes"*: Woodward, *Bush at War*, p. 4.

31 *Bush seemed eager to kill:* Woodward, *Bush at War*, p. 53.

32 *U.S. officials viewing the videotapes . . . could make out a lone child's swing*: Coll, *Ghost Wars*, pp. 528–29.

32 *"I was not on point"*: Bush quoted in Woodward, *Bush at War*, p. 39.

33 *the U.S. could vanquish Al Qaeda and the Taliban in just a matter of weeks*: Woodward, *Bush at War*, p. 53.

33 *"going to have to cut their heads off"*: Former administration official interview with the author.

33 For background on Robert Mueller, see Shenon, *The Commission*, p. 47.

34 *"rule-of-law be damned"*: Michael Rollince interview with the author.

35 Scheuer went on to write a tirade about the CIA's failure to stop Bin Laden, *Through Our Enemies' Eyes*, by Anonymous.

35 *Pavitt kept Scheuer's farewell*: A spokesman for Jim Pavitt denied that he displayed Scheuer's letter.

36 The CTC knew KSM through his nephew, Ramzi Yusef, the convicted plotter behind the first World Trade Center attack, in 1993.

36 *"Don't drive drunk! Life is hard!"*: Cofer Black, "Address to the Association of Foreign Intelligence Officers," Association of Foreign Intelligence Officers Meeting (keynote address, Tysons Corner, Virginia, September 8, 2006).

36 *"They said it was our highest priority"*: Former CIA officer interview with the author.

37 *"These people wish to kill us!"*: Cofer Black, "Address to the Association of Foreign Intelligence Officers."

37 *talk of the urgent need to go on a war footing*: Former administration official interview with the author.

37 *the CIA had no spies inside Al Qaeda*: Wright, *The Looming Tower*, p. 265.

37 *the record of Alec Station was an embarrassment:* For more details about the
    December 3, 2001, briefing when Black discussed this, see Bamford, *A Pretext
    for War*, p. 221.

38 *the CIA hoped to transport Bin Laden from the Afghan cave to Egypt:* Wright,
    The Looming Tower, p. 266.

38 According to James Risen, the MON was silent on the question of interroga-
    tion techniques—deliberately—to create deniability for the President. Cheney
    knew the details of the interrogation techniques, Risen says. But it's unclear if
    Bush did. Either way, it was not spelled out. Interrogations were categorized as
    "intelligence gathering" rather than "covert actions," so technically, according
    to the law, there was no need for specific presidential approval. See Risen, *State
    of War* (New York: Simon & Schuster, 2006), pp. 24–26.

38 *Black emerged . . . to show the project:* Intelligence official present at the meeting
    interview with author.

40 *"Cofer Black and Dick Clarke found themselves suddenly fantastically in power":*
    Former administration official interview with the author.

40 *"wreaking havoc upon and eliminating the sponsors and supporters":* Woodward, *Bush
    at War*, p. 50.

41 *"once you've hit the mercury with the hammer in Afghanistan . . . potential
    destabilizing effect on Middle Eastern countries":* Black did not recall the British
    giving any such warning.

41 *"No . . . Our only concern is killing the terrorists":* For further description of the
    meeting with Black and the British intelligence officials, see also Drumheller,
    On the Brink (New York: Carroll & Graf, 2006).

41 There has been some dispute about whether Black said he expected to be
    prosecuted, or called in front of a congressional hearing. See also Michael
    Isikoff and David Corn, *Hubris* (New York: Crown, 2006), p. 9.

41 *"He was giving his Jack Nicholson,* A Few Good Men *speech":* Black said
    Drumheller was joking.

41 *"Great job!":* Bush quoted in Woodward, *Bush at War*, p. 79.

41 *Gary Schroen . . . was among the earliest to sense the change in America's posture:*
    Gary Schroen, *First In*, paperback ed. (New York: Presidio, 2005), p. 40.

42 *"You'd need some DNA":* Black quoted in Jane Mayer, "The Search for Osama,"
    The New Yorker, August 4, 2003, p. 27.

43 *"After 9/11, the gloves come off.":* Black said these comments have been
    misconstrued and that he was not referring to harsh treatment of detainees.
    He was describing the move to a war footing.

46 *"the legality of the use of military force":* Justice Department memorandum
    quoted in Tim Golden, "After Terror, a Secret Rewriting of Military Law,"
    New York Times, October 24, 2004.

46 *"The Fourth Amendment applies across the board":* Michael Mukasey quoted by
    Carrie Johnson, "Constitutional Exception Not Valid, Mukasey Says,"
    Washington Post, April 11, 2008.

47 *"No penance would ever expiate the sin against free government":* Robert Jackson
    quoted in Charlie Savage, *Takeover* (New York: Little, Brown, 2007), p. 123.

48 *"Our war on terror begins with Al Qaeda":* George W. Bush address to a Joint Ses-
    sion of the United States Congress and the American People, The Capitol,
    Washington, D.C., September 20, 2001.

48 *"never felt more comfortable in my life"*: Bush quoted in Woodward, *Bush at War*, p. 109.

48 *"One of the keys to being seen as a great leader"*: Bush quoted by Mickey Herskowitz in Russ Baker, "Why George Went to War," TomPaine.com, June 20, 2005, tompaine.com/articles/2005/06/20/why_george_went_to-war.php.

48 *"the Commander in Chief"*: Bush quoted in Woodward, *Bush at War*, p. 80.

51 *"fictionalizing the founding"*: Steven Holmes, *The Matador's Cape* (Cambridge, UK: Cambridge University Press, 2007), p. 292.

51 *"When a foreign entity for political purposes can kill 3,000"*: John Yoo interview in *Taxi to the Dark Side*, DVD, directed by Alex Gibney (New York: Jigsaw Productions, 2007).

53 *"We have to!"*: White House staff member interview with the author. David Addington declined to be interviewed.

53 *"Cheney's Cheney"*: David Ignatius, "Cheney's Cheney," *Washington Post,* January 6, 2006.

54 *Bill Clinton liked to remind other lawyers in the administration that he had taught constitutional law*: Abner J. Mikva, " 'Present' Perfect," editorial, *New York Times,* February 16, 2008.

58 *"go-go guys"*: Addington quoted in Ignatius, "Cheney's Cheney."

58 *"the nadir of the modern presidency in terms of authority and legitimacy"*: Cheney quoted in Kenneth T. Walsh, "The Cheney Factor," *U.S. News & World Report,* January 23, 2006, p. 43.

59 Casey's sentiment about congressional overseers was best captured during a hearing about covert actions in Central America, when he responded to his questioners by muttering the word "assholes." After Reagan's election in 1980, the executive branch was dominated by conservative Republicans, while the House was governed by liberal Democrats. The two parties fought intensely over Central America; the Reagan Administration was determined to overthrow the leftist Sandinista government in Nicaragua.

61 *"you naturally express your wishes in law"*: *Olmstead v. U.S.*, 277 S. Ct. 438 (1928).

61 *"the executive power—the whole thing"*: Samuel Alito quoted in Jess Bravin, "Rule of Law, Judge Alito's View of the Presidency: Expansive Powers," *Wall Street Journal,* January 5, 2006.

61 *"If I were a judge"*: Steven Calabresi quoted in Bravin, "Rule of Law."

62 *He earned $4.4 million*: Purdum, "A Face Only a President Could Love," p. 177; Jane Mayer, "Contract Sport," *The New Yorker,* February 16, 2004, p. 80.

62 *Cheney had studied the vice presidency closely*: Barton Gellman and Jo Becker, "A Strong Push from Backstage," from the "Angler: The Cheney Vice Presidency" series, *Washington Post,* June 26, 2007.

63 *"dive into a 200-page bill like it was a four-course meal"*: Bradford Berenson quoted in Savage, *Takeover*, p. 236.

63 *Addington noted that if anyone got in his way*: Former White House official interview with the author.

65 *Yoo reflected on occasion, he would not have attended Harvard*: Savage, *Takeover,* p. 80.

65 *"golden shields"* and *"get-out-of-jail-free cards"*: Goldsmith, *The Terror Presidency,* p. 97.

66 *"The War Council"*: For a full description, see Goldsmith, *The Terror Presidency*, p. 22.

66 *they were led instead to the Vice President's office*: Barton Gellman and Jo Becker,

"A Different Understanding with the President," from the "Angler: The Cheney Vice Presidency" series, *Washington Post*, June 24, 2007.

67 *"They wanted to go on fishing expeditions"*: Former federal prosecutor interview with the author.

69 *"No one at the NSA period had access to the legal opinions"*: Former administration official interview with the author.

69 *"powerful, permanent presence" on the commercial communications networks:* The NSA transition report quoted in Eric Lichtblau, James Risen, and Scott Shane, "Wider Spying Fuels Aid Plan for Telecom Industry," *New York Times*, December 16, 2007.

69 *"After 9/11 the White House asked Hayden what he wanted"*: Former Bush administration interview with the author.

69 *"My spikes will have chalk on them"*: Michael Hayden quoted in Dana Priest, "Covert CIA Program Withstands New Furor," *Washington Post*, December 30, 2005.

70 *{Thompson} reportedly refused to sign the wiretap permission forms*: Eric Lichtblau, *Bush's Law*.

70 *"they blew through them in secret based on flimsy legal opinions"*: Jack Goldsmith, *The Terror Presidency*, p. 181.

70 *"It was the biggest legal mess I had ever seen in my life"*: Jack Goldsmith interview with the author.

70 *"Addington never said"*: Bush administration lawyer interview with the author.

73 *"To tell you the truth, he was really boring"*: John Walker Lindh statement to Tamara Sonn, an expert on Islam and professor at the College of William and Mary. Sonn examined Lindh for his defense team. Sonn interview with the author.

73 *"I came to fight the Northern Alliance, not other countries"*: Lindh to Rohan Gunaratna, a terrorism expert advising Lindh's defense team. Gunaratna interview with the author.

74 *News . . . took a while to reach Lindh*: Lindh defense lawyers interview with the author.

74 *"He's just despicable"*: George H. W. Bush interview with Diane Sawyer on *Good Morning America*, television program (New York: ABC, December 19, 2001).

75 *"When Lindh went there, we were buddies with the Taliban"*: Scott Carrier interview with the author.

75 *three cardboard boxes . . . containing $3 million in hundred-dollar bills*: In *Bush at War*, Bob Woodward says the cash was in a metal suitcase, but in his book *First In,* Gary Schroen says it was packed in three cardboard boxes. See Woodward, *Bush at War*, p. 139, and Schroen, *First In*, p. 38.

76 *"pikes" were requested as well*: Woodward, *Bush at War*, p. 143.

76 *"a big chunk of money"*: Woodward, *Bush at War*, p. 248.

77 *Dave Tyson, sometimes referred to as "Dawson"*: Gary Berntsen, *Jawbreaker,* paperback ed. (New York: Crown, 2005).

78 Johnny Spann, father of Johnny Micheal "Mike" Spann, interview with the author.

78 *spitting blood and dust*: Gary Berntsen, *Jawbreaker,* p. 25.

79 *terrorists do not "deserve to be treated as prisoners of war"*: Gellman and Becker, "A Different Understanding."

79 *adequate security couldn't be maintained in makeshift battlefield prisons*: Goldsmith, *The Terror Presidency*, p. 108.

79 *"When you capture a suspected Al Qaeda terrorist, what do you do with him?"*: Bradford Berenson inverview in "The Torture Question," *Frontline*, television program (Boston: WGBH and PBS, October, 2005). The full interview is available at www.pbs.org/wgbh/pages/frontline/torture/interviews/berenson.html.

81 *"thought it was a great idea"*: Timothy Flanigan quoted in Tim Golden, "After Terror, a Secret Rewriting of Military Law," *New York Times*, October 24, 2004.

81 *a windowless conference room*: Savage, *Takeover*, p. 135.

82 *"Are we going to go with a system that is really guaranteed"*: Flanigan quoted in Golden, "After Terror."

82 *"What the hell just happened?"*: Powell quoted in Gellman and Becker, "A Different Understanding."

82 In their groundbreaking and exhaustive reporting for the *Washington Post*, Gellman and Becker crafted the best account of this phenomenon.

83 *Ashcroft had been "rude" to the Vice President*: Gellman and Becker, "A Different Understanding."

83 *they still could not be subjected to "physical or moral coercion"*: Joseph Margulies, *Guantánamo and the Abuse of Presidential Power* (New York: Simon & Schuster, 2006), p. 55.

85 *"Any dilution of the Geneva Convention"*: Niall Ferguson, "Don't flout Geneva— or the tables could easily be turned," *Daily Telegraph* (London), October 1, 2006.

86 *in the span of little more than a luncheon, Addington's text became U.S. law*: Gellman and Becker, "A Different Understanding."

86 *"you pass a magnet under the table and you see the iron filings on the top of the table move"*: David Frum quoted in Gellman and Becker, "A Strong Push from Backstage."

88 *"perceived as unfair, because it was unnecessarily archaic"*: Tom Romig quoted in Savage, *Takeover*, p. 138.

88 *"Don't bring the TJAGs into the process"*: David Addington and Romig quoted in Philippe Sands, *The Torture Team* (working manuscript, 2007), p. 43.

89 *"No, you don't"*: Haynes quoted in Golden, "After Terror, a Secret Rewriting of Military Law."

91 *"a gross abuse of power"*: Joseph Margulies interview with the author.

93 *3,000 other U.S. prisoners . . . were in Afghan jails*: Margulies, *Guantánamo*, p. 45.

94 *government document obtained by Lindh's lawyers . . . "take the gloves off"*: Richard A. Serrano, "Prison Interrogators' Gloves Came Off Before Abu Ghraib," *Los Angeles Times*, June 9, 2004.

95 *"I have passed you {sic} assessment along"*: De Pue quoted in Michael Isikoff, "The Lindh Case E-Mails," *Newsweek,* June 24, 2002, p. 8. The e-mails are available at www.msnbc.com/id/3067190.

95 *"After 9/11 . . . in the name of terrorism"*: Jesselyn Radack interview with the author.

102 *"'Why the hell would they fly in the middle of the night?'"*: Rajiv Chandrasekaran quoted in Eric Umansky, "Failures of Imagination," *Columbia Journalism Review,* September–October 2006, p. 29; Chandrasekaran interview with the author.

103 *"a little extraordinary"*: Border police quoted in Stephen Grey, *Ghost Plane* (New York: St. Martin's Press, 2006), p. 26.

105 *What followed were joint prayer sessions, and rambling discussions about Mohammed, Jesus, and God:* For a description of the religious conversation between Fincher and al-Libi, see Isikoff and Corn, *Hubris,* p. 120.

105 *"he found out that we were really there to listen":* Law-enforcement source interview with the author.

105 *the Al Qaeda commander told the investigators he knew of none:* Isikoff and Corn, *Hubris,* p. 120.

106 *"They literally came into the room, strapped him to a stretcher":* FBI official quoted in Isikoff and Corn, *Hubris,* p. 121.

106 *"He was transferred":* Source with knowledge of the interrogation of al-Libi interview with the author.

107 *"no one will have to seek revenge for what I did":* Jack Cloonan interview with the author.

107 *Bush preferred the CIA's tough-guy approach:* Woodward, *Bush at War,* p. 147.

107 *"It was the Camelot of counterterrorism":* Former counterterrorism officer quoted in Dana Priest, "Senate Urged to Probe CIA Practices; Intelligence Panel Should Examine the Use of Rendition, Rockefeller Says," *Washington Post,* April 22, 2005.

108 *117 rendition cases after September 11:* Peter Bergen and Katherine Teidemann, "The Body Snatchers," *Mother Jones,* March–April 2008, pp. 58–61.

113 *Walker Jr., the U.S. Ambassador to Egypt, learned about the plan from the CIA:* The meeting between Scheuer and Walker is described in Grey, *Ghost Plane,* p. 139.

113 *"worth a bucket of warm spit":* Michael Scheuer to the International Organizations, Human Rights, and Oversight Subcommittee and the Europe Subcommittee of the House Foreign Affairs Committee, *Extraordinary Rendition in U.S. Counterterrorism Policy: The Impact on Transatlantic Relations,* 110th Congress, 1st Session, April 17, 2007.

113 *"the negative things that the Egyptians engaged in, of torture and so on":* Edward Walker quoted in Grey, *Ghost Plane,* p. 141.

114 *Egypt also sentenced both of the Zawahiri brothers to death in absentia:* For a description of the trials, see Grey, *Ghost Plane,* p. 144. Grey writes that the trials became "a cause celebre."

114 *"the response, which we hope they will read carefully, is being prepared":* Zawahiri quoted in Wright, *The Looming Tower,* p. 269.

114 *President Clinton signed a still-classified directive:* For more details, see Grey, *Ghost Plane,* p. 143.

118 *an FBI agent told him that if he didn't confess . . . {his family} would be tortured:* Stephen Bergstein, "A tale of two decisions (or, how the FBI gets you to confess," Pet Rock: Camera Obscura blog, October 21, 2007); www.psychsound.com/2007/10/a_tale_of_two_decisions_or_how.html.

119 *Al-Libi and . . . the Scorpion maximum security prison in Cairo:* Grey, *Ghost Plane,* p. 31.

119 *"we transferred him to a third country for further debriefing":* Tenet, *At the Center of the Storm,* p. 353. Tenet maintains that contrary to allegations that the CIA knew that al-Libi would be tortured, the Agency was assured that the foreign intelligence service in question, which he identifies elsewhere in his book as Egypt, planned to only hold al-Libi for a limited period of time, before returning him to the United States, where he would be registered with the Red Cross.

120 *"'real difficulties getting actionable intelligence from detainees'"*: Yoo quoted in Gellman and Becker, "Pushing the Envelope on Presidential Power."

120 *only seven copies were kept*: Sands, *The Torture Team*, p. 69.

120 *"the only person in the White House who really knew the rules"*: Former White House lawyer interview with the author.

122 *"unfashionable"*: Douglas Feith quoted in Jeffrey Goldberg, "A Little Learning," *The New Yorker*, May 9, 2005, p. 36.

122 *Feith's argument left captives in the war on terror in legal limbo*: Sands, *The Torture Team*, p. 40.

122 *it would defile the Geneva Conventions to extend their rights*: Sands, *The Torture Team*, p. 45.

123 *"Lawyers have to be the voice of reason and sometimes have to put the brakes on"*: David Bowker interview with the author.

124 Gellman and Becker in the "Angler" series were the first to state definitively that Addington was the author, sourcing it to an unnamed White House insider.

124 *"the United States Armed Forces shall continue to treat detainees humanely"*: George W. Bush "Humane Treatment of Taliban and al Qaeda," memorandum to the Vice President, Secretary of State, Secretary of Defense, Attorney General, et. al., February 7, 2002.

125 *"He has these cowboy characteristics . . . you can really get him to do some dumb things"*: Confidant of Colin Powell interview with the author. Powell declined to comment.

125 *"You can slip a lot of crap over on someone"*: Wilkerson interview with the author.

126 *"Habib was of no intelligence value"*: Australian official interview with the author.

126 They *"wanted him for their own investigations"*: Makhdoom Hayat quoted in Margulies, *Guantánamo*, p. 185.

128 *"they had injected him with drugs, and hung him from the ceiling, and beaten him"*: Jamal al-Harith interview with the author.

128 Habib *"used to bleed from his nose, mouth and ears"*: Margulies, *Guantánamo*, p. 187.

129 *"It certainly pays well"*: Sean Belcher, Jeppesen employee, interview with the author.

131 *an official investigation by the Canadian government found Arar and other prisoners' descriptions credible:* Stephen J. Toope—Arar Commission of the Government of Canada, "Commission of Inquiry into the Actions of Canadian Officials in Relation to Maher Arar: Final Report," October 14, 2005.

132 *"We need to get Al Qaeda before they get us"*: Woodward, *Bush at War*, p. 129.

132 *a closed-door meeting of top intelligence officials*: Suskind, *The One Percent Doctrine*, p. 83.

132 *Other top American officials in attendance* and *Pavitt evidently amplified the tough talk*: Suskind, *The One Percent Doctrine*, p. 83. Another person in attendance at the meeting confirmed this in an interview with the author.

132 *The most upsetting screams . . . were from women, evidently locked up and being beaten while their infants wailed*: Toope, "Commission of Inquiry: Final Report."

132 *The treatment of Arar grew less severe . . . psychologically, the torment only grew:* Maher Arar interview with the author.

133 *After Arar's release . . . made accusations against Arar to the FBI*: CTV.Ca News Staff, "Arar accuser has spotty background: report." CTV (Oct. 20, 2007).

133 *"Judge Trager . . . argues, amazingly, that even invoking the state secret doctrine might prove embarrassing"*: David Luban, "An Asymmetrical Assault on Reality," Balkanization blog, June 12, 2006, balkin.blogspot.com/2006/06/ asymmetrical-assault-on-reality.html.

133 *"They are outsourcing torture because they know it is illegal"*: Arar interview with the author.

134 *"It works—we know it does. The CIA says it does"*: John Yoo discussion with the author.

135 *"He could not come up with a story"*: The Senate Select Committee on Intelligence, "Postwar Findings About Iraq's WMD Programs and Links to Terrorism and How They Compare with Prewar Assessments," 109th Congress, 2nd Session, September 8, 2006, p. 82.

136 *"this was the most chilling"*: Rand Beers, "No Torture. No Exceptions." *Washington Monthly* (January–March 2008), p. 20.

137 *"This is like Genesis"*: Powell quoted by Wilkerson in interview with the author.

137 *"It was a very dramatic moment"*: Wilkerson interview with the author.

137 *"so confusing, it was James Joycean. It required a leap to get to the conclusions"*: Pillar interview with the author.

138 A later report also cast doubt on al-Libi's closeness to Bin Laden, suggesting that rather than being a member of Al Qaeda, he had been part of a broader movement of Muslim extremists. See Michael Hirsh, "The Myth of Al Qaeda," *Newsweek Online,* June 28, 2006, http://www.newsweek.com/id/52476.

138 *"They were killing me"*: FBI officials quoted in Isikoff and Corn, *Hubris,* p. 124.

139 *"There was blood everywhere. It was all over him"*: Kiriakou interview with Brian Ross, "World News" with Charles Gibson, television program (New York: ABC News) December 10, 2007. Kirakou confirmed the interview on ABC but declined to comment further.

140 *"We thought if we could capture him it would deal a significant blow"*: Kiriakou to Ross, "World News."

141 A CIA source said that the FBI took custody of the unnamed suspect with the Arizona driver's license.

141 *the incriminating detritus scattered around a criminal scene*: Risen, *State of War,* p. 173.

141 *The soldering iron . . . "was still hot"*: Kiriakou to Ross, "World News."

142 *"they got themselves a helicopter. We funded the whole thing"*: CIA officer interview with the author.

142 *the best way to make reluctant informants talk*: Jeffrey Goldberg, "In the Party of God," Part I, *The New Yorker,* October 14, 2002, p. 188.

143 *"Who authorized putting him on pain medication?"*: Bush quoted in Risen, *State of War,* p. 22.

143 *"we hauled in a guy named Abu Zubayda"*: Bush quoted in Suskind, *The One Percent Doctrine,* p. 99.

145 Israel's Supreme Court made allowances for ticking time bomb cases, suggesting that a necessity defense could be employed by interrogators facing charges.

147 Operation Box Top was first reported in Risen, *State of War,* p. 35.

147 One possible vessel for the floating ghost prison may have been a ship called

the U.S. *N.F. Gunnery Sgt. (GYSGT) Fred W. Stockham,* a huge, 906-foot-long government-owned maritime pre-positioning ship that carries thirty days' worth of fuel and provisions and ammunition. A spokesman at the Department of Defense dismissed this as unlikely. But according to records compiled by the Military Sealift Command, the Stockham was retrofitted for "the war on terror" with a flight deck, a commercial-type aviation fuel system, and a "medical module." One secondhand source indicated that it had held "Arab-looking" prisoners in appalling conditions, early on after September 11. Vice Admiral David Brewer, commander of Military Sealift Command from August 2001 to his retirement in early 2006, told *Sea Power* magazine that the Stockham was "off doing some real good stuff that we can't talk about."

147 *"a goat fuck"*: CIA officer quoted in Risen, *State of War,* p. 29.

148 *"how to make people disappear"*: Risen, *State of War,* p. 30.

148 *at least eight countries have participated:* Dana Priest, "CIA Holds Terror Suspects in Secret Prisons," *Washington Post,* November 2, 2005.

148 *the Afghan prison operation alone cost an estimated $100 million*: Priest, "CIA Holds Terror Suspects."

148 *the Agency reportedly promoted him:* Priest, "CIA Holds Terror Suspects."

149 *the Agency flew him around the world for three days*: Former CIA employee interview with the author.

149 *"They hate us more than they love life"*: Kiriakou to Ross, *World News.*

150 *"you don't call in the tough guys; you call in the lawyers"*: Tenet, *At the Center of the Storm,* p. 241.

150 *"Everyone was focused on trying to avoid torture"*: Michael Hirsh et al., "A Tortured Debate," *Newsweek,* June 21, 2004, p. 50.

150 For more information, see Frederick A.O. Schwarz Jr. and Aziz Z. Huq, *Unchecked and Unbalanced* (New York: New Press, 2007), pp. 65–96; Sadakat Kadri, *The Trial* (New York: Random House, 2005); Edward Peters, *Torture* (Philadelphia: University of Pennsylvania Press, 1996).

151 *"a no-brainer for me"*: Cheney to Scott Hennen, *WDAY Hot Talk,* radio program (Fargo, North Dakota: WDAY), October 24, 2006.

151 *"Some locutions begin as bland bureaucratic euphemisms to conceal great crimes"*: William Safire, "Waterboarding," On Language column, *The New York Times Magazine,* March 9, 2008.

152 *"power either has no beginning or it has no end"*: Jackson Remarks in *Youngstown Sheet & Tube Co. v. Sawyer,* 343 U.S. 579 (1952).

152 *"the most clearly erroneous legal opinion I have ever read"*: Harold Koh to the Senate Judiciary Committee, "Hearing on the Nomination of Alberto Gonzales to be U.S. Attorney General," 109th Congress, 1st Session, January 7, 2005.

153 *"there is a category of behavior not covered by the legal system"*: Yoo interview with the author.

153 *"They can't prevent the president from ordering torture"*: Yoo interview with the author.

154 *trying to determine if Yoo's torture memos fell below the professional standards*: Scott Shane, "Waterboarding Focus of Inquiry by Justice Department," *New York Times,* February 23, 2008.

154 *Michael Chertoff . . . downplayed his role during his 2005 confirmation hearings*: A spokesman for Chertoff said his Senate testimony was truthful, but also

acknowledged that Chertoff did speak with lawyers for the intelligence community.

154 *"Avoiding prosecution is literally a theme of the memoranda"*: Anthony Lewis, "Making Torture Legal," *The New York Review of Books,* July 15, 2004, pp. 4–8.

155 *Ali Soufan, a passionate young émigré . . . had been tracking Al Qaeda doggedly . . .*: Ali Soufan declined to comment on his involvement in any terrorism case, noting that the details of the FBI's work were classified.

156 *Tenet . . . was under extraordinary pressure from Bush to produce breakthrough intelligence*: Suskind, *The One Percent Doctrine,* pp. 100–101.

157 Retired Air Force Colonel Steve Kleinman said Mitchell had only observed "mock" interrogations in which American military personnel played all of the parts.

158 *"the actions we have taken have been legal and ethical"*: James Mitchell and John Bruce Jessen quoted in Katherine Eban, "Rorschach and Awe," *Vanity Fair Online,* July 17, 2007, http://www.vanityfair.com/politics/features/2007/07/torture200707.

158 *"You get a feeling of utter, hopeless despair"*: Frank Schwable quoted in Margulies, *Guantánamo,* p. 115, note 17.

159 *"Mine was a more subtle kind of torment"*: Schwable quoted in Margulies, *Guantánamo,* pp. 116–117.

160 *"very deep breakdowns can be provoked"*: Alfred McCoy interview with the author. See also McCoy, *A Question of Torture,* p. 36.

160 *"I had no idea what a potentially vicious weapon this could be"*: Donald Hebb quoted in Gibney, "Taxi to the Dark Side."

160 *"they didn't just bring back the old psychological techniques"*: McCoy interview with the author.

163 *Mitchell reportedly closed a private consulting firm he'd opened just a few months before*: Eban, "Rohrschach and Awe."

163 *a second-floor suite of offices behind a locked door:* Karen Dorn Steele and Bill Morlin, "Senate Probe Focuses on Spokane Men," *The Spokesman Review,* June 29, 2007, www.spokesmanreview.com/tools/story_breakingnews_pf.asp?ID=10496.

166 *they reportedly threatened to bury Zubayda alive:* Eban, "Rohrschach and Awe."

166 *they planned to become Zubayda's "God"*: Eban, "Rohrschach and Awe."

166 *took his clothing as punishment*: Eban, "Rohrschach and Awe."

168 *"Arabs only understand force"*: For more information and a discussion of Raphael Patai, see Seymour Hersh, "The Gray Zone," *The New Yorker*, May 24, 2004, p. 42.

168 *heart rates soar, kidneys shut down, and delusions deepen*: McCoy, *A Question of Torture,* p. 46 .

169 *keeping prisoners awake for as long as ninety-six hours*: Darius Rejali, *Democracy and Torture* (Princeton: Princeton University Press, 2007), p. 292.

169 *noise . . . from the Red Hot Chili Peppers:* Eban, "Rorschach and Awe."

170 *it was the favored choice only of witch hunters*: Rejali, *Democracy and Torture,* p. 511.

171 *Los Angeles Times,* "It's torture; it's illegal," editorial, February 2, 2008.

171 Evan Wallach in the *Columbia Journal of Transnational Law* details incidents of waterboarding prosecuted by DOJ itself, including the 1983 federal prosecution of a Texas county sheriff who waterboarded prisoners. The sheriff and his deputies were all convicted.

172 *"Allah had visited him in the night"*: Kiriakou to Ross, *World News.*

172 *the reviewers' report was kept secret, but the verdict was reportedly mixed*: Rejali, *Torture and Democracy*, p. 503.

174 *"When you cross over that line of darkness, it's hard to come back"*: Former CIA officer interview with the author.

175 *"He spent all of his time masturbating like a monkey in the zoo"*: Two former CIA officers' interviews with the author. Another source said, "He masturbated constantly. A couple of guards were worried about it. He wasn't brazen about it—he wasn't facing the camera. He'd do it at night, facing the wall, but it was rigged so there was no place for him to not be seen. This was closed circuit. He complained to the interrogator that he would never have the chance to feel a woman's touch again, and lament that he would never have children. He freaked though, at one point, because there was blood in his ejaculate. He saved it for the doctors in a tissue, to show them in the morning. The doctor said not to worry."

176 *"No one made the connection"*: The National Commission on Terrorist Attacks, *The 9/11 Commission Report*, p. 277.

176 See also Tony Czuczka, "Germany seeks second fugitive in U.S. terrorist attacks," Associated Press, September 21, 2001; Peter Finn and Brooke A. Masters, "Officials Seek Hijacker Who Wasn't," *Washington Post*, November 16, 2001; Russ Buettner, "Manhunt for Hijackers' 3 Pals," *Daily News* (New York), October 24, 2001. The FBI Director referred to Bin Al Shibh as the "twentieth hijacker" and he was discussed in the Zacarias Moussaoui indictment in December 2001.

177 *"In other words, the fat fuck came through"*: Tenet quoted in Suskind, *The One Percent Doctrine*, p. 139.

177 *led to Bin Al Shibh's capture, along with a number of other suspects, on September 11, 2002*: See Rory McCarthy, "Threat of war," *The Guardian,* September 16, 2002.

177 *Abu Zubayda led to Ramsi Bin Al Shibh*: Tenet, *At the Center of the Storm*, p. 242.

178 *"You're not going to let me lose face on this, are you?"*: Bush and Tenet quoted in Suskind, *The One Percent Doctrine*, p. 100.

178 *"Men are pigs"*: CIA briefer quoted in Tenet, *At the Center of the Storm*, p. 243.

178 *"He had a schizophrenic personality"*: Daniel Coleman interview with the author.

178 *"he was just a hotel clerk"*: Coleman interview with the author.

178 *Zubayda . . . reportedly confessed to dozens of half-hatched or entirely imaginary plots*: Suskind, *The One Percent Doctrine*, p. 114.

179 *"It was about face time, and sounding good"*: Coleman interview with the author. ◆

179 *"Waterboarding is probably something that we shouldn't be in the business of doing"*: Kiriakou to Ross, "World News."

179 *For Cofer Black*: Black said he had little or no involvement with "enhanced interrogations" which all took place after he left the CIA.

180 In an interview with *Frontline,* Gary Schroen calls the personnel taken from Afghanistan "essential."

180 *"George had some long nights"*: John Brennan inverview in "The Enemy Within," *Frontline,* television program (Boston: WGBH and PBS, October, 2006). The full interview is available at http://www.pbs.org/wgbh/pages/frontline/enemywithin/interviews/brennan.html.

183 *there were no details of any other sort. Not even a name:* Two former White House officials; interviews with the author.

183 *"among the most dangerous, best-trained, and vicious killers":* Rumsfeld quoted in Gerry J. Gilmore, "Rumsfeld Visits, Thanks U.S. Troops at Camp X-Ray in Cuba," *American Forces Press Service,* January 27, 2002, http://www.defenselink.mil/news/newsarticle.aspx?id=43817.

183 *"gnaw through hydraulic lines":* Richard Myers, comments at the Defense Department Regular News Briefing, January 11, 2002.

183 *"pure chaos":* Michael Gelles, former chief psychologist, Naval Criminal Investigative Service, interview with the author.

183 The first published mention of the unidentified CIA officer's report on Guantánamo appears in Seymour Hersh, *Chain of Command* (New York: HarperCollins, 2004), p.3.

183 *"just caught in a dragnet":* Former CIA analyst interview with the author.

184 *"please shut up and go home":* Military official to Dunlavey, quoted in Tim Golden, "Administration Officials Split Over Stalled Military Tribunals," *New York Times,* October 25, 2004. Dunlavey told Philippe Sands, in *The Torture Team,* that half the detainees in Guantánamo had no connection to terrorism.

184 *only 8 percent were alleged to have associated with Al Qaeda:* Mark Denbeaux and Joshua Denbeaux et al., "Report on Guantánamo Detainees: A Profile of 517 Detainees through Analysis of Department of Defense Data," Seton Hall Law School, p. 2. This report is available at http://law.shu.edu/news/guantánamo_reports.htm.

188 *"I don't do detainees":* Rumsfeld quoted by source at the meeting in interview with the author.

191 *with meticulous detective work, identified the rental car driven by September 11 ringleader Mohammed Atta:* Tim Golden and Don Van Natta Jr., "The Reach of War: U.S. Said to Overstate Value of Guantánamo Detainees," *New York Times,* June 19, 2004.

191 *the FBI had reportedly ascertained that Qahtani had in fact intended to join the other hijackers:* Golden and Van Natta, "The Reach of War." A lawyer for Atta disputed this claim. See Bill Dedman, "Can the '20th hijacker' of Sept. 11 stand trial?" MSNBC.com, October 26, 2006, www.msnbc.msn.com/id/15361462.

191 *Qahtani . . . disclosed that he had attended the key Malaysia planning meeting:* Golden and Van Natta, "The Reach of War."

192 *Becker authorized the guards to wrap more tape around his head and beard, "as a control measure":* Summarized witness statement of Guantánamo employee [Becker] in Randall Schmidt and John Furlow, Report Enclosures Part II of "AR 15-6: Investigation of Detainee Abuse at Guantánamo Bay, Cuba Detention Facility" (the Schmidt-Furlow Report), Army Southern Command Investigation, p. 3751. The released portions of the report and its appendices are avilable through the University of Minnesota Human Rights Library, at http://www1.umn.edu/humanrts/OathBetrayed/general-investigations.html. A spokesman for the DIA declined a written request to interview Becker, and asked that he not be identified. The spokesman also said that Becker was dissatisfied with the way Pentagon investigators had represented his role. But he declined to be interviewed.

193 *"My God . . . did I authorize putting a bra and underwear on this guy's head?"*:
Rumsfeld statement to Randall Schmidt, quoted in the "Testimony of
Lieutenant General Randall M. Schmidt," Department of the Army Inspector
General, Investigations Division, August 24, 2005, p. 25. The released
document is available at Salon.com at http://www.salon.com/news/feature/
2006/04/14/rummy/.

193 *"I got my marching orders directly from the President of the United States"*:
Summarized witness statement of M.G. (Retired) Mike Dunlavey, Report
Enclosures Part II of the Schmidt-Furlow Report, p. 3738.

193 *"Dunlavey's successor . . . with Rumsfeld was described as equally close"*: Michael
Scherer and Mark Benjamin, "What Rumsfeld Knew," *Salon,* April 14, 2006,
http://www.salon.com/news/feature/2006/04/14/rummy/.

194 *"It's immoral, unethical, and it won't get good results"*: Mallow interview with
the author.

194 *"I've talked to the people overseas and they're getting good results"*: Billingslea
declined to comment. Quoted by Mallow in interview with the author.

195 *"That's when the silly stuff started"*: CIA employee interview with the author.

195 *"Many of the aggressive interrogation techniques"*: Summarized witness statement
of Becker, Report Enclosures Part II of the Schmidt-Furlow Report, p. 3753.

196 *"We saw it on cable . . . It was hugely popular"*: Diane Beaver quoted in Sands,
The Torture Team, p. 80.

196 *"There's this stuff that the CIA does—and it works!"*: Gelles interview with
the author.

197 *"which SERE techniques might be useful in interrogations in Guantánamo"*: Deputy
Inspector General for Intelligence Shelton R. Young, "Review of DoD-Directed
Investigations of Detainee Abuse (Unclassified)," Office of the Inspector
General of the Department of Defense Investigation, August 25, 2006, p. 25.

197 *"My predecessor . . . arranged for SERE instructors to teach their techniques"*:
Summarized witness statement of Ted Moss, Report Enclosures Part I of the
Schmidt-Furlow Report, p. 847.

198 *"as they got new ideas"*: Beaver quoted in Sands, *The Torture Team*, p. 81.

198 the *"guy in charge"*: Beaver quoted in Sands, *The Torture Team*, p. 82.

198 stared back with a smoldering hatred: Goldsmith, *The Terror Presidency*, p. 100.

198 how the military was *"managing"* his case: Michael Dunlavey quoted in Sands,
The Torture Team, p. 62.

199 *"This is what habeas corpus is for"*: Goldsmith, *The Terror Presidency*, p. 102.

201 It was a novel theory: Author interview with Pentagon official.

204 *"Lead, follow, or get the fuck out of the way"*: Gerald Phifer quoted in the
Summarized witness statement of Clemente, Report Enclosures Part II of the
Schmidt-Furlow Report, p. 3756.

204 *"If you want to wear the jersey, you've got to be on the team"*: Geoffrey Miller quoted
in CITF staff member and Member of Congress interviews with the author.

204 Bowman's role is described in greater detail in Sands, *The Torture Team*, p. 145.

205 *a fraternity brother of George W. Bush at Yale*: Angie C. Marek, "A Righteous
Indignation," *U.S. News & World Report*, March 20, 2005, p. 36.

207 *"it was okay to subject the terrorist to twenty hour days"*: Summarized witness
statement of Becker, Report Enclosures Part II of the Schmidt-Furlow Report,
p. 3753.

207 *"if the detainee was made to feel 'unclean' he would have to stop praying"*: Summarized witness statement of Becker, Report Enclosures Part II of the Schmidt-Furlow Report, p. 3753.

211 *"a valuable source of information"*: Department of Defense spokesman quoted in Adam Zagorin and Michael Duffy, "Inside the Interrogation of Detainee 063," *Time*, June 12, 2005, pp. 26–28.

211 *"Did it help catch Osama Bin Laden? No"*: Cal Temple quoted in Sands, *The Torture Team*, p. 190.

211 *"too much of an unsophisticated Bedouin"*: Khalid Sheikh Mohammed, "Substitution for the Testimony of Khalid Sheikh Mohammed," *U.S. v. Moussaoui*, 282 F. Supp. 2d 480 (E. Dist. Va., 2003). The statement is available at www.vaed.uscourts.gov/notablecases/moussaoui/exhibits/defense/941.pdf.

214 *The inscription was from the Bible—Isaiah, chapter 6, verse 8*: Alberto Mora, Acceptance Speech as Recipient of the John F. Kennedy Profile in Courage Award (The John F. Kennedy Library, Boston, Massachusetts), May 22, 2006. The speech is available at http://www.jfklibrary.org/Education+and+Public+Programs/Profile+in+Courage+Award/Award+Recipients/Alberto+Mora/Acceptance+Speech+by+Alberto+Mora.htm.

220 *there was a fourth category that disappeared*: Margulies, *Guantánamo*, p. 98.

221 *"intrigue" that was "probably occurring"*: Richard Myers quoted in Phillipe Sands, "The Green Light," *Vanity Fair*, May 2008, p. 280.

221 *"Good to go"*: Haynes quoted in Sands, "The Green Light," p. 279.

221 *Addington . . . had discussed the issue of Qahtani's interrogation with Beaver*: Sands, "The Green Light," p. 279.

221 Mora's twenty-two-page account of his dealings with Haynes and other Pentagon officials was checked with the Office of General Counsel at the Pentagon, which did not deny any of it.

223 *"These approved techniques, say, withholding food, and 50-degree temperature"*: Kelbaugh quoted in Scott Shane, David Johnston, and James Risen, "Secret U.S. Endorsement of Severe Interrogations," *New York Times*, October 4, 2007.

225 *his legs had "basically been pulpified"*: coroner quoted in Tim Golden, "In U.S. Report, Brutal Details of 2 Afghan Inmates' Deaths," *New York Times*, May 20, 2005.

225 *he just "disappeared from the face of the earth"*: American official quoted in Dana Priest, "CIA Avoids Scrutiny of Detainee Treatment," *Washington Post*, March 3, 2005.

226 *Her story, Umansky found, was at the center of an editorial fight*: Umansky, "Failures of Imagination," p. 22. In May, 2005, *New York Times* did run a remarkable investigative story about Dilawar's case on the front page. See Golden, "In U.S. Report, Brutal Details of 2 Afghan Inmates' Deaths."

228 *"I have plenty of advisers, but I only listen to one of them"*: Rumsfeld quoted in family friend interview with the author.

231 *"a monument to executive supremacy and the imperial presidency"*: Eugene Fidell quoted in Mark Mazetti, "'03 Memo Approved Harsh Interrogations," *New York Times*, April 2, 2008.

239 *turning from the predicted "cakewalk" into a horror show*: Kenneth Adelman, "Cakewalk in Iraq," editorial, *Washington Post*, February 13, 2002.

239 *"they suggest that this represents some sort of failure on the part of the Coalition"*: Donald Rumsfeld, "Remarks Delivered to the Veterans of Foreign Wars," San Antonio, Texas, August 25, 2003.

240 *"Politically, the U.S. has failed to date"*: Report quoted in Hersh, "The Gray Zone," *The New Yorker*, May 24, 2004, p. 41.

240 *Rumsfeld loudly disparaged the quality of the information:* Schwarz and Huq, "Unchecked and Unbalanced," p. 86.

241 *"She's soft—too soft"*: William Boykin quoted by an interlocutor in an interview with the author.

241 *Miller advocated using ordinary military police officers:* Blake Morrison and Peter Eisler, "General Promised Quick Results if Gitmo Plan Used at Abu Ghraib," *USA Today*, June 23, 2004.

241 *Miller also recommended using military dogs for interrogation*: "Ex-Warden Tells of Use of Dogs," Associated Press, July 27, 2005.

242 *"'we can do this my way or we can do this the hard way'"*: Janis Karpinski quoted in Morrison and Eisler, "General Promised Quick Results."

242 The ACLU obtained a copy of Sanchez's September 14, 2003, memo, showing that with his permission, dogs could be used in interrogations if they were muzzled, and that detainees could be kept awake for twenty hours of three consecutive days. Stress positions could be used for up to one hour at a time, and four hours during a day.

242 *the first instances of military interrogators removing detainees' clothing:* MG George R. Fay, "AR 15-6 Investigation of the Abu Ghraib Detention Facility and 205th Military Intelligence Brigade," Investigation for the U.S. Army Combined Joint Task Force, August 23, 2004, pp. 20, 41. The report is available at http://news.findlaw.com/hdocs/docs/dod/fay82504rpt.pdf.

242 *"the civilian leaders at the highest levels . . . unleashed the hounds of Hell . . ."*: General Ricardo S. Sanchez, *Wiser in Battle,* p. 154.

243 *"Copper Green"* and *"Special Access Program"*: Hersh, "The Gray Zone," pp. 38, 41.

243 *commandos reportedly had legal authorization, in advance . . . to use lethal force:* Hersh, "The Gray Zone," p. 38.

243 *"'Grab whom you must. Do what you want'"*: Hersh, "The Gray Zone," p. 39.

244 *CIA headquarters refused to give the Baghdad station the resources it needed:* Risen, *State of War,* pp. 144–45. Confirmed by CIA officer interviewed by author.

244 *The Agency reportedly sent a handful of this population—six to eight—outside of Iraq for interrogation*: Risen, *State of War*, p. 145.

244 One such suspect, an Iraqi member of the terrorist group Al Ansar—identified as Hiwa Abdul Rahman Rashul—was captured by Kurdish soldiers in the summer of 2003 and taken outside of Iraq for interrogation by the CIA. See Edward T. Pound, "Iraq's invisible man," *U.S. News & World Report,* June 28, 2004, p. 32.

245 In his investigation into the abuse of detainees at Abu Ghraib, Army Major General Antonio Taguba singled out the CIA's practice of maintaining such "ghost detainees" for special criticism, calling it "deceptive, contrary to Army doctrine and in violation of international law."

245 *"disagreed with what they described as the 'hard-line approach'"*: "Review of DOD-Directed Investigations of Detainee Abuse," p. 27.

246 *the task force . . . was abusing prisoners in ways that could be construed as illegal:*
Josh White, "U.S. Generals in Iraq Were Told of Abuse Early, Inquiry Finds,"
Washington Post, December 1, 2004.

247 *the Iraqi insurgents were not enemy prisoners of war covered by the Geneva Conventions:*
"Review of DoD-Directed Investigations of Detainee Abuse," p. 28.

248 *"not appropriate to use in training interrogators":* "Review of DoD-Directed
Investigations of Detainee Abuse," p. 29.

250 *eighteen-inch hooks hung from the ceiling:* Eric Schmitt and Carolyn Marshall,
"In Secret Unit's Black Room, a Grim Portrait of U.S. Abuse," *New York Times,*
March 19, 2006. *five interrogation rooms ranging in degrees of coerciveness:* "'No
Blood, No Foul': Soldiers' Accounts of Detainee Abuse in Iraq," Human Rights
Watch Reports (Vol. 28, No. 3), July 2006, p. 8.

250 *placards warning against leaving telltale marks on the detainees, with the motto
"No Blood, No Foul":* Schmitt and Marshall, "In Secret Unit's Black Room."

250 *"I'm going to barbecue you if you don't tell me the information":* Soldier quoted in
John McChesney, "The Death of an Iraqi Prisoner," *All Things Considered* radio
program (Washington: NPR Public Radio), October 25, 2005. Available at
npr.org/templates/story/story.php?storyid=4977986.

251 *"I called them disappearing ghosts":* Karpinski quoted in Hersh, "The Gray
Zone," p. 41.

255 *"I am not going down for this alone":* Thomas Pappas quoted by Captain Donald
Reese, the commander of Abu Ghraib military police, in interview with the
author.

260 *"This is going to kill us":* Alberto Gonzales quoted in Goldsmith, *The Terror
Presidency,* p. 141.

261 *"Could I have done something to stop them?":* Goldsmith, *The Terror Presidency,*
p. 141.

262 *Ashcroft convinced Andrew Card . . . that Yoo was . . . not competent to run the
OLC:* Goldsmith, *The Terror Presidency,* p. 25.

263 *Yoo advised that no part of the Geneva Conventions protected "unlawful combatants":*
the Department of Defense Working Group, "Working Group Report on
Detainee Interrogations on the Global War on Terrorism," April 4, 2003,
reproduced in *The Torture Papers,* edited by Karen J. Greenberg and Joshua L.
Dratel (Cambridge, UK: Cambridge University Press 2005), p. 288.
Nonetheless, Yoo later claimed he had always meant for Iraqi fighters to be
covered by Geneva IV.

264 *"Death threats, beatings, broken bones, murder":* Ian Fishback letter to
John McCain, republished as "A Matter of Honor," *Washington Post,*
September 20, 2005.

265 *"he was smart—but he couldn't interpret treaties!":* Colleague of John Yoo
interview with the author.

265 *"They'll respect you more in the morning":* Walter Dellinger interview with
the author.

265 *"It was a huge pain in the ass":* former Iraq-stationed CIA officer interview
with the author.

267 *"the veneer of serious scholarship (abundant footnotes, many citations, long dense
paragraphs)":* Stephen Gillers, "The Torture Memos," *The Nation,* April 28,
2008, p. 6.

267 *"no basis in prior OLC opinions, or in judicial opinions, or in any other source of law"*: Goldsmith, *The Terror Presidency,* p. 145.

267 *Yoo turned out to have based his broad definition of allowable pain . . . not on torture cases but rather on a document defining thresholds for public health benefits*: Margulies, *Guantánamo*, p. 91.

267 *"cursory and one-sided"*: Goldsmith, *The Terror Presidency*, p. 149.

268 *"The President decides who sees what, not you!"*: Addington quoted in former administration official interview with the author.

269 *"They blew right through them in secret, based on flimsy legal opinions"*: Goldsmith, *The Terror Presidency*, p. 181. Michael Hayden, who was then the director of the NSA, has said that the NSA's own lawyers had enough information about the program to independently vouch for its legality. But it remains doubtful that they had access to the OLC's legal work prior to Goldsmith's intervention.

269 *Putting it on "a proper legal footing . . . was by far the hardest challenge I faced in government"*: Goldsmith, *The Terror Presidency*, p. 182.

269 *"We're one bomb away from getting rid of that obnoxious court"* and *"the blood of a hundred thousand"*: Addington quoted in Goldsmith, *The Terror Presidency*, pp. 71, 181.

270 The "Malaysian Scientist" who Khalid Sheikh Mohammed identified as experimenting with anthrax prior to September 11, 2001 was Yazid Sufaat. He was captured by Malaysian authorities before KSM's arrest. According to Malaysian news articles, the FBI interrogated him in 2002.

270 *"We're hearing this too much from the FBI"*: Cheney quoted in Suskind, *The One Percent Doctrine*, p. 252.

270 *"what {they} gave us was worth more than CIA, NSA, the FBI and our military operations had achieved collectively"*: Tenet, *At the Center of the Storm*, p. 256.

271 *"Brutalization became bureaucratized"*: former Afghanistan-based CIA official interview with the author.

271 Sources on Mohammed's interrogation include European and American experts in intelligence, government, and law, as well as former detainees released from CIA custody, and their lawyers.

272 *"We were getting good information, and then they were told: 'Slow it down'"*: Paul Kelbaugh quoted in Shane, Johnston, and Risen, "Secret U.S. Endorsement of Severe Interrogations." *"Things went too far. It was awful. Awful"*: former CIA agent interview with the author.

272 *a carefully choreographed twenty-minute routine, during which a suspect was hog-tied*: Dick Marty, *Alleged secret detentions*, memorandum to the Council of Europe.

273 *"tear clothing from detainees by firmly pulling downward against buttoned buttons"*: William Haynes, "Counter-Resistance Techniques (S.E.R.E. Interrogation Standard Operating Procedure), memorandum to Donald Rumsfeld, The Department of Defense, The Pentagon, Part 3, Section D. December 10, 2002.

273 *the CIA kept Mohammed naked for more than a month*: sources who read Mohammed's statement to the ICRC interviews with the author. *"She thought it would be cool"*: former CIA counterterrorism officer interview with the author. The CIA declined to discuss any details of its detentions and interrogations, other than to describe the program as legal and effective.

273 *"They told her, 'It's not supposed to be entertainment'"*: former CIA officer interview with the author.

273 *Mohammed . . . alleged that he was beaten incessantly, attached to a dog leash*: sources who read Mohammed's statement to the ICRC.

274 *"Plenty lost their minds. I could hear people knocking their heads against the walls and doors, screaming their heads off"*: for more details of his interrogation and detention, see Moazzam Begg's *Enemy Combatant*.

275 *hundreds of different techniques in just a two-week period*: Risen, *State of War*, p. 32.

275 *"What mattered was things done in combination. It can look antiseptic on a piece of paper"*: former administration official interview with the author.

275 See Dick Marty, *Alleged secret detentions*, memorandum to the Council of Europe.

276 *white noise was piped in constantly . . .*: Mohammed al-Asad interview with the author.

276 *Mohammed claimed that even after he started cooperating, he was waterboarded*: Sources familiar with ICRC report, interviews with the author.

277 *there really was nothing "solid" enough to pass on*: former CIA agent interview with the author.

277 *to issue urgent terrorist threat alerts on several occasions, for no real reason*: Sources familiar with ICRC report, interviews with the author.

280 *they accused the CIA of "obstruction," a federal crime*: Thomas Kean and Lee Hamilton, "Stonewalled by the CIA," editorial, *The New York Times*, January 2, 2008.

280 *questions posed by the Commission spurred some thirty extra interrogation sessions*: Robert Windrem and Victor Limjoco, "9/11 Commission Controversy," Msnbc.com, January 30, 2008, http://deepbackground.msnbc.msn.com/archive/2008/01/30/624314.aspx.

281 *"Jim, I've got bad news . . ."*: Goldsmith, *The Terror Presidency*, p. 154.

282 *"Everyone wanted to play the game"*: Former CIA official interview with the author.

286 *"Now there's a record! It will get out—it will become a German political issue"*: Schily quoted by well-informed source interview with the author. Senator Daniel Coats declined to discuss the matter because it was classified.

287 *"Whoever says that's not torture should just have it done to them"*: Khaled el-Masri interview with the author.

287 *"General Patton wasn't popular either, but sometimes it takes a tough person to win a war"*: former CIA official interview with the author.

287 *investigating "seven or eight other cases like Masri" in which the CIA had apparently abducted and jailed the wrong people*: former CIA official interview with the author. Confirmed by two other former CIA officials.

289 *"The whole IG's office was completely politicized"*: A source who spoke with John Helgerson said that the Inspector General briefed the Vice President, but denied that he was politically influenced in any way.

289 *"No good lawyer"*: Comey quoted in Shane, Johnston, and Risen, "Secret U.S. Endorsement of Severe Interrogations."

292 *Tenet had provided graphic details of specific coercive interrogations during Principals Committee meetings*: Jan Crawford Greenburg, Howard Rosenberg, and Ariane de Vogue, "Sources: Top Bush Advisors Approved 'Enhanced Interrogation,'" ABCnews.com, April 9, 2008, http://abcnews.go.com/TheLaw/LawPolitics/

story?id=4583256&page=1; a former administration source confirmed and amplified the report. Rice declined comment to ABC, but Powell said he had no memory of such meetings. *the two cabinet members directed their frustration at Gonzales, neither had the temerity to confront Cheney*: Barton Gellman and Jo Becker, "Pushing the Envelope on Presidential Power."

294 *Addington . . . "stormed out of the meeting"*: meeting participant interview with the author. Another source said he or she did not recall this.

297 *"twisting yourselves into knots"*: Richard Armitage interview in *Torturing Democracy*, documentary, produced by Sherry Jones (Washington: Washington Media Associates, 2008).

300 *"a lawless enclave insulating the executive branch from any judicial scrutiny"*: Gibbons quoted in Margulies, *Guantánamo*, p. 151.

301 *"the very core of liberty"*: Scalia quoted in Margulies, *Guantánamo*, p. 155.

301 *"what is left of American freedom if the government has the authority"*: "It's Called Democracy," editorial, *Los Angeles Times*, June 29, 2004.

302 *"know-nothingness"*: Gellman and Becker, "Pushing the Envelope on Presidential Power."

302 *"slap on the wrist"*: Goldsmith quoted in Margulies, *Guantánamo*, p. 137.

302 *"now it argued that the doors were open, but the building was empty"*: Margulies, *Guantánamo*, p. 159.

302 *"how are we supposed to represent them if we don't know who's there"*: Margulies interview with the author.

303 *"its only purpose was to keep the truth from the world"*: Clive Stafford Smith interview with the author.

303 *Hamdi spent years in prison without ever having the opportunity to contest his status*: Margulies, *Guantánamo*, p. 156.

303 *its case could never have survived the scrutiny of an open court*: The critics who suspected this include Joe Margulies and Clive Stafford Smith, among others. Hamdi's case closely paralleled that of John Walker Lindh, but unlike Lindh, he had not incriminated himself on national television.

305 *"They'll all get lawyers"*: Four participants' interviews with the author. These participants also provided extensive details on the White House meetings on detainee issues. Cheney's office declined to comment.

305 *"Ninety-nine percent"*: Lewis Libby quoted in former Bush administration lawyer interview with the author. Libby did not respond to an effort to reach him for comment.

306 *"they are not covered up, but exposed, investigated and publicly disclosed"*: Rumsfeld to the Senate Armed Services Committee, "Allegations of Mistreatment of Iraqi Prisoners," 108th Congress, 2nd Session, May 11, 2004.

307 *Levin agreed to put in the cryptic footnote whitewashing previous practices*: Three former administration officials' interviews with the author.

307 *mind-altering drugs and mock burials*: Former administration official interview with the author. Reached for comment on rumors that he had approved the use of drugs and mock burials on detainees, John Yoo said, "I can tell you that my opinion, right now, is that neither would be permitted by the anti-torture statute." Asked if that had been his opinion when he was at OLC, he did not respond.

307 *"in the real world of interrogation policy nothing had changed"*: Yoo, *War by Other*

Means: An Insider's Account of the War on Terror (New York: Atlantic Monthly Press, 2006), p. 183.

308 *"Don't pick him"*: Dan Levin quoted in colleagues' interviews with the author.

308 Bradbury's "probation" was first revealed by the *New York Times* in October, 2007. Bradbury denied that he had molded his opinions in order to be nominated: "No one ever suggested to me that my nomination depended on how I ruled on any opinion," he said. "Every opinion I've signed at the Office of Legal Counsel represents my best judgment of what the law requires." See Shane, Johnston, and Risen, "Secret U.S. Endorsement of Severe Interrogations."

308 *"The White House held the nomination over him"*: Former senior administration official interview with the author, confirmed by two other officers.

308 Shane, Johnston, and Risen, in their *New York Times* article "Secret U.S. Endorsement of Severe Interrogations," broke the story of Bradbury's secret memo. Multiple former officials of the Bush Administration corroborated this reporting in interviews.

309 *just "couldn't afford" to pick a fight*: Gonzales quoted in three former Justice Department officials' interviews with the author.

309 Bradbury was nominated to run the OLC but Congress declined to confirm him, so he held the job in "acting" status only.

310 *"haunt" both Gonzales and the U.S. Department of Justice*: Isikoff and Corn, *Hubris*, p. 340. James Risen, who broke the story of Bradbury's memo, described Comey as saying Gonzales and America would be "ashamed" by the Bradbury opinion. See Savage, *Takeover*, p. 338.

310 *"he's changed his mind"*: Several colleagues of Comey in interviews with the author.

310 Gonzales agreed with the criticism of torture, according to interviews with former administration officials who were familiar with Comey's conversations.

310 *"There's a gap"*: Philip Zelikow interview with the author.

312 *"Some of them did pay a price for their commitment to right"*: James Comey quoted in Daniel Klaidman, Stuart Taylor Jr., and Evan Thomas, "Palace Revolt," *Newsweek*, February 6, 2006.

313 *"Just shut it down and plow it under"*: Thomas Friedman, "Just Shut It Down," editorial, *New York Times,* May 27, 2005.

313 *a request . . . from Senator Jay Rockefeller...to see over a hundred documents*: John Rockefeller, "Chairman Rockefeller Says Intel Committee Has Begun Investigation into CIA Detainee Tapes," press release, December 7, 2007, http://rockefeller.senate.gov/press/record.cfm?id=288567.

313 *the existence of any videotapes of terror suspects in U.S. custody*: Dan Eggen and Joby Warrick, "CIA Destroyed Videos Showing Interrogations," *Washington Post*, December 7, 2007.

320 *"legitimizing an agent of the government engaging in torture"*: John McCain quoted in Savage, *Takeover*, p. 222.

321 *"To a spectator it would look like torture"*: Gannon quoted in Shane, Johnston, and Risen, "Secret U.S. Endorsement of Severe Interrogations." Hayden claimed that the tapes were destroyed because they posed a "serious security risk." Six or seven CIA employees were apparently visible on the tapes along with the terror suspects, including a member of Rodriguez's personal staff, according to former officials.

323 *Harriet Miers . . . was strongly influenced by Addington*: Addington and Cheney favored a one-page piece of legislation reversing the impact of the Hamdan decision, according to "Pushing the Envelope," by Barton Gellman and Jo Becker, *The Washington Post,* Monday, June 25, 2007.

326 *"Yuck! Special procedures? It sounds scary!"*: Confidant of Karen Hughes interview with the author. Hughes failed to respond to requests for comment.

328 *many of the administration's own top authorities . . . acknowledged that . . . waterboarding was torture*: McConnell quoted in Wright, "The Spymaster," p. 53; Ridge quoted in Eileen Sullivan, "Tom Ridge: Waterboarding Is Torture," Associated Press, January, 18, 2008; Kiriakou quoted in Ross, *World News.* 329 *"it's not about them, it's about us"*: McCain interview with Bob Schieffer, "Face the Nation," television program, (New York: CBS News, November 13, 2005).

330 *"we lack metrics to know if we are winning or losing the global war on terror"*: Donald Rumsfeld, "Global War on Terrorism," memorandum to Gen. Dick Myers et. al., The Department of Defense, October 16, 2003, reproduced at http://www.usatoday.com/news/washington/executive/rumsfeld-memo.htm.

330 *"coercive interrogations can lead detainees to provide false information"*: John Rockefeller, "Statement on President's Veto of the Intelligence Authorization Bill," press release, March 8, 2008.

331 *threats to U.S. interests at home and abroad will become more diverse*: The National Intelligence Council, "Declassified Key Judgments of the National Intelligence Estimate," Directorate of National Intelligence, April, 2006.

331 *"our greatest sin was robbing Muslims of hope"*: Eric Haseltine interview with the author.

332 *two countries in the world supported the U.S. war on terror—India and Russia*: The Pew Global Attitudes Project, "America's Image Slips, But Allies Share U.S. Concerns Over Iran, Hamas," June 13, 2006.

332 *we were right from the beginning in using all means*: Hosni Mubarak quoted in Agence France-Presse, "Mubarak Says Egypt's Military Courts Vindicated by U.S., Britain," December 15, 2001.

332 *"If we've been holding these guys for so long, how can we explain letting them get off?"*: Haynes quoted by Morris Davis in Ross Tuttle, "Rigged Trials at Gitmo," *The Nation,* March 10, 2008, p. 4.

333 *"in our zeal to get information, we had compromised our ability to prosecute him"*: Stuart Couch quoted in Jess Bravin, "The Conscience of a Colonel," *The Wall Street Journal,* March 31, 2007.

334 *"I was legally prevented from further investigation into higher authority"*: Antonio Taguba quoted in Seymour Hersh, "The General's Report," *The New Yorker,* June 25, 2007, p. 61.

BIBLIOGRAPHY

BOOKS

Bamford, James. *A Pretext for War*. Paperback ed. New York: Doubleday, 2004.

Begg, Moazzam. *Enemy Combatant: My Imprisonment at Guantánamo, Bagram, and Kandahar*. New York: New Press, 2006.

Bergen, Peter L. *The Osama bin Laden I Know*. Paperback ed. New York: Free Press, 2006.

Berntsen, Gary. *Jawbreaker*. Paperback ed. New York: Crown, 2005.

Bovard, James. *Terrorism and Tyranny: Trampling Freedom, Justice, and Peace to Rid the World of Evil*. Paperback ed. New York: Palgrave Macmillan, 2003.

Bumiller, Elisabeth. *Condoleezza Rice: An American Life*. New York: Random House, 2007.

Burstein, Dan, and Arne J. De Keijzer. *Secrets of 24*. New York: Sterling, 2007.

Cohn, Marjorie. *Cowboy Republic: Six Ways the Bush Gang Has Defied the Law*. Sausalito, CA: PoliPointPress, 2007.

Cole, David, and Jules Lobel. *Less Safe, Less Free: Why America Is Losing the War on Terror*. New York: New Press, 2007.

Coll, Steve. *Ghost Wars*. New York: Penguin, 2004.

Danner, Mark. *Torture and Truth: America, Abu Ghraib, and the War on Terror*. Paperback ed. New York: New York Review Books, 2004.

DeYoung, Karen. *Soldier: The Life of Colin Powell*. Paperback ed. New York: Vintage, 2007.

Draper, Robert. *Dead Certain: The Presidency of George W. Bush*. New York: Free Press, 2007.

Drogin, Bob. *Curveball: Spies Lies, and the Con Man Who Caused a War*. New York: Random House, 2007.

Drumheller, Tyler. *On the Brink: An Insider's Account of How the White House Compromised American Intelligence*. New York: Carroll & Graf, 2006.

Faludi, Susan. *The Terror Dream: Fear and Fantasy in Post-9/11 America*. New York: Metropolitan, 2007.

Goldsmith, Jack L. *The Terror Presidency: Law and Judgment Inside the Bush Administration*. New York: Norton, 2007.

Gordon, Philip H. *Winning the Right War: The Path to Security for America and the World*. New York: Times Books, 2007.

Greenberg, Karen J., and Joshua L. Dratel, eds. *The Torture Papers: The Road to Abu Ghraib*. Cambridge, UK: Cambridge University Press, 2005.

Greenberg, Karen J., ed. *The Torture Debate in America*. Cambridge, UK: Cambridge University Press, 2006.

Grey, Stephen. *Ghost Plane: The True Story of the CIA Torture Program*. New York: St. Martin's Press, 2006.

Hersh, Seymour M. *Chain of Command: The Road from 9/11 to Abu Ghraib*. New York: HarperCollins, 2004.

Holmes, Steven. *The Matador's Cape*. Cambridge, UK: Cambridge University Press, 2007.

Isikoff, Michael, and David Corn. *Hubris*. New York: Crown, 2006.

Kadri, Sadakat. *The Trial*. New York: Random House, 2005.

Kepel, Gilles. *Jihad: The Trail of Political Islam*. Trans. Anthony F. Roberts. 2nd ed. Cambridge, MA: Belknap Press of Harvard University Press, 2002.

Kessler, Ronald. *The Terrorist Watch: Inside the Desperate Race to Stop the Next Attack*. New York: Crown Forum, 2007.

Mackey, Chris, and Greg Miller. *The Interrogators: Inside the Secret War Against al Qaeda*. New York: Little, Brown, 2004.

Mann, James. *Rise of the Vulcans: The History of Bush's War Cabinet*. Paperback ed. New York: Penguin, 2004.

Margulies, Joseph. *Guantánamo and the Abuse of Presidential Power*. New York: Simon & Schuster, 2006.

Marks, John. *The Search for the "Manchurian Candidate": The CIA and Mind Control*. 1979. Paperback ed. New York: Norton, 1991.

McCain, John. *Faith of my Fathers*. Paperback ed. New York: Perennial, 2000.

McCoy, Alfred W. *A Question of Torture*. New York: Metropolitan, 2006.

McKelvey, Tara. *Monstering: Inside America's Policy of Secret Interrogations and Torture in the Terror War*. New York: Carroll & Graf, 2007.

Nance, Malcolm W. *The Terrorists of Iraq: Inside the Strategy and Tactics of the Iraq Insurgency*. Privately printed, 2007.

The National Commission on Terrorist Attacks Upon the United States. *The 9/11 Commission Report*. New York: Norton, 2004.

Nichols, John. *The Rise and Rise of Richard B. Cheney*. Paperback ed. New York: New Press, 2005.

Parry, Robert, Sam Parry, and Nat Parry. *Neck Deep: The Disastrous Presidency of George W. Bush*. Arlington, VA: The Media Consortium, 2007.

Paust, Jordan J. *Beyond the Law: The Bush Administration's Unlawful Responses in the "War" on Terror*. Paperback ed. Cambridge, UK: Cambridge University Press, 2007.

Peters, Edward. *Torture*. Philadelphia: University of Pennsylvania Press, 1996.

Rejali, Darius. *Torture and Democracy*. Princeton: Princeton University Press, 2007.

Risen, James. *State of War: The Secret History of the CIA and the Bush Administration*. New York: Free Press, 2006.

Rose, David. *Guantánamo: The War on Human Rights*. New York: New Press, 2004.

Roth, Kenneth, and Minky Worden, eds. *Torture*. New York: New Press and Human Rights Watch, 2005.

Sanchez, General Ricardo S. *Wiser in Battle*. New York. HarperCollins, 2008.

Sands, Philippe. *The Torture Team*. Working manuscript. Privately printed, 2007.

Savage, Charlie. *Takeover*. Paperback ed. New York: Little, Brown, 2007.

Schroen, Gary. *First In*. Paperback ed. New York: Presidio, 2005.

Schwarz, Frederick A.O., Jr., and Aziz Z. Huq. *Unchecked and Unbalanced*. New York: New Press, 2007.

Shenon, Philip. *The Commission*. New York: Twelve, 2008.

Stafford Smith, Clive. *Bad Men: Guantánamo Bay and the Secret Prisons*. London: Weidenfeld & Nicolson, 2007.

Suskind, Ron. *The One Percent Doctrine*. New York: Simon & Schuster, 2006.

Tenet, George. *At the Center of the Storm*. New York: HarperCollins, 2007.

Timberg, Robert. *The Nightingale's Song*. Paperback ed. New York: Touchstone, 1996.

Toobin, Jeffrey. *The Nine: Inside the Secret World of the Supreme Court*. New York: Doubleday, 2007.

Unger, Craig. *The Fall of the House of Bush*. New York: Scribner, 2007.

Weiner, Tim. *Legacy of Ashes: The History of the CIA*. New York: Doubleday, 2007.

Weisberg, Jacob. *The Bush Tragedy*. New York: Random House, 2008.

Woodward, Bob. *Bush at War*. New York: Simon & Schuster, 2002.

———. *State of Denial*. New York: Simon & Schuster, 2006.

Wright, Lawrence. *The Looming Tower*. New York: Knopf, 2006.

Yoo, John. *War by Other Means: An Insider's Account of the War on Terror*. New York: Atlantic Monthly Press, 2006.

Zegart, Amy B. *Spying Blind: The CIA, the FBI, and the Origins of 9/11*. Princeton, NJ: Princeton University Press, 2007.

PERIODICAL AND ONLINE SOURCES

Adelman, Kenneth. "Cakewalk in Iraq." Editorial. *Washington Post*, February 13, 2002.

Agence France Presse. "Mubarak Says Egypt's Military Courts Vindicated by U.S., Britain." December 15, 2001.

Associated Press. "Ex-Warden Tells of Use of Dogs." July 27, 2005.

Baker, Russ. "Why George Went To War." *TomPaine.com*, June 20, 2005, tompaine.com/articles/2005/06/20/why_george_went_to-war.php.

Bergen, Peter, and Katherine Teidmann. "The Body Snatchers." *Mother Jones*, March-April 2008.

Bergstein, Stephen. "A tale of two decisions (or, how the FBI gets you to confess)." *Pet Rock: Camera Obscura*, October 21, 2007, http://www.psychsound.com/2007/10/a_tale_of_two_decisions_or_how.html.

Bravin, Jess. "Rule of Law, Judge Alito's View of the Presidency: Expansive Powers." *Wall Street Journal*, January 5, 2006.

Bravin, Jess. "The Conscience of a Colonel." *Wall Street Journal*, March 31, 2007.

Buettner, Russ. "Manhunt for Hijackers' 3 Pals." *Daily News* (New York), October 24, 2001.

Czuczka, Tony. "Germany seeks second fugitive in U.S. terrorist attacks." Associated Press, September 21, 2001.

Dedman, Bill. "Can the '20th hijacker' of Sept. 11 stand trial?" *Msnbc.com*, October 26, 2006, www.msnbc.msn.com/id/15361462.

Department of Defense. "Working Group Report on Detainee Interrogations on the Global War on Terrorism." April 4, 2003. Reproduced in *The Torture*

Papers. Eds. Karen J. Greenberg and Joshua L. Dratel. Cambridge, UK: Cambridge University Press, 2005.

Dorn Steele, Karen, and Bill Morlin. "Senate Probe Focuses on Spokane Men." *Spokesman Review*, June 29, 2007, www.spokesmanreview.com/tools/ story_breakingnews_pf.asp?ID=10496.

Eban, Katherine. "Rorschach and Awe." *Vanity Fair Online*, July 17, 2007, http://www.vanityfair.com/politics/features/2007/07/torture200707.

Eggen, Dan, and Joby Warrick. "CIA Destroyed Videos Showing Interrogations." *Washington Post*, December 7, 2007.

Ferguson, Niall. "Don't flout Geneva—or the tables could easily be turned." *Daily Telegraph* (London), October 1, 2006.

Finn, Peter, and Brooke A. Masters. "Officials Seek Hijacker Who Wasn't." *Washington Post*, November 16, 2001.

Fishback, Ian. Letter to John McCain. Republished as "A Matter of Honor." *Washington Post,* September 28, 2005.

Friedman, Thomas. "Just Shut It Down." Editorial. *New York Times*, May 27, 2005.

Gellman, Barton, and Jo Becker. "A Different Understanding with the President." The "Angler: The Cheney Vice Presidency" series. *Washington Post*, June 24, 2007.

———. "Pushing the Envelope on Presidential Power." The "Angler: The Cheney Vice-Presidency" series. *Washington Post*, June 25, 2007.

———. "A Strong Push From Backstage." The "Angler: The Cheney Vice Presidency" series. *Washington Post*, June 26, 2007.

Gellman, Barton. "In U.S., Terrorism's Peril Undiminished." *Washington Post*, December 24, 2002.

Gillers, Stephen. "The Torture Memo." *The Nation,* April 28, 2008.

Gilmore, Gerry J. "Rumsfeld Visits, Thanks U.S. Troops at Camp X-Ray in Cuba." *American Forces Press Service*, January 27, 2002, http://www.defenselink. mil/news/newsarticle.aspx?id=43817.

Goldberg, Jeffrey. "In the Party of God." *The New Yorker*, October 14, 2002.
———. "A Little Learning." *The New Yorker*, May 9, 2005.

Golden, Tim, and Don Van Natta Jr. "The Reach of War: U.S. Said to Overstate Value of Guantánamo Detainees." *New York Times*, June 19, 2004.

Golden, Tim. "Administration Officials Split Over Stalled Military Tribunals." *New York Times*, October 25, 2004.

———. "After Terror, a Secret Rewriting of Military Law." *New York Times*, October 24, 2004.

———. "In U.S. Report, Brutal Details of 2 Afghan Inmates' Deaths." *New York Times*, May 20, 2005.

Greenburg, Jan, Crawford, Howard, Rosenberg, and Ariane de Vogue. "Top Bush Advisors Approved Enhanced Interrogation," ABCnews.com, April 9, 2008, http://abcnews.go.com/TheLaw/LawPolitics/story?id=4583256.

Hersh, Seymour. "The Gray Zone." *The New Yorker*, May 24, 2004.
———. "The General's Report," *The New Yorker*, June 25, 2007.

Hirsh, Michael. "The Myth of Al Qaeda." *Newsweek Online*, June 28, 2006, http://www.newsweek.com/id/52476.

———. "A Tortured Debate." *Newsweek*, June 21, 2004.

Ignatius, David. "Cheney's Cheney." *Washington Post*, January 6, 2006.

Isikoff, Michael. "The Lindh Case E-Mails." *Newsweek*, June 24, 2002. Available at www.msnbc.com/id/3067190.

Johnson, Carrie. "Constitutional Exception Not Valid, Mukasey Says." *Washington Post*, April 11, 2008.

Johnson, Glen. "Bush Fails Quiz on Foreign Affairs." Associated Press, November 4, 1999.

Kean, Thomas, and Lee Hamilton. "Stonewalled by the CIA." Editorial. *New York Times,* January 2, 2008.

Klaidman, Daniel, Stuart Taylor Jr., and Evan Thomas. "Palace Revolt," *Newsweek*, February 6, 2006.

Lewis, Anthony. "Making Torture Legal." *New York Review of Books*, July 15, 2004.

Lichtblau, Eric, James Risen, and Scott Shane. "Wider Spying Fuels Aid Plan for Telecom Industry." *New York Times*, December 16, 2007.

Los Angeles Times. "It's Called Democracy." Editorial, June 29, 2004.

Luban, David. "An Asymmetrical Assault on Reality." *Balkinization* blog, June 12, 2006, balkin.blogspot.com/2006/06/asymmetrical-assault-on-reality.html.

Mann, James. "The Armageddon Plan." *Atlantic Monthly*, March, 2004.

Marek, Angie C. "A Righteous Indignation." *U.S. News and World Report*, March 20, 2005.

Mayer, Jane. "A Deadly Interrogation." *The New Yorker*, November 14, 2005.

———. "Contract Sport." *The New Yorker*, February 16, 2004.

———. "Junior." *The New Yorker*, September 11, 2006.

———. "Lost in the Jihad." *The New Yorker*, March 10, 2003.

———. "Outsourcing Torture." *The New Yorker*. February 15, 2005.

———. "The Black Sites." *The New Yorker*, August 13, 2007.

———. "The CIA's Travel Agent." *The New Yorker*, October 30, 2006.

———. "The Experiment." *The New Yorker*, July 11, 2005.

———. "The Hidden Power." *The New Yorker*, July 3, 2006.

———. "The Manipulator." *The New Yorker*, June 7, 2004.

———. "The Memo." *The New Yorker*, February 27, 2006.

———. "The Search for Osama." *The New Yorker*, August 4, 2003.

———. "Whatever It Takes." *The New Yorker,* February 19, 2007.

Mazetti, Mark. "'03 Memo Approved Harsh Interrogations." *New York Times*, April 2, 2008.

McCarthy, Rory. "Threat of war." *Guardian*, September 16, 2002.

Mikva, Abner J. "'Present' Perfect." Editorial. *New York Times*, February 16, 2008.

Morrison, Blake, and Peter Eisler. "General Promised Quick Results if Gitmo Plan used at Abu Ghraib." *USA Today*, June 23, 2004.

Pound, Edward T. "Iraq's invisible man." *U.S. News & World Report*, June 28, 2004.

Priest, Dana. "CIA Holds Terror Suspects in Secret Prisons." *Washington Post*, November 2, 2005.

———. "CIA Avoids Scrutiny of Detainee Treatment." *Washington Post*, March 3, 2005.

———. "Covert CIA Program Withstands New Furor." *Washington Post*, December 30, 2005.

———. "Senate Urged to Probe CIA Practices; Intelligence Panel Should Examine the Use of Rendition, Rockefeller Says." *Washington Post*, April 22, 2005.

Purdum, Todd. "A Face Only a President Could Love." *Vanity Fair*, June, 2006.

Safire, William. "Waterboarding." On Language column. *New York Times Magazine*, March 9, 2008.

Sands, Phillipe. "The Green Light." *Vanity Fair*, May, 2008.

Scherer, Michael, and Mark Benjamin. "What Rumsfeld Knew." *Salon*, April 14, 2006, http://www.salon.com/news/feature/2006/04/14/rummy.

Schmitt, Eric, and Carolyn Marshall. "In Secret Unit's Black Room, a Grim Portrait of U.S. Abuse." *New York Times*, March 19, 2006.

Serrano, Richard A. "Prison Interrogators' Gloves Came Off Before Abu Ghraib." *Los Angeles Times*, June 9, 2004.

Shane, Scott, David Johnston, and James Risen, "Secret U.S. Endorsement of Severe Interrogations." *New York Times*, October 4, 2007.

Shane, Scott. "Waterboarding Focus of Inquiry by Justice Department." *New York Times*, February 23, 2008.

Sullivan, Eileen. "Tom Ridge: Waterboarding Is Torture." Associated Press, January, 18, 2008.

Tuttle, Ross. "Rigged Trials at Gitmo." *The Nation*, March 10, 2008.

Umanksy, Eric. "Failures of Imagination." *Columbia Journalism Review*, September-October 2006.

Walsh, Kenneth T. "The Cheney Factor." *U.S. News & World Report*, January 23, 2006.

Weisberg, Jacob. "Fishing For a Way to Change the World." *Newsweek*, January 28, 2008.

Windrem, Robert, and Victor Limjoco. "9/11 Commission Controversy." Msnbc.com, January 30, 2008, http://deepbackground.msnbc.msn.com/archive/2008/01/30/624314.aspx.

White, Josh. "U.S. Generals in Iraq Were Told of Abuse Early, Inquiry Finds." *Washington Post*, December 1, 2004.

Wright, Lawrence. "The Spymaster." *The New Yorker*, January 21, 2008.

Zagorin, Adam, and Michael Duffy. "Inside the Interrogation of Detainee 063." *Time*, June 12, 2005.

ALL OTHER SOURCES

Amnesty International. *Below the Radar: Secret Flights to Torture and 'Disappearance.'* Amnesty International Report (51/051/2006), April 5, 2006, http://www.amnesty.org/en/library/info/AMR51/051/2006.

Black, Cofer. "Address to the Association of Foreign Intelligence Officers." Keynote address to the Association of Foreign Intelligence Officers. Tyson's Corner, Virginia, September 8, 2006.

Bush, George H.W. Interview with Diane Sawyer. *Good Morning America*. Television program. New York: ABC, December 19, 2001.

Bush, George W. "Humane Treatment of Taliban and al Qaeda Detainees." Memorandum to the Vice President, Secretary of State, et. al. Washington, D.C., February 7, 2002. www.pegc.us/archive/white_house/bush_memo_20020207_ed.pdf.

Bush, George W. Address to a Joint Session of the United States Congress and the American People. The Capitol, Washington, D.C., September 20, 2001. www.whitehouse.gov/news/releases/2001/09/20010920_8.html.

Clarke, Richard A. "Presidential Policy Initiative/Review—the Al-Qida

Network." Memorandum to Condoleezza Rice. Washington, D.C., January 25, 2001. Reproduced by the National Security Archive of the George Washington University, www.gwu.edu/~nsarchiv/NSAEBB/NSAEBB147/index.htm.

Denbeaux, Mark and Joshua Denbeaux et. al., "Report on Guantánamo Detainees: A Profile of 517 Detainees through Analysis of Department of Defense Data." Seton Hall Law School. http://law.shu.edu/news/guantánamo_reports.htm.

"The Enemy Within." *Frontline*. Television program. Written and produced by Lowell Bergman and Oriana Zill de Granados. Boston: WGBH and PBS, October, 2006. www.pbs.org/wgbh/pages/frontline/enemywithin/interviews/brennan.html.

Fay, MG George R. "AR 15-6 Investigation of the Abu Ghraib Detention Facility and 205th Military Intelligence Brigade." Investigation for the U.S. Army Combined Joint Task Force. August 23, 2004. http://news.findlaw.com/hdocs/docs/dod/fay82504rpt.pdf.

Haynes, William. "Counter-Resistance Techniques" (S.E.R.E. Interrogation Standard Operating Procedure). Memorandum to Donald Rumsfeld. The Department of Defense, the Pentagon, December 10, 2002.

Hennen, Scott. *WDAY Hot Talk*. Radio program. Fargo, North Dakota: WDAY, October 24, 2006. www.whitehouse.gov/news/releases/2006/10/20061024-7.html.

Human Rights Watch. "'No Blood, No Foul': Soldiers' Accounts of Detainee Abuse in Iraq." Human Rights Watch Reports (28.3), July 2006. www.hrw.org/reports/2006/us0706.

Human Rights Watch. "Ghost Prisoner: Two Years in Secret CIA Detention." Human Rights Watch Reports (19.1), February 2007. http://www.hrw.org/reports/2007/us0207.

Kiriakou, John. Interview with Brian Ross. *World News with Charles Gibson*. Television program. New York: ABC News, December 10, 2007.

Marty, Dick. *Alleged secret detentions in Council of Europe member states*. Memorandom to the Parliamentary Assembly of the Council of Europe Committee on Legal Affairs and Human Rights. January 22, 2006. http://assembly.coe.int/Main.asp?link=/CommitteeDocs/2006/20060124_Jdoc032006_E.htm.

McChesney, John. "The Death of an Iraqi Prisoner." *All Things Considered*. Radio program. Washington: NPR, October 25, 2005. npr.org/templates/story/story.php?storyid=4977986.

Mora, Alberto. Acceptance Speech as the Recipient of the John F. Kennedy Profile in Courage Award. The John F. Kennedy Library, Boston, Massachusetts, May 22, 2006. http://www.jfklibrary.org/Education+and+Public+Programs/Profile+in+Courage+Award/Award+Recipients/Alberto+Mora/Acceptance+Speech+by+Alberto+Mora.htm.

Myers, Richard. Comments at the Defense Department Regular News Briefing. The Pentagon, Arlington, Virginia, January 11, 2002.

The National Intelligence Council. "Declassified Key Judgments of the National Intelligence Estimate." Directorate of National Intelligence Report, April, 2006.

The Office of the Inspector General. *The OIG Report on CIA Accountability*. June, 2005. www.mideastweb.org/cia_911_oig.htm.

Olmstead v. U.S. 277 S. Ct. 438. Supreme Court of the United States. April 9, 1928.

The Pew Global Attitudes Project. "America's Image Slips, But Allies Share U.S. Concerns Over Iran, Hamas." June 13, 2006.

Rockefeller, John. "Chairman Rockefeller Says Intel Committee Has Begun Investigation into CIA Detainee Tapes." Press release, December 7, 2007, http://rockefeller.senate.gov/press/record.cfm?id=288567.

———. "Statement on President's Veto of the Intelligence Authorization Bill." Press release, March 8, 2008.

Rumsfeld, Donald. "Remarks Delivered to the Veterans of Foreign Wars." Address at the 104th VFW National Convention. San Antonio, Texas, August 25, 2003. http://www.defenselink.mil/speeches/speech.aspx?speechid=513.

Rumsfeld, Donald. "Global War on Terrorism." Memorandum to Gen. Dick Myers et. al., The Department of Defense, October 16, 2003; http://www.usatoday.com/news/washington/executive/rumsfeld-memo.htm.

Scheiffer, Bob. *Face the Nation*. Television program. New York: CBS News, November 13, 2005.

Schmidt, Randall, and John Furlow. "AR 15-6: Investigation of Detainee Abuse at Guantánamo Bay, Cuba Detention Facility." The Schmidt-Furlow Report. Army Southern Command Investigation. June 9, 2005. Available through the University of Minnesota Human Rights Library, www1.umn.edu/humanrts/OathBetrayed/general-investigations.html.

Schmidt, Randall. "Testimony of Lieutenant General Randall M. Schmidt." Department of the Army Inspector General, Investigations Division. August 24, 2005. Available at www.salon.com/news/feature/2006/04/14/rummy/.

Sifton, John. "Information about Detainees Previously Held In Secret or in a Third Country." Human Rights Watch Memorandum. December 20, 3006.

Taxi to the Dark Side. DVD. Written and directed by Alex Gibney. New York: Jigsaw Productions, 2007.

Toope, Stephen J. *Commission of Inquiry into the Actions of Candian Officials in Relation to Maher Arar: Final Report*. Arar Commission of the Government of Canada. October 14, 2005. www.ararcommission.ca/eng/ToopeReport_final.pdf.

"The Torture Question." *Frontline*. Television program. Written, produced, and directed by Michael Kirk. Boston: WGBH and PBS, October, 2005. www.pbs.org/wgbh/pages/frontline/torture/interviews/berenson.html.

Torturing Democracy. Documentary. Produced by Sherry Jones. Washington: Washington Media Associates, 2008.

U.S. Congress. House of Representatives. International Organizations, Human Rights, and Oversight Subcommittee and the Europe Subcommittee of the House Foreign Affairs Committee. *Extraordinary Rendition in U.S. Counterterrorism Policy: The Impact on Transatlantic Relations*. 110th Congress, 1st Session, April 17, 2007.

U.S. Congress. Senate. Armed Services Committee. *Allegations of Mistreatment of Iraqi Prisoners Hearings*. 108th Congress, 2nd Session, May 11, 2004.

U.S. Congress. Senate. Judiciary Committee. *Hearing on the Nomination of Alberto Gonzales to be U.S. Attorney General*. 109th Congress, 1st Session, January 7, 2005.

U.S. Congress. Senate. Select Committee on Intelligence. *Postwar Findings About*

Iraq's WMD Programs and Links to Terrorism and How They Compare with Prewar Assessments. 109th Congress, 2nd Session, September 8, 2006.

U.S. v. Moussaoui. 282 F. Supp. 2d 480. United States District Court of the Eastern District of Virginia. April 22, 2004.

Young, Shelton R. "Review of DoD-Directed Investigations of Detainee Abuse Unclassified." Office of the Inspector General, Department of Defense. August 25, 2006. www.dodig.osd.mil/fo/Foia/DetaineeAbuse.html.

Youngstown Sheet & Tube Co. v. Sawyer. 343 U.S. 579. Supreme Court of the United States. June 2,1952.

A NOTE ON SOURCES

This book grew out of thirteen articles first published in *The New Yorker* magazine since September 11, 2001. That reporting, which involved hundreds of interviews, was supplemented by hundreds of hours of additional interviews with a range of authorities, including many current and former officials from the Bush administration, the intelligence community and other parts of the government. Many of them could only discuss sensitive issues on the condition of anonymity. There has been much criticism of the use of anonymous sources of late, yet any reporter covering the subject of national security knows that there is no other way to get many of the most important stories to the public. That said, I have tried wherever possible to put sources on the record, or to give readers an indication of their relationship to the story. Many took risks to share sensitive information that they felt the public needed know. I owe them a huge debt of gratitude. I also am indebted to the work of many of my colleagues in the press. It's become common to criticize the "mainstream media," but print reporters have performed brilliantly and honorably against long odds in covering the hidden stories beneath America's war on terror. Among those whose work I would not have been able to write this book without are Jo Becker, Steve Coll, Barton Gellman, Tim Golden, Stephen Grey, Seymour Hersh, Dana Priest, James Risen, Charlie Savage, Scott Shane, Bob Woodward, and Lawrence Wright.

Shortly before this book went to press, the CIA responded with the following statement:

> The CIA has declined to confirm or deny many details about the terrorist interrogation program. But an Agency spokesman stressed

that it has been conducted in accord with the law, and has been the subject of repeated legal reviews within the Executive Branch. It has, in addition, been briefed in detail to the intelligence oversight committees of Congress. The CIA also said that the program—involving under a hundred detainees, less than a third of whom have required any special form of questioning at all—has produced information that has foiled terrorist plots and saved innocent lives. Such methods, the agency notes, have been used only when traditional tactics like rapport-building have proven ineffective.

INDEX